M000289633

791.43   Fox, Julian,
Fox
          Woody : movies from
          Manhattan

DATE

BAKER & TAYLOR

Plainfield Public Library
1120 Stafford Road
Plainfield, Indiana 46168

Woody

Woody

Movies from Manhattan

Julian Fox

THE OVERLOOK PRESS
WOODSTOCK • NEW YORK

For Jane and Annabel

First published in The United States of America in 1996 by
The Overlook Press
Lewis Hollow Road
Woodstock, New York 12498

Copyright © 1996 Julian Fox

All Rights Reserved. No part of this publication may be reproduced or
transmitted in any form or by any means, electronic or mechanical, including
photocopy, recording, or any information storage and retrieval system now
known or to be invented without permission in writing from the publisher,
except by a reviewer who wishes to quote brief passages in connection with a
review written for inclusion in a magazine, newspaper or broadcast.

Library of Congress Cataloging-in-Publication Data

Fox, Julian
Woody : movies from Manhattan / Julian Fox.
p. cm.
Includes bibliographical references and index.
1. Allen, Woody—Criticism and interpretation.
Originally published in the United Kingdom by BT Batsford Ltd.
I. Title.
PN1998.3.A45F68 1996
791.43'092—dc20
96-18135 CIP

Manufactured in The United States of America
ISBN: 0-87951-692-5

First American Edition

Contents

Preface & Acknowledgements   7

1   Introduction   11

2   Balancing on an Eye   17
    Woody Allen: Film-Maker

3   From this he makes a Living?   25
    1935-64: The Early Years

4   Small Portions   29
    1965-9: *What's New Pussycat?* to *Don't Drink the Water*

5   The King of Comedy   47
    1969-75: *Take the Money and Run* to *Love and Death*

6   City Stories   83
    1976-80: *The Front* to *Stardust Memories*

7   The Changing Man   129
    1981-5: *The Floating Lightbulb* to *The Purple Rose of Cairo*

8   All in the Family   163
    1986-9: *Hannah and Her Sisters* to *Oedipus Wrecks*

9   God, Guilt, Sex, Death - The Whole Damn Thing   201
    1989-92: *Crimes and Misdemeanors* to *Shadows and Fog*

10 Crimes & Whispers   227
    1992-5: *Husbands and Wives* to *Mighty Aphrodite*

    Filmography   259
    Shorts & Documentaries   271
    Woody on Stage   272
    On Woody Allen   274
    Production Information   276
    Selective Bibliography   279
    Index   281

Preface & Acknowledgements

Woody Allen stands today as the most extensively documented film comedian-auteur after Chaplin. It is even possible that, taken simply as a public personality, he has attracted more print and media analysis within a relatively shorter time than any other comic performer of the twentieth century.

Notwithstanding his reputation for reclusiveness, Woody has granted any number of interviews about his life and work. His sets have remained open to selected observers, including journalists, in spite of the almost obsessive secrecy in which his films are reportedly made. Numerous television programmes and critical studies have attempted to explain Woody and his art to the world, comparing him, in the process, with every major comedian and notable director whose style or subject matter are supposed to have influenced him. We also have the invaluable memoirs of close collaborators, as well as a vast accumulation of other insights from associates past and present without which no full-length study of Woody, the film-maker at work, can be undertaken.

'A plethora of people have written about Woody Allen', John Lahr told me 'and they either like him or dislike him. But no one has yet managed, I think, to interpret him.' Perhaps it is foolish even to try, though, as with any creative artist, a number of approaches are possible. Lahr's efforts at defining Woody are admirable, while American comedian Steve Allen, in a brilliant 1981 essay, has done more than anyone to evaluate Woody's skills as a stand-up performer. However, what we may laugh at spontaneously can become correspondingly *less* funny when we try to interpret it for others. We have seen, all too frequently, how numerous comedians of the past have all but disappeared from comic view under the cumulative weight of critical examination. Indeed, as Graham McCann has noted, 'No form of culture is more unfriendly to rational analysis than the incongruity that causes laughter.'

In Woody's case, any discussion of his work, as comedian or film-maker, is bound to take cognizance of a life and its concerns which, more than for any other contemporary American film artist, seem to have been so overtly reflected in his movies that we feel we know him better than we actually do.

His use of real-life names and anecdotes as colour for his screenplays has never been denied, even though the actual incidents from his experience have been imaginatively distorted through the creative process. As he has been the first to admit, by setting his movies, mainly, in his favoured environment, with personal friends in the cast and his own choice of music on the soundtrack, it is almost as if he were inviting us to make an analogy between that real-life experience and the stories which unfold on screen. Appearing in many of the films himself, as characters whose occupations are familiar to him may also serve, agrees Woody, to 'double the intensity of that misconception'.

Although I shall be giving a brief account of Woody's early life and career and the way he has been perceived as a gag writer, stand-up comedian, TV personality, short-story writer, essayist, dramatist, universal sage and moral philosopher, the body of the book will concentrate, as its title implies, on the movies themselves - both those which Woody has written and directed and those in which he has appeared for others. The first group represents a series of highly individual and recognizably auteurist works which, if not all physically *made* in Manhattan, at least owe the genesis of their creation to that epicentre which Woody has chronicled and idealized more extensively and attractively than any other film-maker in recent memory.

No book of this nature can be written in perfect isolation and I should, first of all, like to express my gratitude to all those earlier authors, who, in over 50 books and countless newspaper and magazine articles, have proved invaluable either in helping to crystallize my views or in firming my opposition to received notions of a film-maker who seems to divide opinion more sharply than any equivalent talent on the American movie scene today.

I should also like to offer grateful thanks to the many friends and fellow *aficionados* who have given their help and encouragement, especially Ian Bremner, Donald Campbell and Joel Finler. My particular thanks to Joel whose suggestion it was I write this book and who has been more than generous with advice, comments on the text, the loan of archive material and of many of the stills herein. I would like to thank my ever-patient editors at Batsford (Pauline Snelson, Timothy Auger and Richard Reynolds) and my talented copy-editors, Jeanne Brady and Martina Stansbie, and hard-working publicist, Teresa Howes. My best thanks also to Xandra Barry of the BBFC; Isobel Begg, Michelle King and Tom Piethura of Miramax; Helene Blanc of Columbia Pictures (LA); Steve Bryant of the National Film and Television Archive; Graham Bury; Amanda Casson of BBC TV; Norma Lee Clark of Untitled Productions Inc; Marion Cres of IDHEC; Mickey Eberhardt of the Monmouth County Department of Public Information and Tourism (NJ); David Garside of Rank; Denis Gifford; Mark Gilbert of *The Jazz Journal*; Kirsty Hanson of Channel One; Amanda Hobbs of *The South Bank Show*; Marion Koltai-Levine of PMK (NY); Linda Kurland of the Rollins-Joffe office; Ralf Ludemann and Ritchie Paterson of *Screen International*; Jennifer Lyne of ICM (Los Angeles); Tim McDonough of Hallmark Entertainment; Angela Mesher and Sue O'Brien of *Variety;* Barry A. Norman of The Theatre Museum, London; Andrew Ormsby and Phil Wickham of the BFI; Ceris Price of CJP; Alex Sapirstein of ABC News (UK); Michelle Sewell and Darryl Finer of Buena Vista; David Shipman; Claire Soper of the Nuffield Theatre, Southampton; Anna Whelan, Stephen Oliver and Philip Rose of Columbia-TriStar; Michael Whitehorn; Fred Zentner; the staffs of the Kew and Richmond public and reference libraries, Surrey; Colindale Newspaper Library; and Peter Collins and the staff of the Central Reference Library, Westminster, London.

My very warm thanks, obviously, to all those who have contributed personal comments on and/or recollections of Woody and his work, most notably: Claire Bloom, Patricia Brake, Betty Buckley, Philip Casson, Julie Christie, Stuart Craig, Clive Donner, Norman Dorme, Larry Gelbart, Robert Greenhut, Val Guest, the late Jack Hildyard, Clive Hirschhorn, Ian Holm, Charles H. Joffe, Gérard Krawczyk, Jeffrey Kurland, Michael Kustow, John Lahr, Fran and Jay Landesman, Gaila and James Leahy, James Lindemuth, Andrea Marcovicci, Bob Monkhouse, Stephen Moore, Tim Piggot-Smith, the late Donald Pleasence, Beth Porter, Herbert Ross, Maureen Stapleton, Daniel Toscan Du Plantier, Gary Waldhorn and Matthew Walters. My deep gratitude to Woody Allen for consenting to answer some quite obscure questions, and without whom this book would have no subject. Above all, I should like to thank my wife Jane and daughter Annabel who have borne years of my Woody Allen obsessions with remarkable forbearance.

Most of the photographs in the book are from the Joel Finler Collection, except those for *Bananas*, *Stardust Memories* (kind permission of the BFI), *The Subtle Concept* (graciously loaned by Gérard Krawczyk), *Shadows and Fog*, *Manhattan Murder Mystery* (kind permission of Columbia-Tristar), *Bullets over Broadway*, *Mighty Aphrodite* (kind permission of Buena Vista), and were originally issued to publicize or promote films made or distributed by the following companies: AIP, Cinerama, Columbia, Columbia-Tristar, Miramax, Orion, Palomar-ABC, Paramount, Rank, Sweetland Films, Touchstone-Buena Vista, United Artists and Warners. To all of whom, my thanks.

1

Introduction

> You go to a Bergman film and you know he will be dealing
> with God's silence. Whenever you see a Scorsese film you
> know there's going to be a sociopath in it. With me it's this
> thing, the unfathomableness of desire. It's there over and over
> again. You can't help it, you need to deal with it and live.

> *Woody Allen*

More, perhaps, than any other contemporary American film-maker, Woody
Allen has been both consistent in his enthusiasms and, in his choice of themes
and subject matter, infuriatingly difficult to categorize. Apparently settled in
during the late 1960s and early 1970s as a sort of hip, urban neurotic suc-
cessor to Chaplin, Keaton and the Marx Brothers - as well as a master
parodist of everything from science fiction to Russian literature, Italian
movies to Third World politics - he then assumed the role in the following
decade of a middle-class, New York Jewish Chekhov, dealing with the moral
and sexual complexities of intellectual over-achievers like himself.

From that base, he was soon branching out into dazzling experiments with
fake documentary, Pirandelloesque fantasy and bizarre goings-on in country
houses. Critical eyebrows have been raised at some of Woody's more perverse
departures, especially, the so-called 'serious' films, while, in the 1990s, a not
altogether valuable foray into 'German Expressionism' and a well-publicized
off-screen 'scandal' have led to widely-voiced speculation that his ongoing
love affair with an admittedly specific audience must finally be coming to
an end.

However, long-time fans of Woody's multifaceted talent (confirmed at the time of writing by a triumphant return to comic form) have stayed with him through many a change in his life and cinematic fortunes. The wider, more commercial audience, which prefers Spielberg and Schwarzenegger and has turned less than half a dozen of Woody's movies into anything even approaching a blockbuster, has continued to stay away in droves. Part of the problem is that Woody's films have always reflected the concerns of his own generation: though many of his fans from the 1970s and 1980s have remained loyal, the bulk of today's youth audience simply isn't there.

'But what Woody does brilliantly', wrote Steven Schiff, 'is reinvent himself with every film'. Those of us who are still switched on to his largely minority brand of movie-making have been delighted to follow him on his personal, highly idiosyncratic progress which, in American cinema as a whole, is formidable in terms of invention, imagination, insight, visual imagery, literacy, humanity and range of expression.

Early in his career, Woody insisted that he does not see society as the focus of art and says that he has never deliberately presented himself as a moral commentator. He has also claimed, through the character of Sandy Bates in *Stardust Memories*, that his themes are psychological, not political. However, despite his once-held view that whether comic or serious, 'in the end it's all entertainment', to some observers Woody's moves towards the more sober side of his artistic muse have always been problematic. One of Woody's early collaborators, Larry Gelbart, has identified the dilemma of the funny man wanting to play Hamlet as being largely the fault of those who fail to give credit where credit is due. 'Serious people somehow are more admired than clowns', said Gelbart, 'it's the idea that serious ideas should be rewarded more than comedic ideas and that comedy is easier and trivial.' Gelbart's view has been voiced often enough by Woody himself. Although he admires the talent of filmmakers like Spielberg, Woody admits that he finds their subject matter uninteresting. 'Spielberg has said he makes the kind of pictures he enjoyed as a child', says Woody, 'I like to make the kind of pictures I enjoy as an adult.'

A great deal of his international appeal has undoubtedly been due to the romantic humanization of the Allen screen character through his personal and professional relationships with Diane Keaton and Mia Farrow. In his early comedies, often featuring Woody's second wife, the improvisational comedienne Louise Lasser, the female characters were little more than appendages to his comic persona - even though, in *Take the Money and Run*, Woody's easy rapport with the excessively pretty Janet Margolin does lend that agreeably hit-and-miss entertainment some moments of appealing Chaplinesque lyricism.

He is known as a great admirer of women and, as a child, the female influence in his family was strong. He noted that, until quite recently, he rarely thought in terms of male characters, except where his own screen persona was concerned, and this, in turn, placed certain proscriptions on the subjects he chose. 'I'm not interested in all that stuff that others like to direct', he told *Hot Press* in May 1988. 'Action, gangster movies. That's not my bag. I'm into human interest. And my main interest is what makes women tick ... psychologically.' Yet those who have nothing but praise for Woody's sensitive handling of the female characters in his recent films may be surprised to be reminded that in the 1970s he was lumped together with the likes of Hugh Hefner of *Playboy* by the Women's Liberation Movement. Indeed, as Adam Gopnick has recently suggested, the social trend of feminism has continued to pull against Woody's work and may well be an important factor in the failing box office of his recent films in America.

Other commentators have insisted that Woody, in his films, is the antithesis of the arch male chauvinist frequently complained of and point, quite justifiably, to the way he has employed female characters to reflect more sensitive areas of his work and personality which could not be expressed by male protagonists. John Updike, in discussing the main trend in American fiction, has referred to 'a narrow stoic universe' where the hero always acts right and looks good and the heroine exists simply to satisfy his needs. 'But I love the relationship of women to women', says Woody, and he has intimated that he would dearly have loved to make a movie featuring Mia Farrow, Diane Keaton, Dianne Wiest, Judy Davis and Meryl Streep - all his favourite actresses together. Sharon Stone, an early Allen cast member, has noted that 'When a man writes in the voice of a woman, he writes his fantasy of a woman.' Woody, on the other hand, writes roles for women who are recognisably women. In a July 1991 BBC radio interview, he spoke of his earlier inability to create women characters but how, having cracked it, it had become one of his 'greatest strengths'. He also paid generous tribute to his two most famous co-stars who, he said, had always given him a great deal of feedback, advising on his scripts, with Diane, in particular, demonstrating 'a wonderful story sense' which he found invaluable.

Woody's involvement with Mia Farrow and Diane Keaton led directly to his three biggest box-office successes to date - *Annie Hall*, *Manhattan* and *Hannah and Her Sisters*, which represent an unofficial trilogy on the way sophisticated New Yorkers would like to see themselves. Along the way, Woody has made seven appearances in the Top Money-Making Stars lists and was revealed in a Quigley Poll survey as the eighth biggest drawing card of the 1970s - trailing Clint Eastwood, Burt Reynolds, Barbra Streisand, Paul Newman, Robert Redford, Steve McQueen and John Wayne. He won a Best Director Oscar for

Annie Hall and Best Original Screenplay Oscars for that film and *Hannah*. He is the only film-maker, apart from Orson Welles and the twice cited Warren Beatty, to have been nominated as actor, writer and director for the same film.

At the same time, Woody has never achieved the more potent box-office success of his erstwhile chief comedy rival Mel Brooks. Though they are both Jewish, refugees from Brooklyn, literate, hypochondriacs and graduates of the Sid Caesar comedy-writing team, they are not otherwise much alike, especially since Woody has long since developed his talents beyond mere genre parody which has remained Brook's mainstay. Woody has described genre parody as simple and pleasurable, and that it is very tempting to be 'doing your comic version of the thing you'd like to be doing for real'. Given that opportunity, however, Woody's propensity for homage, especially as regards his idol, Ingmar Bergman, has often been blatant.

Early on, Woody had named Bergman as one of the two artists (the other being Martha Graham) 'who had most profoundly affected him'. He also admitted that his interest in 'doing' Bergman was to see how well a Scandinavian sensibility could be transferred into an essentially American, middle-class, setting.

The influence of Martha Graham on Woody has been less in terms of his films than of his artistry in general; if he draws much of his philosophic and artistic sensibility from Bergman, from Graham he derived a sense of movement and form. He also wrote the first draft of a film script, *Dreams and Furies*, 'heavily influenced by Martha Graham's exploration of the hidden connection between psyche, myth and dramatic movement'. It would be one of an increasing number of Allen movie ideas to remain unrealized.

As well as paying repeated homage to the various artists he admires, Woody has proved especially adept at 'plagiarising' himself. Characters and plot lines from his night club routines have turned up in his TV sketches and short stories. Ideas from all of these have, in turn, fuelled his stage plays and movies. Gags and episodes from his films have appeared again, honed and amended, within the pages of *The New Yorker*, *The Evergreen Review* and other prestigious periodicals to which he has contributed. 'A man in his life tells only one story', said Jean Renoir, and Woody, quite recently, admitted that, like any artist, he has only so many good ideas in him. It is to be hoped that his ability to continue to recycle himself with uncommon ingenuity does not, finally, descend into mere repetition.

Like a number of his contemporaries, Woody has combined the best of traditional Hollywood story-telling with the more innovatory techniques and aesthetic leanings of the European film-makers he admires. However, unlike some other directors, he has resisted the more recent massive swing back to overtly American-style movies, retaining the same closeness to the influences which have, to some observers, all but disembodied him from the Hollywood mainstream. His films, like those of the French New Wave, have long assumed a degree of culture and intelligence in the audience which may flatter but can also irritate. At the same time, his wide appreciation of European culture has been tempered with elements of American popular art (old movies, city architecture, classic jazz) which he patently adores.

Critic Elvis Mitchell's recent view - that the concerns of Woody's movies 'are increasingly out of touch with contemporary America' - has been echoed by any number of commentators. Indeed, the progress of Woody's career has been marked by some dramatic shifts in critical opinion. Although the likes of Vincent Canby and Richard Schickel have remained loyal, Woody found particularly galling the hostility of one-time admirer Pauline Kael. Falling into the convenient trap of equating Sandy Bates in *Stardust Memories* with reflections on Woody's life and personality, Kael declared herself personally 'betrayed' by the film and barely had a kind word to say about his work thereafter.

Earlier, Kael had described Woody as 'an erratic comic genius' and, with the release of *Zelig* in 1983, Jack Kroll in *Newsweek* echoed the view of many in recognizing him as 'Our most intelligent comic and most comic intelligence'.

At least in recent years, Woody's films have been better received by European critics and there has been a simultaneous increase in the world audience. Until *Annie Hall*, few European countries, apart from France and Italy, were on Woody's wavelength. He was notably slow to catch on in Britain where, accompanied by fairly downbeat reviews, his earliest films were invariably released some time after being shown in the US. However, as his films have become more expensive and, in most instances, more difficult to market, the profit margin has been small to non-existent. It has been said that the takings on such films as *September, Another Woman* and *Shadows and Fog* barely paid for the processing costs. *September* and *Another Woman* only received limited distribution, while a great deal of Woody's work has yet to be shown in rural areas where his backers fear it might prove indecipherable. None of this, surprisingly, seems to have damaged Woody's credibility with his successive studios, while his stock company approach and freedom to make what he wants regardless of success or failure has meant that, in the 1980s at least, he was able to turn out more movies in total than almost any other US director. The fact that each one of his films has been inimitable and in most cases, highly regarded, may be considered one of the consistently sustained miracles of contemporary American cinema.

2

Balancing on an Eye

Woody Allen: Film-maker

Now the veteran in a number of creative guises (even, on one occasion, composer) of over three-score movies, Woody remains something of a maverick
within the mainly conformist American film industry. Yet his films, though
highly individual and independent in spirit, still acknowledge the prerequisites
of commercial film art. Established players, often lush production values,
major studio backing and distribution, are allied to a skilfully negotiated
autonomy over the finished product which, in recent years, has been granted
to relatively few directors on the American film scene. Possibly no contemporary American film-maker enjoys as much creative control as Woody, certainly
not one who so successfully fulfils the tripartite functions of director, writer
and star ('*L'auteur des auteurs cinématiques*', as Norman Mailer playfully dubbed
him, when introducing Woody at an international PEN conference in
December 1985).

Woody's consecutive relationships with, mainly, three major studios, have
granted him extraordinary auteurist privileges. His contracts call for, in his
own words, 'a number of neurotic proscriptions' about secrecy, hermetically-
sealed working conditions, the freedom to shoot in black-and-white if he so
wishes, and to supervise the final cut from his own post-production complex
- fashioned out of a converted ladies' bridge parlour on the first floor of the
old Beekman Hotel. Woody's 1980 'dream deal' with Orion stipulated that he
could make any film he liked, without submitting a script, so long as he kept
within a moderate $8-$10m budget.

Certainly, until recently, the prestige of having Woody under contract far
outweighed the risk element at the box-office, and being writer, director and
sometime actor, he has said, makes it a whole lot easier to control a film, without endless time-and money-wasting argument. His perfectionism is, by his

own admission, obsessive and, in his quest for work which meets his exacting standards, friends and fellow workers may be peremptorily sacrificed. Work is what drives him, and he scarcely pauses between the final edit of one picture and scripting the next, often, as was the case in early 1988, working on three separate projects simultaneously.

Insistent on staying close to his safe Manhattan base, Woody has, invariably, made his films exclusively within the environs of the city itself, with only occasional expeditions to California, New Jersey, New York State and, more recently and uncharacteristically, to Italy and France. Until the late 1980s, he ventured but reluctantly on to a sound stage, preferring to film cheaply on actual locations. However, the highly untypical *Shadows and Fog* was filmed entirely in the studio, due to his unwillingness, he has said, to make a complete movie out on the streets at night-time which was the ambience the subject demanded. The film was expensive by Woody's then standards - and a flop.

New York has been described as everyone's and no one's but it is certainly Woody's; although he doesn't see himself as its official chronicler, he has intimated that in years to come the cityscapes and locales he so lovingly records may be the only things of value to be drawn from his movies. This is in spite of the fact that, for example, at the time of *Manhattan*, Woody had difficulty finding the attractive, romantic locations he required.

Woody says that the ideas for his films usually come to him by accident but, sometimes, he will just sit down deliberately in a room, and start to imagine a story. Occasionally, he will 'kill the loneliness' with a collaborator, like Mickey Rose, Marshall Brickman or, more recently, Doug McGrath. He says he tends never to write a synopsis, treatment or even notes, but retains an idea in his head, writing the first 'bad' draft straight off. This he does, usually, lying on his bed, writing in longhand on large legal pads, or typing on the same little German portable that he has used for 40 years. The first draft is exploratory, to see if the characters and theme can be properly developed beyond the first ten pages. He does his first rewrite instantly, revising as many times as necessary. This process takes about a month and the rough script is only presented so that his production team can have something to budget. The period between final screenplay and actual shooting is also relatively brief.

Once filming is under way, Woody tends to shoot quickly and methodically. Retakes, he says, are just like correcting proofs are for a novelist. To facilitate this process he has a clause in all his contracts stipulating that he can come back during post-production - and reshoot 20-30 per cent of any film, or even more. Reshoots are costed in advance and, in recent years, upwards of 50 per cent of his footage has often been altered in this way. This constant tinkering and changing is part of the reason why Woody has invariably embarked on his films without an official title, a ploy used by a number of his European idols. Since his backers and the studio publicists are also denied even a general synopsis, the progress of his movies from script to screen follows Woody's long-established practice of whetting the audience's appetite in advance and avoiding publicity overkill.

Although he appears to know the script backwards by the time he comes to filming, Woody says he rarely looks at it after completing the final draft, only memorizing his own part ten minutes before playing a scene. The opposite of a Spielberg or Hitchcock, he is also dismissive of storyboards: '99.9 per cent of the time I haven't the faintest idea what I'm going to do with the camera when I come to the set.' It's a matter of instinct, he says, and he does very few takes, on average only four. But 'there *have* been times when I've done more. In *Broadway Danny Rose* I did fifty takes at one point. For a scene where Nick Apollo Forte and I are just crossing the street. But that's very rare.'

In recent years, Woody has developed his own distinctive editing style, making fewer and fewer cuts and preferring to shoot in long continuous takes. With his current editor Susan E. Morse he has now reached the stage where he can, as Woody told Stig Björkman in 1994, 'put the whole picture together in just one week, starting from scratch because there are just master-shots. Forty master-shots, and then it's finished'. Woody says that this technique is 'more fun and less boring', and that he is never very comfortable with short sequences.

That he owes an enormous debt to some of his early associates is a matter of record, his education in film form owing much to the sympathetic tutelage of editor Ralph Rosenblum. Gordon Willis, who photographed eight of Woody's most innovative films, helped, more than anyone, to shape his specific visual style. From Willis, Woody learned the value of off-screen acting - the technique of shooting on empty sets with voices off which Woody regarded as a 'revelation'. Like Willis, Woody prefers to shoot a sequence exactly as he wants to see it on screen, offering no alternatives for the editor to play around with. Both men share a propensity for fantasy, conjured photographically rather than with special effects, and each has made something of a fetish of darkly-lit interiors. For exterior filming, Woody and Willis favour overcast days which offer 'an unchanging, soft, even light' and Woody, in particular, 'loves rain shots' said Willis, 'which occur in many of his films. Clouds and rain are his kind of weather. For him, a nice day is a rainy day'. Woody has described Willis as 'probably the greatest American cameraman, and he taught me a ton about photography and about lighting. So I really feel I have learned from the best person we have.' Although Woody's recent films (under his two

subsequent cinematographers, Sven Nykvist and Carlo Di Palma) have continued to be supremely good looking, one may regret the ending of the
Allen-Willis partnership which reached its magical apogee with *The Purple Rose
of Cairo*. With Carlo Di Palma, Woody has not only returned to the black-and-
white experiments inaugurated with Willis, but has drawn increasingly on the
services of firms like R.Greenberg Associates and Balsmeyer and Everett for
some elaborate visual effects. Di Palma has also supported Woody in his recent
enthusiasm for Louma crane shots, flying sequences, double exposure, hand-
held camera and 'Play on Film'. Woody has said that the basic difference
between working with Willis and working with Di Palma is that he was in awe
of Willis, who taught him a great deal, but by the time he began his association
with Di Palma (on *Hannah and Her Sisters*), he had more confidence in what he
was doing and was moving his films towards a more European style with
longer takes - 'So he just fit in perfectly for me'.

Woody is, in fact, the perfect blend of auteur and collaborator: even though
his control over the finished product is total, on-set observers have recorded
that he is likely to accept an idea from a grip or even an extra if it strikes him
as valid. Indeed, his modest title credit - 'Written and directed by Woody Allen'
- democratic alphabetical cast lists and willingness to give due appreciation to
everyone concerned with his movies has been much remarked upon.

Woody does not tend to socialize with his associates, except for a few close
friends; it has been said that working with Bergman on even his most serious
films is a great deal of fun, compared with Woody on his comedies. For all that,
there is, invariably, a friendly camaraderie amongst actors and crew, and, on
'family' films like *Hannah and Her Sisters* and *Radio Days*, the cast usually
includes a number of youngsters with whom Woody plays and jokes between
set-ups. There are also the unexpectedly amusing incidents, like the occasion
recalled by actress Betty Buckley who, cast as the first wife of Ian Holm in
Another Woman, had to turn up and disrupt his character's engagement party
with spouse number two. Buckley, who welcomed Woody's ability 'to create
this atmosphere on set' and give actors the 'confidence to go in and try things',
was instructed to enter the scene 'shouting and throwing my weight around
and wreck the party. It was great, and fun to do, but Woody had me do it over
and over again, this way and that but, at first, it wouldn't come out the way he
wanted. And then he had this temper tantrum and ran into the door - it was
very funny!' Woody's tendency when directing actors is to 'get them on the
side quietly' rather than offer voluble instructions on the floor and very rarely
does he get rattled. Actor Sam Waterston has recalled that, one day, on
Interiors, Woody suddenly decided to have all the furniture on set changed at

the last minute, 'which cost half a day's shooting time. On most sets that would have caused a crisis, but he just waited patiently'. Jean Renoir once referred to his chosen team as 'accomplices' and Woody has described his own film-making as being like 'a small store operating out of New York with the help of some close friends'. Indeed, this is the way he has nearly always worked and, as his manager and former producer Charles H. Joffe told me, 'It's a very loose organization, as you probably know, and Woody likes to change the company name from film to film, as we used to do. It's still run very much on stock company lines, with people working from several different offices, often quite independently of each other, and though, to outsiders, it might seem a bit chaotic, somehow it all comes together'. Woody's loyalty to his regular associates is legendary and many have been with him almost since the beginning. Unlike some directors, Woody remains on set throughout, persistently refusing to work with a video monitor. He prefers, he says, to watch the actors close to, retaining for that purpose a favoured 'repertory company' of not only leading players but also small-part artists, a number of whom are pals and non-professionals. Sometimes the group is augmented by people who just happen to be passing and *look* right. Many actors, in fact, have been so eager to work with Woody that they have cheerfully paid their own air fare and hotel bills, turning up on his sets, script unseen, apart from their own pages or, in some instances, scarcely that. Even 'A-list' actors, it has been reported, have been happy to work with Woody 'for scale', plus a token $10,000 a week. This is in contrast with the attitude of some of the more firmly-entrenched stars - for example, Jack Nicholson, who although admiring of Woody, was unwilling to drop his then usual $6m fee to accept the role subsequently played by Michael Caine in *Hannah and Her Sisters*. George C. Scott, who has confessed to an active dislike of Woody's films, refused even to *read* the script of *Another Woman*.

On his early films, Woody has said he felt so intimidated by celebrities that he eschewed working with stars - except those he had specifically created. Later, he would be accused of casting stars in derisory roles, almost as if he were getting some kind of revenge for his early insecurities. Woody, quite obviously, respects actors, though Mia Farrow has said she considers him hard on them, with a tendency to be intimidating. 'Woody Allen is *very* difficult to work for', Ian Holm told me, 'I felt I was out of my depth on *Another Woman*, despite having words of praise from the master's mouth. Yes, I *do* think he is a master. But there are so many toings-and-froings on Woody's movies, it's sometimes hard to know who's playing what. Another thing is, you have to give him two free weeks to reshoot the reshoots!'

The late Donald Pleasence had similarly mixed feelings about working on *Shadows and Fog*. During much of the time, he told me, he was completely in the dark about what was supposed to be going on. Nor was he helped by Woody's almost wilful failure to communicate:

Woody is very difficult, I think, to talk about or write about at the moment because of all his problems. He is very cold, I suppose, very far from being the great comic - something I've noted about a lot of the great comedians. But I really did like Woody, liked him a lot, even though, for me, making the film was very different. I'm used to being very close to the people I work with and, on his films, you really do find yourself accommodating some strange kind of moodiness. Having said that, I enjoyed working on the film and, on one occasion, he said to me that I was his favourite actor!

Sam Shepard, who replaced Christopher Walken and was replaced in turn by Sam Waterston on *September*, subsequently attacked Woody in an *Esquire* article, complaining that he and Robert Altman 'had no understanding of actors whatsoever ... individually each understands zip about acting'. But director Sydney Pollack, signed for an acting role in *Husbands and Wives*, remains sanguine: 'I found the whole experience fascinating. He says very little. He does most of the work in the writing, in the casting.' Actress Beth Porter who appeared in *Love and Death* agrees. 'It's true he doesn't give much direction', she told me. 'He trusts the people he's cast, only giving slight adjustments. So some of the actors feel cheated.'

By contrast, with certain of his long-term associates, Woody can be surprisingly vocal. Mia has revealed that, since their split, she found it a relief to work with another director (John Irvin) who didn't 'go on and on about what you should do the way Woody did, soul-searching and analysing'. Mostly, Woody says, he doesn't believe in pre-rehearsal and leans less towards direction than 'misdirection' to obtain the unexpected results which excite him. Ideally, he prefers to work with actors with no prior meeting or socializing, using them as 'virgin parchment' from the moment they walk on set. Camera moves are prepared beforehand using stand-ins, and when the actors come in, Woody gives them their key moves while running through their lines: 'The first time you hear the dialogue is when we shoot the scene. And sometimes that take is the best ever.' He also confirms that his casts are usually so good that he practically never has to tell them anything at all. 'I would say' he told Melvyn Bragg, 'that 90 per cent of the directing that I've done, over all the movies I've done, is for me to say "Faster" and "Don't do so much, do a little

less, you're being too big." ' Actors tend to relish Woody's now well-established practice of shooting mainly in long fluid master shots and without
unnecessary camera flourishes, a technique which avoids the choppiness of
much present-day filming.

Although several actors have won Oscars for their work in Woody's films
he is against the usual kind of histrionic flamboyance which can win awards of
this kind and he mainly casts according to suitability and proficiency rather
than star aura. Though he admires artists like Brando and De Niro, Woody
claims he could never work with a Method actor and complains that the average American leading man is usually too charismatic to play the ordinary guy
and is, generally, unwilling to appear weak or vulnerable. Hence Woody's casting of European actors who, accustomed to playing in adult relationship films,
have the ability to be convincingly nondescript. Another problem, of course,
is that Woody is less interested in action than the usual run of American directors, preferring to concentrate on the workings of the human mind. Taking his
cue from his own performances, he encourages his actors in the kind of stuttering speech which has been taken to epitomize naturalism in the movies. The
result can be just as stylized as the more traditional, theatrical delivery; it is
significant that those performers who are permitted to speak in complete sen-
tences tend also to produce a deliberately powerful effect.

Woody has often claimed he became a director primarily to protect his
own writing and that he makes movies out of compulsion rather than pleasure.
What he really enjoys, he says, is working on the script, particularly the
moment when the idea first strikes him. He then likes to get filming over as
quickly as possible, so he can indulge himself playing around with the footage
in his Park Avenue editing suite, writing his next script or practising the clarinet in the privacy of his apartment.

Indeed, though he often finds the day-to-day elements of movie-making
laborious and, by his own admission, not altogether pleasant, Woody's filming
method and preferred way of working have long since been established to
cushion him against the interference and outside distractions which assail the
average American film-maker. 'I think I was lucky' he told *Esquire* 'in that I did
comedy exclusively when I started, and I have a theory that the studios always
think there's some mystery to that … I got off on that foot with them and
they've always left me alone. That's the way it's been with every film.'

3

From this he makes a Living?

1935-64: The Early Years

I wish younger

Woody Allen was born Allan Stewart Konigsberg on 1 December 1935 in Brooklyn, and brought up there, mainly in Long Beach and Flatbush. His parents were of Austrian and Russian descent, first-generation Americans, born on the Lower East Side of Manhattan. Though he did develop a facility for essay writing, Woody played hookey from school, preferring to listen to the popular radio shows of the day and to practise magic tricks in the privacy of his room. His other interests included sport and the movies, while his enthusiasm for Dixieland jazz led to him taking up several instruments, notably the clarinet.

At the age of 16, after enjoying the comic routines at the local Flatbush Theater, he was inspired to start writing gags, sending them under his *nom de guerre* to a number of New York columnists. Within three weeks he was being published and was subsequently hired, at $25 a week, to supply jokes in batches of 50 for the well-known clients of a New York press agent. Woody, through the recommendations of his mother's relative, Broadway librettist Abe Burrows, was soon writing for radio and TV, enrolling, at Burrows's suggestion, for a course in Communications Arts at New York University. This, and a later spell studying dramatic writing, photography and motion picture production at City College, were short lived, but he was signed in late 1955 to a $169-a-week contract with the NBC Writers' Development Program in Hollywood. His work on the by that time disastrously failing *Colgate Comedy Hour* brought him into contact with writer Danny Simon (brother of Neil) whom Woody credited with having taught him how to structure a comedy script. He would also name the writer, along with his manager Jack Rollins, film critic Vincent Canby and United Artists and later Orion head Arthur Krim as being 'the four most important people' in his career.

In March 1956, Woody married 17-year-old philosophy student Harlene Rosen who encouraged him to make up for his lost education. Meanwhile, Woody continued to write material for popular performers, including a TV sketch starring Bob Hope and Kathryn Grayson. Woody's efforts brought him to the attention of Max Liebman, discoverer of Sid Caesar and Danny Kaye. After a brief sojourn writing for Buddy Hackett and Carol Burnett on the unsuccessful comedy series *Stanley* (1956), Woody took a job at Camp Tamiment, a popular Jewish summer resort in Pennsylvania. Starting at $150 a week, Woody stayed three seasons, writing, directing and even acting in sketches which were not only funny but, in many cases, daring and surrealistic. Significantly also, his marriage broke up, Harlene finding it difficult to adapt to the world which increasingly concerned him.

In between his summer camp engagements, Woody continued his TV work, fulfilling his long-time ambition to write for Sid Caesar on a 1958 special for *The Chevy Show*. Woody's co-writer was Larry Gelbart and their efforts, co-starring Art Carney and Shirley Maclaine, were much praised. A subsequent show with Gelbart, Art Carney's *Hooray for Love*, included a sketch, 'Strange Strawberries', which at Woody's suggestion, wittily satirized the style and subject matter of Ingmar Bergman. Woody went on to work, without Gelbart, on a 30-minute Sid Caesar comedy series for ABC, but in 1960 he was fired from his $1700-a-week job on *The Garry Moore Show*, due to his 'almost pathological invisibility'. He had, though, in 1958, entered into a handshake deal with his future managers, Jack Rollins and Charles H. Joffe and was encouraged by them to try stand-up comedy.

His early efforts were disastrous, but, gaining in technique, Woody was soon appearing at The Village Gate, 'the hungry i' in San Francisco and other leading clubs, like Mister Kelly's in Chicago. As Woody's skill and confidence grew, and he pushed his distinctive idiosyncratic routines into ever more absurd flights, the public began to take to him. He had also, by this time, achieved his ambition to write for the theatre, contributing some of his Tamiment material to Hermione Gingold's short-lived two-act revue, *From A to Z*.

Woody's reputation as a stand-up comedian, however, was now assured. He would write hours and hours of material, honing it down to about 35 very funny minutes, turning his stage nervousness into an asset by wrapping the microphone cord around himself and timing his act by seemingly casual glances at his wristwatch. With the same horn-rims and casual clothes which would become his trade mark, Woody was to become a universal comic voice, in appearance and complexity so like the audience he was entertaining that, within two years, he was being widely touted as the most popular stand-up comic in America.

In his act Woody emerged as a typical product of his time, less trenchant than his great idol, Mort Sahl, but one of an expanding group of artists and writers who presented what appeared to be their own real-life experiences as their main source of fictionalized autobiography and self-revelation. It was a technique which

Woody would find relatively easy to adapt to the movies and, as with his short stories, night-club and TV routines, audiences have persistently refused to believe that the public and private Woodys can be anything but the same.

Like Lenny Bruce, Mort Sahl, Nichols and May and others of the New Wave of American humorists, Woody helped change conceptions of what stand-up comedy should be. His themes, since familiar to us through talk-show appearances and his films, ranged from his supposed inadequacy, counterpointed by boastful bravado about his inordinate sexual appetite, to gags about his Jewish roots ('God and carpeting'), religion, food and psychoanalysis. He denied being either a political or an intellectual comedian; rather he was, at least on stage, a universal philosopher on such interdependent themes as thwarted ambition, the fear of discovery and the comedy of anti-climax, master of an act, wrote Maurice Yacowar, which 'seemed less like a public performance than a private confession'.

Our view of the stand-up Woody today, strutting his stuff on re-runs of 1960s' television shows or on the five albums he recorded of his best routines, is of a true original whose time had come. In the space of only two years, he had progressed dramatically from some of the seedier halls to Las Vegas and the top TV variety shows. In 1964, *Variety* placed Woody amongst 'the first rank of cerebral comedians', while the New York *Daily News* dubbed him 'the hottest comic on the show business scene today'. Between the fall of 1963 and spring of 1964, his earnings shot up from $1000 to $5000 a week and, by the end of 1964 he was making $10,000 an appearance. He was, for instance, booked for a single, packed-house stand-up gig at the Carnegie Hall, in December 1963, in support of Count Basie, and would serve as a one-week replacement for *Tonight Show* host, Johnny Carson.

Woody had less luck, initially, in developing his own vehicles. In 1962 he conceived and wrote a TV pilot show, *The Laughmakers*, with Louise Lasser, Alan Alda and Paul Hampton, but ABC failed to develop it into a series because its highbrow humour failed to attract a sufficiently large audience to satisfy a national sponsor.

Concurrent with his new career as a comedian, in the mid 1960s Woody began contributing stories and comic essays to *The New Yorker, Esquire, Playboy* and other magazines, his material heavily influenced by S.J. Perelman and Robert Benchley. A catalogue of sophisticated parodies and word pictures, often veering towards the lunatic or macabre, they appealed to a readership which didn't demand, unlike the audience for Woody's club act, that his humour be instantly comprehensible. Before long, other writers' parodies began to read like his and, as Woody's work in this field grew increasingly elliptical and cinematic in style, it would furnish actual source material for his screenplays. It was, though, his talents as a writer and performer of stand-up material which would lead directly to Woody's entry into the world of film in the summer of 1964.

4

Small Portions

1965-9: What's New, Pussycat? to Don't Drink the Water

What's New, Pussycat? Rollins and Joffe had already begun fielding several movie offers on behalf of their client, including one for Woody to appear with Richard Widmark in *The Bedford Incident*. According to Woody, there had also been the possibility of a script for Sophia Loren and Marcello Mastroianni. His chance finally came at the behest of Charles K. Feldman, a former agent turned producer, who had once handled some of the top names in Hollywood. Feldman was on the look-out for someone to write a movie starring Warren Beatty and Feldman's then girlfriend, Capucine.

The source material was a frothy boulevard comedy, *Lot's Wife,* by the Hungarian-born novelist and screenwriter Ladislaus Bus-Fekete. The English-language rights had been bought some years before for Cary Grant, and several writers, including I.A.L. Diamond, had tried to lick the story, without success. Feldman, at Shirley Maclaine's urging, caught Woody's act at The Blue Angel and became convinced that the comedian's 'unusual ability to deal with sexual yearnings and inadequacies with such charm and wit' would be ideally trans-ferable to the screen.

Woody was signed to a $35,000 writing contract (Feldman had been pre-pared to offer $60,000!), plus a further fee for his services as an actor. Woody, reportedly, scarcely glanced at Diamond's script, merely acceding to Feldman's supplication that he 'write something where we can all go to Paris and chase girls'. It also gave Woody the opportunity to air a number of his favourite pre-occupations - sex, death, food, old movies and psychoanalysis. The eventual screenplay was in some ways different from the original text; after the film's release, *Variety* reported that Bus-Fekete's widow intended to sue the film's pro-ducers 'for either some financial or credit recompense'. Woody's version dealt with a fashion magazine proprietor, Michael James, pathologically distracted by gorgeous women, who consults a similarly afflicted psychoanalyst, Dr Fritz Fassbender. The good doctor, this being comedy, is nuttier than any of his patients, while the hero's 'cure' does little but foment even wilder sexual and romantic complications.

Neither Feldman nor Beatty liked the first draft. 'Woody couldn't quite grasp what was funny about being a compulsive, successful Don Juan', complained Beatty, who further disliked the overconfident Jewish heroine, the numerous film references and, especially, the fact that Woody's role was funnier than his own. Woody's rewrites were more to everyone's taste and Feldman decided to go ahead. The film's title, *What's New, Pussycat?*, was derived from Beatty's standard telephone greeting to his numerous girlfriends which, as Feldman's long-term house guest, he was frequently heard to utter.

As director, Feldman signed London-born Clive Donner, having initially offered him a choice of four projects - including a Ben Hecht script for *Casino Royale* and what Feldman described as 'a spoof comedy by an unknown young writer'. As Donner told me in February 1994:

I flew to New York and worked with Woody for six weeks on the script of *Pussycat*, during which time we not only got on very well but, as Woody had not written a film script before, we were able to revise, reconsider and polish his first version, nevertheless still keeping the very free-form farce/light comedy structure which we thought would find a reasonable audience who were open to something fresh. It was not in any way a mess nor, in my opinion, did it finish up as a mess.

Although in essence Woody had been allowed to write anything he liked and, unusually on a Feldman film, was to receive sole credit as screenwriter, the film which emerged was scarcely the one he wrote. As Beatty has recalled, Woody must also take part of the blame. Initially, Woody's role ran to only about six pages, but, in the rewrites, said Beatty, it gradually increased until it became 'almost half the script. Mine was as large but not quite as good'. At this point, Beatty quit the project, reputedly due to Feldman's changes, though it was also reported that he called the producer's bluff when Feldman refused to cast Beatty's then inamorata, Leslie Caron. Beatty, who later called Woody's screenplay 'the funniest script I've ever read', discovered he had 'another commitment' and his role was offered to Peter O'Toole. By this time, the film was growing from a relatively small romantic comedy into a lavish 'Swinging Sixties' entertainment which everybody wanted to be in. 'Everything they did was big and jazzy', complained Woody, 'They couldn't do anything small.'

Overriding Woody's suggestion that Groucho Marx play Fassbender, Feldman, at Donner's urging, signed Peter Sellers. Sellers had only recently recovered from a series of massive near-fatal heart attacks, and Feldman set aside $350,000 of his own money to insure against the awful possibility of the actor's further incapacity. Woody had long been a fan of Sellers and was, much to the latter's annoyance, frequently mistaken for the older comic. This led to a subsequent, but unsustained rumour that Woody would star in a biopic of the comedian for producer Robert Evans. From August onwards Woody sat it out in London, appearing on TV and working on his play ideas, while Feldman juggled deals in various countries. Ignoring Woody's reminder that the script, as per his brief, had an essentially Gallic flavour, Feldman tried to move the production to Rome, finally consenting to Paris only when his two male stars refused to film in the Holy City due to previous unfortunate experiences with the *paparazzi*.

Although *Pussycat* got under way with a degree of optimism on Woody's part, 'It was', he recalled, a 'nightmarish experience in many ways'. Much has been made of Feldman's artistic indecision and lack of feel for the material, as well as of the reports of the two main stars significantly dominating the production, demanding rewrites which would increase their comic opportunities at the expense of the script.

About halfway through filming, Woody instructed Charles Joffe to inform Feldman that he wanted his name taken off the picture and that he would refuse to make any more changes. Most of the subsequent ones were, reportedly, 'made by practically everyone connected with the film' - except Woody.

Donner, however, remembers the filming as a relatively cheerful experience: 'The script went through the usual stages of change and polish which occur in most productions.' The picture's major difficulty resided in making allowance for Sellers's recent health problems:

Indeed, scheduling his sequences in the film was very difficult and depended on my finishing his role by a point of no return so that if he was taken ill, to recast and reshoot would have been contained within a given cost. Feldman was anxious to overcome Sellers's caution and encouraged him to be in as many additional scenes as possible, and, as he and O'Toole who had not previously met, worked very well together, they frequently had suggestions and ideas which they offered to me and which I always cleared with Woody. I told Woody the first time I changed dialogue on set, and he gave me the freedom to do so. He said he believed if an actor found a way of saying something that was more comfortable for him, he should be free to do so,

providing it was appropriate and funny ... Woody was quiet and co-operative, very in awe of O'Toole and especially Sellers to begin with. He knew
a great deal about movies (as is apparent from various 'quotes' in the film)
and movie-making. He has developed greatly, of course, but Woody then
and Woody now are very consistent. I'm glad he did, finally, get the contract
to make his own films and that I helped start a truly independent spirit in
film-making to reach the great heights he has.

For all his dissatisfaction with the film, Woody did, on Joffe's advice, agree to
act as chief pitchman for *Pussycat* in the US. He was given full credit for his
script and invited on talk shows, receiving, in the process, more exposure than
the other participants.

Pussycat opened in New York to an almost universally hostile critical reception. 'Salacious', 'leering', 'oversexed', 'neurotic and unwholesome' were
among the epithets bandied about, while *Variety* suggested that a 'better title
for the achievement might be *What's New, Copycat*', none of which prevented
the film's initial six-week booking at two New York theatres from being
extended as word of mouth brought the public in. British critics, due to an
inherent fondness for Sellers and sympathy for his 'resurrection', were somewhat kinder. Critical approbation was even more to be noted in France where
a number of writers read meanings into a movie which was patently not to be
taken *too* seriously. In Paris *Pussycat* won an award as the 'Best Directed
Comedy' of 1965.

Though we can scarcely credit Woody's tongue-in-cheek claim that he
'dropped the original script getting out of a taxi so the pages ended up in the
wrong order and the film no longer made sense', it does have that (now dated)
off-the-cuff feel to it which characterizes so many comedies of this period. In
spite of some well-choreographed chase sequences by second unit director
Richard Talmadge, much of it goes for nothing due to the general frenzy and
lack of a consistent comic style among the participants. Both Sellers and
O'Toole disappoint, mainly on account of over-exertion, and appear to be acting in quite different movies. The women in the cast fare somewhat better,
especially Capucine (in a role bearing her real-life surname - Lefebvre), and
Ursula Andress is a magnificently languorous golden-haired vision in a snake-
skin jump-suit. However, Romy Schneider's natural sweetness is insufficient to
overcome an underwritten role, while the statuesque Paula Prentiss is, for
once, unfunny as a habitually suicidal stripper. Other players include Woody's
then fiancée, Louise Lasser (massaging Sellers's back in the sauna scene) and
France's then-favourite recording star, Francoise Hardy, in a cameo role.

Woody, meanwhile, as chief spokesman for the film that might have been, is the sexually-frustrated Victor Shakapopolis and he lends a wry, semi-desperate persona to one or two good little scenes.

Prior to filming, Woody had described the script to a reporter as being about 'two Americans and their romantic adventures in Paris'. Unfortunately, the idea of having Victor as a sort of minuscule, romantically less-successful *alter ego* for Michael somehow got lost in the rewriting. Woody had, in fact, been persistently flattered by Feldman into creating suitable scenes for his own character, only to see the role diminish as these were reassigned to his co-stars. One was a *Cyrano de Bergerac*-style wooing sequence which Woody had written for himself and Capucine but which was finally played by Sellers. Marvin H. Albert's subsequent 'novelization' of Woody's original screenplay also hints at a number of differences between the initial concept and the completed film. Missing, for instance, is a key scene, set in a gym, where Michael is seemingly unaware that Victor is trying to strangle him for love of Carol (Romy Schneider). According to the stills accompanying Woody's August 1965 *Playboy* piece, 'What's Nude Pussycat?', there was a great deal more naked flesh on display than we see in the finished picture. However, perhaps the most significant difference as far as Woody was concerned resides in the fate of Victor who, in the novel (and anticipating Woody's preferred ending for *Take the Money and Run)* goes down in a hail of police bullets in Chicago after trying to rob a bank!

In one version of the script, Woody got the girl but, as he would recall in 1985, Schneider had it in her contract that she must end up with O'Toole - because 'her press agent felt it would be bad for her international image to come away married to me at the end of the movie'. According to Donner, even this ending proved to be problematic and would be one of the sequences which *were* rewritten without Woody:

> The final scene with O'Toole and Romy Schneider getting married, with Sellers as best man, was written over a long weekend at Sellers's country house in England with the two Peters working on it with me until I felt satisfied with the open ending for both of their on-screen characters. Charlie Feldman believed if the scene had been cut and the final fade-out had been on O'Toole and Romy Schneider holding hands at the end of the go-kart chase, the audience would have been on their feet cheering. Maybe, but I disagreed.

If something of an artistic failure, *Pussycat* was scarcely a commercial one. With a gross of $17.2m, it went on to be the fifth Biggest Money-Maker of 1965 and is often referred to (erroneously) as the highest-grossing comedy up to that time. 'If they had let me make it', said Woody, 'I could have made it twice as funny and half as successful.' Although he admitted to 'an enormous affection for Feldman', he said he considered the producer 'crap to work for' - laying what he considered the 'massacre' of his screenplay squarely on Feldman's shoulders: 'I wasn't happy with *Pussycat*. It was clearly a star vehicle. But I think small and Charles Feldman thought big. Consequently, he was a millionaire when he died and *I* gotta work Vegas.' Feldman, reportedly, made at least $2m, personally, out of *Pussycat*.

Casino Royale As a result of *Pussycat*, the work began to pour in. Woody guested on TV for George Plimpton and Andy Williams, appeared on NBC's one-hour rock'n'roll programme, *Hullabaloo*, and was invited to direct a Broadway show, adapt books for films and act in others. One vaguely discussed project was to co-star Julie Christie, of whom Woody was a great fan. The feeling was mutual. 'I knew Woody a little and liked him a lot', she told me, 'He is a hero of mine as I suppose he is of yours. If only the plan had materialized into a reality!' Woody had, however, signed a three-picture deal with Feldman at the time of *Pussycat*, and did agree, officially as an actor only, to work on the producer's massive James Bond spoof, *Casino Royale*.

Made at the very height of the swinging sixties and one of the most bizarre big-budget projects ever to touch down in London, *Casino Royale* had its origins in the very first of the James Bond novels. Published in 1953, it had been sold by Ian Fleming to CBS for $1000, entitling the network to produce a one-hour TV version during the same year. Under the title *Too Hot to Handle*, the show was transmitted on 21 October as the fourth play in the CBS *Climax* series. The show made little impact and plans to adapt further Bond stories for television were scrapped. However, Fleming then sold the film rights for $6000 to actor-director Gregory Ratoff, a move he instantly regretted. In late 1960, with Fox backing, Ratoff, just prior to his death, announced plans to produce *Casino Royale* in Britain with Peter Finch and Robert Morley. Feldman subsequently acquired the rights from the Ratoff estate and 'For some reason or other', director Val Guest told me, 'Charlie found out, when he bought the book, that all he had got was the title. The rival Bond producers, Saltzman and Broccoli had already used everything in the book except the baccarat game, so the whole thing had to be structured around that.' The result, said writer Wolf Mankowitz later, 'was total lunacy'.

Failing to make deals for Connery and Shirley Maclaine to star or Bryan Forbes or Clive Donner to direct, Feldman decided to go for a multiplicity of directors, with the role of Bond shared between several different actors, and a number of 'gag' cameos, including former Bond, George Lazenby, in an unbilled bit. The picture would be filmed mainly on a closed set, in a rather half-hearted attempt to keep the identity of the 'real' Bond secret. Since, like Saltzman and Broccoli, Feldman had a distribution deal with United Artists, he agreed to circumvent the company's possible embarrassment by taking the project to Columbia.

Feldman's brainstorm casting of Peter Sellers (for a fee of $1m) in what was originally intended as the lead role was responsible, according to several sources, for a great number of the problems which subsequently beset the movie. Filming began under Joe McGrath's direction at Shepperton in January 1966, without a finished script and with a number of the *Pussycat* team on hand. The vast sets, which would monopolize the studio for several months, were designed under the general supervision of Michael Stringer who was eventually responsible for over 50 - from the 30 originally contracted for. These included the spectacular psychedelic fun palace of Woody's character, Dr Noah. As new ideas were incorporated into the misconceived enterprise, filming spilled out into Pinewood and MGM-British, Borehamwood, often with three or more units shooting simultaneously.

The film's opening sequence - a wild and woolly preamble set in Scotland (but filmed in Ireland) starting in April - was directed by John Huston. Robert Parrish completed the baccarat sequences started by McGrath as well as the bulk of the suspense scenes. The remainder was divided between Guest, Ken Hughes and second unit directors Richard Talmadge and Anthony Squire. As Guest recalled:

> We had standing sets in each studio and Dr Noah's fun palace was on two stages at Pinewood, but Woody's little studio - whatever you call it - where he gets Dahlia Lavi on the couch, was at MGM. But we leapt around all over the place.

Extensive locations in Paris, the South of France and West Berlin also escalated the budget and played havoc with even the most rudimentary pretence at continuity.

The film was already being referred to as Columbia's 'little *Cleopatra*' and a major problem, as assistant designer Norman Dorme told me, was that 'No one was given a script in advance, which is something, in my experience, which never happens'. The situation was further exacerbated by the disconnected contributions of a plethora of (surprisingly distinguished) writing talents, who had been hired by Feldman to try and pump life into the constantly changing screenplay. Although this was finally credited to Mankowitz, John Law and Michael Sayers, also involved, at one time or another, were Huston, Sellers,

Terry Southern, Billy Wilder, Ben Hecht, Joseph Heller, Dore Schary, Frank Buxton, Orson Welles - and Woody. The bulk of the Sellers scenes had, initially, been the responsibility of Mankowitz, but a dispute developed when Sellers found Mankowitz closeted 'far too closely' with Welles and, 'After about eighteen months', Mankowitz said, 'I really couldn't take any more of it and I withdrew'. Val Guest:

> When Charlie Feldman first approached me to come in on *Casino Royale* he gave me four screenplays to read. They were as widely varied as you could get and Charlie said to me, 'See if you can get a script out of these.' Well, the answer is, we couldn't! And in the end, all those scripts were flung away, we didn't use any of them. Then Charlie flew Woody Allen in and I worked with Woody on the script for a long time, which was great - he's fun to work with. Finally, Charlie asked me to try and pull the whole mess together, with some linking scenes, which I did, using David Niven and Ursula Andress. I didn't meet the other writers at all. I was only presented with the horrible mess at the end which Charlie lumbered me with.

Despite Woody's initial contention that 'I was responsible for only one scene in *Casino Royale* - the execution scene - and that I ad-libbed', his final contribution was actually quite substantial. As he later admitted to Edwin Miller in *Seventeen*:

> I wrote the last part of the script, my part, and at first they said it went in a different direction from the rest of the script. Then, months later, they wrote and asked me if I had a carbon of the pages. I sent them because now they were heading in my direction and would reshape the whole of the script to fit it.

Woody's original idea for the grand finale had previously been scrapped as being too farcical but was now used, at least in part, in an attempt to salvage the enterprise. As Val Guest told me:

> I directed all of Woody's scenes, every single one, which we wrote together. Woody would come over to our house, Pear Tree Cottage in St John's Wood, and he would do a scene and I would do a scene and Woody would work over mine and I would work over his. And sometimes the scenes would come through the office, which Charles Feldman had suggested, and it was all perfectly smooth. I found Woody *completely* smooth, no problems

at all. I mean, he was a very pleasant young man, but he seemed to live in a world of his own. Feldman was the one person Woody hated because he had a terrible habit of making changes. We had a hell of a job trying to keep the script away from him and prevent him cutting our laugh lines. He'd go through all our stuff we'd beaten out, cut out all the gags but leave in the build-up! He had no *idea*. So Woody spent his time moaning to me, 'This murderer! This murderer!' So I said, 'Don't worry about it, we'll put it back, on the floor.' Which we did.

Filming ran on for over ten months, finally wrapping in October. Fifteen hours of printed footage produced a rough cut of three hours - to deliver a running time of 129 minutes. The film's basic plot revolves around retired agent Sir James Bond (David Niven) who is recalled to active duty and dispatched to comfort a colleague's widow in Scotland. She (Deborah Kerr) turns out to be working for the other side. MI6 decide to confuse the enemy by creating dozens of other 007s, one of whom, Evelyn Tremble (Sellers), a small-time cardsharp, challenges the villainous Le Chiffre (Orson Welles) to a baccarat duel. Le Chiffre has been accumulating funds on behalf of SMERSH and the attempt to defeat his plans forms the central sequence of the film. It is also about as far as the original Fleming novel is taken, the rest of the enterprise being a madcap and only intermittently hilarious parody of various cinematic genres.

The film's conflict of intent was anticipated by Sellers's indecision about his character, his refusal to appear in the same shots as the magisterial Welles, his sudden three weeks' disappearance with '2000 extras' standing by, and his quarrels with and the eventual removal from the film of his old friend Joe McGrath - who had been hired at the actor's behest.

Things were bad enough already when, in mid-April, Sellers suddenly quit, and the production was thrown into a flurry of panic and injurious speculation. Although Columbia were to single out the actor as a convenient scapegoat for the debâcle, also quite disastrous was Feldman's uncertainty as to what kind of film it was to be, not to mention the rising costs. A recent Sellers biographer, Roger Lewis, suggests that the decision to swamp the film with a multitude of Bonds was a last-minute brainstorm on Feldman's part to fill the gap left by Sellers. Certainly, the producer had been so desperate to outdo the Saltzman-Broccoli series in flair and spectacle that he continued to pour talent (and Columbia's money) into the project. The frenetic casino climax alone, which was overseen by Richard Talmadge, cost $1m and took two months to shoot. By the end of filming, the picture had doubled its original budget to $12m - or as much as $28m, according to Mankowitz!

Although plans were briefly set in motion to build up Woody's role at the moment of Sellers's departure, various other ploys to fill the gap were also discussed. There was even a suggestion that Sellers be substituted with drag star Danny La Rue. La Rue was to play the role of Mata Bond, the result of a long-ago liaison between Sir James and Mata Hari. This character was eventually played by British-born actress Joanna Pettet. As for Woody, 'I was flown to London and given a big salary and expense account and sat there and just when my salary had run out I was on overtime and they started shooting and I shot for a week or so.'

Woody's original six-week schedule had stretched to six months and he utilized a great deal of this time visiting museums, playing high-stakes poker (his winnings furnished the basis of his extensive art collection) and appearing on TV. In early August he acted as one of the celebrity hosts for *Hippodrome*, a US-UK co-production, introducing a mélange of musical stars and European circus acts. This was recorded in London as a summer replacement for *The Red Skelton Hour*. In September, Dusty Springfield (who would record Burt Bacharach's 'The Look of Love' for *Casino Royale*) invited Woody to appear on her weekly variety show, *Dusty*. He also guested for Bob Monkhouse on *Chelsea at Nine* and was noisily upstaged by Spike Milligan on *The Eammon Andrews Show*. Whilst still in London, Woody was roped in to perform at the opening of The Playboy Club in Park Lane.

Although Woody's work on *Casino Royale* tended to be overlooked at the time, he gives, apart from the diminutive Scots comedian Ronnie Corbett (as a German-accented robot), the only genuinely funny performance in the whole fiasco. Woody makes his first appearance about 35 minutes into the film when, in a brief two-minute sequence, he escapes from two separate Latin American firing squads. In spite of what Woody has claimed, Val Guest told me that the ad-libs were kept to a minimum.

At any rate, the material in the Latin American sequence (a loose blueprint for *Bananas*) is insufficient to establish Woody's character, 'Jimmy Bond', who is, in fact, Sir James's illegitimate nephew. Later in the film he turns out to be the real villain of the piece, Dr Noah - something of a problem, since this character is only belatedly referred to. Although the earlier scenes don't really clue us in, Woody's role is still of strategic importance because, despised by his uncle as jealous and incompetent, Jimmy is plotting to replace world figures with robot lookalikes and, with the aid of a virulent bacillus, eliminate all men over 4'6". His vision of a latter-day Utopia where 'all men are created equal, where a man no matter how short can score with a top broad' is a reflection of Woody's stance as a sexual inadequate, and intimates some of the 'perfect' soulless elements he would bring to bear in his own film, *Sleeper*. The sets Dr Noah inhabits are similarly futuristic and the film's imaginative use of Woody's persona during the final sequences make one regret that he wasn't more fully employed. Norman Dorme:

> Woody's stuff was shot at MGM, and ... as I remember, he stood or sat behind this vast magnifying set, a huge lens kind of thing, and there was this enormous shadow of him behind it. He was small and he had to look large and when David Niven, now 007, shatters the glass, there's Woody in this sort of throne chair he's sitting in. And the gag was that there was this tiny man who finally comes out, but who had only *appeared* to be enormous.

Casino Royale opened at the Odeon, Leicester Square on 14 April 1967, where it broke every single opening record in the theatre's history. Wisely, critics had been kept at bay until after the première, by which time, fearing the worst, most of them had sharpened their scalpels. 'Many hands make light weight', said *The Times*, 'but who knows, maybe there will be someone to love it somewhere. Unless everyone believes the posters and waits to see "the real James Bond" in *You Only Live Twice*.' Which to some extent they did, although in the US, *Casino Royale* peaked as the biggest three-day opener up to that time in Columbia's history and went on to be the year's third Biggest Money-Maker (after *The Dirty Dozen* and *Casino*'s better Bond rival). However, it somehow failed to emulate that very cycle of films it had set out to satirize. 'I never bothered to see *Casino Royale*', said Woody later, 'I knew it would be a horrible film. The set was a chaotic madhouse. I knew then that the only way to make a film is to control it completely.'

What's Up, Tiger Lily? In between the two Feldman films, and as a sort of test piece for the gems to come, Woody involved himself in an enterprise which he found far more to his taste. Never intended as more than a modest joke, *What's Up, Tiger Lily?* was developed on a whim by producer Henry G. Saperstein who had purchased the rights, for $66,000, to a Bond-style Japanese thriller, *Kagi No Kagi/Key of Keys*. AIP had already made a dubbed version of the film called *Keg of Powder*, but an executive screening provoked such gales of derisive laughter that it was decided to go the whole hog. Woody was invited to look the movie over.

His first viewing of the film was minus the soundtrack and he and Saperstein hit on the idea of retaining much of the Japanese footage, but with Woody and a group of friends dubbing a new send-up version of the story on top of it. For a fee of $75,000 Woody moved his cast to a room at the Stanhope Hotel where, during the course of several screenings, they improvised gags and dialogue. Whatever Woody liked got into the script which was recorded at the Teachers Sound Studio on Broadway. Convinced that something more was needed than the simple over-dubbing of zany dialogue, Woody also spliced in a number of gag effects and some new scenes featuring himself.

Amongst the contributors were Lenny Maxwell, Frank Buxton and Louise Lasser, whom Woody married on 2 February - Groundhog Day - in a brief break from production. Daughter of a wealthy East Side tax lawyer, Louise was a Brandeis University drop-out (she had been reading political theory) and a gifted comedienne and singer who had understudied Barbra Streisand in *I Can Get it For You Wholesale*. She had met Woody while he was appearing at the Duplex in 1961 and represented for him something of an ideal, having been raised in a Jewish family with staunch upper-class WASP values. Although the couple were to remain friends, the marriage broke up after three years, reputedly due to Louise's violent mood swings. These had been exacerbated by the tragic suicide of her mother during the filming of *Pussycat*.

During the making of *Tiger Lily*, Woody was also doing stand-up at the Americana Hotel's Royal Box at night. His last show was at 3am and Woody was in the recording studio at eight. For his return engagement, in May 1967, the Royal Box paid him $6000 a week. As for *Tiger Lily*, 'it was done at such a low price and the idea was so novel', said Woody, 'that it was almost hard for them not to make money with it.'

Although a somewhat scrappy enterprise (he was later to dismiss it as 'stupid and juvenile') Woody was still prepared to stand up for his efforts when Saperstein tried to make him finish before he was ready. Nor was he happy with the result. He hated the title and argued over the producer's insistence on a full-length feature. Woody, preferring a tighter, more frenzied 60-minute version, considered this to be unduly padded. 'Other writers were brought in to add stupid jokes', complained Woody, 'and even my voice was dubbed, at times, by another actor.' Saperstein also interpolated clips from other Japanese adventure films, along with appearances by The Lovin' Spoonful, a popular US rock group, and some current dance crazes like 'The Twist' and 'The Frug'.

Woody felt that his conception had become so inflated that he sued the producers for tampering with his work and tried to halt the film's release. His dissatisfaction was borne out by several reviews which suggested the movie could have been cut by about 20 minutes. The finished entertainment did have its adherents, sufficient in number for Woody to drop his lawsuit, and the film came to represent, even at this early stage, what Maurice Yacowar has held to be 'the essential Woody Allen work'.

The original Japanese film, albeit exotically photographed, would appear to have been, even by the prevailing standards of its cycle, too terrible ever to have enjoyed a profitable release in America. The new version, although not actually very funny when viewed today, is such a peculiar entertainment that it astonishes with its effrontery. The incongruous soundtrack and narration, Woody's 'live' intrusions and generous outpourings of New York Jewish one-liners do go some way, wrote Joel Finler, to demonstrate 'a wacky inventiveness in establishing a totally new and disjointed comic relationship between sound and image. With its rich selection of puns, wisecracks and *non sequiturs*, the script provides a memorable example of Woody Allen's verbal humour run wild.' This, allied to a plot, at least in Woody's version, involving a conspiracy to steal the best egg salad recipe in the world, made *What's Up, Tiger Lily?* an esteemed if, in the long run, spottily attended, cult success.

Woody makes four appearances in the film, first as a cartoon character on the opening titles, then as an interviewee, giving the impression that what we are about to see is a documentary about the making of 'the definitive spy picture' rather than a film in the true sense. Woody and Louise later appear as superimposed silhouette lovers, clandestinely kissing and shadowing the lens from the projection booth. Finally, Woody appears in the last scene, settling down on a couch and eating an apple, as a stripper, played by former *Playboy* centrefold China Lee (the wife of Mort Sahl), begins to disrobe. 'And if you have been reading this instead of looking at the girl', leers Woody, as an optician's chart is run off to right of frame, 'then see your psychiatrist or go to a good eye doctor.' *Tiger Lily* did not, initially, receive many screenings outside of the US - Woody thought it had something to do with the rights problems of the original Japanese movie - and, even five years later, he told *Rolling Stone*, none of the participants had seen any money from it. It didn't turn up in Britain until ten years later when Woody's fame and popularity were a *fait accompli*. As in the US, it succeeded in finding its own audience, *Sight and Sound* describing the film as 'a frantic counterpoint of sound and image as deliriously silly as a Tex Avery cartoon ... this inspired screwball one-off remains as fresh as the day it was born.'

Don't Drink the Water Quite apart from his film projects, Woody was scarcely out of the public eye. He combined well-paid appearances at Las Vegas and other venues with a slew of TV work. For NBC he starred with Liza Minnelli, William F. Buckley and Aretha Franklin on a *Kraft Music Hall* comedy hour segment, 'Woody Allen looks at 1967'. The high point was Woody and Liza in a spoof of *Bonnie and Clyde*. He continued his regular spots on Johnny

Carson and Dick Cavett and in August 1969, appeared, along with Hedy Lamarr and Arthur Treacher, in the première production of Carson's late-night chat-show rival, Merv Griffin - for whom Woody would be an almost weekly contributor. A month later he hosted his own CBS special *Woody Allen*, featuring Candice Bergen, Dr Billy Graham and the musical act, The Fifth Dimension. Included were two short films, *Cupid's Shaft*, a parody of *City Lights* with Bergen in the Virginia Cherrill role, and a loose retake on *Pygmalion*, with Bergen as a dim-witted baker's daughter and Woody as a wise old rabbi. By this time, his first full-length play, *Don't Drink the Water*, had also enjoyed a successful run on Broadway.

Woody's earnings were commensurate with his widening fame. According to *Time*, for a two-week stint at Caesar's Palace just after the play's November 1966 opening his fee was $50,000, and *Current Biography* in the same year was describing him as 'perhaps the most prosperous of today's comedians'. In 1966, from films, TV, personal appearances and published articles, Woody earned a reputed $250,000, double that amount in 1967 and, by the end of the decade, he was making over $1m a year.

Woody had written *Don't Drink the Water* over a two-year period, completing it just prior to leaving for London for *Casino Royale*. Due to that film's protracted schedule, he found himself by the autumn commuting back and forth from London to Manhattan to supervise the casting. Despite the chaotic circumstances of production, including changes of producer and director, 13 cast replacements, the death of an actor's wife and the sudden collapse of one of the leads, *Don't Drink the Water* survived mixed reviews to achieve a run of 598 performances. Had it not been subjected to subsequent moves from the Morosco to two other theatres, it might have played longer than its already impressive 18 months' run.

The film version (1969) was another matter entirely. It was shot mainly in Miami and Quebec, the former chosen to accommodate the film's star, Jackie Gleason, a Miami Beach resident. Seen today, the film is more like a TV movie than a feature and was scripted, without Woody's participation, by two writers, R.S. Allen and Harvey Bullock, who had put in several years with the Hanna-Barbera cartoon division and had gone on to create TV's *Top Cat*. This pair adapted the initial screenplay by Woody's close friend and fellow jazz enthusiast, Marshall Brickman. The film was directed by Howard Morris, the diminutive, energetic Sid Caesar sidekick from *Your Show of Shows* and produced by Woody's managers, Rollins and Joffe.

The play was inspired by Woody's firsthand impressions of what it was like to be in a foreign country, deprived of the everyday necessities of New York life, while the plot, said Woody, posited the idea of what might happen if his own family were let loose abroad, even though they had never had that experience. Woody's version deals with the reluctant implosion of a family of loud New Jersey tourists into a fictitious American embassy - around which idea Woody constructed a well-developed, if not altogether subtle, comedy of manners. Depending on such surefire comic elements as the American tourist abroad (Woody's original title had been *Yankee, Go Home!*), the play also exploits the Cold War as a source of black humour and is fuelled by the self-deprecatory nature of the Jewish joke. This latter element, despite the leading character's origins and profession (he is a caterer from Newark), is scarcely touched upon in the film version. Gleason, the archetypal, blustering Yank in Europe - resentful, homesick, xenophobic, with his loud check shirt and rasping voice - is some way removed from the subtler, more shaded comedy talents of the Broadway version's Lou Jacobi. Gleason's brash, redneck personality, a big screen expansion of Ralph Kramden in *The Honeymooners,* though funny in itself, tends to off-balance the film and as Woody would recall, 'I adored him. He's a genius. But he's the wrong guy.'

American critics took the film roundly to task for vulgarizing the play, as well as for broadening and sentimentalizing the leading characters. These are the Hollanders (Gleason, Estelle Parsons, Joan Delaney), named by Woody after some childhood Flatbush neighbours. In a dire pre-credit sequence we see the family making semi-slapstick preparations for their summer vacation in Greece. En route to their destination, their plane is hijacked so that a minor agent can return to his own country, the aptly named Vulgaria, located behind the Iron Curtain. While awaiting some action, Marion Hollander (Parsons) insists that her husband take her photo. However, they are standing dangerously near some restricted installations and, accused of being spies, they take refuge in the American Embassy. Axel McGee (Ted Bessell), the wimpish attache, left in charge by his ambassador father who is now in Washington, tries to unravel the mess and reason with the Vulgarian secret police chief Krojack (Michael Constantine). Ted also falls in love with the Hollanders' daughter Joan - Daphne in the play - who is engaged to a dull lawyer back home.

Once in the embassy, the film begins to betray its stage origins and only intermittently can we discern the wit and distinctive voice of Woody himself so broadly directed and played is the result. Howard Morris had been the producers' fifth choice as director and although he had already handled two quite successful comedies, one of which had starred Doris Day, they still considered him a novice and dispatched an experienced editor, Ralph Rosenblum, to Florida to keep an eye on things. 'He [Morris] didn't do a very good job on it',

Joffe told me, 'He missed the whole point of the thing. It should have been in these very cramped little quarters of this foreign embassy and he blew it up, made it much too lavish. It finally cost about $8m but no one came to see it. It was a terrible failure'. Indeed, according to Rosenblum, Morris was the antithesis to Woody, being insecure, insensitive, unable to accept ideas that weren't primarily his own and obsessed with playing the role of the important director on set. Matters came to a head in the cutting room where, finally, said Rosenblum, 'I abandoned all efforts at collaborating and simply followed his orders. And, in the end, when the people at Avco Embassy saw his cut, they ordered him to let me recut it my way.'

Woody was subsequently asked by *Time* why he hadn't considered taking a role in the film, possibly as Axel, an early example of the lovelorn wimp whom Woody would delineate in *Play it Again, Sam*. It is significant that, in the Broadway version, the role was played by Tony Roberts, so often to be in films a more upfront *alter ego* for the 'insecure' Woody.

Although Woody *had* been asked to appear in the film, he refused because he was convinced that it wouldn't be as successful as the play and he wanted to concentrate on his writing. He also had an offer to work on the screenplay but, as he told *Boston After Dark*, 'I wrote it as a play and I have no desire to re-work it into something else.' Especially into a film which could not make up its mind whether it was a sort of *Honeymooners* on location, a satire on American foreign policy (*à la Bananas*) or a screwball farce - like some of the 1930s comedies Woody so much admired.

Don't Drink the Water has never achieved a general release in the UK and, apart from the rare National Film Theatre screening (July 1986) and a couple of late-night transmissions on independent television, it remains for Woody's fans the most obscure of all his movie enterprises. Judging by its negligable US gross (just over $1m), the film's lack of commercial appeal to distributors outside its country of origin was not merely a simple matter of 'translation'. In light of the above 'it must have been some self-destructive impulse', suggested *Variety* in December 1994, that had induced Woody to remake *Don't Drink the Water* as a telefeature. Produced as the first of three projected small screen offerings, under his deal with the recently formed Sweetland Films, this version starred Woody, Julie Kavner, Mayim Bialik (of TV *Blossom* fame) and Michael J. Fox. The project was backed with a $3.5m budget by ABC.

Woody's decision to embark on a new film of the play was, apparently, due not so much to disappointment with the first screen version - which he claimed never to have seen until starting the remake - than to the fact that, during the play's original Broadway run, he had found himself watching the performances from the back of the stalls wishing he were old enough to have played, not Axel, but Walter Hollander. 'And it was perfect for me', said Woody, 'because it's my father and mother. Then suddenly I looked up and I was twenty years older - *more* than twenty years older', just the right age to play the part.

On this occasion, the Hollanders (Woody, Kavner, Bialik), unlike their counterparts in the 1969 film, were authentically Jewish, while Woody's direction of the material was obviously more assured than Morris's for the earlier version. Although Woody remains relatively faithful to the play, there are one or two important differences from the first film. One is that the foreign country in which the Hollanders are trapped is now unnamed; another that the characters of the renegade priest, Father Drobney (Dom De Luise), with his inexhaustible repertoire of magic tricks, and the Arab emir, travelling with his 14 wives, are brought into greater prominence than in the Morris film.

The problem with the remake, though, is that some of the material seems even more antediluvian than it had appeared 25 years previously. As *Variety*'s Tom Jacobs drily noted, 'This hopelessly dated comedy is the sort of work that should be kept hidden in a shoe box in his bedroom closet, to be unearthed by future historians who can use it to show how far Allen has progressed over the years.' Although there was praise for the one-liners, Woody's own 'basic exasperated-little-man schtick', the appealing performance of Bialik and De Luise's unusual restraint as Father Drobney, the film was criticized for the thinness of the characterizations, Woody's failure to update the material, the 'cultural insensitivity' of the Arab caricatures and the way that several of the plot developments were 'telegraphed in advance'. Jacobs, whose negative view was echoed by some of the daily critics, indicated in summing-up that audiences would be better served by the concurrent *Bullets Over Broadway* which demonstrated how 'Years of practice have made Allen a much better writer than this early effort would suggest.' Indeed, when the new *Water* was transmitted at 9pm on the ABC network on 18 December 1994, a large proportion of viewers failed to sit through it until the end, and the programme achieved less than half the ratings share of the evening's top attraction, NBC's *A Christmas Romance*.

5

The King of Comedy

1969-75: Take the Money and Run to Love and Death

Take the Money and Run In May 1966 Charles K. Feldman had taken an option on an unproduced treatment by Woody called *Take the Money and Run*. Derived very much from the style of his monologues, it was the story of an ineffectual crook who had known 'five aliases by the time he was 25' but is destined to be a loser. United Artists expressed themselves willing to put up $750,000 for a film version, but this was rejected as insufficient. 'It would have killed the project', said Charles Joffe.

Meanwhile, Val Guest had been approached to direct and he and Woody spent some time together in London discussing the possibility. Progress was stalled, however, on Feldman's prior claim to the property. When the producer's death in 1968 - hastened, it was said, by the stresses of *Casino Royale* - freed the rights to the script, Rollins and Joffe decided to produce it between them but, although they had already been angling for Woody to turn director, neither of them thought he was quite ready.

Guest was now involved elsewhere and an offer to direct the picture was made to Jerry Lewis. Lewis, in need of a career boost, agreed on principle. He told Woody he thought the film should be in colour, whereas initially Woody favoured black-and-white. But meetings between the two were cordial, at which point, to everyone's surprise, United Artists decided not to commit to Lewis. ('It would have been a disaster', agreed Guest). Joffe now let it be known that anyone who took the project on must also accept Woody as director; after much haggling, it fell to the independent Palomar Pictures (a short-lived subsidiary of ABC and backers of the Broadway version of *Play it Again, Sam*) to put up the $2m budget. 'And from that day on', said Woody, 'I never had any problem in the cinema from the point of view of interference in any way.'

Although Woody has maintained that film courses are a waste of time and that 'You can learn all about cameras and lighting in two weeks', prior to starting *Take the Money* he did consult a few established directors for advice, notably Arthur Penn, of whose *Bonnie and Clyde* Woody was a fan. The result was a good natured pastiche of both the Warner Brothers gangster thrillers of the 1930s and the more grittily realistic prison break-out dramas of a later era, like *Brute Force* and *Riot in Cell Block 11*. In his own movie Woody would combine conventional storytelling with a spoof *cinema verité* technique; straight-to-camera interviews and linking commentary delivered by a portentous *March of Time*-style narrator. This was Jackson Beck, the voice behind the old Paramount newsreels, who had also narrated the radio version of *Superman* in the 1940s.

Woody plays Virgil Starkwell, a characteristically inept criminal, persistently frustrated that he 'never made it to the ten most wanted list'. Although Woody says he was thinking of John Dillinger while making the film, the character's name, if not the letter of his exploits, was apparently 'inspired' by one Charles Starkweather, a notorious public enemy of the late 1950s who has been the subject of at least three recent Hollywood movies. *Take the Money and Run* traces Virgil's career from petty larceny in childhood through his involvement in more serious crimes, frequent imprisonment and an ambitious bank robbery which goes wrong. In the original draft, Woody had typed in his own name rather than 'Virgil' and, indeed, there are a number of autobiographical references, like the satirical treatment of his parents, echoes of his childhood and boyish run-ins with the Brooklyn cops. Woody had worked intermittently on the screenplay in late 1966 while nursing *Don't Drink the Water* to Broadway success. As co-writer he selected his old Midwood school pal Mickey Rose, but the strained circumstances of *Water*'s production had again put the project in limbo. Finally, *Take the Money* began filming in San Francisco in the summer of 1968, the location chosen when it was realized that New York or Florida would add $500,000 to the budget. Woody and his team did their best to make 'Frisco resemble locations as widespread as New Jersey, Ohio, Baltimore and Georgia, while the prison scenes were shot in San Quentin where Woody and his cast were frequently mistaken for real guards and prisoners. The warden advised Woody to keep his actors separate from the 4000 or so real cons to avoid hostage-taking, but Woody remembers finding the inmates 'very co-operative and very nice'.

Take the Money was only the second picture to make use of the single truck mobile studio that had been designed and developed by cameraman Fouad Said for the weekly TV show *I Spy*. This meant that, with a brisk 15-minute turn-around, Woody was able to shoot as many as six locations a day, three times the normal for the average Hollywood film unit. Unsurprisingly, the picture came in at $470,000 under budget and a week under schedule, even though Said was replaced some weeks into shooting by Lester Shorr.

Using his script only as a guideline, Woody encouraged his cast, many of them amateurs, to improvise wildly, often shooting as many as three different gags for each scene. Woody said later that his first films were as much as 50 per cent improvised on set and he went in for a lot of coverage, because he thought that's what film directors did. 'I am operating on the principle', he told Kevin Thomas, 'that the less you know about directing, the better off you are.' And, in spite of Woody's apparent contempt for what he regarded as TV-style sloppiness, the lightweight Arriflex cameras did help establish just the kind of natural, documentary look he was aiming for.

Along with his editor, James T. Heckert, Woody then spent eight months trying to whittle down the existing footage into something of manageable length. A number of demoralizing previews left audiences silent, even hostile, and Palomar executives, who regarded the movie as unfunny and formless, now threatened not to release it. In January 1969, Woody's worried production manager, Jack Grossberg, called in editor Ralph Rosenblum, who had gained a reputation for saving 'hopeless' comedies like *The Producers* and *The Night They Raided Minsky's* from disaster. He had also in the early 1960s proved himself adept at cutting low-budget gangster biopics like *Mad Dog Call*. Both of these factors made him an eminently suitable choice to 'salvage' *Take the Money and Run*.

Rosenblum was to note that the movie as he found it, 'was a very unusual experience, a film that seemed to be flying all over the place, with highs as high as the Marx Brothers and lows as low as a slapped-together home movie'. The problem, Rosenblum recalled, was that the film lacked rhythm, had poor continuity and weak cuts and was hampered further by Woody's tendency to throw away much of the film's funniest material, rather than 'patch it or revise it in the cutting room'. This was more due to impatience on Woody's part than self-criticism and, appalled by such potential loss, Rosenblum asked to see the script before committing himself. Delighted to discover 'that it contained a wealth of jokes, many of them very funny' which were not in the film, he agreed to take on the job of re-cutting the picture. He was also immediately impressed by Woody's modesty and lack of pretence. As he got down to work, Rosenblum was also relieved to find that much of the discarded material was still extant and 200 boxes of outtakes were duly delivered to the editor's private cutting room in New York.

At this point, Woody had to go on the road for about three months with his second theatre piece, *Play it Again, Sam*, leaving Rosenblum a free hand with the material in his absence. In his frankly detailed account of his working relationship with Woody, Rosenblum relates how he was able to restore and restructure the film: putting back a number of scenes, extending or recutting others, juggling the material to create a rhythm and, in some cases, moving complete scenes from one part of the film to another, trimming almost everything to quicken the pace. The pretitle sequence, for instance, which ends with Virgil opening fire on the cops in the alley with what turns out to be a cigarette lighter, was lifted from the middle of the movie. The sequence of the two gangs holding up the same bank simultaneously was taken from the beginning and moved towards the middle.

To get a sense of continuity Rosenblum made more use of the staged interview material, like the scenes with Virgil's Groucho-masked parents, much of which had been abandoned, and this, together with the parodic Beck commentary and interviews and Woody's own voice-over, now gave the film an effective frame. It was Rosenblum's idea to have Woody add comic narration to the somewhat maudlin initial scene between Virgil and Louise (Janet Margolin) which, otherwise, Rosenblum felt, seemed to belong in another picture. A number of dead spots due to Woody's 'obsessive desire to keep a strain of seriousness running through the film' were also eliminated.

Rosenblum, in fact, did much to restore Woody's confidence but, although their relationship was amicable - leading to their collaborating on five subsequent movies - there was a less comfortable rapport with the film's composer, Marvin Hamlisch. Grossberg recalled that Woody's apparent indifference to a main title ballad with which Hamlisch was 'justifiably pleased' caused the composer to fall on the floor and weep. The misunderstanding was put down to a failure of communication rather than deliberate malice on Woody's part and Hamlisch was subsequently rehired for Woody's second directorial effort, *Bananas* - 'One of the great unacknowledged film scores', said Rosenblum. For *Take the Money* Woody also persuaded Oscar Peterson to compose a blues.

Seen today, a great deal of the sloppiness Woody was afraid of is still evident in the movie and, like many another tyro comedy director, he often falls into the trap of 'illustrating' visually what has already been verbally described. Woody, not for the last time, also had enormous problems with the film's ending and, when examining the rushes, Rosenblum discovered that Woody had shot about six different ones, 'all of them sentimental, weakly amusing or sad'. The exception, which Woody wanted to use, was a particularly gruesome *Bonnie and Clyde*-type climax in which Virgil is slain in a gun battle with the police. It was, felt Rosenblum and others who saw it, far too chilling for comedy.

Even the ending finally chosen failed to satisfy everybody, especially Pauline Kael of *The New Yorker*, who, at least at that time, was one of Woody's supporters. Like a number of observers, she regretted Woody's failure to get the girl at the end, and she was also not alone in castigating him for the lack of care and concern he seemed to take, certainly in his early films, with his supporting casts. Woody was inclined to agree with this judgement, as well as with Vincent Canby's view that the film was a 'visual monologue'.

He would also confess that it was merely 'abject humility' which made him reluctant to stray too far from his usual vein of routine-based comedy. *Take the Money* is less a narrative than a series of hilarious black-out sketches, sight gags, *non sequiturs* and loose endings - virtually a comic collage so haphazard in execution that, as Vincent Canby would also suggest, 'You have the feeling that scenes and, perhaps, entire reels could be taken out and rearranged without making much difference in total impact, which is good because it all looks so effortless.'

The satirical elements are juxtaposed with a sweetly charming love story, wherein the late Janet Margolin plays, delightfully, the young launderess Louise, who likes to sketch in her lunch hour. Virgil meets her during a despondent bag-snatching stroll through the park - and later marries her. Margolin, who had enjoyed her first big success as the disturbed girl in *David and Lisa* (1961), described Louise as her 'first grown-up role'. Woody found her 'beautifully and hysterically funny' and their scenes together were largely improvised. Also on hand were Louise Lasser, in an entirely ad-lib cameo as Virgil's old friend 'Kay Lewis', Marcel Hillaire as the Fritz Lang-like 'film director' and assistant Stanley Ackerman, a former actor, who was pressed into service to play the photographer who, quite by chance, makes a movie of Virgil's spectacular arrest. Everything, in fact, is grist for Woody's comic observation and recall of Hollywood's old crime movies including a dextrous spoof of the earlier Chain Gang cycle - which climaxes with the entire chain, shuffling, single file like a 'human bracelet' off to freedom. We also have the botched prison escape, (parody of an actual incident involving John Dillinger), in which Virgil's gun, modelled out of soap and painted black, melts in the rain and is reduced to a mass of bubbles. Then there is the big job itself - engineered by a 'film company' shooting a bogus bank heist, while the real one is being enacted under cover. This idea has been a popular movie stand-by but Woody's version, being more farcical and succinct, is undoubtedly the funniest variation on a familiar routine.

Take the Money opened in New York in August 1969 while Woody was appearing on Broadway in *Play it Again, Sam*. He had made the film for a fee and a small percentage which, at the time, he doubted would ever pay off. None the less, the film did quite well on home ground; although it opened quietly, Vincent Canby's warm *New York Times* review turned it around and, after breaking house records at one theatre, another was added. Playing on only 18 screens (and 15 cities) in the US, the film built in popularity and also enjoyed an at least qualified success elsewhere, notably (and improbably) in Greece. Woody, though, has said the film took about seven years to break even and is unlikely, from a creative accountancy standpoint, ever to go technically into the black. As with *Tiger Lily*, a cult following for the movie has grown up almost of its own accord. Each of Woody's subsequent comedies would go on to increasingly better business.

Bananas None of the above was lost on United Artists. Regretting having missed out on *Take the Money*, they now came up with a deal which would grant Woody absolute control over his future projects - including script, casting and final cut - once UA president David Picker had agreed the basic story. It had taken Charles Joffe 18 months' hard slog to obtain these favourable terms: three films on an average 10-12 weeks' shoot, at $2m each. Woody would receive $350,000 per picture, Rollins and Joffe $125,000 as producers. There would also be deferred payments of $200,000 and $50,000 respectively, as soon as any film had recouped 2.7 times its production cost. The deferments would be paid prior to profit participation which worked out at 50 per cent of the net profits, after UA had taken 30 per cent off the top for distribution and kept 50 per cent for itself. Woody's 50 per cent would be split among himself, Rollins and Joffe and others. This was in recognition of the hard work they had done to launch his career. Any excesses on budgets would come out of their fees. Were any excesses to top that amount, UA would cover the remainder. Providing a film were profitable, Woody and his partners would have any losses in their fees made up to them.

For his first project, Woody, to everyone's surprise, offered a serious script, *The Jazz Baby*. 'The guys were white faced', he recalled, 'it was a period jazz story. But probably too ambitious.' He was persuaded to substitute something which would establish his comic image more forcibly before branching out into the serious stuff. Within two weeks Woody came up with *Bananas*, derived from a project he had been working on at MGM in 1966. This had been a satirical book, *Don Quixote USA* by Richard Powell, dealing with a naive American Peace Corp volunteer in an unnamed Caribbean country which is ruled by a dictator. MGM saw it as a comedy vehicle for Robert Morse and also negotiated a possible deal for Woody to direct. Woody and Mickey Rose had a great deal of fun working on the script, tentatively entitled *El Weirdo*, which later contained elements of Woody's *Evergreen Review* story 'Viva Vargas'. But the 40 pages they originally completed were not much liked and the duo had switched to *Take the Money and Run* prior to Woody's departure for London to work on *Casino Royale*.

Bananas began shooting in Puerto Rico in May 1970 - a location facilitated by Governor Luis G. Ferre who, to attract film production to the island, was offering studio facilities and favourable tax concessions to visiting US moviemakers. Sequences were shot in the streets, plazas and docks of old San Juan and, during one particularly gruelling week, at Cerra Gordo which necessitated a 4am departure from the crew hotel and a 90-minute drive so that Woody could obtain just the right light for a scene at dawn. Very much improvised, like *Take the Money*, with a strong cartoon-like approach, the filming, according to Woody, relied strongly on suggestions from the actors and crew. He didn't rehearse in advance or know where he was going to put the camera, and some scenes were shot over and over again, comic business being changed along with the dialogue. As for the film's mainly static camera style, this, he explained later, had been his 'reaction against the tracking shots that tended to muffle and displace the gags' on *Take the Money and Run*.

The result of all this was a riotously funny, if not entirely satisfactory entertainment, which parodies the Cuban Revolution, American interventionism, Black Studies, the CIA, TV advertising, the military Right, the loony Left, machines, profits and a number of sacred cows dear to Middle America - while, at the same time, spoofing such solemn revolutionary biopics as *Viva Zapata* and paying homage to the Marx Brothers and *Duck Soup*. The pretitle sequence takes its cue from the *cine verité* on-the-spot reportage of its predecessor, as an inflexionless, pontificating announcer (Don Dunphy) gives an insistent up-to-the-minute newscast from the troubled Latin American state of San Marcos. The president's assassination has been 'advertised' in advance and the commentator now hands over to a roving reporter who proceeds to present the whole incident as a boxing commentary, plunging through the throng to grab the president's dying words. For this sequence, Woody hired real-life sportscaster Howard Cosell to put it over like an authentic segment of ABC's *World World of Sports*. It is a game self-parody ('Well, you've heard it with your own eyes', rasps Cosell in winding-up), to be capped subsequently, in *Sleeper*, by Woody's definition of Cosell's back-'em-up-against-the-wall style as a suitable 'Punishment for twentieth-century traitors'. Cosell would also appear in

Broadway Danny Rose, but turned down the role of a sex pervert in *Everything You Always Wanted to Know about Sex* because it would 'irrevocably damage his image'. His stint on *Bananas* was filmed in two hours, with Cosell flying in to Puerto Rico and back to New York in a single day.

We now meet Fielding Mellish (Woody), products tester for a large corporation. He is first seen battling it out with the 'Execuciser', a grotesque all-purpose 'exercise while you work' machine for busy execs. The sequence is one of many in the film which pay lip service to Woody's now well-established accident-prone guise and lifelong 'bad relationship' with mechanical objects. In no time at all, Fielding is being assaulted by muggers on the subway (an early brief appearance by Sylvester Stallone) and failing to make it with various girls. Until, that is, a fresh-faced City College student activist, Nancy (Louise Lasser), turns up at his door. To prove himself to her, Fielding decides to become involved with Third World politics, setting off to San Marcos where, after a series of increasingly farcical and improbable misadventures, he becomes rebel leader and, finally, president.

Fielding, disguised *à la* Castro, is sent by the rebel government to negotiate a US loan. This is signalled by a society fund raiser in New York, with a cast drawn, authentically, from the real-life international diplomatic corps. Gaila Leahy, then a young anthropology student on a visit to the city, recalled for me Woody's somewhat singular way of filming this sequence:

> The fund raiser, as I remember, was shot over one day, at a hotel in Manhattan, a proper banquet hall, all set up for the purpose. I happened to be in New York and there was a call to several of the foreign embassies, United Nations people, mostly, for extras who looked like the real thing and had the duds for it ... I had a friend who worked at the French Embassy in a minor role and she said 'Why not go along?' ... Now, the one thing that really struck me was that, when they were filming, Woody didn't actually appear to be making a speech at all, but was sort of mouthing into the microphone, with nothing coming out, and I got the impression that whatever it was he was going to say hadn't yet been decided but was all going to be dubbed on later ... All we saw of him on the day was just his mouth going up and down, up and down, and either no sound coming out or just 'Rhubarb, rhubarb!' I must say it was kinda weird.

The fund raiser is a success and, his confidence already boosted by his coupling with a girl rebel (played by *Playboy* centrefold Natividad Abascal), Fielding finally makes it with Nancy. But he is arrested as a 'subversive impostor' and put on trial - a sequence dictated by the fact, explained Woody, that they 'didn't have the money for the traditional chase. So I made it a trial. It's always much cheaper!' The scenes which follow, reported by actual newscaster Roger Grimsby on the evening news, are Kafka-as-farce at the end of which Fielding is given a 15 year sentence, suspended by the judge on Fielding's firm promise 'that he will not move into my neighbourhood'. Nancy then agrees to marry Fielding and their wedding-night encounter, a 'discreet' under-the-bedclothes affair, takes place in the gold and white bridal suite of the Royal Manhattan Hotel, with Cosell breathlessly announcing the proceedings in a 'play-by-play description'.

This final sequence came about at the suggestion of Rosenblum who felt that Woody's original ending, though funny, failed to work 'in transition'. This had involved Fielding, invited to make a revolutionary speech at Columbia University, falling foul of black protesters, only to emerge from a sudden explosion, in blackface. He is instantly recognized as a 'brother' by three black guys with rifles. Rosenblum suggested that Woody do something which linked the film's ending with the beginning, a device which would subsequently be employed to frame the main narrative of *Anne Hall*.

As with *Take the Money*, Rosenblum was amazed by Woody's willingness to throw out material which didn't work. Cut was a promising sequence in which government troops, disguised as a rumba band, cha-cha-cha through the jungle to take the rebels by surprise. Despite a sudden downpour, it was successfully filmed but, as Rosenblum recalled, 'It was a hit with cast and crew, but it wasn't funny on the screen.' Another scene, with a bogus 'Bob Hope' acting as decoy so government planes could bomb the rebels, looked too much like a war documentary to be funny and, like several other sequences, though hilarious when filmed, failed to make it to the finished movie. Some of the surviving gags, though, are supreme, like the silent, miming quartet at General Vargas's dinner party, a divinely surrealistic moment, reportedly necessitated by the actual no show of the musicians' instruments. The musicians themselves had been recruited from a local old folks' home.

Bananas opened in New York's Coronet Theatre in April 1971, the media noting with interest that Louise, from whom Woody had been divorced for nearly two years, was his leading lady. She is an appealing and accomplished foil, but the film's strength resides, once again, in our response to Woody as a screen comedian. He was the first to admit, though, that the balletic talents of a Chaplin initially eluded him.

Public reaction to the film was, mainly, positive. The French, in particular, 'went mad' about it, though early on, said Woody, his comedies were not particularly successful outside the US. But in spite of the hit-and-miss circumstances of its production, certain themes and obsessions were already beccomming evident. There are, for instance, a number of references to sexual inadequacy and a strong vein of political satire which Woody insisted was purely 'coincidental'. Although his barbs had grown somewhat sharper than during the nightclub years, as a film-maker he realized early on that political criticism is best served with a goodly dose of mockery - as in *Bananas*, with its Marx Brothers view of the trial of the Chicago Seven.

In the same year Woody embarked on one of his most overt political acts as an entertainer: his 'wickedly satirical' 30-minute sketch on Nixon and Kissinger ('Dixon' and 'Wallinger') which he made for New York's Channel 13 TV station (the Public Broadcasting Service network) in December, with Diane Keaton. Part of a one-hour special, *The Politics - and Comedy - of Woody Allen*, it juxtaposed archive footage with dramatic inserts. The show's sudden cancellation in February 1972 evoked only muted protest from Woody who was content to let the scandal surrounding the implications of political suppression and bureaucratic secrecy to speak for itself. Since he had accepted only a nominal $135, the enterprise was quite obviously a labour of love.

Play It Again, Sam During the pause between *Bananas* and Woody's third directorial effort, he busied himself preparing his first volume of short stories and essays for publication, co-hosting the Peabody Award-winning family educational TV series *Hot Dog* for NBC and scripting and starring in the film of *Play It Again, Sam*.

The stage version of *Sam* had opened at the Broadhurst Theater, under Joseph Hardy's direction, in February 1969, and ran for 453 performances. After the success of *Don't Drink the Water*, Woody had wanted to write a funny play he could also act in and found his inspiration in the behaviour of his married friends who, when his second marriage was breaking up, kept trying to introduce him to 'suitable' women - with often embarrassing results. Writing the play mainly at the Astor Towers Hotel in Chicago in 1968, Woody combined the married friends idea with the story of a film critic who has fantasies about his favourite movies. The figure of 'Humphrey Bogart', a late addition to the piece, was quickly transformed into a leading character.

Many critics at the time regarded *Sam* as merely a pleasant evening's diversion but (as witness the extended subtlety of the 1973 film version) it remains elemental to an understanding of Woody's creative development from this time on. More importantly, the growing relationship with his new love and co-star, Diane Keaton (after the final, amicable split with Louise four months into the play's run) seemed to give Woody a wholly new perspective in his life and work.

As in the film, Woody played Allan Felix, a nervous, sexually frustrated film buff, trying to revive his love life and self-respect after his wife has left him. In his despair, he somehow conjures up the reassuring shade of Humphrey Bogart (Jerry Lacey), the star whose romantic aura and seduction technique he would most like to emulate. After a number of unsuccessful encounters with young women, Felix moves to a successful climax (in both senses of the word) with Linda, his best friend's wife, played by Diane.

The play is an insouciant conjuring trick, one of a number of examples of Woody's sleight-of-hand in respect of such questions as 'What is myth?' and 'What is true?' - plus the constant blurring of the same. The play's title is itself mythical - a much misquoted line, supposedly from *Casablanca*, but actually from *The Spoilers* (1955), and never spoken in that precise form in the earlier film by any of the characters.

It is, though, *The Maltese Falcon* which Allan is watching on TV at the beginning of the stage version - the scene where, in spite of his attraction to her, Bogart tells Mary Astor she will have to take the rap for her crimes. In the screen version, *Casablanca* seems in every way more appropriate and many fans preferred the Bogart interpolations of the film, notwithstanding the wonderful theatricality of the apparitions in the play.

The irony of *Sam* is that Linda, who knows the *real* Allan Felix, is drawn to him in spite of the false Bogartian image he tries to project; it could be successfully argued that, seen in this light, the Bogart character is a *non sequitur*. Though offering his own variations on the essential Bogart dialogue, Felix knows full well that he can never *be* Bogart. Until his *rapprochement* with Linda, he is marked down for amorous disaster. Even then he is too nervous to relay Bogart's romantic promptings to the letter and it is only by being recognized and accepted for his true self that Felix can score - this almost at the expense of his friendship with his best buddy, the phonoholic Dick (Tony Roberts).

With *Sam* settled into a healthy run in New York, the play opened in London in September with Dudley Moore as Allan Felix. The casting had come about at the suggestion of Val Guest, who told Woody that Moore would be 'fabulous' in the part and subsequently urged the younger comedian to accept. When producer David Merrick asked Woody what he thought of the idea of Moore as his West End surrogate, Woody replied, simply, 'Great', and, as Guest told me, 'I like to think I helped to get him into that and started his career as an actor.'

Fans of Moore's crumpled charm - rather than of Woody's essentially New York Jewish humour - kept a much anglicized version of the play running for ten months at the Globe Theatre after a brief try-out in Cambridge. 'It was his first acting part', that production's Nancy, Patricia Brake, told me, 'and he was very nervous. But *Play It Again, Sam* was really his thing. The part *was* Dudley and he was very good in it.'

Woody has been the first to admit that any number of actors may have played the role of Allan Felix better than himself and *Sam* has remained a regular item in the repertoire. It was, until recently, the eleventh most popular play in the American amateur theatre - as opposed to *Don't Drink the Water* at fifth. 'The surprising preference of *Water* over *Sam*', quipped Maurice Yacowar, 'is presumably due to the dwindling supply of Bogart impersonators.'

By the fall of 1971, Woody was starring in but not directing the film version of *Sam*, which would blend the mystique of *Casablanca*, San Francisco and Woody's (by this time defunct) affair with Diane Keaton into a dreamlike, if verbally-hip homage to Hollywood romanticism. Although some critics were to find the result more ordered and coherent than his own initial directorial efforts, others bemoaned the loss of Woody's disjointed free-flight gag style. 'I'm hoping *Sam* will be a nice, solid, funny, commercial picture', he told a San Francisco press conference, 'and hopefully entice a broader audience for me than I get with my own films.'

According to Charles Joffe, Woody had been reluctant to adapt *Sam* to the screen, preferring, as with *Water*, to sell the rights for a handsome sum and forget about it. Although he originally wrote the play for himself, he apparently tried to persuade Richard Benjamin and Paula Prentiss to star in the film version. Neither were available and another of Woody's choices, Dustin Hoffman, was also tied up with movie contracts. 'I was', said Woody, 'the only one who was available.' The rights had been acquired prior to the Broadway opening by Arthur P. Jacobs, best known for the popular *Planet of the Apes* series, who planned to produce the film, together with Rollins and Joffe, under the latter's set-up at United Artists. But because UA, in spite of the play's success, were too cautious to back it, Jacobs took the project to Fox where he had an ongoing distribution deal. The latter studio then had second thoughts after $700,000 had been spent on pre-production. This included $400,000 for the rights to the play. Happily, Paramount, under the then aegis of Robert Evans, agreed to take the project off Fox's hands for a mere $250,000.

Woody had not been part of the original package and Paramount were only persuaded to have him in the film due to the unexpected success of *Bananas*. Diane, for a fee of $21,000, was signed to recreate her stage part, along with Roberts and Lacey, and 'To the best of my knowledge', the film's director Herbert Ross told me, 'no one else was considered for the roles.' Initially curious that Woody had not chosen to direct the picture, Ross soon realized that he 'wanted it to be different as a film, to have more dimension'. As he also told me, there had never been any attempt on Woody's part to assume even minor directorial responsibility on *Sam*: 'Woody didn't ever direct a scene nor did he ever evidence any desire to do so. I asked him during rehearsals why he had not wanted to direct himself and he replied, "Well, this is a story with plot and character and I couldn't do that." So it was a learning experience for him.' As Woody told Hellmuth Karasek in 1987, Ross 'directed it the way he wanted and I just did what I was told to do. But he had seen the play and wanted to retain in the movie that which worked in the play, he wasn't looking for radical changes.'

Ross subsequently confessed that he had been initially nervous about working with Woody, but actually found him 'terribly open and modest ... delightful to work with, unassuming, no cranky kicks' and very co-operative over making changes to the adaptation which had taken Woody about ten days to write. 'It was easy to do', he recalled, 'and Herb had some very good suggestions for the screenplay.' Chief among these was Ross's more visual approach to the material. He has recalled that Woody's initial draft script had been a virtually unadulterated version of the play, complete with stage directions. Ross suggested that Woody eliminate Allan Felix's opening monologue and write a number of additional scenes to move the characters on from one setting to another.

It was originally intended to shoot in New York but, within two weeks of the start date, the production was hit by a film technicians' strike in the city. Due to what Paramount regarded as exorbitant 'below-the-line' New York labour costs and the fact that official six-day working on the West Coast could take a whole week off an average eight-week schedule, the studio decided to switch the film's location from Manhattan to San Francisco - a change which, considering Woody's frequently verbalized distaste for southern California and his deep-rooted New York persona, could well have damaged the material. But he had not always disliked Los Angeles - he had relished his time working on *The Colgate Comedy Hour* in the early 1950s - and has frequently named San Francisco as his second favourite American city. Ross had refused to consider Los Angeles 'because it was the wrong atmosphere for the story', and, although Woody was 'a bit nervous about it' he agreed to the change, mainly due to the fact Ross recalled, that 'San Francisco did have all the elements the story required - a university life, a film culture and beaches.'

In opening out the play, Ross and Woody were able to set the story in some very charismatic locations selected only a week before the start of rehearsals. These included the bandshell of Golden Gate Park, the San Francisco Museum of Art, the Trident Restaurant on the Bay, Cunio's Italian Bakery, Ray's Laundromat, the Spaghetti Factory cabaret and a couple of very attractive hillside apartments. Allan Felix's apartment was actually the home of a real-life amateur film-maker and local film critic, while the beach house used in the film belonged to a couple very like the characters played on screen by Tony Roberts and Diane Keaton. Apart from a few scenes shot at Paramount's Marathon Street Studios in Hollywood, virtually all the interiors were also filmed on location and, notwithstanding a few bleak gags aimed at the values of West Coast living, *Sam* thus becomes, at first glance, an on-screen love affair with San Francisco, as potent in its way as Woody's ongoing relationship with Manhattan.

Much of *Sam*'s undoubted appeal resides in Ross's direction. As befits a former choreographer, he always 'moves' the film well, retaining audience interest through a great deal of expository dialogue by having the leading characters in almost constant transition from one attractive locale to the next. In all of this, cinematographer Owen Roizman's contribution to the proceedings is incalculable. 'Owen is a wonderful cameraman', Ross told me, 'I had told him I wanted the film to look like pastel-coloured popcorn. He told me later, after the success, that he never thought anything we had done was funny. He was very surprised when he heard the laughter.' Roizman's use of low light levels and shallow depth of field, against real backgrounds, has been influential and, as he noted to Dennis Schaefer and Larry Salvato in 1984, '*Play It Again, Sam* was one of my favourites. I think it was a really good picture. I'm not known as a comedy cameraman but I did three of them and I just find that you end up shooting it a little bit brighter and using more light. There isn't much else you can do.'

Filming began on 4 October 1971, with the scene where Felix is introduced to Julie (Joy Bang) in the Trident Restaurant, and claps his hand in the salad. The first shot, panning with Allan and Dick as they walk through the restaurant, was satisfactory, but a little scene at the end, where Felix's ice-cream pop flies up in the air, required 37 takes, because Woody couldn't get the business right. Ross has recalled that, having printed all the takes and decided on the very last one, he received a message, three days later, from a perturbed Robert Evans, saying, 'Do you think you will have to do as many takes for *every* scene?'

There were also problems, said Ross, in directing the cast to play more subtly than they had in the stage version: 'It was an adjustment in tone, which in the movie is far more refined. The play was broader and cruder.' As Ross told Richard J. Anobile in March 1977, 'When we began rehearsals I suggested that we forget that we were doing a comedy, I wanted it to be funny, but played more for the play. For example, Tony's character could have ended up a mere caricature if it had been taken too far.'

Although the material was tightly scripted, a certain amount of freedom, as in Woody's own films, was, Ross told me, very much par for the course in his handling of the scenes:

Woody and Diane were directed as much or as little as any actor may be in a movie. And the approach did lend itself to a degree of spontaneity. The bit with the flying record in the blind date scene happened in the course of a rehearsal and we kept it in. The scene of Woody preparing for the date in his bathroom, with the out-of-control blow dryer, was improvised by both of us and was, in fact, unscripted. Sometimes, in filming, we found ourselves very near the edge, like when the cinemobile we were working out of caught fire and burned up the day of the bridge shots, but we continued to work through the crisis and there was a replacement up in San Francisco two days later. Taken all in all, though, things went very smoothly and for all the problems of filming mostly, on location, we shot the picture, I think, in forty days, or maybe less. It was also done quite cheaply. The budget was $1.6m and the picture came in about $1.3m. I've no idea what the P & A were but I assumed minimal. It was all very pleasant. Just about everything was done by ourselves. We just set out, determined to make a movie, and it always *was* a movie in everyone's mind, not a mere adaptation.

The film is, indeed, thoroughly cinematic and, although Woody told Diane Jacobs that 'the play's tight structure forbade new material, so most of the options are directional', there are, in fact, a number of departures. The most significant is in having the play's fantasy figures, like the 'dream' Bogart and Felix's ex-wife Nancy (a 'flashback' in the play) appear as fully rounded characters, just as Allan Felix envisions them. In the film, Nancy (Susan Anspach) is also a far more pleasant person, instead of, as on stage, a figure of grotesque fantasy. But Graham McCann still noted in Woody's approach a 'tendency for a Bob Hope style of boyish misogynism' which is nowhere more apparent than in his treatment of the latter character who manifests a number of traits derived, apparently, from Woody's first wife Harlene.

The slight softening of Nancy in the film version does point toward Woody's continuing affection for Louise, who would also partially inspire a number of key moments in *Annie Hall*, as well as the character of Dorrie in *Stardust Memories*. Unlike Harlene, Louise never took Woody's digs too seriously. 'I did say some of those things', she told Tim Carroll in 1993, 'like

"I wanna be free! I wanna laugh all the time! I wanna go skiing!" but he was
horrible and took them out of context.'

A number of feminist writers also expressed themselves weary, as they
would at the time of *Annie Hall*, of seeing the Allen character struggling 'to
make out with women'. But, as Ross told Richard Anobile, 'That theme runs
though *all* his films ... it was the subject of the story. There is no plot without
that story! It is a classic theme. Chaplin had the same thing in every movie as
well.' In order, though, to make the Allan Felix character more sympathetic -
especially in light of the fact that he actually sleeps with his best friend's wife
- Ross made a conscious decision to direct the famous seduction scene in
Linda's apartment as if she were the aggressor, so that 'What Allan responds
to is that for the first time a woman, because of her own particular problems,
is interested in him. Her interest is the catalyst that ignites the flame which
produces that response in him.' It was, as Ross also commented 'a dangerously difficult scene to play within the context of the film', but was obviously
softened, to some extent, by Woody's increasing skill in writing convincing
female characters. Linda, for instance, is somewhat expanded from the play
version. She is a much more real character and, for Diane, the role was something of a breakthrough. Ross was to praise her as 'a splendid actress, mature
for her age'.

Other changes from the play include the turning of Felix's straight-to-
audience asides into voice-overs, but the main transformation, apart from
questions of scale, resides in the quite different use of the Bogart legend as a
springboard for the action. On stage, notwithstanding some famous quoted
lines, the character of Bogart seemed nearer to Sam Spade in *The Maltese Falcon*
than to *Casablanca*'s Rick. In the film, *Casablanca* predominates, notably in the
use of clips at the beginning and end of the movie, for use of which Warners
demanded $250,000. The Bogart/*Casablanca* motif under the opening titles
was Ross's idea and, inspired by a study of Bogart's movies prior to the commencement of shooting, Ross also decided to paraphrase the final
'renunciation' scene of *Casablanca*, shot for shot, with the three stars of *Sam*
playing their parts as 'honestly' as Bogie, Bergman and Paul Henreid had in the
original. 'We shot that on a very windy night at San Francisco airport', said
Ross, 'You can imagine what it was like trying to get that fog into shot!'

A major problem of the film resides in matching the real Bogart (in the
clips) with his ghostly counterpart in the story, the actor Jerry Lacey. Although
Ross declared Lacey to be 'the best imitation of Bogart I've seen', the actor is
less successful on screen than on stage because, unlike the theatre, where distance and lighting facilitate suspension of disbelief, we are only too aware, in

the screen version, that he is patently *not* Bogart. But Lacey, best known, otherwise, as a star of the hit TV series *Dark Shadows* (1966-71), was so remarkable in both media that the role of Bogie, which he also played in a number of commercials, was to cast a shadow on his subsequent career. ('I don't know where Jerry is now', Ross, told me, 'He seems to have disappeared. Nice man.')

The choice of Bogart, the idol of Woody's own generation, as his screen character's role model, was a significant one. It was the first time, on screen, according to the evidence of friends and other observers, that Woody had engineered a more than *passing* connection between his on-screen and off-screen identities. Although Woody, taking his customary stance, was quick in his denials, the one autobiographical element which he would never be able to deny is the way he has exploited his lifelong addiction to cinema. *Sam,* through the very nature of its hero's occupation, is ideally suited to a veritable stream of captivating old movie references. Billy Goldenberg's score likewise authenticates the film's cult credentials, along with the (obligatory) Dooley Wilson singing 'As Time Goes by'.

When *Sam* came out in April 1972, it did, as a number of his associates had predicted,usher in for Woody a whole new public. 'The picture opened at the Radio City Music Hall - an amazing booking for Woody', Ross told me, 'It was one of the last movies to play Radio City. It was moved to an East Side house still in the first run about three weeks later.' Apart from its commercial success, the film also offered Woody a brand new perspective and maturity for his future career; starting with *Sam,* a popular image of him had begun to appear which, for movie audiences at least, was taken to be both a reflection of themselves and all the things they were to assume Woody was about. The film itself attracted a plethora of warmly appreciative notices: Vincent Canby, echoing the thoughts of many, declared that 'Woody Allen ... is, I'm convinced, the premier comic intelligence at work in America today ... and probably even tomorrow.'

Sam took over $11m in the US, Woody making $1m plus out of his ten per cent of the gross. *The Motion Picture Herald* placed him, for the first time, in its annual list of Top Money-Making Stars, at number 13. He would remain in the list until 1979, the year he made it to fourth, and there would be a further, final appearance in 1986.

Everything You Always Wanted to Know About Sex* (*But Were Afraid to Ask) Woody's initial showing in the lists had been augmented by the concurrent box-office success of *Everything You Always Wanted to Know About Sex* (*But Were Afraid to Ask),* a portmanteau movie, only loosely derived from the

best-selling question-and-answer sex manual of that name by Dr David
Reuben. Woody claimed only to have glanced at the book, though one sketch,
at least, in the movie, is drawn from Reuben. 'I think we learned more from
Woody Allen's film than we did from the book', said a subsequent sex researcher,
Dr June Reinisch of The Kinsey Institute. As Maurice Yacowar has rightly noted,
the film is less an adaptation of Reuben than Woody's reaction *against* the book
and sex manuals in general. Woody's decision to make the film came about by
accident. Watching late-night TV with Diane, he heard someone remark that,
were Reuben's work ever to be filmed, the only person who could do it justice
was Woody. He immediately instructed his managers to negotiate the rights
from producer Jack Brodsky, who had originally acquired the book as a vehicle,
with Paramount backing, for his then partner, Elliott Gould.

In the interim, the book's pat blend of reassurance had grown dated and
Gould's popularity as a symbol of early 1970s counter-culture had waned. The
Gould-Brodsky partnership had also recently been dissolved and Rollins and
Joffe had little difficulty acquiring the property. Woody's version of *Sex* was to
be the first of the team's productions to be made almost entirely in a
Hollywood studio. The budget was $2m: Woody would receive 20 per cent of
the gross receipts, with Brodsky and Gould retaining credit as co-producers.

A number of writers before Woody had tried to come up with a viable
script, but had failed. Working on the screenplay prior to filming *Sam*, and
with an uncredited contribution from Marshall Brickman, Woody felt that the
relaxation of censorship had only just made possible the kind of sexual satire
he had in mind.

The idea, though, according to Joffe, was to eschew any kind of sensation-
alism and to treat the subject through the eyes of an 'irreverent comic'. Since
the book contains several hundred forthright questions on sexual matters,
Woody contented himself with boiling them down to six, adding one of his
own invention and substituting satiric revue sketches in lieu of Reuben's 'jaun-
ty self-confident replies'.

'I didn't enjoy the movie', Reuben would complain later to the *Los
Angeles Herald-Examiner*, 'because it impressed me as a sexual tragedy. Every
episode in the picture was a chronicle of failure which was the converse of
everything in the book.' But, as Douglas Brode has averred, it is the key
point of the movie 'that none of the questions are answered by the individual sketches at all. The film, then, is a paradox: a movie that flatly rejects the
book it's based on.'

As Woody sees it, the film became a satire on America's well-established
obsession with sexual topics, and a comment on those (the media, film-makers

and 'learned sexologists') who feed on that obsession. 'R for Rabelaisian', was Woody's wry comment on the picture's inevitable MPAA rating!

One of the better sketches (the fourth in the film) has Lou Jacobi as a man with a sudden-to-strike cross-dressing urge. Escaping, *en travestie*, from the bedroom of his future son-in-law's parents, he has 'his' purse snatched in the street and ends up perversely enjoying the dangerous possibility of having his true gender discovered by a curious crowd of bystanders. Jacobi's Tatiesque reactions to this predicament are oddly endearing, while the sketch also pokes gentle fun at the fiancé's snobbish Jewish family with their African carvings and musical evenings. Doubtless recalling his own lower-middle class Brooklyn origins, Woody treats all of these characters with a mixture of horror and affection.

The above sketch replaced another - which was filmed but discarded by Woody - called 'What Makes a Man a Homosexual?' In this, Woody was a male spider, trying to make it with a black widow (Louise Lasser) who seduces and devours him. Finally, the camera zooms away to reveal Woody, again, but human size as a gay, lisping entomologist who has been spying on the 'lovers' through his microscope. The sketch was highly elaborate and, when the scheduled three-day shoot stretched into two weeks, Woody threatened to have a nervous breakdown. After abandoning filming it in LA, he had a portion of the giant-sized steel cable cobweb transported to New York where he tried again, with just cameraman and sound. Finally, after undergoing maximum discomfort with the suffocating spider costume he had to wear, and dissatisfied with the various endings he'd come up with, he scrapped it. Read today, the sketch is still funny and, amusing though the transvestite episode is, we can only mourn the loss of the bizarre entertainment it replaced.

The third sketch in the film, 'Why Do Some Women Have Trouble Reaching Orgasm?' is an effective parody of a certain kind of Italian movie, wherein Woody marries a mature virgin (Louise Lasser), who can make it sexually only in 'endangered' public places. The idea is a nodding reference to the plot of Monicelli's *Casanova 70* (1965), in which Marcello Mastroianni is a would-be seducer, pathologically impelled to place himself in extreme jeopardy in order to succeed in the boudoir. The implications are somehow unnerving - an element which Woody plays upon wonderfully, at the same time transmuting his established 'inadequate' persona, through the medium of the settings and the witty pidgin Italian dialogue (learnt phonetically!), into a suave Latin lover.

Interestingly, this sequence was also a replacement, substituting for a sketch dealing with masturbation. Woody and Louise were to play Onan and his wife, Tamar (*Genesis*, Chapter 38!) and a desert location in Palm Springs had been selected. Louise happened to read a version of the Italian script which Woody had decided to cut. The original blue print was a pastiche of an old De Sica-Lollobrigida peasant village movie, in black and white, which Woody planned to shoot in the style of the Neo-Realists. 'No, no', Louise insisted, 'I hear footsteps in a large corridor and I see Ferraris and that kind of thing.' Convinced that this would work, Woody, according to Eric Lax, approached Paula Prentiss and Richard Benjamin, then John Cassavetes and Raquel Welch, all of whom turned the sketch down. The sequence finally featured Woody and Louise - the latter with blonde hair and make-up *à la* Monica Vitti. 'I really started to feel that piece', recalled Woody, 'I just loved it. Some of the shots in there are dynamite ... the colour is great ... It would take up to three hours to do one of those [Bertolucci] shots, but I never had anything to do except worry about imitating one of those styles.'

Visually, the sketch was Woody's most mature work to that date, due largely to the efforts of set designer Dale Hennesy and cameraman David M. Walsh. Walsh, unimpressed by the technical quality of Woody's earlier films, initially resisted his invitation to light *Sex* but, as he would subsequently recall, although technical decisions were left to him, Woody took more and more interest in finding things out. He also experimented with different uses of colour and stylized decor, like the white-on-white look of the Italian piece (a motif used again, for comic effect, in *Sleeper*), and the glowing yellow lighting of the 'Sodomy' sketch, which would resemble a glossy De Luxe women's picture from the 1950s.

Woody's confidence had also grown to the extent that he was less concerned with staying within budget; Walsh recalled that they 'over-covered a lot on *Sex*' and there were always problems in getting Woody to prepare in advance. Against this, 'Woody will find a frame that's really a classic and has a lot of merit in it that some cameramen and artists couldn't find in a lifetime.' The Italian sketch is a case in point. It represents, in embryonic form, a clear exposition of Woody's theory that 'Serious directors have all the fun' and, of all his early film work, it would remain his favourite.

The remainder of the sketches are a mixed bag. A medieval sequence, 'Do Aphrodisiacs Work?' has Woody as a court jester, floundering in a desperate Henny Youngman-style routine, cracking comforting bad gags and trying vainly to get inside Lynn Redgrave's chastity belt. She's the Queen, Anthony Quayle is the King and, as in *Play It Again, Sam*, Woody is called Felix. The sketch includes a parody of Hamlet's 'To be or not to be' soliloquy, revamped in medical terminology, and also has the idea of the ghostly father, like Bogart, egging Felix on to seduce the Queen. Aided by a frothing aphrodisiac, Felix nearly succeeds but, foiled by the chastity belt, he is discovered and beheaded. The stylistic model here is *A Man for All Seasons*, the homage to Bob Hope and the pseudo-medieval comic-strip dialogue and game, behavioural swagger of the principals are straight out of Moreland's *Humours of History*. The sketch also pays tribute to such essentially Yank-angled chain-mail and tights nonsenses as *Prince Valiant, The Court Jester* and *The Black Shield of Falworth*. Woody, with his modern neurotic mien, obligatory spectacles and schoolboy smut dialogue, echoes his avowed fondness for Bob Hope's famous gift for anachronism, and is as deliriously out of place as he would be subsequently in *Love and Death*. But, in spite of Woody's skill and Redgrave's charm, the initial joke runs out of steam.

The film's second sketch, 'What is Sodomy?' is a genuine curiosity about a respected medic in love with a sheep - an affliction he has 'inherited' from a patient, an Armenian shepherd. After a number of embarrassments and professional disgrace, the good doctor runs amok in a restaurant and ends up on Skid Row, guzzling on a bottle of Woolite. Like the Jacobi sketch, the story relies on the 'comedy of embarrassment' and deals with the tragedy, in comic terms, of the man of probity (cf. Hurstwood in Theodore Dreiser's *Sister Carrie*) who suffers social and moral decline due to his obsession with a love object from an 'inferior class'. Although Dreiser could not have envisaged his unfortunate protagonist's self-destructive aberration as an ovine one, Woody was in no doubt about his *chief* model when, reportedly, he offered the role of the doctor to the star of *Sister Carrie*'s film version: Sir Laurence Olivier! In the event, Gene Wilder's wonderful moon face, with its constant look of surprised innocence, is perfect for the part. He was 'terrific', said Woody.

'What are Sex Perverts?' is a skit on TV panel shows, shot throughout in fuzzy 'Kinescope' blow-up, wherein contestants are asked to participate in a show called *What is my Perversion?*. Presided over, with mock seriousness, by such real-life TV personalities as Jack Barry of *What's My Line?* and Pamela Mason, the show offers prizes to contestants with the most fascinating sexual hang-ups. Although the satire of the sketch is dimmed today by such genuine equivalents as *The Love Connection*, there's a funny bit about a man who exposes himself on subways. But the winner is a rabbi from 'the heartland of innocence', Muncie, Indiana, who gets an opportunity to act out his favourite fantasy on air. In an obvious dig at the coyness of prime-time TV's handling of matters sexual this turns out to be little more than a purely *dietary* aberration. The sight of the bound and gagged rabbi, however, flogged by an attractive model, while his wife is forced to eat pork at his feet, was, to some, an offensive image. Each of the sketches, as Douglas Brode has noted, plays up the connection between sex and food - an element somewhat over stressed, elsewhere, by this particular analyst of Woody's work.

The sixth sketch, 'Are the Findings of Doctors and Clinics Who Do Sexual Research and Experiments Accurate?' poses a question not to be found in Dr Reuben's book and, significantly, this is the one item which most closely parodies an existing film genre. It burlesques the themes of such classic Universal horror pics as *The Mad Doctor of Market Street* (1942) but, because we have seen too many such spoofs, this sketch comes across as one of the weaker items in the film. John Carradine is Dr Bernardo, a reject from Masters and Johnson (!), conducting arcane experiments in a rambling old house on a hill. He was, in fact, the first man 'to measure the sound waves produced by an erection', and his assistant Igor, a pathetic Dwight Frye-like hunchback, apparently got that way due to a scientifically induced four-hour orgasm. 'Posture, posture', murmurs Woody, in passing, as visiting sexual researcher Victor Shakapopolis.

Bernardo, a sinister combination of Frankenstein and Dr Moreau, has evil designs on all visitors, and when Victor's companion, Helen Lacey (Heather Macrae), a Sunday supplement reporter, is about to be gang-banged by a bunch of slavering boy scouts, Victor springs to the rescue, firing a gun in all directions. They escape from the suddenly exploding laboratory, but a vast vat of silicone overflows and the couple are pursued across country by a mammoth marauding breast (very Philip Roth!). Woody also guys the traditional Hollywood cupcake fetish, in having Victor co-operate in imprisoning the rampant mammary expansion in a gigantic brassière.

The film's final sequence, 'What Happens During Ejaculation?' is the one for which the movie is chiefly remembered, and the only one for which there would be any sort of critical consensus as to the quality of the individual sketches. It draws its inspiration from Dr Reuben's analogy of the reproductive process as a sort of anatomical missile launch, Woody setting the whole segment inside a NASA-like rocket base (the human body), while outlining the physiological and psychological workings of intercourse and male orgasm in space-age terms. It is inspired nonsense, and Woody's own turn as the terrified (Jewish) Sperm No.2 ('What if it's a homosexual encounter', he wails, while awaiting to be ejaculated) affords us some brilliantly lunatic comedy. The sketch itself is framed by a couple trying to make love in a car. Woody, increasingly nervous, prepares to take his first trip into 'Space', playing 'Red River Valley' on his harmonica. He contributes a sense of owlish alarm to a sequence which, if again overlong, equals the Italian parody for cinematic virtuosity.

The set design of this sketch is superb, the costuming ingenious, the guest stars suitably tongue-in-cheek. The Big Screwing itself is conveyed subjectively. The sight of burly hard hats slaving away in the 'boiler room', ankle deep in bodily fluids, and striving to raise a 45° erection in the subject, being yet another mind-boggling absurdity conjured out of Woody's extraordinary imagination. He even manages to transpose his own New York-based anxieties on to his 'sub human' role as the pre-ejaculated sperm cell, all too aware of a world out there which literally bristles with unknown terrors. The cinematic models are, in this instance, Hennesy's own 1966 designs for *Fantastic Voyage*, Kubrick's *2001* and Fritz Lang's vision of sweating labourers working to maintain the city of the future in *Metropolis*. The imagination, otherwise, is Woody's.

Sex opened in New York only four months after *Sam*, with Woody cutting the final print right up until an hour before the première. Due to the fact that Rosenblum was busy directing the documentary feature *Turner,* the editing on this occasion was supervised by James T. Heckert. The film received some of Woody's most encouraging reviews yet, though some critics (Vincent Canby, Paul D. Zimmerman *etc.*), while recognizing the cleverness of the enterprise, adamantly refused to find it funny. *Sex*, like *Bananas*, was very well received in France, where Woody had become a cult figure, while in Italy, actor and theatre director, Oreste Lionello (who would dub Woody into Italian for over 20 years) was quick to note how much Woody's humour was 'based on elements of European culture'.

Sleeper Since Woody's income from *Play It Again, Sam* and *Sex* was reliant on future profits, he had received no real money for a year. In October 1972 he took himself off on a gruelling six-week tour of his stage act, including Chicago, San Francisco and Las Vegas. The latter venue paid him $85,000, warming up the audience for his managers' other top client, Harry Belafonte. This was to fulfil his final engagement on an old 1965 contract and represented his first stand-up tour since 1968. It was also to be his last. Characteristically, he wore the same dark brown tweed jacket on stage as he had in *Play It Again, Sam*. Woody devoted his spare time to working on the three one-act plays, *Sex, God* and *Death*, and preparing for the late spring shooting of *Sleeper*.

Billed as 'A Love Story about Two People who Hate Each Other ... 200 years in the Future', *Sleeper* was a spectacular elaboration on the last sequence from *Everything You Always Wanted to Know About Sex*. Set in the year AD 2173, it pokes fun at certain American institutions, as seen through the eyes of a present-day health-food store owner, Miles Monroe (Woody), who is unfrozen from a time capsule after two centuries of suspended animation. The film is a chaotic narrative, drawing on sources as wide ranging as Mayakovsky's *The Bed*

Bug, Godard's *Alphaville,* Kubrick's *A Clockwork Orange,* Harold Lloyd, Buster Keaton and, especially, H.G.Wells's *When the SleeperWakes* - which had in 1964 been a putative AIP project for Vincent Price.

Again Woody fulfilled a three-way function as actor, director and writer, sharing the latter chore with Marshall Brickman who would collaborate on three further Allen projects. Brickman, former chief writer on *The Johnny Carson Show*, was an ex-country singer and banjo player whom Woody had met when they were both appearing in cabaret, and had been inducted as a sideman into Woody's New Orleans Funeral and Ragtime Orchestra, a group of gifted amateurs, playing for fun and worthwhile charities. Already, in 1969, Woody and Brickman had worked together on an abortive screenplay, *The Filmmaker,* which no one thought 'special enough to produce'. In the late summer of 1972 Brickman took official leave from *The Dick Cavett Show*, of which he was now producer and creative director, and joined Woody on the new project.

According to Woody, he got the idea for *Sleeper* while walking down the street at the time he was working on *Sex*. Although he has claimed 'never to have been up in science fiction', he admits that the trigger was probably the 'sperm' sequence from the latter film: 'It was fun to make that, and the "scientific" backdrop worked for comedy. So I decided to extend it'. Woody's initial plan was for a three-hour movie, set half in the present, half in the future, with an intermission. But, when he started to write it, Woody realized 'it was a Herculean task. I mean, "Forget it, we'll just do the futuristic part of it".' After discarding a number of other ideas, Woody was soon able to show a finished draft to David Picker at UA who liked it and approved the project, in spite of the fact that its locations and special effects would be expensive. Woody said he wanted it to look like 'a great big cartoon ... cute and funny' but the making of the film was to be the opposite of light-hearted. *Sleeper*, recalled Ralph Rosenblum, was 'a monstrous challenge and tension pervaded every aspect of its production'.

The film began with two-and-a-half months of pre-production in Los Angeles starting in February 1973 - for a project which required at least six. Woody, guarding his script with utmost secrecy, worked from a pretty three-room cottage, doubling as a cutting room, which had once been Clark Gable's *Gone with theWind* dressing room, located on the remnants of the old Pathé-Selznick lot at Culver City. Although there was talk of shooting exteriors in Brasilia, this was ruled out for logistical reasons and the locations finally selected ranged from the rolling hills above the sea at Monterey, to Colorado, the Mojave Desert and the Rockies. As usual,Woody took no pleasure in looking for locations, often leaving decisions to the very last minute. He was, though, reportedly, delighted with the motorized wheelchair Miles is put in after his 'defrosting' and had great fun doing gags with it. He also spent some time shooting black-and-white tests of his 'robot' walk to get the movements absolutely right. Meanwhile, architect Charles Deaton designed the gadget-infested house of scientist Dr Melik, and Dale Hennesy constructed sections of the story's futuristic city and the 12 foot-high vegetables for the 'future farm' sequence which, it was claimed, made the Monterey countryside 'look like Long Island!' and were inspired by another Wells novel, *The Food of the Gods*. Here, as on *Sex*, Hennesy's patience was sorely tried by the fact that sets which looked good on paper frequently failed to meet Woody's expectations when they were built. The problems were scarcely alleviated when the design budget shrank from $267,000 to $130,000.

Filming began in Denver on 30 April, on a 50-day schedule which eventually stretched to 101. It would prove to be Woody's most difficult movie to that date. There was rain on the first day, snow on the second, a plague of spotted-fever ticks blew in from the Rockies and there were problems with the colour of the set. After lunch on the second day, Woody did manage to make an appearance, in a wet-suit and goggles, for a sequence which was subsequently cut. The following scenes were shot in the Rockies above Denver, where, although it was sunny, the temperature was only 20°C.

Inevitably on a science-fiction comedy, the special effects proved far more difficult than anticipated. 'This is a movie about wires', Woody would quip during a final screening while editing. There were also problems with the robots and the bubble-topped cars which were driven by levers. Woody, still expressing his real-life impatience with machinery, kept adding gags and, as first assistant Fred T. Gallo would complain, 'We had time enough for test shooting to know we didn't want what we saw, but not enough to figure out what we did want. Woody just doesn't know what he wants until he sees it.'

As on *Sex*, the schedule and budget were under constant revision. Producer Jack Grossberg realized quite early on that there was no way *Sleeper* could be made for $2m. On one occasion, some weeks into shooting, Woody waited several hours for the sun to go down behind the Rockies so that it would be in exactly the position he wanted. This was a marked departure from *Take the Money* when he worried himself sick if he got a single day behind. As filming fell further and further back, Woody was forced to break his usual practice of not editing until the end of shooting. With a mid-December release looming, Ralph Rosenblum flew in from New York (Woody usually edited at Rosenblum's apartment-cum-post-production suite in Manhattan) to work on the cut. By this time, Woody's $350,000 fee had been swallowed up by the overages, though his and Joffe's share of the eventual profits, by the end of 1974, would amount to around $2m.

Arriving in California in August, Rosenblum found Woody despondent:

> The robots, the mechanized props, the stunt shots and, most exasperatingly, his own performances were either failing or not meeting his exacting standards. In some cases the failures were so repeated - wires and towropes snapping or flying into frame - that after innumerable takes he moved on and left perfection to the editing.

Woody and Rosenblum now got down to cutting alternate sequences, comparing notes and collaborating on changes until they had whittled down 35 hours of exposed film to a rough cut of 2 hours 20 minutes. This was reduced to approximately 90 minutes' screen time. *Sleeper* relied more on slapstick and sight gags than Woody's previous films and many promising scenes revolved around elaborate visual jokes which, although funny in execution, 'interrupted the essential flow of the narrative'. These were either cut straight away or discarded when they failed to get a laugh at preview screenings.

One of the *visually* most satisfying sequences had been a dream fantasy with Woody as a terrified white pawn on a vast chess set (both he and Brickman are fanatical about the game), shot on a salt flat in the Mojave Desert. Pursued by a vicious black knight, Woody ends up in white tie and tails in an opera house, where he is seen as the leader of a small orchestra. The sketch 'climaxes' on a hilarious impotence gag as Woody's violin bow sags, to his embarrassment, 'like a wet noodle ...The scene worked magnificently on the screen', said Rosenblum, 'and though it failed to fit the needs of *Sleeper*'s plot and comic pace, I saw in it a forecast of major future accomplishment.'

Another cut scene has Miles and his futuristic girlfriend Luna (Diane Keaton) having dinner. Miles, the suave lover, performs magic tricks to charm her out of her initial dislike of him. In the release version, Miles sets out to 'seduce' Luna, instead, with his clarinet. The original sequence did turn up in the French-release print, *Woody et les Robots*. This title, along with *The City Neurotic* (the German version of *Annie Hall*) so incensed Woody that he obtained a contractual proscription against the unauthorized retitling of his films in Europe.

Sleeper begins in 1973 where Miles, having 'died' from a routine exploration for a peptic ulcer, undergoes cryogenic immersion and is illegally resuscitated in the 22nd century by a trio of scientists, secretly on the side of the 'Revolution'. A Big Brother figure, 'Our Leader', presides over a negative Utopia called The Central Parallel of the American Federation, in Southern California. A seemingly benign old party in a wheelchair, he waves at the populace from the top of a cliff on late-night TV.

The scientists have homed in on Miles because they require 'a man with no identity' (an anticipation of *Zelig*) to aid them in overthrowing the government - represented, as in *1984* and *Brave New World*, as a soulless technocracy run by computer, where logic rules and emotions and individuality are punishable by brainwashing or death. Miles, disguised as a robot valet, takes refuge in the home of a socialite poet Luna Schlosser, whose atrocious verses were, apparently, modelled after Diane's real-life 'literary' idol, Rod McKuen! After battling it out with a giant expanding pudding, Miles proceeds to wreck Luna's dinner party. Taken along for robot 'reservicing', he kidnaps her but is recaptured and brainwashed into a state of hedonistic apathy. Luna, now convinced of the sinister forces which control the people's lives, escapes and is in her turn indoctrinated by the rebel underground.

Sleeper's basic plot device is merely a peg for placing the outsider, Miles, in a world not simply alien, but one which, farcically for us, horrendously for him, resonates his fears of what the world he had long since left is threatening to become. Taking a further leaf from Orwell and Huxley, Woody aims verbal and visual sling shots at the perfect 'faceless' society: uniformity on all its levels, as in the robots' ludicrous costumes and white Langdonesque faces, technological imperialism and the way in which a society of the future might well reflect the political and bureaucratic excesses of our own. In acknowledgement of both this uniform way of life and the influences which would shape the film's visual style, Woody decreed that all the costumes (except for the red ones worn by the 'security police') should be black, white or grey and the sets black and white, wherever possible. This was a deliberate attempt to make the whole film resemble a pre-Technicolor comedy.

As his antidote to the dire Orwellian warnings reflected in the early scenes, Woody presents us with a typically facetious view of revolution at work while the film's upbeat denouement would have assuredly found favour with Huxley who, in his introduction to the 1950 reprint of *Brave New World*, recanted the 'unutterably despairing tone of the 1931 original'. Woody's ending had also been subject to revision, with Rosenblum again objecting to Woody's initial idea 'which was flat and relied entirely on a corny visual gag'. Woody shot his new ending on a Sunday, so that Diane could fly in for the day from the New York location of *The Godfather Part II*. 'It was only through a whirlwind of overlapping labour', recalled Rosenblum, 'that we made the Christmas release', and noted that it was the unnerving experience on these early films which prompted Woody, by the time they got to *Annie Hall*, specifically to budget for two weeks of post-production cinematography. From then on, all the scripts Rosenblum was handed anticipated Woody's usual problem, with a final caption, 'Ending to be Shot'!

After a year's work and an almost record number of answer prints, *Sleeper* was ready for screening with only two days remaining before the premiere. The film garnered Woody's best all-round reviews to that date and went on to be the 16th Biggest US Money-Maker of 1974. It also further consolidated Woody and Diane as a popular screen team. Woody, with his self-deprecatory patter, bemused but quizzical mien and diminutive, oddly expressive frame - notwithstanding Dilys Powell's contention that, unlike Jacques Tati and Buster Keaton, his comedy is not in his legs - provides, yet again, an irresistible centre for semi-serious fun. More importantly, although he continued to find comedy antithetical to the visual aspects he was increasingly trying to exploit, he was, said Rosenblum, fast becoming a genuine movie professional: 'I think *Sleeper* was Woody's first real film.' This was nowhere more apparent than in his choice of music. After much discussion, it had been decided against using the usual kind of synthesized score most frequently associated with futuristic movies and, as befits the fact that Miles, in the story, had once been leader of a small band, The Ragtime Rascals, Woody duly opted for a combination of jazz standards and originals. These were played by the New Orleans Funeral and Ragtime Orchestra at Michael's Pub in New York. He also used a group of genuine New Orleans professionals who had never heard of Woody's movies. He recorded them in October 1972, for a fee of $12,000, and has said he never had more fun on any movie than his work on the *Sleeper* score. The results added much to the film's efficacy and charm.

Love and Death The aggregate gross on Woody's first four films as director had come to around $40m (though *Sex* alone, according to later reports, would go on to achieve rentals of $16m by the end of 1985). This represented a $10.5m profit on a combined negative cost of around $8.75m. UA quickly signed Woody to a new five-picture deal, extending the original to seven years. To everyone's surprise, Woody refused to renegotiate the terms of his own contract, except for an extra $25,000 in production fees. Woody was soon toying with script ideas for his next film, working in New York from January 1974 on with Mickey Rose. None of their possibilities took. Meanwhile, Woody had also started playing around with 'a more serious idea to shoot in New York in the beginning of summer'.

This was the embryo for *Annie Hall* which started life as a murder mystery involving two clever New Yorkers, Woody and Diane, who solve a crime. After some preliminary work on the screenplay, however, Woody lost interest; yet another script played out, due to the difficulties of aligning Woody's comic persona with the 'deeper comedy' he had in mind. Thoughts of doing a Hepburn-Tracy farce were also dismissed - 'Keaton and I are not Hepburn and Tracy. Our chemistry is completely different: theirs can't be duplicated.' Woody was to recall a number of other possibilities, not to be taken too seriously, but, throwing his various ideas into the drawer and with time running out, he 'just happened' to come across a Russian history book on the shelf which, he claimed, immediately inspired him to embark on the script which became *Love and Death*. With the proposed start date for his new movie already passed, Woody wrote an average two pages a day, completing a draft screenplay in three weeks.

By the end of July, he had decided this would definitely be his next film. UA, recalled Woody, were more difficult to convince, especially when he explained that he had 'written a comedy about man's alienation in a world of meaningless existence'. But, finally, invoking the artistic prerogative clause in his contract, Woody had a deal.

Plans were made to film in France, Hungary and Yugoslavia but when it was realized that the bulk of the picture could be shot in and around Paris over a six-month period Woody was delighted, due to his popularity in France and the fact that he likes Paris more than anywhere, except New York. The film's inevitable logistical problems were exacerbated by the fact that Woody could only take his first assistant Fred Gallo along with him, when the idea of having his usual US crew on the picture proved prohibitive. Gallo was credited as associate producer on the film and, because he had parted company with Jack Grossberg over the mounting pressures on *Sleeper*, Woody again had Charles Joffe as on set producer.

Actors for the 54 supporting roles (ranging from several hundred feet to a few frames) were recruited in the US, Britain and France, with Woody's near-pathological 'withdrawal' during the casting process already passing into legend. 'It was a very peculiar interview', British actor Stephen Moore told me, 'Miriam Brickman, when she was alive, was the casting director at the London end and I had all my conversation with her. Woody Allen sat down one end of the room, reading, virtually in the dark. We never exchanged a word. I didn't get the job!'

Woody has excused this remoteness as being due to the fact that, ideally, he'd like to cast everyone who applies and this is his way of distancing himself from the actors' sense of rejection. 'I cast quickly', he said, 'I see actors only for a minute. Not that much is required. What interests me is the look.'

Shooting started in September 1974, with units based in Paris and Budapest - the latter being 'suitably made up for the part'. Service facilities were provided in the former city by Studios Billancourt, in the latter, by Hungarofilm and Mafilm. 'There was no actual studio filming on *Love and Death*', Joffe told me, 'certainly not in Paris. There may have been the odd bit, but not very much. In recent years, of course, Woody's done more in the studio, and always in the same studio, the Kaufman Astoria, in New York - but, in the early days, scarcely at all'. Due to language difficulties no one knew what Woody was talking about, couldn't understand his humour and most of the cast had to play their scenes 'cold'. The first day's shooting was a disaster and this was followed by a chain of misadventures, wittily recalled by Woody in a July 1975 article in *Esquire*:

> When good weather was needed, it rained. When rain was needed, it was sunny. The cameraman was Belgian, his crew French. The underlings were Hungarian, the extras were Russian. I speak only English - and not really that well. Each shot was chaos. By the time my directions were translated, what should have been a battle scene ended up as a dance marathon. In scenes where Keaton and I were supposed to stroll as lovers, Budapest suffered its worst weather in twenty-five years.

The catalogue of disasters seemed unparalleled. An actor, hired because of a first-rate reading, broke both legs in a car accident; an actress who'd completed half her part fell off a horse, breaking her nose; a lens from London proved defective, leaving scenes with thousands of horseback extras looking 'like underwater shots by Jacques Cousteau'. Halfway through filming, Paris suffered an outbreak of flu, Charles Joffe succumbed to food poisoning, and Woody sprained his back 'falling on some ice in front of the Eiffel Tower'. This was followed, shortly afterwards, by treatment for second-degree burns when he backed into a floodlight. Woody also claimed he accidentally stuck a violin bow in Diane's eye, causing production to shut down for half a day. At Christmas time, the negative for a spectacular banquet scene with 600 extras 'went through the developing bath and came out with large white spots on the actors' faces'.

Woody, unsurprisingly, according to Ralph Rosenblum, was at his most miserable during the shooting of *Love and Death* and 'By and large, the more people he has to come into contact with, the more taxing he finds the production.' Budapest was windy and cold, the Hungarian crew undependable and the battle scenes, with hundreds of extras, plus special effects flown in from London, something of an ordeal. Since the film was, ostensibly, a spoof on *War and Peace*, Woody engaged the services of the Russian army of occupation, who were delighted, by all accounts, to have relief from their boredom. But the thousand or so soldiers he had at his disposal would take orders only from their own officers, with the translations having to travel through four languages. By the time these instructions reached them, the pre-set dynamite charges had already been exploded and the whole process had to start again. The sheer scale of the enterprise put the film months behind schedule and, by Woody's account, $1m over budget. 'It was not my idea of a good time', said Woody afterwards, 'It worked ... but at great expense to my emotional life.'

Woody's stay in Paris, a city he normally loves, was also made unendurable by the attentions of the *paparazzi*. Other observers have taken a more idyllic view of the proceedings and for actress Beth Porter, at least, filming in France 'was great. And the production took very good care of us.' Porter played the role of Anna, sister-in-law to Woody's character:

> I remember the first scenes I was involved in were shot in this wonderful old house near Versailles. The whole set-up was beautiful. It was the scene where Woody's handsome brother Ivan announces he's getting married and Diane thinks it's to her, but it's to me. I liked working with Woody, but I did notice he'd never personally give any direction to the assembled company, always relaying it through his AD, Fred Gallo. It's true some of them were French, but I know, while we were shooting, Woody was asked to speak at the Cinémathèque and I believe he spoke French then. I never heard him speak French to the crew, though. He is very shy, of course, or he was then, but he had a special rapport with Ghislain Cloquet who was an absolutely brilliant cameraman. Woody told me how happy he was to be working with Cloquet. He said he'd been really impressed by his work and knew he would give him exactly the look he wanted.

So enraptured was Woody by Cloquet's invaluable contribution to the pictorial flavour of the film that he later appended the cameraman's surname to the hero of his November 1977 *NewYorker* story, *The Condemned*.

When not involved in the actual filming, Woody would invariably retreat into a room in the Versailles house to read or practise the clarinet, keeping very much to himself. Occasionally, though, according to Porter, he was 'very amenable to conversation', at least on a one-to-one basis:

> He was always very serious, charming and very intelligent. I remember, on one occasion, he said he had to cast the part of a Russian countess and he was

trying to decide whether to go with Carol Kane or someone unknown who was absolutely gorgeous. He asked me what I would do. I asked whether it were essential that the woman be so gorgeous. He said he guessed not. I said I'd always go for the best actor, you can always make someone look beautiful. In the end, of course, he went for the gorgeous unknown.

This particular role had (or so she claimed) been earmarked for Erin Fleming, the constant companion of Woody's friend Groucho Marx, who had played the girl in the car in the last sequence of *Sex*. She had asked Woody if she 'could be the one to have a little red-haired baby at the end of the film', but this particular scene was cut and, to her dismay, she found herself in Paris, being fitted for the big seduction scene, in corset and black garters. Alarmed that the role of the heavily décolleté Countess Alexandrovna would intensify the publicity which had already attended her relationship with Groucho, she decided not to go ahead. 'I don't want to play the hooker', Fleming complained, 'I'm tired of being cast in that part.' The role, finally, went to Olga Georges-Picot, best known to English-speaking audiences for her appearance in the 1969 Bette Davis movie *Connecting Rooms*.

According to advance publicity, Woody's character was to be called Pierre Bezhukhov, after the 'thinker hero' of *War and Peace*, but the name was lost along the way, together with the character's aristocratic connections. In his revamped role of Boris Grushenko, Woody needed two youngsters, aged seven and twelve, to play him as a child. The older boy, after a long search, was Alfred Lutter III from New Jersey, whose blonde hair was dyed to match Woody's dark-reddish, but equally disarrayed thatch. The slightly bemused gaze which stares out at us from the screen, complete with something resembling Woody's characteristically small-boned facial structure and the inevitable horn-rims, is remarkably suggestive of the adult Woody.

Love and Death is an anarchic, irreverent, expansive burlesque of all things Russian. Thus customs, plays, films and, even, a typically revisionist approach to the Napoleonic Wars become satirical targets in an enterprise which was to represent Woody's most dramatic departure from previous form. His increased mastery of narrative in *Sleeper* had advanced him, quite logically, to philosophic parody, musings on the existence of God and, as the title implies, love and death. Woody now found himself only too eager to move beyond the pastiche elements which the subject matter afforded, extending his visual range as far as he could.

After much discussion with Cloquet, he decided to go for the autumnal look, an aspect which, for Woody, has become something of a signature. 'That movie required it', he told Ken Kelley in *Rolling Stone*, 'You know, in Paris, you get that weather all the time - foggy and gray. If you shoot in California, it's sunny and it doesn't look so nice'.

Having now begun to develop into a visual stylist of no mean skill, Woody had also gained a degree of cinematic maturity on the human level. Beth Porter:

> Something Woody revealed to me was his gratitude to Diane for teaching him to see the natural beauty in people's faces, especially old people. She'd been doing a lot of photography and he said it was through her enthusiasm and appreciation of old faces that he learned to see. I've worked with three performer/directors: Barbra Streisand on *Yentl*, Warren Beatty on *Reds* and Woody. Woody was certainly the one who had the most confident vision.

In other ways, *Love and Death* is true to earlier form. It contains, for one thing, a typical strain of *gefiltefisch* humour ('Jewish women don't believe in sex after marriage'), and recurrent food imagery. Woody, at one point, thought of calling the film *Love, Food and Death* or *Love, Death and Food*. During a key battle scene a man with a tray goes around passing out red hot blinis to the troops and, in another sequence, filmed in Paris but eventually cut, Boris and Sonja (Diane) had stopped off on their way to see Napoleon, at the home of a Jewish couple. It is Yom Kippur and the four of them settle down to eat a 'full' meal off plates with no food on them. Throughout the film, Woody's flip, New Yorker asides are as anachronistic in the world of Tolstoy and Dostoyevsky as is the black drill sergeant to Woody's version of the Russian army or the recaps of old routines from *Shoulder Arms, The Great Dictator* and *Monsieur Beaucaire*. Taking his cue from the latter, Woody continues to demonstrate a Bob Hope-like complicity with the audience, but the film also anticipates, in its more reflective moments, the close-knit psychological complexities of his later chamber works.

The story begins in 1812. Boris is a craven country lad, first glimpsed within the film's framing device as a prisoner in the death cell, looking back on his all-too-brief life and the exploits which brought him to this pass. As befits the new-found seriousness in Woody's comedy, Boris is given a voice-over monologue, wherein, like Raskolnikov, he muses darkly on the meaning of guilt and redemption and about mankind's misfortune in being 'ultimately executed for a crime it never committed'. Then, with gnomish irreverence for his literary models, Woody turns seriousness aside with a gag about a smart lawyer who, by putting in a successful plea of leniency, has gained Boris an extra hour of life!

The narrative flashes back to earlier days - when Boris was shamed by his fellow villagers into joining the army to fight the French. We are also introduced to Boris's cousin Sonja with whom he is in love. On the rebound from his butch older brother, Ivan, she marries an ill-fated herring merchant. She also dallies with a family friend and, indeed, the film at this point becomes, in a neat reversal of *Sleeper*, almost a story of woman's sexual role in the early nineteenth century - as viewed through the post-Freudian microscope of our own.

Meanwhile, while trysting with an Anna Karenina-like countess, Boris is challenged to a duel to the death by her lover. Refusing to kill his adversary when, by a fluke, he is left with the only loaded pistol, he inadvertently becomes a hero, forcing the man, a noted marksman, into a quasi-Tolstoyan reformation. Sonja, convinced that Boris would be killed, had agreed to marry him on the eve of the duel. Understandably, their initial married relationship is tense but, in a series of idyllic sequences, reminiscent of *Doctor Zhivago,* they 'find each other'. There follows an interlude of quite perfect romantic lyricism, abruptly terminated when Sonja decides they should remember their duty to Mother Russia and assassinate Napoleon. Boris, confused by Napoleon's official *doppelgänger,* stops short to air moral imperatives according to St Thomas Aquinas and Socrates. He botches the assassination, is arrested and sentenced to death.

Languishing in his cell, Boris is visited by an angel who assures him that God and Napoleon will spare his life. It is a lie. The final scene of the film, in which Boris and the Grim Reaper skip in and out of a row of trees by the river bank, ends the story on a perfect Bergmanesque flurry. The sequence acknowledges Woody as an uncanny imagist, capturing, in perfect detail, the style and flavour of his actual model, *The Seventh Seal*, which he admitted to having seen at least eight times prior to making *Love and Death*.

Musically, the picture looks forward to Woody's later films, being the first time he had relied exclusively on existing works rather than a specially commissioned score. He now regards his selection of music as important as the casting of actors and, although briefly acceding to Bergman's long-held view that film music (except for source music) is 'barbaric', Woody came swiftly to the conclusion that it was vitally connected with his own material and the emotions he was trying to express. His ongoing predilection for using the motion picture medium as a means of conveying and sharing his own personal taste, in both the popular and classical repertoires, has tended to border, by his own admission, on the messianic. It was Rosenblum who showed Woody the art of editing *with* music, even though the discs used weren't necessarily the ones to be laid on the final track. It was as a result of this process (cutting his films against music he really liked) that Woody gravitated towards the vintage jazz and popular standards he favours today.

For *Love and Death*, Rosenblum talked Woody out of Stravinsky in favour of Prokofiev, notably the symphonic score for the 1934 Russian classic *Lieutenant Kitje*, which has also been reused memorably in a number of other films. Other borrowings are from *Alexander Nevsky*, 'The Scythian Suite' and *The Love of Three Oranges*, while the Act 1 'Valse' from Tchaikovsky's *The Sleeping Beauty* adds the obligatory coating of sugar.

At the Berlin Film Festival in June 1975 Woody received a Silver Bear 'for his achievement in creating a new style of comedy', and critics on both sides of the Atlantic were mostly in favour. A notable exception was Stefan Kanfer in *Time* who complained that 'Allen has not altered his technique since the earliest films. The only plot that ever concerns him is the one in which he will be buried.' Clive Barnes, however, called the film Woody's 'best yet' and 'After *Love and Death*', quipped Andrew Sarris prophetically, 'can Strindberg be far behind?' Woody has recalled, ruefully, that his most devastating review ever was for this film - 'He should only ever play a sperm or a worm' - but adverse opinions were far outweighed by the positive ones and the film went on to achieve rentals of $7.4m in the US alone.

6

City Stories

1976-80: The Front to Stardust Memories

The Front Quite apart from his personal plans, Woody had still been receiving numerous offers of finance for projects and directing jobs in Europe, as well as for roles in other directors' films. Although he has said, even recently, that he is quite prepared to appear in a 'silly movie' for lots of money, he insists he would never make one of his own pictures for financial reasons alone. As Woody noted around the time of *Love and Death*, 'occasionally somebody will send me a preposterous script, either a crazy, surreal thing about spiders taking over the world, or a dirty story about a sex clinic' - offers all too easy to refuse.

In more serious vein was a project called *The End* which, according to its eventual director and star, Burt Reynolds, had been hanging around since 1972 and had originally been written specifically for Woody. Its author, Jerry Belson, had been inspired by Woody's remark that death could be funny, 'if it was dealt with properly'. Belson embarked on the screenplay, consulting with its projected star, but Woody then decided to go on developing his own material. According to Reynolds, the studios had then passed around the property from Dustin Hoffman to Paul Newman (who had taken an option on it) until, finally, it ended up with himself.

In 1975, Woody agreed to star in Martin Ritt's *The Front*, a bleakish tragicomedy, conceived and put together by a group of talents who had been blacklisted during the McCarthy era. Woody had been sent the script while working on *Love and Death* in Paris and has said the subject immediately appealed to him due to his sympathy with the participants' ideals and his longtime respect for Ritt's work as a film-maker.

Intended as a comic look - with serious overtones - at the problems faced by artists during that uneasy period, *The Front* was virtually the first cinema feature to confront the way many workers in the entertainment industry and,

indeed, elsewhere, had suffered under a system where a simple denounce-
ment, regardless of evidence or court proceedings, was deemed sufficient to
deprive people of their livelihood.

The film takes as its starting point the experiences of Ritt and screenwriter
Walter Bernstein in being blacklisted by the House Committee on Un-
American Activities (HUAC) while working on the US TV series *Danger* in the
early 1950s. 'I didn't understand at the time *why* I'd been blacklisted', recalled
Ritt, 'I was never called a Red but it was known that there were some genuine
Communists in my circle. But I wasn't about to denounce them.' Ritt had
wanted to make a film on the subject for 25 years and had spent 11 of them
actively trying to get backing. He finally accepted a three-picture deal with
Columbia, with a stipulation that his first film would be *The Front*. This was
made only with the support of studio chief David Begelman who had formerly been Ritt's agent. The film was produced, on New York locations, with an
assist from Woody's own producers, Rollins and Joffe. The subject matter
though, still presented problems: 'I needed certain locations and certain
equipment' Ritt told *Screen International*, 'The only locations and equipment of
television studios from that time that I could find were at NBC and CBS, and
they both turned me down.'

Another problem was the casting. Ritt has denied that signing Woody for
the lead role was in any way a commercial consideration - there had previously been talk of Dustin Hoffman, Peter Falk or Al Pacino - 'but I had seen
Woody's films and thought he was terribly sweet in them. It was the sweetness
I wanted'. As a former actor, Ritt later admitted that he would love to have
played the Zero Mostel role of the desperate Borscht Belt comic, Hecky
Brown. In fact, said Ritt, around 1973, he and Bernstein had been working on
a script about Hecky - 'And halfway through, we stopped and looked at each
other one morning, and we said: "This film is going to be morbid, a trifle hysterical and maybe even self-pitying - things that we want to avoid".' So they
changed tack and began developing the idea of 'the front', with Hecky now a
subsidiary character. The only other actor to be considered for Hecky had been
Jackie Gleason, but Ritt and Bernstein felt the character should be a Jew.
Mostel turned out to be the perfect choice and, like Herschel Bernardi, who
plays the role of programme producer Phil Sussman, had been a victim of the
blacklist; a factor which gives the film an added dimension of autobiography.
The Cold War atmosphere and nervous goings-on in a typical New York TV station of the time are further authenticated by the end titles. These inform us
which of the film's participants were real-life victims of the blacklist -
and when.

The film starts promisingly with newsreel footage of the demagogic McCarthy in action, along with Truman, Eisenhower, MacArthur, Korea, the Rosenberg trial and the young Richard Nixon, as well as Marilyn Monroe and other 1950s icons, chillingly counterpointed by Frank Sinatra singing 'Young at Heart' on the soundtrack. Howard Prince (Woody), a restaurant cashier and small-time bookie, is hired by old high-school chum and blacklistee Alfred Miller (Michael Murphy) to lend his 'politically safe' name to the TV scripts Miller is no longer permitted to sign. Such is 'The Front's' apparent success that he is soon lending his name to a number of other victims, and the way this group pulls the wool over the network's eyes is both fascinating and histori-cally true. The trouble with *The Front* is that, though it is a brave attempt to deal with the HUAC's purges on the TV industry, it seems insufficiently devel-oped. The casting of Woody - on the face of it, a master stroke - confuses the issue. Although his typical one liners are apt in their own right, they are ulti-mately a distraction and, augmented by Woody's established sexual hangups and loser's diffidence, make Howard's courageous stand against The Committee at the end of the film seem optimistic rather than likely. This last is occasioned by the network's decision, lacking other 'ace' writers to sacri-fice, to offer up Howard to the HUAC on the grounds that his 'scripts' are so good he must, by inference, by a subversive! The scene of Howard toughing up to his inquisitors rather than rat on his friends is not out of character for Woody - his 'cowardly' persona, like Hope's, has frequently been rounded up by last-minute acts of bravado - but is simply unconvincing in the light of the 'rock-bottom moral values' established for Howard Prince at the outset. His moral reformation and 'conversion' to the side of the angels by a sweet, clever, middle-class story editor Florence Barrett (Andrea Marcovicci in her debut) also lacks total conviction, due to some oddly out-of-context exchanges: 'In my family' says Florence, 'the biggest sin was ... raising your voice.' 'In mine', is the reply, 'it was buying retail.' This *is* Woody talking - not Howard Prince.

Such chilling asides as the suicide of the despairing Hecky - an incident based on the real-life death of 1940s TV star Philip Loeb - and the frightening implication that the *Red Channels*-reading wife of a chain-store proprietor may dictate to the networks precisely which writers and artists to employ, would be all the better were the treatment not *quite* so blackly jokey. Although real-life blacklistee Larry Adler has expressed the view that *The Front* is 'a more honest film' than Irwin Winkler's *Guilty by Suspicion* (1991), perhaps the for-mer presents us with the wrong kind of comedy. It needed something even darker, more scathing, with a possibly less sweetly ingenuous hero in the cen-tral 'charlatan' role than Woody. He has admitted that he was, quite patently, being himself in the part and had actutally suggested that Jack Nicholson might have been a better choice. As Walter Bernstein has noted, 'It would be very tough for Woody to act in a completely serious film. The audience comes prepared to see *Woody*, and they have a response to *him*.' More than one observer, however, pointed to the curious similarity in appearance, even down to the horn-rims, casual pullovers and thin, scruffy hair, between Bernstein and Woody himself!

Although, shortly after appearing in the film, Woody's recently purchased 5th Avenue duplex was raided by the FBI, he did not personally consider *The Front* an angry movie, nor a particularly devastating indictment of the blacklist. Ritt, though, was to speak at some length of the problems inherent in making the open score implications of the story palatable to a potentially unreceptive and, in many cases, disbelieving audience. This was borne out by the fact that 'the film did pretty well in Europe but only fair in the United States'.

Some critics found *The Front* to be Ritt's best work in years and it certainly brought Woody, billed on the ads as 'The Most Unlikely Hero of Our Time ...' a completely new reaction as a 'serious actor'. Andrea Marcovicci told me in December 1994 that she found him 'very pleasant, professional and eager to learn', though, it being her first film, she was 'more nervous than he was'. As Woody himself was to recall in 1987, the experience of making the film and being directed by Martin Ritt 'was perfectly pleasurable, it was fun to be able to go in, in the morning and act and go home, and leave the burden of the film on somebody else. That was pleasurable.' More importantly, his involvement with Ritt undoubtedly rubbed off on him, not least in its approach to the film's central romantic relationship. This would point the way to Woody's own more mature treatment of women characters in *Annie Hall* and *Manhattan*.

Annie Hall If we accept Woody's view of his early comedies as apprentice works which were fun to do and drawn from what he calls 'secondary material', dealing only marginally with the serious concerns he was hoping to express, then *Annie Hall* is clearly the first film of his maturity. Taking as its theme its protagonist's view that 'life is divided into the horrible and the miserable' so you'd best make the most of it, Woody wrought a warm, funny, romantic but at the same time deeply thoughtful movie which seemed to hit a nerve with a whole generation, and not only in America. It was also the first of his films, apart from *Play it Again, Sam,* to make more than just peripheral use of 'autobiography' as a basis for the narrative. But, since co-writer Marshall Brickman comes from a similar background and experience, we may safely assume, as he and Woody have intimated, that at least some of the film's real-life resonances are his.

The film has been seen by many observers as a cinematic love-letter to Diane Keaton and, indeed, makes use of the couple's off-screen relationship as well as the entrancing quirkiness Woody and Brickman discerned in Diane's personality. In interview, Woody has said that he and Diane had not been lovers for four years prior to the release of *Annie Hall*, though they had actually stopped living together as early as March 1970 when Diane moved to her own apartment on East 68th Street. The affair's progress and its eventual break-up, said Woody, were quite different from the way they were portrayed on screen. Or, indeed, from the play-*within*-the-film which Alvy Singer (Woody) writes near the end of the story and to which he appends a different, happier ending.

At least one critic has suggested that you could *only* treat *Annie Hall* as autobiographical and should come to it armed with a full knowledge of the real-life relationship behind it. That said, we do know that the couple did not meet (as in the film) during a game of tennis but when Woody auditioned Diane for the stage version of *Sam*. Diane does not hie from Chippewa Falls, Wisconsin (the actual birthplace of Woody's friend, folk singer Judy Henske), but from Los Angeles, and she did not move back to California after her break-up with Woody, but remained in New York. Woody's father did not have the job he has in the film, nor did the real-life Woody live as a boy under the shadow of the giant 'Thunderbolt' roller-coaster on Coney Island. Alvy's father in *Annie Hall*, just like little Joe's in *Radio Days*, was originally to have been a cab driver, and the boyhood scenes were to be shot on the site of one of Woody's earliest homes at Avenue K, Brooklyn. But, after spotting the roller-coaster house on a Coney Island location recce, he put in a bid for it, changing the script to make Alvy's father the man who runs the bumper-car concession.

Woody had originally wanted to call the film *Anhedonia* - a 'cute' and 'superior' title, scoffed noted Woody Allen detractor Joan Didion - which refers to a chronic inability to experience pleasure. Although reports that Woody had been prevailed upon to change it only three weeks prior to the film's release are not strictly true, *Anhedonia* had become sufficiently entrenched for UA to approach an advertising firm to think up a campaign to sell the title and explain its meaning to the public. In what was to become his usual practice, however, the project, during the actual filming, was simply referred to as 'Woody Allen's New Movie', and cast and crew grew more than slightly annoyed, it was reported, at only receiving two or three pages of script per day, with no inkling from their director as to what the film was about.

At first, the film had been intended, said Woody, to be 'about me exclusively ... my life, my thoughts, my ideas, my background', and Brickman later told their friend Susan Braudy that he and Woody had conceived the screenplay 'in a gradual process of highly stylized conversations' while strolling up and down Lexington Avenue until, finally, it had been impossible to pick out who had contributed what. These lengthy discussions were followed by Woody, physically, doing the writing, followed by more discussions. Aided by Brickman, Woody made a concerted move away from his previous writing form, where his own characters had tended to talk in wisecracks, like Bob Hope or Groucho Marx, rather than in cohesive 'behavioural dialogue'.

The genesis of the script lay in the abortive murder mystery Woody had been trying to write in the winter of 1973-74, elements of which would also turn up, years later, in *Crimes and Misdemeanors* and *Manhattan Murder Mystery*. For *Annie Hall*, the murder plot had been interwoven, said Rosenblum, with glimpses of the Allen character's problematic life and career, childhood and romantic experiences while 'in the process satirizing much of our culture'. It ended with the spectre of a middle-aged man, incapable, as Woody's preferred title suggests, of experiencing joy. According to Rosenblum, however, the story of Alvy and Annie 'so insistently overwhelmed the others that *Annie Hall* was born'. Moving in that direction, Woody and Brickman decided to go for a contemporary love story, duly 'pirating' the lead characters and some basic sit-uations from an unfinished novel Woody had started earlier. This had begun, like the film, 'with a monologue, but you don't realize it's a monologue, because it's written'. As Woody was to recall to Caryn James, he felt that audiences might well be interested in such an idea, even though 'I knew there would be fewer laughs than in my other films'.

With a $3m budget, rising to $4m, filming began at Long Island's South Fork (the lobster scene) on 10 May 1976. Since details were kept secret from the media, the film's progress generated maximum curiosity, especially since, apart from a few scenes shot at the Pathé Studios at 106th Street and Park Avenue, the crew were to be seen all over New York, Long Island, Coney Island and the Upper West Side at a time when movie-making in the city was not as prevalent as it is now. Indeed, in a year when the city was all but teetering on the edge of bankruptcy, Woody almost single handedly promoted the idea of New York filming as one of its biggest sources of future income. Locations ranged from St Bernard's School in West Village - for the Alvy classroom scenes - to Englewood, New Jersey, standing in for Chippewa Falls. The Adlai Stevenson rally was shot at the Statler Hilton Hotel, the waterfront scenes between Alvy and Annie, at dusk, at the picturesque South Street Seaport Museum by the East River in Lower Manhattan, and Annie's night-club scenes, where she sings two songs, at the popular Grand Finale on West 70th Street. The second of these, where Annie's singing is altogether more assured, becomes a key moment in her life with Alvy: her meeting with smarmy record tycoon Tony Lacey (Paul Simon). The scene was improvised, Woody's only instruction to Simon being 'Try to get to the word "mellow" eventually because I have a joke I want to tell.'

Several sequences in the film take place in or outside movie theatres. These were the Beekman, the Thalia, the New Yorker and Paris, while the beach scenes (for Alvy's house in the Hamptons) were at Amagansett, Long Island. Annie and Alvy were also filmed eating lunch at a restaurant across the street from the New York State Theater at the Lincoln Center and some scenes were shot at the apartment of Richard Runes, a lawyer who lived at the Hotel des Artistes nearby. Annie's apartment was in a beautiful art deco building on 70th Street, between Lexington and Park, which, said Woody, 'is my favourite block in the city ... the best architecture and it hasn't been ruined'. Alvy's childhood home, by the roller-coaster, was an actual wood-framed shack which had pre-dated the 'Thunderbolt' by some years and had required one of the latter's hair-raising plunges to be angled round it. Long derelict, the house burned down in May 1991.

Not all of the above locations were utilized during the initial ten-week shoot - there would be two weeks of addititional filming and completion of principal photography in LA - but if any movie justifies Woody's contention that his films are not so much made as remade, then *Annie Hall* is the premier example. The whole thing, said Woody, like the later *Stardust Memories*, was originally 'supposed to take place in my mind. Something that would happen would remind me of a quick childhood flash, and that would remind me of a surrealistic image ... None of that worked.' Woody's original footage, complained Rosenblum, was an 'untitled and chaotic collection of bits and pieces that seemed to defy continuity, bewilder its creators, and, of all Allen's films, hold the least promise for popular success'. Misanthropic and abstract, it was saddled with 'stream of consciousness ... rambling commentary and bizarre gags which completely obscured the skeletal plot'.

It seems entirely likely however that the film's problems could easily have been anticipated, had anyone had the temerity to talk Woody out of the kind of movie he originally had in mind. Beth Porter:

About two years after the *Love and Death* filming, I was living in LA and part of the time I stayed with Fred Gallo and his wife. While there and completely by accident, I read an early draft of what turned out to be *Annie Hall*. And I have to tell you it was terrible. It didn't have a title, just 'Woody Allen project'. And it was a series of pretty disconnected scenes of Woody chasing various women. Fred explained to me that the deal Rollins and Joffe had with the financiers was that there had to be a document, a script of sorts to placate them, in order to raise the money. They weren't going to read it anyway, but it allowed them to justify a budget. Then when Woody was ready, he could address the real script. I don't know if that was true, but that's what I was told.

However much of that original draft ended up in the film which finally emerged, it is certain that, far from being the story of a love affair, the first version dealt almost entirely with the Alvy character's highly flawed life and inner tensions. Annie, at this point, was but one of a number of subsidiary characters and, during the first 15 minutes, made only one brief appearance. The first cut of 2 hours 20 minutes took about six weeks to complete and Woody had shot enough material for three films - 50 hours or a ratio of 31:1 by the time of the final edit. It was then left to Rosenblum and his assistant, Susan E. Morse, to whittle down 100,000 feet of exposed film to a running time of 93 minutes. Though readily acceding that the first rough-cut assembly contained 'some of the freest, funniest, and most sophisticated material Woody had ever created', Brickman expressed himself 'devastatingly disappointed'. He felt that 'the first 25 minutes were a disaster and that the film did not get going until Paul Simon appeared.' Brickman also felt strongly that they would be humiliated by the eventual reaction and was all for halting the project.

Deciding to treat the first version like the draft of a novel, Rosenblum now suggested to Woody that they extrapolate the best material, concentrating less on the character of Alvy than on his relationship with would-be singer Annie. In the original version, Annie had only begun to emerge as a character in the second half of the story, most of which involved the 'present tense'. It was to discover Annie and her relationship with Alvy that Woody and Rosenblum embarked on their biggest exercise in reconstruction to that date. Woody, as Rosenblum recalled, now had no hesitation in trimming away some of the first 20 minutes in order to establish Annie more quickly.

The opening monologue was finally reduced to six minutes, retaining, in abbreviated form, Alvy's childhood visit to the doctor, the classroom scene and the early TV clips, but much else was discarded, leading directly to the scene on the sidewalk with Alvy and his friend Rob (Tony Roberts), and Alvy's meeting with Annie outside the movie theatre. So as not to stray too long from the Annie character, Alvy's first and second wives (Carol Kane and Janet Margolin) were reduced to flashbacks lasting four-and-a-half and three minutes, respectively. A number of overly academic one-liners and several minor characters were also dropped. The scene at the Wall Street Tennis Club was now placed 24 minutes into the film, though Brickman, who had suggested scrapping the picture's time-shifting structure in favour of strict chronology, was all for putting this first meeting between Alvy and Annie at the beginning - a logical argument if we consider the warm reaction which the tennis club scene elicited amongst most audiences.

In order to bring the central love affair into even greater prominence, elements of the murder mystery, a French Resistance fantasy, a dream sequence set in the Garden of Eden, a run-in betwen the teenage Alvy and a gang of bikers, as well as a spoof on *Invasion of the Body Snatchers*, were now eliminated. Also cut was part of the sequence involving Alvy's intellectually ambitious second wife Robin (Margolin) who forces him into a party swarming with representatives of the more celebrated New York magazines - 'I heard *Commentary* and *Dissent* had merged and formed *Dysentary*', quips Alvy. This scene was reduced to a walk-through and a key moment in the couple's bedroom, where Alvy has slipped away to follow the Knickerbockers' game on TV. Out went the follow-up fantasy in which Alvy joins in the game, playing on a team alongside 'Kafka' and 'Nietzsche', but losing the ball to the real-life Earl Monroe. Although shot elaborately at Madison Square Garden with the actual Knicks, Woody decided that the sequence slowed the narrative. Also excised was a surreal fantasy, beginning as a pastiche of the 1946 movie, *An Angel on my Shoulder*, in which Alvy, Annie and Rob are transported by the Devil on a guided tour of Hell's nine layers. Level Five, for instance, is for 'organized crime, fascist dictators and people who don't appreciate oral sex'.

To avoid stalling the dramatic flow, even scenes involving Alvy and Annie often had to be drastically pruned, including a major portion of Colleen Dewhurst's role as Annie's mother. Also cut, albeit temporarily, was the scene where Annie's brother, Duane (Christopher Walken), confesses his neurotic impluse to drive headlong towards oncoming traffic. A week before the film's completion, the sequence was restored. 'We were getting such good responses', said Woody, 'we started to put back one or two things that we liked.' Additional shooting included the transition of the leading characters to California and the scene where Alvy inadvertently sneezes away $2000 worth of cocaine. The sneeze and Diane's reaction to it were, apparently, spontaneous and at many venues, it would get the biggest laugh in the picture.

In the first version of the film, Annie was just a neurotic New York girl, based not only on Diane but, partially, also, on Brickman's observations of a 'high strung journalist' he had once known. It was soon realized, however, that this would leave no room for 'dramatic transition', and the various changes wrought in her character, through the rewriting and additional filming, led to Annie being made less harsh and more appealing. Originally, she came from New York but, gradually, the character was transformed into more of a country hick. Incorporated were a number of Diane's own quirks and distinctive speech patterns, though the famous 'lah-de-dah' catch-phrase was an invention. But it was Diane's endearing stop-start manner of speaking, apologetic, almost self-effacing acting style, and abrupt embarrassed giggles which Woody and Brickman found so captivating and indicative of the character. These elements, combined with Diane's real-life semi-naive/semi-wise sayings, were duly worked into the screenplay. And, although, as Brickman recalled, there were problems in adapting Woody's own character into the script - specifically in finding motivations for Alvy's pessimism - it was on Annie that the emotional heart of the movie finally fastened and thus provided for America, as elsewhere, a feminine ideal for the late 1970s.

Essentially, *Annie Hall* is about two people who cannot decide if they need each other more than their freedom and, in real life, as with Louise Lasser, Woody's relationship with Diane would not end with their romantic separation. Something of this maturity of approach is reflected in the film itself, an element which helped it strike a chord with a much wider audience than Woody had enjoyed thus far.

Except when it deals with Alvy's quite separate soul-searchings, the story is largely a series of amusing, often touching, two-handed confrontations between Alvy and Annie, as they meet, become friends, fall in love, quarrel, break up, get back together and part for good. The film employs flashbacks, flash forwards, split screen, double exposure, instant replay, free association, interior monologue, subtitles, pseudo-documentary and even animation - as though, wrote Graham McCann, 'Allen were trying to capture in images the variety of impressions, and subjectivity of interpretations one experiences in the mind'.

Since Alvy, in the story, is a comedian, Woody uses routines culled from his old night-club act and, elsewhere, includes other recycled stuff - fragments from his short stories and repeat gags from earlier movies. All of this augments the strong autobiographical nuances to be found in both the film and the character Woody plays. As with the audience participation sequences in *Radio Days,* he mostly shot the reactions to Alvy's stand-up patter separately. Woody was actually performing his act on one occasion to an empty room and, when the audience was finally filmed, they had no idea what they were supposed to be laughing at! For another sequence, set in Coney Island, Woody, not for the last time, emulated David Lean - when he doesn't 'feel' it, he can't shoot it - and with 200 extras on tap, he kept everyone hanging around all morning with nothing filmed. There were difficulties with the famous scene where Marshall McLuhan in the *New Yorker* lobby 'annihilates' the bore who is waiting in line to see *The Sorrow and the Pity*. Woody had tried to persuade several different celebrities to fill the McLuhan spot, his first choice having been Fellini. This was logical 'casting', as it linked up with a previous dialogue but, said Woody, Fellini was unwilling to come to the United States for just this one sequence. In the event, McLuhan was not very convincing, even playing himself, and the scene was later reshot. At which point, Woody, according to one observer, 'didn't want to talk to him any more. It was very embarrassing.'

Woody has suggested that the film's real impetus revolves around his character's ability to talk directly to the audience and, initially facing camera, Alvy begins the film on a couple of typically pessimistic Jewish jokes. The second gag derives from Freud and both this and the joke at the very end of the film had been in the repertoire of Groucho Marx. The final joke also deals with an analyst and his patient and thus, in one fell swoop, Woody succeeds in framing his story alongside at least two of his essential influences: traditional Jewish humour and psychoanalysis. He also links himself with a number of classic movies, like *Sunset Boulevard* and *Rebecca* which, adopting as their initial thesis what has been defined as the 'anticipation of retrospection', begin with a narrator, telling us the end of the story, before working backwards to the beginning. In the process, to alleviate the sense of despair emanating from his own on-screen character, Woody allows Alvy to find in the 'stumbling self-critical ineptitude' of Annie and their shared interests an antidote to his own loneliness. It was Woody's friend, Nora Ephron, who described such a relationship as 'just two neuroses knowing theirs is a perfect match'. But, in no time, Alvy is encouraging Annie to 'improve' herself up to his level. He also persuades her to develop her singing talents, losing her when she becomes successful. In real life, Diane's Oscar and success in dramatic roles put her somewhat beyond Woody's influence, though from him she inherited a noted reclusiveness and ambitions to be a director. Woody uses the cipher of Diane's off-screen success to mark the beginnings of the on-screen break-up.

As protagonist-narrator, Alvy witnesses scenes from his own past from the vantage point of his adult presence in them, and he would return to this Bergmanesque device in a number of later films. In this instance, though, he breaks the convention by also having Annie and Rob party to the game. Alvy's visits to his childhood and lower-middle-class Jewish family are an affectionate parody of the Flatbush, Brooklyn milieu Woody grew up in. Here we meet Alvy's younger self, hilariously played by the carrot-topped Jonathan Munk, glimpsed among his peers in the old school-room, with each kid prophetical-ly representing for us what he or she might well become as adults. Classrooms are a recurring motif in Woody's films and, intriguingly, in an early (but cut) version of the flashbacks, the object of Alvy's schoolboy crush was played by an 11-year-old Brooke Shields.

This school-room sequence was shot, like the other flashbacks, in a nostal-gic golden-yellow glow, as part of the film's preordained 'three-colour' approach. For Woody's admittedly idealized view of New York, cameraman Gordon Willis, who has said he 'hates the colour blue', agreed to film delib-erately at sundown or 'on gray, overcast days, so it would look more moody and romantic'. For the scenes in southern California - Woody's 'symbol for the culture of narcissism' - 'we shot in hot light', he said, 'because that is what strikes me about LA, that bright sunlight', with the result that 'people seem to evaporate'. Fellow cameraman Conrad Hall once dubbed Willis 'The Prince of Darkness', due to his ability to turn under-exposure into an art form, and photographically, *Annie Hall* was Woody's most innovative film thus far. Willis, enthused Woody, is 'a technical wizard. He's also a great artist. He showed me things about cameras and lighting; it was a real turning point for me in every way.' One thinks, in particular, of the split-screen sequence involving Alvy and Annie's respective analysts, and the scene where Alvy is trying to make love to Annie and her bored 'ghost' gets out of bed to observe the action. 'It's an interesting sequence if you know it's been done with a mirror', recalled Willis, 'because it all takes place in one shot.' Willis, with his enthusiasm for shooting colour as if it were black-and-white and actually filming the occasional movie in monochrome, was to be the ideal interpreter of Woody's work.

Alvy's childhood scenes are in marked contrast with those involving Annie's anti-Semitic WASP family in Chippewa Falls - split screen is again employed to contrast the Halls' comfortable, middle-class lifestyle with Alvy's less privileged background and bickering parents. Annie's folks spout typical country-club aphorisms and are not sure how to take their daughter's new beau who, as well as being bohemian and Jewish, has in a reflection of Woody himself, spent 15 years in analysis. All these characters, surprisingly for a film-maker with no first-hand knowledge of such an essentially middle-American upbringing, are beautifully understood, understated and observed. Woody's portrait of Alvy's own family was, of course, wrung painfully from life.

Lester D. Friedman, in his excellent study, *The Jewish Image in American Film* (1987), has characterized Alvy Singer as 'the most Jewish of all his screen char-acters, a man obsessed with paranoia, guilt, sexual hangups, death and childhood fantasies'. There is also the antithesis to this - the elements which have laid

Woody open to charges of anti-Semitism by his peers: the fact of his self-con-fessed agnosticism, the vein of Jewish caricature in his films and monologues and, most importantly, perhaps, that the Jewish ex-wives and girl friends who inhabit his stories, remain unsympathetic fictionalizations of his first wife, Harlene, while 'true love' is usually found, as in his off-screen life, with a succes-sion of WASP 'dream women' or 'villagey blondes'. It is a type towards which Woody, amongst Jewish artists, has been scarcely alone in his leanings, but *Annie Hall*, dealing to some extent with urban show-business values, demonstrates for us a way in which Jews and Gentiles can and do come together. Not for nothing is Alvy a moderately successful Jewish comic and gag writer, seen on various occasions in action and appearing, in flashback, on *The Dick Cavett Show*. The fact that it is Woody, rather than Alvy, in the clip, and that the show originally trans-mitted in late 1969 is genuine, offers us yet a further frisson of real life versus fiction. There is also a wry moment of celebrity *angst* which combines tradi-tional ideas of Jewish alienation with thoughts on the artist's relationship with his audience. This occurs when a couple of guys hustle Alvy outside the Beekman Theater, for no other reason than that he's 'on TV'. This touches on a theme which would increasingly obsess Woody - 'the concept of celebrity being both an attractive and difficult status' - and anticipates the idea of the fan-assas-sin in *Stardust Memories* who, though still insisting that Sandy Bates is his 'hero', finally blows him away.

Another major theme is the ongoing conflict between good and false values. It is Annie's eventual success and 'discovery' by Tony Lacey which leads to her removal to Southern California, a place where Alvy finds himself totally alien-ated. For Alvy, as for Woody in real life, the West Coast is an environment where artistically, intellectually and, in this case, emotionally, he cannot func-tion. Tony Lacey represents the Devil's Messenger, seducing Annie with promises of false fame from which, for largely unexplained reasons, she finally escapes, returning to New York, a new lover and, finally, an amicable reunion with Alvy.

As with several of his earlier films, Woody was to find the ending of *Annie Hall* highly problematic. At one point he had wanted to close the picture on the jailhouse scene which forms the climax of Alvy's desperate attempt in Hollywood to be reunited with Annie. This, at Rosenblum's urging, was much abbreviated and placed earlier and 'Of all the things we removed from the film the cut that Woody resisted most strongly'. Woody, apparently, shot additional material for the film's last segment on three separate occasions in October, November and December, 'much of it an attempt to show the process by which Alvy comes to miss Annie'. One sequence, where Alvy and Annie meet awkwardly outside the Thalia, again showing the *The Sorrow and the Pity*, was, said Rosenblum, 'a real downer', and was eventually confined to a single long shot, reducing Sigourney Weaver's cameo as Alvy's date to an imperceptible walk-on. Weaver had actually auditioned for a larger role, but gave it up for a stage part. Woody insisted she at least do a bit but, as Weaver has recalled, 'Unless you know my raincoat, you'll miss me.' Another sequence, shot on the last day of filming, had Alvy in Times Square wondering what to do about Annie, when he looks up at a flashing sign which reads, 'What are you doing, Alvy? Go to California. It's OK. She loves you.' Viewing the scene in dailies, Woody hated it so much he went to the nearest reservoir and threw the reels in.

It was Rosenblum, prompted by Woody's chance remark on the denouement of the original murder script, who finally suggested ending the film on a continuation of Alvy's opening monologue - with a brief series of flashbacks to the Annie affair, accompanied by Alvy's final voice-over. Against this was played a reprise of Annie's 'Seems like Old Times' from the second night-club scene. This complementary montage ends on the famous 'We need the Eggs' dissertation which Woody, apparently, composed in the back of a cab on the way to work. The joke was put in at 5.30 that night and it stayed forever'. And, as Brickman was to recall, 'Suddenly there was an ending there - not only that, but an ending that was moving ... The whole film could have gone down the toilet if there hadn't been that final beat on it.'

The film thus ends with Annie and Alvy reconciled in friendship but romantically apart and, although UA execs were initially nervous and some fans shocked by this sweet but melancholic outcome, audiences in the main seemed satisfied with it as well as with the various questions on life and art which Woody provocatively raised. It is a tribute to both the writing and casting that such concerns are both accessible and humorous. Tony Roberts for instance is aptly deployed as Alvy's perennial sidekick, though at least one US critic found the character of Rob 'glib' and 'annoying'. But it is in the portrait of Annie that we find the perfect combination of actress and role. Annie's adorable daffiness is amusingly demonstrated, though, as Diane plays her, her essential loveability does not limit our awareness that she can be thoroughly exasperating.

Alvy's first meeting with Annie in her characteristic androgynous get-up and with her nervous giggling 'Oh yeah? So do you ... Oh God, Annie, Oh God ...' and sing-song 'Lah-de-dah' catch-phrase as she hesitantly tries to exit from a smart Manhattan tennis club, brought spontaneous applause from hardened New York theatre audiences. There was, wrote Nicholas Fraser, in *The Sunday Times*, something like 'a shared perception, not just that a star has emerged, but that someone has managed to articulate, for the first time, the distinctive way in which many people survive the bizarre rigours of social and erotic life in New York'.

In accord with Woody's artistic (and box-office) growth, he had begun to move towards the kind of Grade-A support casts which would grace his future movies. Colleen Dewhurst had been chosen, said Woody, because she looked like Diane's real mother and had 'that real American pioneer look, very classic' which the role required. Shelley Duvall (who had replaced Jessica Harper some way into filming) is *Rolling Stone* reporter Pam, while future stars Jeff Goldblum, Beverly D'Angelo and Shelly Hack rub shoulders in cameo roles with old Allen pals John Doumanian ('The Coke Fiend') and Walter Bernstein (Annie's theatre date). Mark Lenard ('Sarek' from *Star Trek*) has a brief bit as a naval officer, while future Allen regular Danny Aiello ended on the cutting room floor. Amongst the real-life figures guying themselves is Truman Capote: 'Here comes the winner of the Truman Capote lookalike contest', quips Alvy to Annie in Central Park as that genuine literary lion minces by.

Largely at the behest of Woody, UA shrewdly refrained from publicity overkill, a move which helped engender a degree of unexpectedness. Exerting his contractual control over advertising, Woody also insisted on subdued print ads and no TV spots until the film had been running several weeks. Added to which, he prohibited any mention of the film's subsequent Oscar wins being incorporated into bill board advertising anywhere within the environs of New York. As was by now his norm, the plot of *Annie Hall* was kept secret right up until its première at the Los Angeles Film Exposition in March 1977. Woody, ensconced in a suite at the Beverly Wiltshire, agreed, for the last time with one of his movies, to make himself available in LA to promote it. Pessimistically, he declared it, like a number of his films, 'a personal failure': a view scarcely borne out by its enormous critical and commercial success.

Most reviews were unadulterated raves. Richard Schickel in *Time* called the film 'a walking compendium of a generation's concerns comically stated', while *The New Yorker*'s Terence Rafferty noted that, when he first saw *Annie Hall* in a cinema in Santa Cruz, California, 'It was the film that drove me back to New York. Most of the people in the audience were transplanted New Yorkers, and it was like pouring water on people crawling through the desert.' This reaction was echoed in the Big Apple itself where there were lines two blocks long for most screenings, people going back several times to see the film. In the 'nervous romance' of Annie and Alvy they saw something of themselves and their environment, and attained through these two kindred spirits a warm insight into their own insecurities, plus the comfort to be derived from meaningful relationships and the film's distinctively upbeat homage to East Coast iconography.

Apart from the approbation heaped deservedly on Diane and the film itself, several reviewers were to comment on the marked development in Woody's screen character. But although his fans were startled by his new confidence with women, Graham McCann was to see in him aspects of the urban worrier personified by Jack Lemmon in the 1960s, with Woody following that actor in 'playing a lover who exhibits all the anxieties and sexual frustrations that Hollywood denied existed'.

When the year's US film ratings were tabulated, *Annie Hall* found a place on 30 out of 32 leading critics' 'Ten Best' lists. After cable screenings on LA's Z Channel which had 'a geographical monopoly on Academy voter's homes' *Annie* achieved Oscar success when it won awards for Best Picture and Best Actress, though Woody, who had been nominated as Best Actor, lost out to Richard Dreyfuss in *The Goodbye Girl*. No one was surprised, however, when Woody, who has persistently refused to become an Academy member or have his name included in the 'For Your Consideration' pre-Oscar blurbs in the trades, declined to turn up in person to accept his Best Director and Original Screenplay Oscars - preferring, he said, not to let down his jazz musician buddies at their regular Monday night gig at Michael's Pub.

Although *Annie Hall* achieved an estimated first-year US gross of $25m (rising to a reputed $80-$100m world-wide by 1987), the film's real box-office breakthrough came about only in the wake of the Oscars. Woody has noted that the picture did less well, commercially, than any other Best Film Oscar winner of recent years, and failed amongst comedies to achieve the blockbuster success of *Airplane!*, *Animal House* or the Mel Brooks films. He has also claimed, wryly, that even a middle-of-the-road Peter Falk comedy, *The In-Laws* (1979), was to do better at the box office than *Annie Hall, Manhattan* and *Stardust Memories* put together.

However, the characters and themes of *Annie Hall* were to be highly influential on a number of subsequent movies, like *Crossing Delancey, Over the Brooklyn Bridge* and, especially, *When Harry Met Sally*. The trend-setting costume designs, partially elaborated from Diane's own idiosyncratic dress sense, also did much, said British designer Bill Gibb, 'to promote the trend towards an easy, casual look, and the mode for women to dress in a more masculine fashion: baggy shirts and pants, loosely knotted ties, waistcoats and easy trilbies - a far cry from layers of frothy chiffon'. Curiously, *Annie Hall*'s costume designer, Ruth Morley, had been initially resistant to Diane's 'crazy' way of dressing, but Woody, considering the actress something of a sartorial 'genius', persuaded

Morley to let her have her own way. Indeed, the involvement of Ralph Lauren in promoting the 'Annie Hall look' both on-and off-screen (he would continue to design clothes for Woody) led to something of a fashion landmark and helped pave the way for a whole cycle of designer-driven movies.

Interiors If *Annie Hall* marked the turning point in Woody's film fortunes, his next movie, the infuriating (to many) *Interiors* was to inaugurate an increasing difference of opinion as to how his future work should be perceived.

Described by Woody as 'a drama in the traditional sense', *Interiors* was actually a far-from-disguised Bergmanesque examination of the problems and tragedies of family life. Bristling with Scandinavian resonances, albeit grafted on to a post-Eugene O'Neill-style American middle-class setting, the film seemed something of a talkathon and a number of Woody's regular fans were dismayed by this quite drastic change of pace and mood.

Woody had, in fact, long voiced his ambition to make a movie inspired by European culture, largely because American films, by concentrating on action, he said, rarely gave their protagonists time 'even for such simple acts as sitting down at table and eating'. He also took the deliberate decision not to appear in the picture himself. As he argued, quite logically, 'My presence is so completely associated with comedy that when the audience see me, they might think it's a sign for them to begin laughing.'

UA's granting of blessing to *Interiors* could not have come at a more traumatic time in the studio's history. Amidst the elation over the *Annie Hall* phenomenon, it was also being widely reported that the company was in trouble. Woody's own situation, though, remained largely unchanged. As befitted the benign administration of Robert Benjamin and Arthur Krim, there were few constraints on Woody's film-making methods. He was merely limited to submitting two copies of his initial script - one to Krim, the other to Lehman 'Lee' Katz, 'the formidable one-man production and budget estimating department' - and, once approval had been given, no one bothered him until he was ready to show the completed film. Woody was most punctilious, at least at that time, in staying moderately within budget and not offering UA anything they had not previously bargained for.

According to Woody's manager, Jack Rollins, not one of his first 14 films lost money. Not all returned sizeable profits but each, apparently, satisfied its backers. As long as that continued, said Woody, his respective studios were happy: 'They leave me alone and I deliver them a finished movie.'

Benjamin and Krim had, since 1951, successfully pulled the ailing UA out of the doldrums into which it had fallen during the 1940s. But, from an awesome $250m income in 1968, the company had sunk in two years to a pre-tax loss of $35m. With the cutting of a sixth of its world-wide work-force and in 1973, a domestic distribution and syndication deal for the films of MGM, UA had been somewhat turned around, though the earlier 1967 take-over of the company by TransAmerica, a financial services and insurance conglomerate, had signalled an escalating series of problems for the studio's top brass.

By January 1978, things had come to a head. Feeling themselves unable to function under what they considered TransAmerica's oppressive and non-contributable aegis, Krim and Benjamin led a defection of five top executives, including president Eric Pleskow and production head Mike Medavoy, away from the studio. In a move headlined by *Variety* as 'HIGH NOON AT UA', the group swiftly formed a brand new company, Orion - its name claimed to be based on the astronomical factor of its being 'a five-star constellation' (the *real* Orion is actually seven) - and announcing at the same time a financing and distribution agreement with Warners.

Several of UA's existing contractees would sign deals with the new company but Woody, who still had three films to go on his existing contract, carried on much as before - though on its expiry, he too would move his whole production team to the cosier climes of Orion. During this uneasy period - leading up to the *Heaven's Gate* disaster, TransAmerica's divestment of UA and the latter's uncomfortable absorption into MGM - Woody was still considered to be one of the treasured linchpins in the company's ongoing prestige.

The new team, however, knew nothing about his new film beyond the fact that Woody wasn't in it, it wasn't a comedy and that it was thought to be a departure from his usual style. Whatever the fate of *Interiors*, Woody promised that his next project would be a lighter work; this suited UA fine and, ironically, two of the executives with whom he now had to deal (Steven Bach and Chris Mankiewicz) had been together, in the early 1970s, at the New York-based Palomar Pictures which had produced *Take The Money and Run*.

'I would like to take a chance', said Woody, 'I would like to fail a little for the public' and, to many, *Interiors* was exactly the failure he had promised. Views, like that of Robert Benayoun, that the picture was 'received with ear-splitting hostility' are part and parcel of the now-hazy recollections of the event but, in fact, though disliked by some of Woody's hitherto staunchest supporters, the film did receive much favourable attention, especially in Europe, winning several awards for its cinematography and acting. Even in America, 16 out of 31 leading critics placed it on their 'Ten Best' lists for 1978 and it went on to win five Oscar nominations - for Best Director, Actress, Supporting Actress, Original Screenplay and Art Direction. Woody and his producers have insisted that the film actually turned 'a modest profit'. Certainly, it is a tribute to Krim who, despite his doubts, recognized the importance of *Interiors* to Woody's creative development.

The film's opening titles (Woody's trademark plain white typeface on an all-black screen) set the tone but, as he has since noted, this style was less inspired by Bergman than due to the fact that, after using fancy titles on earlier films (like the cutesy colony of white rabbits in *Sex*) he felt it was silly to waste money and, from *Love and Death* on he decided to go for the cheapest titles he could. The credits on *Interiors* are run off against total silence and, elsewhere, except where source music is overheard, natural sound only is used throughout. Characters are photographed against blank walls, exteriors are almost colourless, desolate landscapes. The sessions between Renata (Diane Keaton) and her analyst are played, as in later Allen films, as direct 'confessions' to camera (these were staged, on the first day of filming, in Jack Rollins' New York office). Flashback scenes, as in *Annie Hall*, give the impression of being 'observed' by the characters' present selves, and even the Long Island oceanside setting, where the last third of the film takes place, resembles the barren Baltic island of Faro where Bergman shot *Through a Glass Darkly*, *The Shame* and a number of his other later movies. Location shooting for *Interiors* was extensive since 'each set had to reflect the sparse and exquisite perfection' of the film's leading character, Eve (Geraldine Page). Production designer Mel Bourne looked at no less than 50 different beach houses until Woody agreed to one in Southampton whose owners were away for the summer.

The film is in fact a departure from such photographically adept works as *Love and Death*, where the visuals, however carefully composed, still had to be subservient to the needs of comedy. Woody expressed himself doubtful whether any comedy film could be as well designed as *Interiors*. In this respect, the contribution of Bourne to the look of the film is almost beyond praise - though it was achieved not without problems. 'I'd say *Interiors* was the trial of the age for me', he told Gerald McKnight, 'That was the worst. He [Woody] would change sets suddenly - because he'd last minute decided he didn't like them. Yet ... in the end it turned out exactly right. The way he'd seen it.'

Interiors was Woody's second film with cinematographer Gordon Willis and, just as he had often sat down to write scenes with Diane in mind, so 'I began creating situations hospitable to Gordon Willis's sensibility. I know the way he thinks and I try to give him something he can do.' Variously described as 'the finest American cinematographer' and, by Woody, 'the master of chiaroscuro', Willis had photographed his first feature in 1969, going on to light some of the best films of the 1970s. He turned, somewhat reluctantly, to directing with *Windows* (1980) which had, ironically, been one of Woody's working titles for *Interiors*. Versatile, adaptable and influential, with a distinctive visual style, he has, like Woody, a reputation as a perfectionist.

Interiors revolves around a not-too-typical upper-middle class American family and the dramatic changes wrought upon it by a sudden upheaval. Three sisters, Renata, Joey (Marybeth Hurt) and Flyn (Kristin Griffith), have grown up and sought a degree of independence. One morning, at breakfast, their father, Arthur (E.G. Marshall), a wealthy 62-year old lawyer, breaks the news to their mother Eve that he wants to live on his own. The daughters have their own problems and, in the course of the film, agonize over their anxieties, insecurities and resentments, especially during the final traumatic stages of the drama at the family's beach house. The action also veers between the homes of two of the three young women and their mother's Manhattan apartment.

Woody has claimed that the subject matter had been long in gestation. He had apparently based Eve at least partially on Louise Lasser's late mother and several details of the film family's circumstances and leanings were drawn from life. This was linked to the idea of a man who had deserted his very gifted wife, finding her impossible to live with, and had then found that by marrying a vulgarian, life was much simpler. Woody incorporated these elements into the story of two sisters he met later, each of them going through a difficult emotional crisis. 'It was at the back of my mind', he said, 'even while I was making several other films.' The rest of the story was made up to supplement this basic premise.

Eve, unable to accept that her husband will never return to her and moving towards a breakdown, throws herself into interior decorating, a visual cipher for the film's psychologically motivated title. Unable to take it any more, she seals up the windows of her apartment with black and white tape in a vain attempt to gas herself.

The idea of being sealed in, physically and emotionally, is something Eve has in common with several of the other characters. She is echoed most notably, by Joey (a stunning debut performance by Hurt), a directionless, unfocused dilettante, obsessively worried about being creative rather than simply settling into marriage with her lover, Mike (Sam Waterston), a political film-maker. 'I feel a need to express something', she says, 'but I don't know what it is I want to express or how to express it.' Joey is the first fully-fledged version in one of Woody's films of 'the frustrated female creator' - a character which would reach its most notable expression with the Holly role in *Hannah and Her Sisters*.

Problems of creativity also assail Renata who, somewhat unsympathetically played by Diane, is a tormented, Sylvia Plath-like celebrity poet,

subsidized by a monthly cheque from her father. She is resentful of the latter's lifetime close attention to Joey. Accused of being artistically aloof and
uncommitted to family concerns, Renata, like her mother, is in analysis. She
is now trying to cope with creative impotence and bolstering the ego of her
now unfashionable alcoholic writer husband Frederick (Richard Jordan).
'I'm sick of your needs!' cries Renata, at one point. 'I'm tired of your idio-
syncracy and competitiveness! I have my own problems!' - a line which,
according to a sceptical Joan Didion, gives us 'one of the few lucid moments
in the picture'.

That all had not been well with Arthur and Eve's marriage (though Eve was
oblivious to this) is summed up by Arthur's opening voice-over monologue at
the office window, a scene which originally took place later in the film but
which Woody and Rosenblum, during the editing, thought would be more
'interesting' at the beginning. Here he harks back to the rigidity of an existence where everything, due to Eve's impeccably sterile taste, seemed perfect.
She had, he complains, been building an 'ice-blue-grey palace around herself'
and the seeds of his resentment may also stem from the fact, revealed in a later
scene, that it was Eve who paid his way through law school and, in a sense,
according to Renata, her mother thinks of him 'like he was her creation'.

It is Eve's tragedy that she has failed to recognize the warning signs, while
her later (successful) suicide attempt is prompted, not by self-doubt, but as
her reaction aginst another unforeseen circumstance - Arthur's second marriage to the more life-enhancing Pearl (Maureen Stapleton). Eve's obsession
with tone and colour, echoed wonderfully in Bourne's design, her belief in
balance, scale and 'exact science', denote how far she has retreated from the
ordinary realities of daily life. In common with the typical victim of obsessive
compulsion, particularly now she is bereft of her normal wifely or 'active'
mother role, she has also become an interferer.

To spare himself, if not necessarily the other family members, Arthur, the
'dedicated father and responsible husband' delicately refers to his wanting out
as a 'trial separation'. The casual way in which he does this prefigures the secondary couple's matter-of-fact revelation of their marital break-up at the
beginning of *Husbands and Wives* and, significantly, the fact that Arthur's
announcement takes place at the breakfast table, rather than in private, further
serves to 'protect' him from its immediate effect. The scene is very strong and
Woody admitted that it was based on two actual incidents related to him by
friends. In one of these the wife, given her husband's ultimatum at the dinner
table, went straight to her room and killed herself. 'Now, in *Interiors*', said
Woody, 'I didn't want to take it that far. But I am imitating the incident.'

It is also significant, as in so many of Woody's films, that a number of the key incidents in *Interiors* take place when the family is gathered together, literally, for physical sustenance. One of Pearl's former husbands was an amateur chef and, if we see her character as the one person in the film capable of offering *emotional* sustenance to what remains of this dessicated family group, then all of the alimentary symbolism becomes apt. But so entertaining is she as a character, that, as Woody later admitted, it was 'a failure of the dramaturgy' that he brought her into the drama far too late. Indeed, the later scenes are, thanks to Pearl's energizing influence, certainly more riveting than the film's deliberately low-key beginnings.

Although Pearl's 'Jewishness' is not specifically stated, there are a number of clues which gear her towards the 'Yiddisher Momma' figure to be found elsewhere in Woody's films and indeed, in the work of such contemporaries as Paul Mazursky and Neil Simon. Odd then, to contemplate Woody's own comment that, although no religion is mentioned, there were those in New York who thought 'that Eve, of all people, is the complete Jewish mother, that she has all the traits - compulsively clean, domineering, nagging, possessiveness with her children' that that particular archetype is supposed to have.

Robert Benayoun considers Joey to be the only person in the story with whom Woody feels any affinity. Yet Woody, in interview, has insisted that, although he also identified with Pearl and Eve, it was Diane as Renata who was employed to get his personal concerns across. 'Renata speaks for me', he told Melvyn Bragg, 'without question. She just articulates all my concerns ... my personal feelings. And she did, just said them plain, straight out.' Interestingly, Renata's 'mortality' speech was inspired, said Woody, by his very first meeting with Groucho Marx, then near the end of his life. Old and frail, Groucho reminded Woody of his own uncles and he fell to thinking 'no matter what the great man's achievements, all he had to look forward to was death'.

Everyone dies is a major theme and both the attempted and 'actual' suicides of Eve in the film are also said to have been inspired by tragic incidents involving Louise Lasser's family. Her mother apparently had tried to kill herself when Louise was 21. Louise had saved her mother's life, whereupon Mrs Lasser, after three days in a coma, declared, 'I'll never forgive her.' Her mother's eventual suicide, during the making of *What's New Pussycat* in 1964, left scars on Louise which time did not heal and, as she noted later, the quite obvious parallels she discerned in *Interiors* were difficult to cope with.

The closing stages of the film bring into sharper focus the third sister, Flyn, a minor actress, who has recently been making a TV movie in Denver. She is unattached, her love life is something of a mystery and, due to her long absences from the story, her character seems underdeveloped. A clue, though, is offered by Frederick who, comparing her with one of his books, describes her as 'a perfect example of form without content'. Drunkenly, he makes a play for her at the wedding party. 'It's been a long time since I made love to a woman I didn't feel inferior to', he tells her, coming upon Flyn, snorting coke, alone, in the garage. She repulses him. 'You flirt!' he insists, 'You like to be looked at. All right. You don't exist, except in somebody else's eyes.' Unsurprisingly, this thumbnail sketch of the clichéd, potentially self-destructive glamour girl, reduced to a male-orientated sex object, plus the fumbled rape attempt which follows, would only serve to fuel the complaints of Woody's feminist detractors.

The catalyst is the good humoured Pearl, a warm-hearted vulgarian whom Arthur discovered on his Greek vacation. To emphasize her 'otherness' from the family group, she is dressed in vivid primaries. This enhances her refreshing 'life-force' personality, in contrast to the mainly, harmonized, 'tastefully' designed outfits of the other characters. As Maureen Stapleton told me:

> Woody and the costume designer [future director, Joel Schumacher] and that very good cameraman, Gordon Willis, planned the whole thing, it was all charted and planned, colour-wise, so that everything would be muted - grey, beige, bland sand colours. And the woman I played wore that red dress, and they designed the colour and the dress and everything. I don't remember all the details, but I *would* say that anybody showing up in that red dress would be *bound* to catch your eye!

Stapleton offers us the film's most winning performance and is the repository of the movie's rare moments of humour. Woody denied, though, that he deliberately set out to create a humourous figure and says he was 'just trying to be true to the character. It just came *out* funny. Maureen has a very comic delivery. She's purely unselfconscious.'

Eve, as played by Geraldine Page, with her dogged pursuit of the visually beautiful at the expense of the purely sensual, is by contrast joyless and judgmental. This, again, is thoroughly reflected in the film's staging and production design - often to its detriment. Woody was particularly stung by Pauline Kael who, although praising the acting, dismissed *Interiors* as 'a handbook of art-film mannerisms: it's so austere and studied that it might have been directed by that icy mother herself - from the grave'.

Robert Benayoun, who has done much to redefine Woody in European terms, was, perhaps, the first to note how his 'aspirations were fed by such artists as Emil Nolde and Edvard Munch'. Many of the individual set-ups, irradiated by *clair obscur* lighting, are clearly influenced by the latter, while the haunting beach shot of Renata and Flyn, where they discuss creativity and the problems of growing old, is a characteristic homage to both Bergman's *Persona* and Nolde's celebrated watercolour, 'Am Ufer' ('On the Beach').

Woody has said that he tried very hard not to be influenced by such sources, but he failed, almost inevitably, since 'It's a film where the predominant action takes place on a grey sea shore.' And it is in this setting, after Eve's tragic drowning, that the film ends, with all three sisters, united in grief, gazing out through the beach house windows at the now calm, dark waters of the ocean. Only the very uncharitable might enquire of them, how long before they get to Moscow? It is also possible that, notwithstanding some splendid moments of pure cinema, *Interiors* might have worked somewhat better as a play.

The acting is keyed mainly in a mood of quiet desperation - except, notably, in Eve's famous candle-smashing scene in St Patrick's Cathedral - than towards high-register histrionics. Page, with her loose flowing robes and odd conical hairstyle, always wittering and hoping, is superb. Woody considered her one of America's greatest actresses and this her best screen performance, primarily because he was able to cure her 'tendency to be theatrical and overact. Certainly she was over the top when she started to do her scenes in *Interiors* and I had to say, "Do less".'

As Page recalled, she initially found working with Woody 'exasperating and very difficult', because he would do constant retakes, urging her to simplify but merely shaking his head when he wasn't satisfied. 'He didn't have any of the Method's verbiage', Page told Joanmarie Kalter, 'or even the non-Method director's vocabulary at all. All he ever says is, "Well, I don't like it...".' Page also recalled that Woody was totally 'paranoid' about letting actors see the dailies, so she had no opportunity to check what she might be doing wrong. 'But what was wonderful was that I agreed with his taste. When he said he didn't like it, I believed it; I knew that if I saw it, I would agree with him.'

Maureen Stapleton told me that she also had warm memories of *Interiors* and of being directed by Woody:

Well, I liked Woody and I liked all those other actors in the film - like Geraldine Page, though, sadly, we had no scenes together. I don't know exactly what Woody *did*, but I found him a very *useful* director. He just seemed to sense, from scene to scene, when it was more righter than when it was wronger! He just said, when a scene wasn't ringing true, he said 'Do it again.'

Page went on to win an Oscar nomination and a BAFTA Award for her performance, while Stapleton and the others came in for almost uniform praise.
Marshall, in a role once mooted for Denholm Elliott (Elliott, said Woody,
couldn't do a convincing American accent) turns self-justifying selfishness
into an art form, and Jordan is particularly good as the frustrated drunk
writer, confessing to actual pleasure in his unnessessarily cruel review of an
untalented friend's book. A major casualty was actor Harris Yulin who,
according to Woody, had been playing one of the husbands but had asked to
be replaced because he felt 'uncomfortable' with his role in rehearsal. (He
was later 'compensated' with the part of Marion's unsuccessful brother Paul
in *Another Woman*). Despite the favourable response of several of the cast, the
making of *Interiors*, recalled Ralph Rosenblum, was scarcely a cheerful event,
as Woody rewrote, reshot and all but wrestled the film into shape.

Interiors had been processed on a new film stock and, such was Woody's
perfectionism, that for early press and industry screenings on the West Coast,
he insisted on having the prints returned to the lab after each occasion to be
washed. The editing, which had taken four months, followed Woody and
Rosenblum's usual practice of working irregular hours at the latter's second-
floor apartment-cum-studio on West 84th Street in Manhattan. Here, Woody
anguished over the film's final shape, cutting not only the Yulin scenes, but
making significant reductions to the Hurt-Waterston relationship - one exci-
sion being a sequence in which Waterston breaks down, crying that he is 'only
able to care for people en masse, not as individuals'. Rosenblum to Eric Lax:

> He [Woody] was against the wall. I think he was afraid. He was testy, he was
> slightly short-tempered. He was fearful. He thought he had a real bomb. But
> he managed to pull it out with his own work. The day the reviews came out,
> he said to me, 'Well, we pulled this one out by the short hairs, didn't we?'

If we take congnizance of Red Skelton's famous quip that 'imitation is not the
sincerest form of flattery - it's *plagiarism*', then we cannot be surprised by the
line taken by any number of the critics, especially in America. '*Interiors*',
wrote Jack Kroll in *The New York Times*, 'has the look of a Bergman film, helped
by Gordon Willis's Nykvist-like cinematography, but it does not have the creative elation that triggers elation in the audience, no matter how dark the
artist's vision.' 'His style is Bergmanesque', wrote Richard Schickel, 'but his
material is Mankiewiczian, and the disunity is fatal.' There were similarly
downbeat reviews from James Monaco, Stanley Kauffman and others but,
although these mostly winced at Woody's all-too-obvious assimilation of his

chosen sources, many recognized in *Interiors* a logical development and exposition of the painful concerns which had already bristled not too far from the
surface of even his wildest comedies. Vincent Canby, for instance, didn't like
the film, but praised Woody for making it, devoting four separate articles to
Interiors in both the daily and Sunday editions of *The New York Times*. In favour
was Penelope Gilliatt who, describing the film as 'a giant step forward'
declared it to be 'as true a tragedy as any that has come out of America in
my memory'.

Manhattan *Manhattan* was a return to a number of the themes and interests
Woody had aired in *Annie Hall*. The film was widely acclaimed and US critics,
in particular, noted Robert Bookbinder, 'immediately fell head-over-heels in
love with it and began an outpouring of praise virtually unparalleled in the history of cinema.' Although it failed to win a single Oscar (it was nominated for
Best Original Screenplay and Supporting Actress) it managed to pick up so
many other trophies and appeared on so many international 'Ten Best' lists that
it might be all too tempting to accept Andrew Sarris's contention that
Manhattan was, indeed, 'the only truly great film of the 70s'.

Charles Joffe has described *Manhattan* as 'A drama with comedy rather than
a comedy with drama' and Woody's success in maintaining the balance
between the two was defined by him as 'a happy accident'. But ever his own
harshest critic, he confessed himself so appalled with the film that on completing it he had his agent Sam Cohn offer UA another one for nothing if
they'd agree not to release it!

The film, according to Woody, deals with 'the problems of trying to live a
decent life amidst the junk of contemporary culture - the temptations, the
seductions'. It opens with a glittering montage of Manhattan itself - the initial
shots taken from the terrace of Woody's Fifth Avenue apartment. Over this,
Woody's character, Isaac (Ike) Davis, is heard dictating his feelings about the
city he loves into a tape recorder. It is the first chapter of a novel and the opening montage revolves around a perfect idealization of New York.

Woody's vision of his chosen milieu is nothing if not distinctive. Although
we glimpse the garbage piling up in the street, workmen mending the road
and, in a later sequence, Ike and Mary (Diane Keaton) running for shelter
from a suddenly threatening rainstorm, this is not the New York of a Weegee
or a Lionel Rogosin nor even, for that matter, a Sidney Lumet. It is an ongoing pilgrimage from Park Avenue apartments to the Guggenheim, the Museum
of Modern Art, the Whitney, the Studio Cinema, the Russian Tea Room, the
Stanhope Café, Elaine's, Central Park and the Hayden Planetarium. As Woody

told Caryn James in 1986, 'While I was doing *Manhattan* ... I was very selective, and I did the same thing on *Hannah*. I presented a view of the city as I'd like it to be and as it can be today, if you take the trouble to walk on the right streets.'

There are no opening credits and the film's title is confined to an illuminated hotel sign, winking away to left of frame. As the camera cuts from one breathtaking vista to another, one's pleasure in the sheer beauty of the skilfully edited images is augmented by the strains of 'Rhapsody in Blue', reverberating on the soundtrack. The original idea for the picture, Woody told Silvio Bizio, actually 'evolved from the music. I was listening to a record album of overtures from famous George Gershwin shows, and I thought "This would be a beautiful thing to make a movie in black-and-white, you know, and make a romantic movie." '

As in *Stardust Memories* and *Hannah*, Woody plays the artist in mid-life crisis, struggling to come to terms with his emotional life and about where his talents are taking him. And, although Ike has decided that the best way to artistic fulfilment is to pen an autobiographical novel, the self-image he wishes to project bears only a marginal connection with reality - which is writing scripts for a TV show and audience he despises.

Ike's second wife Jill (Meryl Streep) is a bisexual feminist who has left him for another woman. She has written a revelatory best seller which exposes their married life to ridicule. (His first wife was an infant teacher and drug addict who took up with the Moonies.) There is a deep strain of misogyny running through the film, and also the customary element of masochism in the Allen character. Ike had married Jill despite his analyst's warnings because she was 'so beautiful' and, although there are dark gags about her militant lesbianism and the possibility of their son, Willy, 'ending up wearing a dress', this particular aspect of the story, suggested Martin Sutton, may tell us more about Woody's own sexual insecurities than about lesbianism *per se*.

As a significant advance on the 'unreconstructed 1960s man' of the nightclub routines, Woody's screen character is, otherwise, a much more confident figure. Although, by his own admission, Ike is 'the winner of the August Strindberg Award when it comes to relationships with women', he has, like Alvy Singer in *Annie Hall,* little trouble in getting to know them. He smokes, he drinks, he drives, he dresses up-market and he stands up to his TV bosses when disgust at the pap he's been churning out impels him to quit his job. He still has doubts - about the value and meaning of his work and the desirability of emotional commitment - but, when Ike's married friend, Yale (Michael Murphy) suggests that Ike 'can't function anywhere but in New York. Very

Freudian', and Jill castigates him in print for being subject to 'fits of rage, Jewish liberal paranoia, male chauvinsm, self-righteous misanthropy and nihilistic moods of despair', these are the stark failings of a man who is, in other respects, in control of his daily life and professional destiny.

At an art exhibition at the Guggenheim, Ike is introduced to a neurotic, irresolute author, Mary Wilke (Diane Keaton), who, though prone to waffle pseudishly about 'art' and write 'in-depth' pieces for minority magazines, actually earns her living 'novelizing' popular movies. She's been having an affair with Yale, who represents here a sort of intellectual equivalent of the Tony Roberts character in earlier films. Yale is less venal, more thoughtful than the Roberts character. He also has something of a conscience and, to extricate himself from a relationship he feels is wrong, Yale virtually pushes Ike and Mary together. Although they initally rub each other up the wrong way, a rapport begins to be fomented at the couple's second meeting when they find themselves as fellow guests at an Equal Rights Amendment party at the Museum of Modern Art.

To the accompaniment of Gershwin and further misty-eyed views of the city, the relationship develops into a brief, romantic affair. Ike finds himself torn between Mary and his 17-year-old drama student girlfriend, Tracy (Mariel Hemingway), who is about to go to LAMDA in London. Against this background, Woody, through Ike, presents us with a very clear evocation of his own needs: artistic fulfilment, to be taken seriously and, above all, love.

Ike is nervous of his liaison with Tracy, but it is with her, he finally realizes, that his best bet lies. Their relationship in the film is exquisite: Woody is very tender in his scenes with Hemingway, combining romantic playfulness and paternal humour with a number of somewhat uneasy jokes about Nabokov, school homework and the fact that Tracy's father is younger than himself. She is young enough to enjoy ice cream and buggy rides in the park, suggesting the 25-year gap between them is perhaps less a matter of age than of culture.

The casting of Hemingway in the role came about when Woody saw some photographs of her in *Interview* magazine and 'I thought - and still do think - that she's probably the most beautiful woman that the world has ever seen.' She was also one of his tallest co-stars which led to the curious situation where, in selecting Hemingway's equally tall and beautiful stand-in, Woody was astonished to discover 'her' to be a *him*! Woody has recalled that Hemingway, aged 16 at the time of filming, was young for her age and 'had an inordinate amount of trouble with any kind of intimate moment'. In contrast with the youthfulness of her appearance, the script offers Tracy a degree of sexual maturity which also, in context, disturbs, and it was this 'Lolita' aspect in the movie which led to its somewhat cynical New York revival in the summer of 1992.

UA's new senior vice-president, Steven Bach, who loved the picture, had successfully campaigned for the lifting of the MPAA's adult 'R' rating - which had been mainly imposed on account of Diane's three times use of the 'F' word, but the moment the board's chairman saw *Manhattan* for himself and realized it concerned the relationship between a teenager and a 42-year-old man, the 'R' rating was restored. None of this harmed the film unduly and, as one well-known woman reviewer was to note (at the time of *Husbands and Wives*), 'not one critic had looked askance at the Ike-Tracy, May-December romance in any of the original 1979 reviews of *Manhattan*'.

A number of observers *were* shocked, however, and some of the most intense criticism came from Lee Guthrie, a strongly feminist Southern writer (and mother of actress Sean Young) whose 1978 book on Woody had been withdrawn as a result of his legal action. She had already taken him to task for what she considered his 'ascendant male chauvinism' in *Annie Hall*. This time, she would complain that *she* 'couldn't ever imagine having an affair with a 17-year-old *boy*' and suggested, cuttingly, that Woody was 'nymphet-related'. All of which, again, presupposes, in spite of the extensive 'autobiographical' input of co-writer Marshall Brickman into the screenplay, that Woody and his film character are one and the same.

'Maybe he *was* most like himself in *Manhattan*,' said Jack Rollins, 'I can't be specific, but in my mind it's the closest to what he actually is.' And this in spite of the fact, wrote Philip Thomas, 'that Ike Davis ... is probably Allen's least likeable character'. Much has since been made of the apparent parallels between the Ike-Tracy affair and Woody's real-life two-year relationship with the actress Stacey Nelkin, who would go on to star in such deathless epics as *Halloween III*. She had first met Woody when, aged 17, she had been cast by him in a small, left-on-the-cutting-room-floor role in *Annie Hall*: a short scene in which Alvy fantasizes, in flashback, over a schoolgirl he had always wanted to date but never dared ask.

In Tracy, there are also apparent echoes of Woody's 13-year-old 'pen-pal', Nancy Jo Sales. Their only actual meeting, at his apartment and chaperoned by Sales's stepmother and a family friend, was reportedly brief. In his letters to her, Woody, according to Sales, had encouraged her literary tastes, plying her with questions about her life and interests - as 'unconscious' (?) raw material for the subsequent movie.

Woody had begun writing *Manhattan* just after finishing *Annie Hall* and prior to filming *Interiors* and, although it can be properly argued that Nelkin and Sales did indeed serve as unwitting guinea pigs for Tracy, there were, according to writer Tim Carroll, some even earlier models. As for Nelkin, she has since claimed that Hemingway played Tracy as a much younger, more innocent character than she remembered being at the time she was going out with Woody, and it was undoubtedly this factor, rather than the character's actual age, which unsettled some commentators. The idea of an older man-younger woman benefiting each other is a consistent theme in Woody's work, so much so that years later, elements of Nelkin and Sales would also creep into the character of college student Rain in *Husbands and Wives*, including the fact that Rain, like Nelkin, had been born during a hurricane!

The delineation of the female protagonists in *Manhattan* marked an all-round advance on *Play It Again, Sam* where the women, agreed Woody, had been reduced, for comic effect, to mere lust objects. Diane's character in *Manhattan*, 'an exponent of the fake intelligence', is also a step forward from what Woody denoted as its 'cartoon equivalent' in *Love and Death*. Interestingly, the characters of Mary and Jill in *Manhattan* were both loosely derived from Woody and Brickman's old friend, journalist Susan Braudy - she had, in fact, the same shaggy hair style and speech patterns as Diane, while Mary's Braudy-ish line, 'No, I'm from Philadelphia. We never talk about things like that in public', comes to the screen all but verbatim.

In spite of some initial reservations, UA had agreed to Woody shooting *Manhattan* in monochrome, a process, notwithstanding some recent black-and-white successes, which was still considered commercially doubtful. As Bach has recalled however, even though the triumph of *Annie Hall* had helped promote popular foreign reissues and video releases of some earlier Allen movies, Woody's value to UA had never been a purely economic one. After much discussion between Woody and Gordon Willis, it was also decided to shoot the film in 'Scope which, according to Willis, seemed to be the ideal way 'to graphically get the best visual structure on the sreen'. It would also, as Woody has noted, 'give us a great look at New York City, which is sort of one of the characters in the film'. As Willis recalled to Dean Goodhill in the November 1982 edition of *American Cinematographer*:

I felt that Panavision wide screen, 2.35 to 1, was the most appropriate form. I like wide screen, because of the way you can use it graphically. That was superimposed on the basic idea of romantic reality. Put them together and you have something that was, in my opinion, very workable and quite good looking at times. It was a better way to deal with scale, people in the city and the city in itself.

By shooting wide screen, Willis also succeeded in giving the lie, yet again, to the old saw that 'Scope is somehow unsuited to the needs of intimate, personal movies. *Manhattan*'s visual style takes its cue from Ike's opening monologue: 'Now ... to him ... no matter what the season was, this was still a town that existed in black-and-white ...'. And, although the line was actually written during post-production, it did serve to crystallize a sentiment Woody and Willis had shared from the outset. Luminously shot, not so much in black and white, but in a 'subtle mixture of greys', *Manhattan* comes close to Woody's affectionate recall of the kind of New York movies he grew up with. Shooting in a wide-screen process, though, presented certain problems and, to compensate for the Panavision camera's anamamorphic lenses and their somewhat shallow depth of field, Willis shot the film on an ultra-fast monochrome stock, Kodak's Double-X, which has a relatively wide stop.

Due to the comparative rarity of black-and-white features being made at that time ('Black and white tends to be a lost art!' said Willis) he had to shop around for a New York laboratory which was equipped to develop the negative. In the end, said Woody, they had one built for the purpose, which took care of *Manhattan*, as well as Woody's subsequent four films shot in that process. Printing was undertaken by Technicolor, though Willis specified that *Manhattan*'s release prints be made on Agfa positive. It is a mixture popular with many black-and-white stills photographers, and Agfa's monochrome stock, said Willis 'like their enlarging paper for still use, contains more silver and produces noticeably richer blacks'.

The use of Panavision, magical in capturing the New York panorama, is just as effective, as Sam B. Girgus has noted, in helping 'to expose a whole dimension of meanings and feelings'. This is nowhere more apparent than in conjuring the events of the evening which lead to that famously evocative shot, where Ike and Mary sit, silhouetted, side by side, on their promenade bench in Sutton Place, with the Queensborough Bridge to left of frame. The tonal quality of the camerawork and the heart-stopping strains of 'Someone Who'll Watch Over Me' as the couple gaze out across the East River towards Roosevelt Island and Queens, help make the scene both 'irresistible and wonderfully romantic'. The sequence was to serve as the logo for the film and was shot, between 3.45 and 4.30am, just as it was beginning to get light. Willis did about six takes within a 20-minute period and, to augment the natural lighting, had the bridge lights left on.

The scene conjures up an image of every New York movie ever seen and loved; both the romantic situation and hazy view across the East River help symbolize the film's central theme: Woody's attempt to set 'the romantic vision of New York against the mess that people make of their lives', and to expose to ridicule the kind of New Yorkers - TV executives, phoney intellectuals, fast-food proprietors and car drivers - who mar the city as a perfect living space.

Even more effective, from a dramatic point of view, is the imaginative handling of the film's final sequences, starting with Ike's headlong 'rush for love' through the New York streets, from Second Avenue to the Yorkville section of Manhattan - arriving, breathless, just in time to catch Tracy prior to her departure for drama school in London. The finale is then played out in a series of huge, meaningful close-ups, virtually the last time Woody would have recourse to this device in such a highly concentrated and emotive way. The playing is spot on, an object lesson in doing little but conveying everything, while Ike's touching happy-sad reaction to Tracy's final line ('You have to have a little faith in people') and the ambivalence it implies in terms of their future relationship, reminded a number of observers of that exquisite moment in Chaplin's *City Lights* - the nervous smile on Charlie's face as he wonders whether the blind flower girl, her sight restored, will still love him for himself.

The film's design, like the camerawork, also serves to key the story and the mood of the characters with maximum effectiveness. Ike's affair with Mary, for instance, is conveyed in darker tones (dark clothes, the rainstorm, the very Wellesian sequence in the Hayden Planetarium) while the Tracy scenes are altogether brighter, incandescent. The film is so carefully composed, in fact, that when it was subsequently sold to cable TV Woody insisted on a contract stipulation that it be transmitted in the original 'Scope shape, with masking borders. (In 1993, he sued Dutch television for screening *Manhattan* in the arbitrary pan-and-scan format).

The material for *Manhattan* had been prepared over a two-month period, with Woody writing the first draft ('I think I've integrated things more'), developing it further with Brickman's help. But, although the results were closer to their original intentions than *Annie Hall* had been, Brickman felt the resulting film to be rather too dark and brooding to be entirely enjoyable.

Indeed, Woody made the point of establishing 'a tone on the working out of relationships' by eschewing any number of comic possibilities. He resisted, for example, the temptation to play a sad drunk scene for laughs and cut out a lot of other gags in the editing. 'They were very funny', he told Frank Rich in *Time*, 'not one-liners, but sight gags - but in the context of the film, they looked like they had dropped down from the moon.'

Filming took place, from July 1978 on, in various New York locations, plus Nyack and Englewood, New Jersey. Engelwood, a little town across the

Hudson River, had previously been used in *Annie Hall* but, when Woody returned there to shoot in front of a local theatre, the townsfolk found it so disruptive they took out an injunction to prevent further filming in the area. Although Woody has since claimed that *Manhattan* was shot 'all on location', he did film a number of sequences at the old Filmways Studios in East Harlem. These included part of the Hayden Planetarium set which Woody had custom-built, though about three-quarters of what he filmed was the genuine article, located in Central Park. Logistically, *Manhattan* was one of Woody's most taxing New York-based projects, exemplified by a sequence at Rockefeller Plaza where, with the camera sticking out of an upper-floor window, the cast and crew, trying to go about their business unobserved, were driven mad by passers-by. Reshoots, as per the 'second chance' provisions written into Woody's original budget, were extensive, but the film's cost, just over $8m (the same, more or less, as for UA's concurrent *Cuba*, which flopped), was considered usual for a medium-high priced picture at this time - or three or four smaller ones.

A notable absentee from Woody's regular team was Ralph Rosenblum, who had now edited six of his previous films. 'Woody felt I was overqualified as an editor', Rosenblum recalled, 'and I had a great desire to leave the cutting room and move on.' He later stated, though, that the opportunity to work with Woody was the one thing that had kept him in a field he had long since outgrown. The final parting was friendly and Rosenblum, who, prior to his death in September 1995, would go on to direct a clutch of praised TV movies, was succeeded as Woody's editor by his assistant Susan E. Morse.

Manhattan also marked Diane's last appearance in one of Woody's films until 1987. The other leads, apart from Murphy, were all working with him for the first time. These included Meryl Streep, concurrently playing 'Shakespeare in the Park' and filming her role in *Kramer vs Kramer*. Feature casting included Anne Byrne, former ballerina and ex-wife of Dustin Hoffman; Woody had met her by chance at a Knicks game and offered her the role of Yale's wife Emily. Smaller parts went to radical feminist and US Congresswoman Bella Abzug, playing herself at the ERA party; *New York Magazine* critic Judith Crist; future name Karen Allen as a TV actress and Tisa Farrow - with one line as the blonde with the 'wrong kind' of orgasm!

Steven Bach had initially expressed his nervousness over the project - its cultural references, the (subsequently cut) Skokie-like sequence of neo-Nazis on the march in New Jersey - but, after reading the script he had given it his blessing. A major structural problem, recalled Brickman, was, once more, the lack of an effective 'third act', and it was his idea to include the scene between

Ike and Yale with the classroom skeleton, which meant that 'Woody would be required to do on screen what he never does in real life, yell and scream and get upset by a friend'. Another addition was the Central Park fireworks display, filmed after the rest of the opening New York montage had been shot. This took place near the end of filming, when, taking advantage of an actual display, the crew went to the Central Park West apartment of one of the production staff's parents and the cameraman recorded the scene, hanging out of the bathroom window. The resulting sequence was added to the 'nearly three dozen quintessential New York images' which open the picture.

Manhattan opened simultaneously on 14 screens in both New York and Los Angeles in the last week of April 1979, and Woody broke off a rare vacation in Paris to give two days of interviews in conjunction with the film's subsequent screening at the Cannes Film Festival. It then received its UK première at the Edinburgh Festival in August and went on to win a BAFTA award as the year's Best Picture. It was also to establish a year's-end US net of $16.9m - somewhat more than the pre-Oscar take of *Annie Hall*, though it failed to equal the latter's impressive aggregate gross on the world market. *Manhattan* would also be Woody's last real box-office hit for some time.

Stardust Memories While *Manhattan* was in early release, Woody directed a 62-minute film tribute to Bob Hope, entitled *My Favourite Comedian*. The project had come about at the instigation of Joanne Koch, director of the Lincoln Center's Film Society which was honouring Hope at a fund raiser at the Avery Fisher Hall. Koch had heard Woody on *The Dick Cavett Show* refer to Hope as his 'favourite comedian', and the resulting celebrity packed occasion, co-narrated by Woody and Cavett, raised $100,000 for the charity. Woody had viewed many hours of the comic's work for the compilation and 'I had more pleasure looking at Hope's films', he said, 'than making any film I've ever made.' The result was also shown, to some success, at the New York Film Festival in September.

By the fall of 1979, Woody was busy at work on his next feature, *Stardust Memories*. It was described by him as 'a serious cartoon in the baroque style; but, by many observers, as 'Woody's *8½*' - due to the quite noticeable influence on the finished movie of another of his idols, Federico Fellini.

Woody plays Sandy Bates, a successful comedy director in mid-life and career crisis, attending a long weekend retrospective of his work at the Hotel Stardust in New Jersey. Moving even more demonstrably than in previous Allen movies between present reality, personalized interpretations of the past, stream of consciousness, free association and the most bizarre of fantasies,

Sandy calls up recollections of his childhood, the women in his life and his early success, while drawing parallels with his current creative anxieties and the problems of his latest, highly experimental movie which studio executives are even now trying to wrest from his control.

In the process, Woody turns a baleful gaze on a number of targets, notably those who almost wilfully misinterpret works of art; and as the present becomes ever more confused with the past and Sandy's dazzling fantasies, the movie develops into not so much a film in the conventional sense as a series of surreal digressions on what makes Sandy (Woody?) tick. The story is told from a number of different perspectives, the sum total of which anticipates the Pirandelloesque resonances Woody would bring to bear on the most captivating of his 'middle period' films, *The Purple Rose of Cairo*.

However, *Stardust Memories* is an altogether darker work, a fascinating Chinese box of a film, photographed, once again, by Gordon Willis in black-and-white. 'It takes a certain amount of clout, I'm afraid', Woody told Penelope Gilliatt, during the filming and, even when working with a warmer film stock than had been employed to create the grittier, more urban feel of *Manhattan*, he again agreed that the medium's box-office potential was limited. But, although, on a craft level, Willis has said he drew no real distinctions between the two films, 'On an interpretative level', he told Schaefer and Salvato in 1984, 'they were two different things ... *Manhattan* was, by its very nature romantic reality again. And *Stardust Memories* a more theatrical and poetic approach to shooting a piece of material. So it's different from that standpoint. Whether you like the one or the other, the difference was laid out at that level.'

Woody has said that he had wanted 'a more idyllic and piercing' look than before to point up Sandy's 'existential despair' and to challenge the audience to take the movie seriously as an examination of the artist's predicament when he finds himself at a creative crossroads. He has also insisted that its main theme, as in so many of his films, lay in his attempt to show 'man's relationship to his own mortality' that, no matter how rich and successful one may become, each of us comes to the same end.

Britsh critic Alan Brien suggested at the time of the film's release that it was 'programmed to be critic-proof' but, in spite of the fact that Woody felt it came closer than any of his earlier work to what he had wanted to achieve, it remains his most misunderstood movie to date. So much so that it has alternately fascinated, angered, exasperated, been dismissed out of hand and praised to the skies, emptied cinemas or been perceived, by this writer, amongst others, to be Woody's masterpiece. That it fits none or all of these categories may well depend on predilections and prejudices that have little to do with what is actually up there on screen.

Sandy's misanthropy is not entirely evident at the start of the film, which promises some agreeable, if satirical fun at the expense of Woody's own film-making success. The opening sequence is a pastiche of the pretentiousness many artists are prone to when they wish to be taken seriously. A group of glum, zombie-like people, their faces distorted by the camera's unkind emphasis on their evident grotesqueries, sit in a rattling railroad carriage attended by a Grim Reaper-like conductor. Sandy becomes distracted by a parallel train which is full of attractive, joyful, partying revellers. He is unnerved when a blonde goddess on the other train, brandishing an 'Oscar', plants a kiss for him on the window. He vainly tries to get out. The train he is on, we have to assume, symbolizes the ride of life, whose occupants are representative of the artist's lack of pleasure in it, whereas the briefly glimpsed vision on the passing train demonstrates to him the delightful time he might have had if he hadn't simply got on the wrong track.

The sequence though, is not a dream, but the opening of Sandy's new movie and, appalled, studio executives set about trying to subvert the ending into a 'Jazz Heaven' musical extravaganza, an obvious pastiche of the 'Going to Heaven on a Mule' sequence from the Al Jolson musical *Wonder Bar* (1934). Woody defines Sandy's dilemma as being derived from the invented symptom, 'Ozymandias Melancholia', an idea central to some other Allen films which have allied themselves to the theme of 'perishing and disillusion'. Sandy's creative impasse stems from an increasing awareness of life's futility in a world that is altogether hopeless.

Those who excoriated Woody for turning gracelessly on his critics and his fans, were swiftly to be reminded that Sandy Bates was not Woody but, like his earlier roles, an 'imaginative presence' who, although sharing many of his predilections, was, said his creator, '... a very sick, neurotic almost nervous breakdown film director. I didn't want this guy to be necessarily likeable. I wanted him to be surly and upset; not a saint or an angel, but a man with real problems who finds that art doesn't save you, an idea I had explored in *Interiors*.'

Stardust Memories becomes easier to interpret if we accept, on face value, Woody's contention that it all takes place in the mind and, taken to extreme lengths, Sandy's mental state forces *physical* changes in his environment, as in the scenes in his apartment where the décor and the wall posters alter from sequence to sequence according to his mood.

Sandy's life, like his new movie, lacks structure and he seeks temporary distraction from his unhappiness in contemplating the various women he has known. Dorrie (Charlotte Rampling) is revealed in a series of flashbacks as a sensuous but disturbed pill-popping minor actress, beautiful but anorexic, whom Sandy 'promoted' after meeting her on the set of a movie significantly entitled *Suppression*. But her drastic mood swings alarm him and Woody has described how he utilized his long-time admiration for cubist paintings to orchestrate Dorrie's eventual breakdown as a sequence of disturbing repetitive jump-cuts. A far calmer companion is Isobel (Marie-Christine Barrault) a nice, politically committed mother of two. She has recently left her husband and there are, briefly, for Sandy, intimations of domestic bliss. Finally, there is Daisy (Jessica Harper), a weird, Winnetka-born, bisexual violinist, who is into prescription drugs and old movies - but, although Sandy is attracted to her, their relationship is inconclusive.

The characters of Dorrie and Isobel oddly beg the contrast between the 'nervy' Diane Keaton in earlier movies and the cause-hungry, child-gathering Mia Farrow, whom Woody started dating in April 1980, and whom Barrault, in some shots, curiously resembles. Elements of Louise Lasser also creep into the character of Dorrie, and Louise herself appears in the film in a brief, uncredited cameo as Sandy's secretary. The name 'Dorrie' had already been appended to a character in *Annie Hall,* and is in fact that of Diane Keaton's younger sister whom Woody also briefly dated. Diane had actually begun her stage career as 'Dorrie Keaton' and in 1982 directed a short film about her sister, *What Does Dorrie Want?* In *Stardust Memories*, Sandy's relationships with the three central women are also contrasted with a momentary confrontation with an importunate, married groupie (Amy Wright) and a nightmare vision of his sister's married life which, it is implied, prevents him making his own commitment to marriage.

By far the most enlivening part of the movie is Woody's sharp parody of the kind of folk who traditionally haunt film seminars. But his view of the proceedings is sufficiently jaundiced to cause maximum injury. Critic Judith Crist, who turns up in person during a flashback fantasy to comment on the boyhood Sandy's magic act, felt herself badly used by the film. Woody had earlier agreed to attend an actual weekend seminar at one of Crist's regular movie events in Tarrytown, New York State. After allowing Woody to utilize Tarrytown as a model for the 'Film Culture' weekend at the Stardust Hotel, she found herself cruelly lampooned in the character of the retro's organizer, Vivian Orkin, played by off-Broadway actress Helen Hanft. The occasion itself is wittily satirized, not only through the gallery of pseudish, Felliniesque grotesques who inhabit the festival and Willis's adept simulation of the master's lighting style, but by what sounds suspiciously like Nino Rota on the sound track!

Sandy's chief bile is reserved for his most adulatory fans, like the woman who wants him to autograph her left breast - a sequence derived from an actual incident involving Groucho Marx. 'I said a lot of true things in that picture that people didn't want to hear', Woody told Stephen Farber; one of the most obvious revolves around the love-hate relationship which often exists between the entertainer and his audience which, in extreme circumstances, can actually be dangerous. In *Stardust*, this theme is demonstrated at its starkest by the fan who, approaching Sandy to declare, 'You know, you're my hero', finally guns him down. 'I always had a fear of being shot', Woody told Edwin Miller of *Seventeen*, 'by a girl, a psychotic fan who imagines some connection between us.' And, in the light of the assassination of John Lennon outside the Dakota apartments in December 1980, the ultimate nightmare Woody had long envisioned turned out to be frighteningly prophetic. But it should be pointed out that the death of Sandy in the film is a fantasy and climaxes with the filmmaker, against lowering clips from *The Creation of the Universe*, accepting a posthumous Oscar nomination ('for his convincing portrayal of God') and conducting a ghostly press conference!

Woody has continued to make insistent denials that he could, in any way, be construed as Sandy Bates, albeit 'there was an enormous amount of focus on me and my personal life, even before it came out, and as people said to me, "If you had someone else play the lead ... you wouldn't have to undergo all that." ' But, even if someone like Dustin Hoffman, as Woody has suggested, *had* starred in the film, would anyone have been fooled? Quite clearly, Woody would like to have it both ways. Sandy, in the film, is an ex-stand-up comic who became a comedy film director, but then switched to drama (*Interiors?*), a move rejected by his fans. As a boy, Sandy, like Woody, hung out at a Brooklyn boys' club and practised magic tricks in the privacy of his room. And, in a childhood flashback - an idea more fully developed in the stage play which would follow the film - Sandy performs the illusion known as 'The Floating Lightbulb'. Sandy's favourite actor, like Woody's, is Tony Roberts, playing himself in the movie. Sandy, like Woody, lives in Manhattan, hates Hollywood and answers questions about his work with some of the same kind of replies Woody gives in real life. Sandy, like Woody, is disappointed with his comedy films and finds them trivial, but is equally dissatisfied with his serious work. 'This is not me', Woody told Robert F. Moss, 'but it will be perceived as me' and, one may ask, if he had no wish to be identified with the on-screen Sandy, why, in the first place, did he choose to tell this particular story?

As in earlier Allen movies, favourite film scenes turn up in new guises. There is, for instance, a brief nod to Barrault's debut role in *Ma Nuit Chez*

Maude (1969), while the idea of a crazed doctor grafting his wife's brains on to his mistress's body, previously aired in Woody's *New Republic* story, 'A Lunatic's Tale', is an amusing parody of *Frankenstein*. One of the most intriguing fantasies is the comic nightmare sequence involving Sydney Finklestein's 'hostility' which breaks loose and is pursued, by police with tracker dogs, through a snowy, leafless Central Park. A lively Bergmanesque pastiche of *The Dybbuk* and *King Kong*, it was derived from Woody's (at that time) unpublished short story, 'Phil Feldman's Hostility'. The sequence also posits a retrospective acquaintance with the *real* Sidney Finkelstein (*sic*), actually the uncle of film historian Joel Finler; the former's exploits as a New York Jewish writer and jazz enthusiast must surely have been known to Woody.

Another fantasy, the bleak 'morning-after' scene of dejected train travellers loafing around a beach-lot junkyard ('Seagulls and dead *cars?*'), may well refer to the kind of lousy, existential 'art' movie Sandy, but not Woody, has been making, but it also, oddly, evokes the final wind-down sequence of Fellini's *La Dolce Vita*. The strange beachside hotel, with its stripped awnings, ornate lintels, fake Gothic towers and pinnacle roof, is even more suggestive of European models. Otherworldly, too, is the ravishing Felliniesque descent of three hot-air balloons on to a UFO convention - to which Sandy's semi-picaresque odyssey has unwittingly, led him. Endearingly, he is confronted at one point by a tiny extra-terrestrial called Og (named after the leprechaun in *Finian's Rainbow*), who, echoing his human counterparts, takes Sandy to task for turning aside from the 'early funny films' Og and his little friends prefer.

Woody's attention to such ciphers, though, is not so much slavish as apt. And certainly respectful. Although, suggests Robert Coursodon, the relationship between *8½* and *Stardust Memories* is 'mostly superficial', Sandy, with his European-style sun-glasses, does recall Marcello Mastroianni's role of Guido Anselmi in the former, while the psychiatrist, Dr Pearlman ('Pearlstein' on the credits) - the man who asks Sandy whether he's 'ever had intercourse with any kind of animal?' - bears a quite alarming resemblance to Fellini! The shot of the joyful revellers, all dressed in white, on the parallel train at the beginning of the film, alludes to one of Fellini's own proposed endings for *8½* which he had decided not to use. Like Guido, Sandy is a film-maker at a moment of indecision who finds himself having to make sense of his work, as well as his private life on which his latest film is based. Sandy, like Guido, dallies briefly with a seductive neurotic, but finds solace with someone altogether calmer. He also finds himself smothered by the women in his life, each of whom has different needs. Sandy seems to manifest a 'repetitive compulsion' towards self-destructive relationships, and Woody's films, in general, tend to reflect the view that *most* real-life relationships are problematic. Even the ones that work are derived from what he has called 'an intermeshing of neuroses'.

When Daisy utters the warning, 'I would be very bad trouble', she is merely echoing the almost identical admonition of Dorrie (in the flashbacks) and Mary Wilke in *Manhattan*. 'I'm fatally attracted to you', says Sandy, on first meeting with Dorrie, thus pointing up the relationship between sex and death which, wrote Douglas Brode, 'runs, almost like a spectre, through Woody's films'. Sandy, like Guido, though, wants to be an artist *and* normal, and the danger he finds in the neurotic love affair with Dorrie is counterpointed by the healthier relationship and lifestyle with Isobel.

Some observers have also drawn analogies between *Stardust Memories* and *Sullivan's Travels* whose influence Woody acknowledged during the filming but subsequently denied having seen. Like *Stardust*, the earlier movie deals with a film-maker who wants to make serious films with a message, the notable difference being, in Og's words, that Sandy is 'not the missionary type' and would never dream of doing without his Rolls-Royce, sophisticated friends or entourage - whereas Sullivan is more than eager to share the miseries of the people he imagines to be his audience. It could also be argued that Woody, as a film-maker, was, as some critics duly noted, guilty of producing just the kind of artily pretentious movie which Sturges in *Sullivan's Travels* was so wickedly satirizing.

Stardust Memories, as it turned out, was perceived as a singular act of defiance on Woody's part. Into the mouths of the on-screen studio executives and critics, he put the words which, surely, he anticipated for real once the final cut had been delivered. In this respect, the result is not so much masturbatory, as some critics have averred, as downright masochistic and full of self-loathing.

In amongst the general sourness, we are granted the odd insouciant moment, like the sophisticated dream sequence in which Sandy sees himself as part of an Astaire-style double act, performing a soft-shoe routine to Kalmar and Ruby's 'Three Little Words'. The scene recalls happier, more innocent times in Woody's screen career and looks forward, with hope, to the Astaire-Rogers resonances of *The Purple Rose of Cairo*. Almost in defiance of the fan who asks Sandy, 'If you're a genius, how come you can't make funny films?', a great deal of *Stardust* is very funny indeed and Woody, who up until *Cairo* named it as his own favourite amongst his films, has always thought of *Stardust Memories* as a comedy.

Woody had spent some time in Paris prior to making the picture and, it was briefly reported, he had actually planned to film there. But, after signing Rampling and Barrault, both French residents, he returned to the States where filming began in September 1979. Details of the production have been respectfully preserved by André Delvaux's simultaneous 40-minute documentary, *To Woody Allen, From Europe with Love*. Like the Princeton-based Harold Mantell's *Woody Allen: An American Comedy* (1977), Delvaux's 'Valentine portrait' does offer a valuable exploration of Woody at the tail end of his first decade as a film-maker. In the Delvaux film Woody discourses on his own favourites, especially, (at that time), *Love and Death*. The conversation also ranges from Woody's apartment, where he is glimpsed playing the clarinet, to the Carnegie Deli - future locale for *Broadway Danny Rose*. Delvaux dutifully follows Woody to the Oyster Bay location for *Stardust Memories*, where he reshoots scenes he isn't happy with, as well as observing him in his new editing suite on Park Avenue.

Exteriors for the film were shot mainly in the Nassau area of Long Island and at the Ocean Grove Camp Meeting Association's popular summer resort in Monmouth County, New Jersey. The chief location was the Ocean Grove Great Auditorium, the Association's 6500-seater Methodist Episcopal Conference Center and concert hall. 'I'm a great Woody Allen fan', the Association's executive director, James Lindemuth told me, 'and we were only too happy to help. He was looking for a Victorian style building and this was used for the exterior of the Stardust Hotel. They removed the centre cross and dressed up the frontage to look like a hotel and that is what you see.'

This majestic Eastlake-style structure, surrounded by the quaint 'tent' houses and pattern-book late ninteenth-century 'gingerbread village' architecture of the area, does afford the film a somewhat otherworldly quality. This is at its most distinctive and romantic in the sequences which follow the unexpected arrival of Isobel, framed against a hazy, dreamlike horizon, as she takes her long *Marienbad*-like walk, up the hotel path, towards camera. Lindemuth:

> Straight ahead of you, as you approach from the shore side is the Auditorium, with the Stokes statue, the Association's founder, to the left, and the Auditorium's large open-air Pavilion on the right. The inside of the Auditorium is vast, almost the size of a football field and too big for the purposes of the picture. So they filmed the interiors on different locations, some in local areas, others in New York. They filmed mostly in the fall, during the off-season, coming back and forth several times. Some scenes were shot in an old Sears Roebuck building, over in the Neptune township, to the west of Ocean Grove, which had been standing empty,

and where they built a number of interiors, including the bedroom set. They also used a few other miscellaneous locations, like the railroad station which was actually the old Casino building to the north end of the Boardwalk, going towards Asbury Park. By 'casino' I don't mean as in gambling, but the Italian for 'small house'. But it's actually quite big and, as I recall, they really doctored the building to simulate a train station. it was not, of course, a *real* train station but whatever Hollywood can dream up!

A couple of sequences were also shot in Asbury Park itself, a decaying old seaside town south of Allenhurst, though little now remains of the carousels and seaside arcades we see in the film and about which Bruce Springsteen sang on his early albums. Studio sequences were filmed, once again, on a closed set, at the old Filmways Studio on West 127th Street, in Harlem. Here, Woody shot on a section of the Stardust Hotel auditorium interior and the night-club sequence mock-up, while a beautiful model train replica was also constructed, realistically rocked with the aid of old motor tyres and heaved around on jacks. For the characteristic bleached-out look of Sandy's apartment, Mel Bourne based the design on Woody's own. The reconstruction included a huge photographic mock-up view, around the right-angled terrace of nighttime Manhattan, stretching from the East 70s to the 59th Street (Queensboro) Bridge. The white-on-white décor and general tone of the set were, apparently, influenced by Woody's long-time friend, Jean Doumanian, who, it is said, had done much to develop his taste. Her ex-husband John had one of his frequent cameos as a hustling Armenian fan. Critic Howard Kissel appears as Sandy's manager; Jack Rollins, UA president Andy Albeck and an uncredited Laraine Newman, from *Saturday Night Live*, play studio executives. Eli Mintz (Uncle David in *The Goldbergs*) is the old man who speaks the last line in the picture ('From this he makes a living?') and *Star Trek*'s Brent Spiner is a fan in the lobby. Sharon Stone (her debut), cast after Woody had seen 'hundreds of girls' for the part, had two brief scenes as the blonde on the train. Instructed by him to kiss the window, 'I gave it my best shot to melt the sucker.'

Like *Annie Hall, Stardust Memories* differed more than somewhat from Woody's initial conception. Early shooting, wrote Graham McCann, suggested 'a Felliniesque comedy with rich colours and many outside locales' but as filming progressed, the movie became the subject of considerable gossip around New York. Writing in *The Village Voice* in December, Arthur Bell noted that the proposed 22-week shoot was already five weeks behind schedule and the mood was becoming increasingly depressing. One of Bell's informants was the extra who played Og the Martian and who filmed his role over several days in Oyster Bay. Og, said Bell, expressed himself completely in the dark as to what he was meant to be doing, while Charlotte Rampling, according to the same source, bolted from Bell in terror. 'Sssh', she said, 'Woody would kill me if he thought I was talking to you. I'm in enough trouble already.'

On another occasion, during shooting of the UFO sequence, delays were caused because one of the balloons was meant to float out to right of frame but the wind was in the opposite direction. An entire week was also wasted when the unit travelled to the same location every day for a sequence supposed to be twilit and overcast, but which Woody and Gordon Willis found far too sunny to shoot. The crew spent their time playing cards or ball, sometimes with Woody joining in, though such lighter moments would appear to have been outweighed by the general gloom of the proceedings and Woody's almost pathological insistence on secrecy. 'If he pulls it off', declared one source, 'Woody's Allen's Fall Project will be devastating, a masterpiece. But it's his most risky and ambitious project to date and may just prove a fiasco.'

After a further trip to Paris with Jean Doumanian and her banker boyfriend Jacqui Safra (who plays Sandy's brother-in-law, Sam), Woody embarked on a series of reshoots in April - one being complicated by the fact that, in the interim, a key actor had undergone a sex change. Among the cuts Woody now made was Philip Anglim's role as Nat Bernstein, the friend who dies of amyotrophic lateral sclerosis ('Lou Gehrig's disease'), and whose fate was now referred to only in passing. Woody had actually turned the cameras for 31 weeks and this, combined with months of pre-production, represented his longest schedule to that date. And, as Mel Bourne was to recall, even though a number of people had faith, for much of the early shooting Woody was in despair. 'When I read *Stardust*', said Bourne, 'I thought it was going to be the greatest movie ever, but that was an editing failure as much as everything else.'

Whatever the reason, something had gone drastically wrong and most nervous of all about the putative reaction was, by his own admission, UA's senior vice-president, Steven Bach. Bach has recalled that he had found the original script 'fresh and funny and frank' but felt that Woody's 'most unguarded and autobiographical movie had soured in execution'. Similarly concerned was Charles Joffe who, in a *New York Times* interview, expressed himself saddened by the sourness Woody had, apparently, directed at his closest collaborators. Though reassured by Woody, Joffe's hurt rankled and, as he told the newspaper, 'I found myself questioning everything. I wondered if I had contributed over the past twenty years to this man's unhappiness.'

The result of all Woody's efforts, Bach averred, was something of a grotes-querie, a view borne out by a deal of the film's unfavourable press and public reaction. 'It was more than unpopular in the US', admitted Woody, 'It engen-dered hostility, enmity'. Most vitriolic amongst the critics was Pauline Kael who dubbed the film 'a horrible betrayal ... a whiff of nostalgia gone rancid', while Britain's Richard Roud was to call it 'an unmitigated failure'. Andrew Sarris in *The Village Voice* suggested that the film seemed 'to have been shaped by a masochistic desire to alienate Allen's admirers once and for all' and sev-eral other critics felt obliged to go along with the view voiced by Andy Albeck (*à propos* Sandy in the film) that 'He's not funny any more.' Although a hand-ful of reviewers, like Vincent Canby ('a marvellous movie') found much to praise, and the film's initial box-office average was better than a number of other multiple openers, it was, recalled Bach, 'scarcely a marvellous hit'. *Stardust Memories* did find its audience, chiefly in Europe, where the French almost inevitably found its various layers of meaning much to their taste. British critics, who still persisted in seeing Woody as a funny man, not as a 'personally relevant moralist', were, on the whole, much kinder to both *Stardust Memories* and Woody's next film, *A Midsummer Night's Comedy*, than their US counterparts.

Stardust Memories netted barely half its (then US average) $9m production cost in the US, though, as Woody has since noted, he knew in advance, as he would later for *September* and *Shadows and Fog*, that 'no one would come to see it'. But, in spite of this, and its confidence not yet shaken by the escalating problems of *Heaven's Gate*, United Artists made a concerted bid to keep Woody within the company. In August 1979, it had been reported that he was the seventh biggest international drawing card after Robert Redford, Clint Eastwood, Jack Nicholson, Warren Beatty, Steve McQueen and Al Pacino. This meant that any one of his movies could attract $3.75m in up front guar-antees from overseas investors. Just trailing Woody, at $3m apiece, were Dustin Hoffman, Barbra Streisand and Paul Newman. Woody was also revealed in a 1980 survey as the average New York woman's 'No.1 Dream Lover', which further intimated that in the right vehicle he was, as a per-former, as potent a box-office attraction as he had proved to be in *Annie Hall* and *Manhattan*.

Although Woody's plans remained vague, Marshall Brickman revealed that they were trying to clear their schedules to work together again, possibly with Brickman directing (he had recently completed his first feature, *Simon*) and Woody as co-writer and star. In the meantime, UA offered Woody a new contract with the same 'total freedom' as before. The company confirmed its

readiness to match any financial offers made elsewhere. Woody's agent, Sam
Cohn, weighed the approaches of several of the majors, notably Fox, but the
only serious possibilities being considered were UA and Orion. Although UA
countered with what Bach was to describe as 'an unprecedented offer' (actually better than Orion's), Woody decided that the latter company, with his old
friends, Krim and Medavoy, was where he belonged.

Top Woody, with Capucine and Paula Prentiss in *What's New, Pussycat?* (1965).

Bottom Woody as James Bond's 'nephew', the nefarious Jimmy, in *Casino Royale* (1967).

Released by Brent Walker Film Distributors Ltd.
Colour **"WHAT'S UP TIGER LILY"** cert.A

Top *What's Up, Tiger Lily?* (1966): an ingenious send-up of an imported Japanese thriller, deconstructed and improved upon with New York Jewish wisecracks, an imposed lunatic plot and Woody's own intrusions as an unlikely master of ceremonies.

Bottom *Take the Money and Run* (1969). In his first film as director Woody cast himself as a bungling bank robber, seen here preparing to dynamite the blackmailing Miss Blair.

Top Woody *à la* Castro in *Bananas* (1971). To many, this early example of 'Woody in the rough' seemed funnier than many a smooth-edged entertainment.

Bottom In *Play it Again, Sam* (1972) Woody is a nervous girl-shy film critic who, after a witty assertiveness course from his idol, Humphrey Bogart, briefly gets the girl (Diane Keaton).

Top Dr Ross (Gene Wilder) falling for 'Daisy' in *Everything You Always Wanted to Know About Sex** (**But Were Afraid to Ask*) (1972). 'Did you ever see *Carrie* with Laurence Olivier and Jennifer Jones?' Woody asked Wilder, 'Well, I'm doing the same thing, except instead of Jennifer Jones it's going to be a sheep. And I either want Laurence Olivier or you'.

Bottom Woody as the accidental time traveller in *Sleeper* (1973), trying to come to terms with his 400lb inflatable hydro suit.

Top In *Love and Death* (1975) Woody turned Tolstoy, Dostoyevsky and other Russian novelists on their heads in, visually, his most ambitious film to that date. Harold Gould is Woody's rival in love.

Bottom The director directed: Woody on location with Martin Ritt for *The Front* (1976).

Top Annie (Diane Keaton) and Alvy (Woody) outside Annie's apartment in *Annie Hall* (1977).
Keaton's quirky fashion style was to catch on in a big way but, 'The trouble with the "Annie Hall
Look"' said a character in a May 1978 *Beetle Bailey* cartoon, 'is that it needs Annie Hall *in* it'.

Bottom Chekhov comes to Long Island in *Interiors* (1978), with Diane Keaton, Kristin Griffith
and Marybeth Hurt. Woody's first serious film devolved on the idea of the 'sisterly trinity', a
popular trend in American drama which would be given a more comic going-over in *Hannah
and Her Sisters* (1986).

Top Woody and Diane amid the sculpture garden statuary at the Museum of Modern Art in *Manhattan* (1979). Although this shot was not in the release version, it attests to Woody's fondness for silhouette as a dramatic device.

Bottom Mary (Diane) and Ike (Woody), romantically inclined in *Manhattan* (1979). The scene was shot at early dawn using a Panavision camera with a 75mm anamorphic lens. The street lamp was turned off, the bridge lights left on and 'I used a grad on the sky', said Willis, 'a filter to darken it a little and keep the bridge strong'. The bench, though, was a prop and Mary's dachshund (just visible) was called Waffles!

Top The famous film-maker besieged by his fans in *Stardust Memories* (1980). Woody has always insisted that Sandy Bates was *not* Woody Allen.

Bottom Allan Wenger as Kaiser Lupowitz in *The Subtle Concept* (1981), Gérard Krawczyk's 20-minute version of Woody's *Mr Big*.

Top Woody and Mia Farrow in *A Midsummer Night's Sex Comedy* (1982), a lush, bucolic romp. The verdant location was situated a few miles from Tarrytown - the original setting for *Rip Van Winkle* and *The Legend of Sleepy Hollow*.

Bottom The faceless man meets Eugene O'Neill (with Shane O'Neill) in *Zelig* (1983).

Top Woody as the title character, with the new look Mia, in *Broadway Danny Rose* (1984). Mia recalled *Danny Rose* as one of the three films she'd most enjoyed doing and 'Although the character didn't resemble me - I had a wig and falsies ... I discovered it was not far from what I am'.

Bottom The film-within-a-film in *The Purple Rose of Cairo* (1985) with left to right, Milo O'Shea, Deborah Rush, John Wood and Edward Herrman.

Top Mia Farrow and Michael Caine in *Hannah and Her Sisters* (1986). Caine's casting was inspired by Woody's predilection for British and European actors capable of expressing ordinariness and vulnerability.

Bottom Mickey (Woody) and Hannah (Mia), on the first day of filming, discuss the problem of his apparent sterility while strolling, in characteristic 'walk and talk' shot, along East End Avenue, New York. *Hannah and Her Sisters* (1986) is the most medically obsessed of Woody's films.

Top Tony Roberts as the 'Silver Dollar' quizmaster and Dianne Wiest as Aunt Bea in *Radio Days* (1987) - the questions are on fish and Aunt Bea knows all the answers! Because of complicated copyright problems Woody mostly created his own radio shows for the film.

Bottom Woody directs Jack Warden, Elaine Stritch and Mia in the second version of the problematic *September* (1987), the first of Woody's movies to be made entirely in the studio.

Top *Another Woman* (1988) marked the first of three consecutive films Woody made with Ingmar Bergman's favourite cinematographer, Sven Nykvist. With his supreme talent for the close-up, photographing the 'inner feeling' of actors and often shooting in small, enclosed spaces, Nykvist was the ideal interpreter of Woody's work at this particular time.

Bottom left Sadie (Mae Questel) and Sheldon (Woody) in *Oedipus Wrecks* (1989). As its title suggests, *Oedipus* deals with man's relationship with his mother - in this case a *Jewish* mother.

Bottom right Anjelica Huston and Martin Landau in *Crimes and Misdemeanors* (1989). One of the crimes was Huston's murder and, when first shown in the US, the film was seen as the flipside of *Fatal Attraction*.

Top Mia Farrow and Joe Mantegna in *Alice* (1990), the story of a young woman's self discovery through magical means.

Bottom *Scenes from a Mall*: Nick (Woody) k.o.'s the shopping mall mime (Bill Irwin) whose white-faced parodies of Nick's quarrels with Deborah (Bette Midler) have been driving him mad.

Top On the Sarrasini circus set Woody directs John Malkovich, Mia and Madonna in *Shadows and Fog* (1992).

Bottom left Woody points the way to Mia and Judy Davis in *Husbands and Wives* (1992), a serio-comic look at marriage breakdown and its aftermath.

Bottom right Woody and Diane, together again, in *Manhattan Murder Mystery* (1993). Though not officially a '20 years on' sequel to *Annie Hall*, it *was* the original script for that film, so just as well *might* have been.

Top Dianne Wiest wearing one of Jeffrey Kurland's stunning Oscar-nominated costumes from *Bullets over Broadway* (1994).

Bottom Woody as doting Dad in *Mighty Aphrodite* (1995), with Jimmy McQuaid and Helena Bonham Carter. Photo: Brian Hamill.

7

The Changing Man

1981-5: The Floating Lightbulb to The Purple Rose of Cairo

The Floating Lightbulb In late 1978 Woody had joined the eight-member artistic directorate which was involved in plans to reopen the Lincoln Center's Vivian Beaumont Theater. He also promised them a play - the result being *The Floating Lightbulb*, which pursued themes and situations previously aired in *Stardust Memories*, *Annie Hall* and other Allen works, but now told in the context of a more realistic comedy drama.

Set in 1945, in a dingy Canarsie, Brooklyn apartment, the play revolves around a sad, disintegrating family, the Pollacks. Father, Max, is a shiftless small-time hood and former bookie, working as a waiter in a low dive to pay off his gambling debts, and busy cheating on his wife, Enid, with a cocktail waitress. Enid, a failed dancer, frustrated in her marriage, is involved, like little Joe's father in *Radio Days*, in trying to launch various mail-order ventures, and longs to be thought of as still attractive. Their eldest son, Paul, is a stuttering, solitary, self-conscious 16-year-old with a high IQ. He plays hookey to haunt magic shops and, like the boyhood Woody, practises sleight-of-hand in the privacy of his room. Younger brother Steve is a wise-cracking escapist, addicted to the radio serials of the day and with incipient pyromaniac tendencies. Each of these characters is blighted by a failure to turn dream into reality. 'Someday is a luxury! We can't wait!' cries Enid at one point but, as for many another Allen character, life just seems to pass them by.

Max, for instance, had once had aspirations to be a big shot, Steve has fantasies of 'hypnotizing Catholic girls', joining the Marines and moving to Texas, while Enid's hopes become centred on Paul's magic skills and the visit of an agent, Jerry Wexler, who, like the later Danny Rose, has been yearning all his life to discover the one performer, 'that million-dollar act', who can make his reputation.

But Paul, unlike the real-life Woody, feels unready for 'success'; his audition, due to nerves and an attack of temperament, is a failure. 'The Floating Lightbulb' fails to rise (!) and Enid takes consolation in the fact that Jerry, primed with liquor, has found her 'beautiful'. He, too, though, voices the uncertainty of all when he tells her he's moving his asthmatic mother to Phoenix. 'You know, there comes a time in a man's life when he has to face up to the fact that his plans haven't materialized.'

The play is Woody in more serious vein and owes an at least passing debt to the structure and certain key elements of such classic American dramas as *The Glass Menagerie* and *Death of a Salesman*. With settings and costumes by regular Allen film associate Santo Loquasto, it opened at the Vivian Beaumont on 27 April 1981. But, in spite of five drafts and substantial changes wrought by Woody between first meeting with the director, Ulu Grosbard and the play's New York bow, Grosbard's unease with the entertainment was never completely assuaged. This was reflected in the mixed reviews, several critics noting the too-obvious influence of Miller, Williams, Odets, Albee and other theatre giants, while expressing regret that the play lacked the stylistic adventurousness of Woody's recent film work. Some reviewers, though, complimented him on the ambition of the enterprise and the dramatic advances he had made on *Play It Again, Sam*. Although there was praise for Danny Aiello (Max) and Bea Arthur (Enid), plus a Tony Award for Brian Backer as Paul, most critics agreed that the real highlight was Jack Weston's turn as Jerry Wexler.

Lightbulb, unlike the two Woody Allen stage hits which preceded it, ran a mere 65 performances on Broadway and has been little seen since. The play's belated UK première took place in May 1990 at the Nuffield Theatre, Southampton, in a production directed by Patrick Sandford. Sylvia Syms played Enid, Sam Douglas was Max, Gian Sammarco was Paul, and Lee Montagu was Wexler. It had some decent reviews but, although there was initial interest in a West End transfer, negotiations coincided with the Gulf War and it was felt that there would be 'insufficient Americans in London to guarantee success'.

The One-Act Plays Although *Lightbulb* was his last full-length stage work to be produced, Woody admitted as recently as 1988 that he had at least a dozen unperformed plays on the stocks. He has also turned out a number of one-acters - *Death Knocks*, *The Query*, *My Apology*, the trilogy *Sex, God* and *Death*, and, more recently, *Central Park West*. Most of these have appeared in magazine and/or story collection form, revue compilations or on radio.

Death Knocks, first published in *The New Yorker*, is a spoof of *The Seventh Seal*, revolving around a 57-year-old garment manufacturer Nat Ackerman who defers Death's request that he accompany him by challenging him to a game of gin rummy. Maurice Yacowar has described the character of Death as 'An image of human fallibility with a Jewish accent' and much of the humour derives from the contrast between this shabby accident-prone character and the traditional black-garbed figure of mediaeval legend.

Sex, God and *Death* were originally to have been staged in the 1973-74 Broadway season by David Merrick, but the playlets required elaborate sets and a $250,000 budget which Merrick considered unrealistic for such a commercially doubtful package. Woody, though, confessed in interview that they were the favourite of all his works to that date - because they were the most 'serious'. *Death*, which he described as 'a German Expressionist comedy', has the same protagonist, Kleinman ('Little Man') and the basic plot of the later *Shadows and Fog*. Both works are Kafkaesque rather than Bergmanesque in flavour and each deals with such weighty themes as guilt, racial prejudice, disorientation and the ordinary man's inability to alter a preordained destiny. In the play, Kleinman is a simple salesman who joins a vigilante group in the hunt for a murderer. Unable to discover what his real function is, Kleinman, like the clerk in *Shadows and Fog*, is accused of being the killer. He evades the lynch mob, not through ingenuity (as in the film) but due to the news that the murderer has been captured. But the latter, who has the ability to assume the shape of his victims, turns out to be Death.

Death is a perfect example in miniature of many of the elements which keep reccuring in Woody's work. Less successful is *Sex*, described by Francine du Plessix Gray as a 'continuation of Woody's bitter-sweet musings about the search for a perfect woman, and the futility of that quest'. *God*, loosely inspired by characters from Robert Benchley's 'Physician's Desk Reference', is an agreeable burlesque of ancient Greek drama and has been referred to by John Lahr as 'Woody's *Waiting for Godot*'. It is set in a large amphitheatre in 500 BC and involves two Greeks, Hepatitis and Diabetes, putting in a frenzied telephone call to the author of the play the pair are currently producing. The play opens in three days and, much to their horror, has neither a beginning nor an end - and as for the middle, forget it. There are references to *A Streetcar Named Desire*, Groucho Marx, Woody's own persona and *Play it Again, Sam*, while a college co-ed called Doris Levine is brought up on stage to answer the question, 'Is freedom chaos?' and dismisses the author's (Woody's) work as 'pretentious'. Near the end of the play, God is strangled.

On a broader level, *God* subscribes to the humorous effects of anachronism, a characteristic to be found elsewhere in Woody's work, and also a notable ingredient in *My Apology*. In this mini-masterpiece, Woody has a recurring nightmare that he's actually Socrates in his death cell. Another variant on this theme is *The Query*, wherein Abe Lincoln ends up sparing the son of a farmer who had been condemned to death for falling asleep on guard duty. The President's 'humanization' is brought about through a shared joke - the Dr David Reuben-like riddle, 'How long do you think a man's legs should be?' Answer: 'Long enough to reach the ground'. And this, apart from Lincoln's very Jewish-sounding plea for food at the playlet's end, is virtually the only joke there is.

Death had been written in the fall of 1972 when Woody was appearing at Caesar's Palace in Las Vegas and, together with the National Radio Theater of Chicago's production of *God*, it was to turn up on BBC Radio 3 in 1985 and 1986. *God*, starring Tony Roberts as 'Hepatitis', had a three-line appearance by Woody himself as 'The Voice of the Author' and, because the show was recorded in front of a live audience, Woody's contribution was, apparently, obtained by telephone hook-up. The third play, *Sex*, was also to have been included in the package but, unbelievably, according to producer Matthew Walters, not a single copy could be found. Stephen J. Spignesi, for one, casts doubt on whether the playlet was ever completed, though Woody has stated categorically (to Stig Björkmann in 1993), that he did indeed write it, even though he has not yet allowed it to be performed.

In March 1995, Woody's 70-minute one-acter *Central Park West* was presented off-Broadway as part of a trilogy of comedies by himself, David Mamet and Elaine May. Woody's contribution deals with the problems of a ball-busting vodka-guzzling lady psychoanalyst who accuses her best friend (married to a 'manic-depressive wimp') of being the reason for her own husband's marital walkout. But he's actually leaving her for one of her patients, a 21-year-old Barnard student. The play, raunchier and more foul-mouthed than Woody's comedy fans had hitherto been used to, was, by critical consensus, very funny and came across, according to some observers, like a sort of X-rated revamp of Noel Coward's *Fallen Angels*.

A number of Woody's shorter works have also turned up in fringe productions, usually in the revue-style format, like John Lahr's 1987 compilation at the Royal Exchange Theatre, Manchester, *The Bluebird of Unhappiness*. Directed by Braham Murray, with music by Obie Award-winning composer Stanley Silverman, this put a versatile cast of seven through a number of pieces, including *Death Knocks*, *My Apology* and dramatized versions of the short stories

'The Kugelmass Episode' and 'Mr Big'. 'Kugelmass' and 'Mr Big' had also been aired in a series of 'platform' performances, directed by Michael Kustow, at London's National Theatre in October 1980. A further play, *Getting Even*, based on Woody's book of that title, was presented by a company called Afterthought Productions at the Edinburgh Festival, in August 1990.

The Subtle Concept/Le concept subtil Woody's short story 'Mr Big' was also the subject of Gérard Krawczyk's 22-minute graduation film, for IDHEC (L'Institut des Hautes Cinématographiques, in Paris) and is one of two tales Woody wrote about the Hammett-style private eye, 'Kaiser Lupowitz'. First published in Woody's 1971 collection, *Getting Even*, 'Mr Big' was filmed by Krawczyk under the title *The Subtle Concept*. A 35mm parody of the American *film noir* B-thrillers of the 1940s, the movie, like the story it's based on, revolves around Heather Butkiss (Rebecca Pauly), a Vassar philosophy student (or so she says!) who hires the detective (Allan Wenger) to find a 'missing person'. This is to enable her to complete a paper on Western religion - but the 'missing person' turns out to be God and the 'student' is revealed as His killer! The final confrontation is a pastiche of the last scene between Sam Spade and Brigid O'Shaughnessy in *The Maltese Falcon* and caps a metaphysical speech about the notion of 'Being' with the line 'It was a subtle concept but I think she got it before she died.'

The Subtle Concept received its film festival première at the Tours Henri Langlois Exposition where it won Krawczyk the Best Director prize. In August 1981 it also received the grand prize for Best Short Film at the fifth World Film Festival in Montreal.

In late 1994 I spoke and corresponded with M. Krawczyk who very graciously provided me with a viewing copy, as well as recalling the details of production:

I had a little correspondence with Mr Allen and his lawyers. They accepted the project because it was a non-commercial film and, when it was finished, I gave a copy to Mr Allen. It was, in fact, Charlotte Rampling who brought the film to Mr Allen when she went to shoot *Stardust Memories*. Mr Allen sent me a very kind letter after he saw my work. We filmed entirely in and around Paris, shooting on the school set (Lupowitz's office); in a funeral parlour at Brie-sur-Marne for the morgue scene; in an Italian restaurant, De Carli's; in St Michel, Paris, for the Vatican; in rue Watt, Paris, for a New York street, and in a synagogue in Paris. I also used black-and-white stock shots from the Gaumont Cinémathèque. Each student at IDHEC had 18,240 francs (about

$3000 US) to make his *film de fin d'études*. So it was both the budget and the final cost of the movie. The school provided editing, music, lighting. All the technical crew were students and friends. Only the actors, who were professionals, were paid. I shot with a BNC Mitchell, made in the 'forties. I was the cameraman. Nobody used this old camera, so it was available for our use only. As I remember, the adaptation is close to the short story, the characters are the same and they have the same names in the film as in the original. I just cut some scenes and modified others in order to be able to shoot them. Also I added a small *clin d'oeil* to the movie *The Big Sleep*, shooting in black and white, in English, with French subtitles, and using Max Steiner's score for the music.

A perfect example of *film noir* in miniature, *The Subtle Concept* demonstrates Krawczyk's ability, like the late Jean-Pierre Melville, to conjure an American-style thriller ambience within a deceptively uncharacteristic French setting. Wenger is a good sound-alike 'Bogart' and the film, like 'Mr Big', contains a series of witty but commendably straight-faced exchanges on a number of religious and philosophic topics.

A Midsummer Night's Sex Comedy Woody's two-year film hiatus ended with the July 1982 release of *A Midsummer Night's Sex Comedy*, the first under his new contract with Orion. As with his UA deal, he had been granted complete control over every aspect of production, from script to final cut, advertising and promotion. In addition to his special auteurist privileges, Woody was guaranteed a percentage on his future films 'from dollar one' - 15 per cent of the gross receipts, split with Rollins, Joffe and producer Robert Greenhut. But, because the deal was more lucrative than under the old UA contract, Rollins and Joffe now insisted on a smaller stake, their share being adjusted downwards. The inclusion of Greenhut in the deal was significant for Woody and pointed towards the former's growing importance in the Allen film set-up. Greenhut had started as associate producer on *The Front*, had assumed full producer status on *Stardust Memories* and has remained with Woody in that capacity ever since. It is important to note, however, that Woody, from around the time of *Love and Death*, had required less active hand-holding on set and 'as time went on', Joffe told me recently, 'and Woody grew more confident and assured, I found I needed to go less and less on the studio floor, there was less for me to do. But if I've retired, it's only semi-retired, and I still manage Woody's career. Let's say I've retired from the agency business, but not from production. We retain our contractual links with Woody, our names are on the credits as executive producers and we're always there if needed'.

The initial Orion project was to have been the (as yet untitled) *Zelig* but, while waiting for the script to be budgeted, Woody got the idea for 'this little summer pastiche', a celebration of warm days and nights, chaotic sexual liaisons and turn-of-the-century nostalgia. He completed the screenplay in two weeks and *A Midsummer Night's Sex Comedy* was filmed during the summer of 1981 as a sort of 'sub project', while the enormously complicated lab work and archive research for *Zelig* got under way. Woody thus found himself involved with both films simultaneously but, due to weather requirements, *Sex Comedy* was finished first.

Early into production, Woody expressed himself 'appalled' by reports that his new film was to be called *Summer Nights* (the title under which it was listed in some of the 'trades') and that it was somehow based on *Smiles of a Summer Night* (1955). This was the Bergman classic which had already inspired Stephen Sondheim's Broadway musical *A Little Night Music*. Possibly it was the connection with the musical version which Woody objected to most strongly, though he had already cited the original film as 'one of the very, very few of Bergman's that I wasn't crazy about'. In a pre-recorded 'press conference' he subsequently sent to accompany *Sex Comedy* to the Venice Film Festival in September 1982, he continued to insist that the film's main influences lay elsewhere.

Although Woody's characters have no exact equivalents in the Bergman film, there are marked similarities between José Ferrer's pompous polymath in *Sex Comedy* and the somewhat stuffy lawyer Fredrik (Gunnar Björnstrand) in *Smiles of a Summer Night*, while the three women in the former could well have strayed from a Bergman movie. The atmosphere of summer magic-summer regret is but one of the visual-emotive strains the two works have in common. There is also the vaguely *La Ronde*-like plot and the way both films conjure echoes of *La Règle du Jeu* - an evocative Renoir classic described by Woody as 'probably the best dialogue comedy ever made'. *Sex Comedy* employs warm references to such favourite Bergman motifs as conjuring tricks and optical illusions, old photos, pioneering contraptions, birds, picnics and woodland revels. Both films contain comic suicide attempts and the semblance of a duel, while there is the odd line in Bergman (Fredrik's 'Lord, if the world is so sinful, I want sin') which could be put into the mouths of almost any of the characters in *Sex Comedy*. Another line ('Sex alleviates tension, love causes it'), this time from Woody, could well serve as a thematic link between the two movies - even if, as Alan Brien has suggested, this particular aphorism 'would be just as true, and rather more original, the other way round'.

Sex Comedy is, perhaps, the most magpie-like of all Woody's films. It evokes Shakespeare, Chekhov and the 'bucolic imperative' of J.M. Barrie and Kenneth Grahame, Burne-Jones and Rossetti. There is even a ravishing picnic scene after Manet's 'Le Déjeuner sur L'Herbe', while the white ducks and straw boaters, pleated blouses and ankle-length skirts, striped jerseys and healthy slap-and-tickle are straight out of *Une Partie de Campagne*, another Renoir classic which Woody had fallen in love with in his teens. He also makes room for some quite appealing nature 'documentary', even if its view of vernal delights is closer to Walt Disney than to Arne Sucksdorff. The period and the setting also suggests such influential 'East Coast primitives' of early American cinema as Blackton and Griffith, and in this respect, Woody gets closer to simulating a specific turn-of-the-century ambience than many a more orthodox purveyor of misty-eyed Americana.

The film explores the relationship between love, sex, death, manners and magic, as three couples (four in Bergman) exchange ideas, as well as partners, during a romantic summer weekend in the country. Mendelssohn's *A Midsummer Night's Dream* 'Overture' (along with bits of his 'Scottish Symphony' and other pieces), is plangently in evidence on the soundtrack, while Willis's Renoir-like deep-focus camerawork captures the story's sexy sun-drenched aura and lush impressionist images to perfection. Indeed, in spite of Woody's avowed dislike of the countryside and general preference for filming on overcast days, the mood of rustic enchantment is lovingly conveyed. He has said that he had 'wanted to do for the country' what he'd done for New York in *Manhattan*, making it look as beautiful as possible and ensuring 'that the light was perfect all the time and that the sun was in the exact right place' (when it was *too* sunny to shoot, the crew would repair to their custom-built house to film interiors). Woody said he had been aiming at a 'light ... small intermezzo with a few laughs' and was disappointed that the film's setting and atmosphere were things which Americans in general, don't appear to care about.

That said, Woody still succeeds in giving his own character an essentially urban, post-Freudian frame of reference. 'Shakespeare seen from a Fifth Avenue penthouse', quipped Robert Benayoun, while Douglas Brode suggests that the period setting confuses, since the contemporary stance assumed at times by the characters gives the impression of present-day people taking part in a costume charade, rather in the manner of Jean Anouilh's *The Rehearsal*. Woody admitted that people don't seem to want to see him in costume and suggested, again, that the film might have been better received if Dustin Hoffman had played his part.

Woody plays Andrew Hobbes, Wall Street broker-cum-amateur inventor. His wife, Adrian (Mary Steenburgen), a wafer-thin faded belle, has not been able to pleasure him for six months. Not since the day, it is later revealed, that she made love to Andrew's best friend Maxwell Jordan (Tony Roberts) in the woods. Maxwell, a 'medical Casanova', is there again, to help celebrate the engagement of Adrian's cousin, academic and art expert, Leopold (José Ferrer) to diplomat's daughter Ariel Weymouth (Mia Farrow). Ariel, as her name suggests, is a free spirit, her ethereal beauty deceptively at odds with her promiscuous reputation. She had once, we are told, serviced the entire infield of the Chicago White Sox, and Andrew has taken to pondering his own failure some years before to make love to her.

The randy Maxwell has a compliant nurse, Dulcy Ford (Julie Hagerty) in tow who immediately catches the eye of Leopold. Dulcy is a good sport and, in no time at all, is cheerfully flirting with Leopold and advising Adrian on how to pep up her sex life with Andrew. To complete the circle of sexual promise, Andrew, though still nursing a yen for Ariel, starts building her up for Maxwell. As these various characters move towards a consummation of their sexual desires, they distract themselves with angling, badminton, butterfly catching and demonstrations of Andrew's inventions - one of which, the so-called 'Spirit Ball', can penetrate the unseen world, emitting light-rays 'to conjure up the future and the past'. Leopold, the rational man, has no belief in fairies and the supernatural and initially scoffs, but it is he, who, posthumously, will become the main recipient of the crystal's magic properties.

The main thrust of the story deals with the aspect of jaded, overly-sophisticated city dwellers, offering themselves up to the heady lure of a summer-exalted paganism. In the course of this, Maxwell, rejected by Ariel, tries to shoot himself; Andrew is restored to the sexual benefits of Adrian; Maxwell and Ariel discover they belong together, and Leopold tumbles Dulcy but succumbs to a massive heart attack at the moment of climax! The link between sex and death is thus brought, in precise Woody Allen terms, to its logical conclusion and, with the aid of the 'spirit beam', Leopold's 'pure essence' is projected far into the distance - assuming, like Tinker Bell, the aspect of a darting green light which will remain in the woods forever, for whoever chooses to go in search of it. In the final sequence, the surviving characters run off into the woods, with fireflies darting about in the undergrowth, moving the film far away from the usual Allen concerns into an enchanted world which is delightful to contemplate.

Sex Comedy is an enjoyable diversion, if somewhat short on good jokes. Although he has expressed affection for it ('It was good for little wisps of fun') Woody, like the critics, has tended not to rate it as highly as some of his other films and it is not included amongst his published screenplays. But, with its accurate evocation of early twentieth-century movements, artefacts and inventions and its depiction of the well-heeled professional classes at play, it is an able recreation of a vanished era.

A key departure of the film is that this was the first in which Woody is not the central character but a member of an even-handed ensemble. In making him both a stockbroker and an actively married man, it was also the closest his on-screen character had yet come to being a normal member of the middle-class 'insider' community. Significantly, Woody gives the line about marriage being 'the death of hope' to Maxwell rather than Andrew and, undoubtedly due to satisfaction in his now well-established off-screen relationship with Mia Farrow, he makes the image of the marital state seem, finally, more hopeful than we might otherwise have expected.

The part of Ariel had originally been intended for Diane Keaton (who was then heavily involved in Warren Beatty's *Reds*) and Woody, at the time, was criticized for trying to turn Mia into 'a pale imitation' of Diane. But, as in the future *Alice*, Woody perceptively employs Mia's aura of Pre-Raphaelite wistfulness to convey the film's more mystical concerns. Although cast against her established gamine victim-type as a rapacious, sexually liberated 'new woman', physically she resembles, especially in the context of the film's final scenes, one of those essential J.M. Barrie heroines like Mary Rose (whom Mia had played on the English stage) or the Dream Child in *Dear Brutus*. With her braids, refined cheekbones and agreeable lack of histrionic clutter, Mia becomes in this environment the most captivating, if unlikely, of nympho enchantresses.

Off-screen companions for the previous 14 months, Woody and Mia had first met some years earlier at a Hollywood party. It was not until the fall of 1979 that they had begun to take notice of each other and started dating during the final stages of the *Stardust Memories* filming after Mia had written to Woody, congratulating him on *Manhattan*. Third of seven children of Australian-born director John Farrow and *Tarzan* actress Maureen O'Sullivan, Mia had made her name in the successful TV series *Peyton Place* (1964-6), going on to star in such important movies as *Rosemary's Baby* and *The Great Gatsby*. She had also been kept in the public eye through a number of 'wild child' pronouncements and stage work with the Royal Shakespeare Company in Britain, as well as two well publicized marriages, to Frank Sinatra and Andre Previn. But, by the late 1970s, Mia's screen career, following its early promise, was thought to be in the doldrums, while Woody, damaged by the commercial and critical *débâcle* of *Stardust Memories*, also found himself at something of a crossroads in his life and career. In the course of time, each would exert a beneficial effect on the other and their relationship would result in a series of films which are quite clearly amongst the most entertaining and innovatory in recent American cinema. Mia in fact would go on to star in every one of Woody's movies of the next 12 years - from *A Midsummer Night's Sex Comedy* through to *Husbands and Wives*.

Mia has confessed that on *Sex Comedy* she was, initially 'paralysed with insecurity' and, at one point, was quite ready to abandon her role. But her performance, and her rapport with Woody, are amongst the chief assets of a film which is one of the best acted of all Woody's movies. José Ferrer amusingly guys the self-satisfaction and vocal pomposity which seemed to be endemic to his screen persona, while, surprisingly for an actress who made her name in genre spoofs like *Airplane!*, Julie Hagerty seizes her comic opportunities with affecting subtlety. Mary Steenburgen, in a role which might more comfortably have gone to Mia, is oddly touching as the (temporarily) frigid Adrian.

True to form, Woody found a suitably verdant location only 40 minutes north of Manhattan - the sprawling 400-acre Rockefeller Estate near the picturesque village of Pocantico Hills in Westchester County. The nearness of the locale meant he could drive home every night and sleep in his own bed, making little attempt to transform himself into a country dweller. Following on from the arduous locations of *Sleeper* and *Love and Death*, Woody has, until recently, refused to work anywhere more than a car's drive away from his own apartment, saying he would prefer to recreate somewhere like Philadelphia within the environs of New York, even if, visually, the results were not so good. He also cites the example of Fellini and Bergman who, during their later film-making careers, never strayed too far from their respective home environments of Rome or the island of Faro. 'I like the city of New York, I like an urban atmosphere', said Woody, and for the scene in *Sex Comedy* where Andrew and Ariel, in a rickety flying machine, get ducked in the lake, this obsessive city dweller insisted on doubles. For the follow-up scene, where the couple emerge ankle deep, from the lake, he had himself sprinkled with Evian water, especially ordered in by the props department!

Filming commenced in late June and the design for the house in the movie was chosen by Woody from a magazine spread. It was so well constructed that a man bought it afterwards for $5000, moved it to another location, installed gas and electricity and lived in it. Filming carried on into the fall and when, by the end of shooting, the leaves on the trees were turning brown and yellow, Woody, taking his cue from Antonioni/*Blow-Up*, ordered them painted green. This created problems with the administrators of the estate who insisted that the film company return later and repaint them brown. But the green paint, being dye, proved difficult to remove and, when the rains came, the brown dissolved and the trees were, once again, green, right in the middle of January! Fortunately, all these shenanigans took place after Woody had completed his usual extensive reshoots, notably a very complicated sequence which involved all six leading characters having three separate ongoing conversations on a country walk. Woody had wanted the dialogue both to overlap and have a natural feel to it, but also to be distinct enough so that every member of the audience could understand. The scene was shot over and over again and, as Tony Roberts recalled to Eric Lax, 'Even after the film had been wrapped and edited, we went back into the woods to do that damned scene.' The results, as ever, attested to Woody's usual attention to detail and to an artistry which finally is rarely accidental.

A Midsummer Night's Sex Comedy divided the critics as thoroughly as Stardust Memories had done. 'Wan and featherlight', wrote Peter Rainer; 'a classy but tepid pastiche' said David Ansen; his 'only trivial picture' (Richard Schickel in Time), while Colin L. Westerbeck Jr in Commonweal noted that '... the plot is about as clever as a porn flick with the explicit sex left out.' But Stanley Kauffman in The New Republic, though taking Woody to task for his use of 'trite pastoral symbols', found it '... easily his best-directed film'. The picture's UK reception (seven weeks in London's top ten) and, mostly warm reviews, somewhat reversed the American one. David Robinson in The Times designated it 'a charming trifle' whose only real problem resided in Woody's inability 'to adapt his distinctive style to suit the rest ... he remains the odd man out in a delightful ensemble'. In the rest of Europe the film was similarly well received but Woody has referred to Sex Comedy and September as his 'two biggest financial disasters' and, based on the old saw that no man is a prophet in his own country, the film's US failure, set against its more favourable showing elsewhere, continued to set a significant pattern for the future.

Zelig If Woody in previous films had demonstrated the idea of a man struggling to come to terms with questions of his personal and artistic identity, Zelig is his most explicit examination of someone who has no identity at all. The movie is an ingenious pastiche of documentary film techniques which in other hands might strain the muscles of invention to breaking point. As Eric Lax has noted, if Woody had any reservations about the entertainment, it resided in the fact that the film's technical achievement 'was so flamboyant that it obscured the points he was trying to make about a man afraid to be himself'.

Using black-and-white photomontage, actual documentary and newsreel footage, staged scenes and colour inserts of real-life 'witnesses' (a spoof of

Warren Beatty's *Reds?*), the film tells the curious story of Leonard Zelig, a man so nondescript no one knows who he really is. Zelig (the name means 'blessed' or 'dear departed soul' in Yiddish) is suffering from a 'unique mental disorder'. He is a 'human chameleon', one whose self-esteem is so low and who is so desperate to please that, as psychiatrist Dr Dennis Friedman has defined it, such a person 'only exists when he takes on the colouring of his surroundings'. Unlike recent well-documented cases of multiple personality disorder, Zelig actually appears to change *physically*, assuming the appearance and values of the strongest personality he meets. He thus becomes a Frenchman, a Scotsman, a gangster, a fat man, an opera singer, a black jazz musician, an American Indian, and, even, a doctor removing an involuntary patient's appendix.

'His one regret in life', wrote Woody, as a flyleaf note for *The Floating Lightbulb* and other works, 'is that he is not someone else.' He intended this widely quoted remark as a gag rather than as an authentic key to his character, but, perhaps, said Woody, 'it is a more revealing joke than I thought at the time'. If Woody couldn't physically become the idols he professes to admire, then *Zelig*, juxtaposing his screen character on the same heroic level with the likes of Chaplin, Jack Dempsey and Eugene O'Neill, is the next best thing. The film also revives the theme of celebrity versus vulnerability which had been a central motif of *Stardust Memories* and would find awkward echoes in Woody's real-life misfortunes of 1992-3.

Originally intended as a TV movie rather than a theatrical feature and, at one point, to be contemporary in theme, *Zelig* grew out of an idea for a short story: Woody's observation on the way 'people have a terrible tendency to say things that will please their friends' and how such a conformist mentality might ultimately lead to fascism. 'That's why I wanted to use the documentary form', Woody told Michiko Kalutani in July 1983, 'one doesn't want to see this character's private life; one's interested in the phenomenon and how it relates to the culture. Otherwise it would just be the pathetic story of a neurotic.'

Similar in style and appearance to such genuine 'found footage' compilations as Philippe Mora's *Brother, Can You Spare a Dime?* (1975), *Zelig* carries off a perfect 'doctoring' of reality, from the distinctive 'period' lighting (for the staged scenes) to the deliberate scratches and 'rain-type' streaks on the film stock. To make his own footage look grainy and imperfect, it is said that the crew were encouraged to take Woody's newly exposed celluloid into the shower and tread it into the water! A series of imperfectly preserved stills also serves an invaluable purpose, being transformed through the film medium into a sequence of iconographic emblems in their own right - becoming, in the

process, a sort of elegiac exercise in between-wars recall. Santo Loquasto's wittily appropriate costumes, John Caglione's special make-up and Dick Hyman's
acutely rendered recreations of the dance tunes of the era also aid immeasur-
ably in conveying 'authenticity'. We are offered at the same time such an
uncanny simulation of how the people of the Jazz Age and the early 1930s really looked or comported themselves, how they glanced at the camera, how Tin
Pan Alley hits of the time were actually sung, that what we get finally is almost
more than truth. In less scrupulous hands than Woody's, as one knows all too
well, such perfect recreations of 'real life' can actually be dangerous!

With its more than passing resemblance to the theme of *The Elephant Man*
(1980), the film examines the plight of an unfortunate being whose contemporaries regard him as a freak but one so unique in his 'complaint' that his only
salvation is to be courted. We learn from one of the 'witnesses' that Zelig was
'the phenomenon of the 20s and was once as famous as Lindbergh'. We first
meet him in 1928 - 'a time of diverse heroes and madcap stunts, of speakeasies
and flamboyant parties'. At a Long Island reception, Zelig rubs shoulders with
gangsters, poets and famous authors, one of whom, the inevitable F. Scott
Fitzgerald, is the first to note the existence of Zelig in print. At one point,
Zelig is wittily conjured as the man between Hoover and Coolidge, and has,
writes 'Fitzgerald', the curious ability to transform himself into a Republican
or a Democrat at will! He is, suggests a present-day witness, psychologist
Bruno Bettelheim, 'The ultimate conformist'.

Retaining this wry, poker-faced tone, the film proceeds, in a series of deft,
cinematic short-cuts, to demonstrate how it is possible for an innocent and unassuming person to attain notoriety, not as a result of any crime he has committed,
but through a most singular gift for ubiquity and change. Zelig's astounding
metamorphoses, it is suggested, are due to subtle make-up, to multiple disguise.
He is taken into medical care. Dr Eudora Fletcher (Mia), a young psychologist
keen to make her name, is convinced that Zelig's problem is psychological rather
than physiological, and takes him under her wing. Through crackly radio reports
and witty montages of Zelig's curative process, the film lampoons the era's penchant for crackpot remedies, psychoanalytic gobbledegook and the age-old
conflict between hidebound and innovative medical techniques.

The theme of the film, as elsewhere in Woody's work, is his screen character's ongoing obsession with assimilation and conformity. But, unlike such
earlier Allen heroes as Alvy Singer and Ike Davis, Zelig is not content merely
to be part of American culture and values and the fair-haired WASP family - he
has a compulsion to play it safe, by becoming everyone in all situations, not
merely through a talent for imitation but in fact. Lester D. Friedman in *The*

Jewish Image in American Film suggests that 'In terms of its Jewish content, *Zelig* represents the most devastating film about Jewish assimilation ever produced', the core of our hero's problem being characterized by his confession, under hypnosis, that, simply, he wants 'to be liked'. He is also, in effect, an outsider within his own culture: he can't even speak Hebrew and, as a child, was always being picked on by his bullying brother and hostile neighbours.

The film's darker moments are alleviated by the good nature of the skits. People marvel at Zelig's repertoire of quick changes; he is immortalized in songs like 'Leonard the Lizard' and 'Chameleon Days' - the latter given the authentic Helen Kane-like treatment by 'Betty Boop' voicer, Mae Questel; while real-life Paris singer and niterie owner Bricktop recalls that Cole Porter once tried to insert him into the lyric of 'You're the Top' but was stumped for a rhyme for 'Zelig'!

Zelig becomes the subject of a movie - Warner Brothers' *The Changing Man* (1935) - which, like *The Chameleon Man* and *The Cat's Pajamas* (a line from the film) was one of several titles Woody tried on friends before settling for *Zelig*. There is also a mordant spoof on the Charles Chaplin-Lita Grey divorce scandal and an almost subliminal verbal gag about Clara Bow and the 'It' Girl's well-documented predilection for group sex. In one of the most delirious sequences, after one of his periodic disappearances, Zelig turns up to disrupt the Easter blessing of Pope Pius XI on the balcony of St Peter's in Rome. His 'cure' is a similarly witty process, worked through a combination of reversal therapy, post hypnotic suggestion and falling in love with his analyst, Eudora. These latter scenes, with their amusing mechanical devices and 'genuine' clinical paraphernalia, come replete with missing frames, jump cuts, over-exposed lighting and disappearing heads. The fact that the amateur cameraman considers nothing unworthy of record means that the 'home movie' of Zelig's curative regime conveniently includes a sweet, Keatonesque idyll. There is also a brisk, aerial jaunt with Eudora's dashing aviatrix sister (Stephanie Farrow) - it is interesting to note that Eudora is also a skilled amateur pilot and that Mia, at times, bears an uncanny facial resemblance to real-life transatlantic pioneer Amelia Earhart!

Although Zelig's cure is 'a resounding success for psychiatry', there are dark clouds on the horizon. Fame brings with it exploitation by unscrupulous relatives, not to mention lawsuits and inevitable disgrace. Zelig, charged with offences he was supposed to have committed while in his earlier condition, reverts to his 'chameleon' state and disappears.

This is not the end of him, however. He turns up once more, disguised as a Nazi brownshirt, disrupting the 1933 Munich rally. Eudora, having already spotted him in a Universal newsreel and flown to Germany, starts waving to Zelig from the crowd. This sequence is the most exquisite joke in the film since, would a Jew, of all people, go this far, 'joining metaphorically with his oppressors simply to become an accepted part of whatever society he currently inhabits?' Zelig, peeping out from behind the Chancellor's shoulder, waves back, causing pandemonium amongst party heads and supporters alike. The couple escape and Zelig, having never flown a plane before, is forced to take over from a suddenly blacked-out Eudora, setting the world record for flying the Atlantic upside down!.

Restored to the public's love and favour, the couple, to the enchanted strains of 'I'll Get By', stroll in true home-movie fashion behind Eudora's summer home. We are left once more with the words of F. Scott Fitzgerald; the use of this literary icon to comment on a life which went well beyond the date of Fitzgerald's own death, suggesting - as with Odon Von Horvath in Christopher Hampton's *Tales from Hollywood* - that the truly famous do not die when the history books tell us they do.

As an assemblage, *Zelig* is both illuminating and fun. 'Events in the Jazz Age move too rapidly … like Red Grange', intones Patrick Horgan's English-accented commentator, as the camera cuts quickly away to a newsreel shot of that legendary ball-player in action. A flapper with a Colleen Moore bob performs the Charleston. Ordinary people pass judgement on the Zelig phenomenon - the uniformity of the film's grading exacerbating our bemusement over what is fiction and what is 'fact', all of which presented particular problems for the technical team. As Susan E. Morse told *The New York Times*:

> I wish we could put Woody into more shots with people speaking, but we just had too much trouble finding shots he could be inserted into … We needed enough room, we needed a reason for him to be standing there, and we needed to be sure that no one walked in front of him.

The results, though, are already quite remarkable, even the film's most astonishing moment being presented as such a throwaway that one is inclined unreservedly to believe in it: Zelig, pumped full of somadril hydrate, begins before our very eyes to walk up the wall - an effect especially clever since the male nurse in the scene, like the 'sideways' Zelig, remains vertical throughout! *The Changing Man* is also a tribute to Woody's skill in encapsulating the look and sound of Warners' studio style of the 1930s. By contrasting two key scenes from Zelig's movie 'life' with parallel incidents described in the 'documentary' we are reminded, yet again, how much the typical Hollywood biopic has always toyed with the 'truth'.

Although *Zelig* owes something to such classic antecedents as *Jekyll and Hyde* and Herman Melville's story 'The Confidence Man', it is closer to more recent novels like Ralph Ellison's *Invisible Man* (featuring a black 'chameleon' rather than a Jew) or Henry Roth's *Call it Sleep*, both of which, wrote Brian Case, have touched, in American literature, 'on the ethnic minorities' subterfuges in search of safety'. Critic Edmund Wilson revealed in his *Journals* that, in 1940, he had worked out a detailed scenario about a man in an autobiographical novel who changes identity and physical appearance through each decade of the twentieth century. Inspiration may well have been drawn from an even earlier 'Zelig', an obscure short story by Benjamin Rosenblatt 'about a lonely and alienated Russian Jewish immigrant', published in the *Bellman* and collected in *The Best Short Stories of 1915*. More recent variations include that witty 1991 'Human Chameleon' TV commercial for Henri Winterman cigars and, quite obviously, *Forrest Gump*, the story of an ubiquitous, semi-imbecilic innocent whose very anonymity makes him a suitable prism for many of the key events of his time.

Although a wonderfully wry figment of Woody's busy imagination, Zelig must also be construed as an at least fictional relative of a number of real-life twentieth-century 'chameleons', most notably the extraordinary Trebitsch Lincoln, whose Munchausen-like exploits during the first four decades of the present century seem remarkable indeed for someone who (just like Zelig!) is barely remembered by history. Lincoln (Ignacz Trebitsch) was born in Hungary but, like many another famous charlatan, might more accurately be described as a citizen of the world. Like the Vicar of Bray in the old song, he adapted himself to each changing social and political situation, giving credence to a now long-forgotten reputation as a man for all places and seasons. If there was a pie for him to get into, he was in it and, when he died, of an intestinal complaint, in Shanghai General Hospital, in October 1942, 'It was probably', said writer and broadcaster Eric Robson, 'the only normal thing he ever did.' It was Reginald Johnston, tutor to the Manchurian puppet emperor, Pu-Yi, who first referred to Lincoln in his own 1934 autobiography as a 'human chameleon' - a phrase picked up on, three years later, by *The New York Times*.

For all its modest, small-scale appearance, the making of *Zelig*, said Woody, involved 'an arduous schedule with incessant technical experiment. Gordon Willis and I had to feel our way through some tough and complicated trick shots.' A great deal of credit must go to the stills photographers Kerry Hayes and Brian Hamill, and the photo retouching team, as well as the optical effects experts at R/Greenberg Associates, Joel Hyneck, Stuart Robertson *et al.* who would contribute, singly or in tandem, to such subsequent Allen movies as *The*

Purple Rose of Cairo and *Oedipus Wrecks*. *Zelig* starts in a deceptively simple way, with a series of more or less static shots but the research for the film - sometimes months of work for a few seconds screen time - was expensive. 'You can't imagine how many crates of film we accumulated', said Willis.

Willis, who would receive, surprisingly, only his first Oscar nomination for his work on the film, recalled in an illuminating interview with Michelle Bogre (*American Cinematographer*, April 1984), that the biggest challenge lay in making the various ingredients so seamless that the observer is, indeed, confused as to what is fiction and what is real. 'Technically', said Willis, 'it was like obtaining a postgraduate degree in lab chemistry, photography and printing' - and so expertly are the many components put together that the staged footage only becomes obvious due to the presence in it of Woody, Mia and the other actors. According to Woody 'we did almost no mechanical things at all in *Zelig*' and he claimed that the only genuinely faked scene was the one where Zelig comes up against Babe Ruth and Lou Gehrig at the Yankees' training camp in Florida. His insistence that even the sequences with the Pope and Hitler were 'staged with actors' has to be taken with a pinch of salt. 'I was never put into any newsreels', said Woody, 'It could be easier to do it digitally today, but I don't know too much about those techniques. I was never a good technical film-maker ... If you could do it now by just computerizing it and get the same effect, it would be great'.

According to Willis, the film actually comprised about 50 per cent reality footage and 50 per cent Woody. As he told *L'Express* in September 1983:

We spent months selecting archival footage, then had to study methods of interpolating Woody's fictional character into real scenes. The principal difficulty derived from the black-and-white film stock which is no longer the same. The chemical composition contains less salts of silver today and there's a very marked difference in the grain. For a scene like the one where Woody appears for the first time behind Hitler, where the footage is authentic, it was necessary to add image to image. For another scene where the actors pose in Times Square in 1930, we had to concentrate very hard on mathematical calculations regarding the depth of field, the grain, light - a job which requires 15 or 16 hours' work ... We had to work with deteriorated documentary footage - copies of copies - and we had to foresee the possibility of further deterioration imposed on it by the different images and different prints, of the new scenes. We have had a lot of surprises, good and bad. The filming of *Zelig*, for me, has been a great game.

The research team had begun obtaining the archive footage some time before the start of filming *Sex Comedy* with Woody, having already written the whole *Zelig* script, changing it to fit each new discovery. 'Millions of feet' of material had been bought from various libraries, and dupe copies of the proposed clips were made so that fine-grain prints could be cut into the film with the same visual consistency as the stages scenes. Willis recalled that the book-keeping on this was a particular headache and that a lot of the post-production entailed 'running the soundtrack and the picture together because the images might be too hot for the track and vice versa'. He continually made adjustments to make the whole thing hang together as though it were all filmed within the period of the story. Willis to Michelle Bogre:

> We averaged around 12 weeks of shooting. Post-production was extensive. It lasted a year because there was a great deal of laboratory work involved. We couldn't simply photograph something and hope to bring it around in the lab. We had to work backwards, start with the original historic material, and visualize how it would match with our photography. Many people are surprised when they find out there are only two matte shots in the movie. The rest was intercut, so the intercutting of the material was extremely important.

To obtain the late 1920s look of much of the film, a degree of undercranking was employed, with about half the footage at sound speed and the rest at silent speed, of 18-20 frames a second. For the Nazi rally there is sound for the actual Hitler footage (with Woody waving from behind the Chancellor) and undercranking from the perspective of Hitler's supporters (with Mia waving back), which was exactly how the original footage (minus Woody and Mia) actually looked. The footage in the staged scenes was carefully exposed to duplicate the lighting techniques of the period and was augmented with flicker mattes (film that is completely transparent, but with flickers), plus deliberate scratches on the negative, much in the way that Gregg Toland had effected the 'News on the March' sequences for *Citizen Kane*. For the Zelig 'interpolations', Willis, by careful study of the original newsreels, was able to match the old-fashioned lighting against the blue screen in the studio. Although various film stocks were tried in the film for both the duping and the staged scenes, Willis decided to simplify, finally shooting on Eastman Double X Negative 5222 'because the movie was so complex to start with'.

A major problem, Willis recalled, was in finding a way to splice the colour 'witness' material (the 'present tense') into the monochrome footage (the 'past tense'), without 'popping the track' every time the cut was made. The actual filming of the witness scenes involved straightforward, direct-to-the-camera confrontations with the likes of Saul Bellow, Susan Sontag and Professor John Morton Blum giving the proceedings, said Woody, 'the patina of intellectual weight and seriousness'. There were also a clutch of witnesses who, purporting to be genuine, were actually fictitious, like the character played by amateur actress Ellen Garrison, an uncanny lookalike for Eudora in old age. The witnesses do afford the film an added touch of authenticity and Woody has recalled that Bettelheim, Sontag and the rest were only too happy to go along with the joke. Amongst those whom Woody failed to fit into the film were the then elderly Jack Dempsey, who was in poor health (though he does appear in the stock footage), and Greta Garbo, who didn't reply to Woody's letter. He did, though, manage to shoot an interview with Lillian Gish but 'I didn't use it, because I didn't like the way it came out.'

Unlike other Allen movies shot in black-and-white, it was not possible to print monochrome on Technicolor stock because, said Willis, 'we would have lost the look and feeling we wanted'. However, working with the materials was pleasurable because the black-and-white medium makes it 'easier to define the emotions and can be very beautiful and very good for story-telling'. Shooting with Panaflex cameras which he had always found 'serviceable and reliable', Willis also managed to get hold of a set of old newsreel lenses from the 1930s which he had remounted for Panaflex and found very 'helpful in establishing the look. Some of them were beautiful, but it was a flatter image and they weren't made of optically-coated glass. I think the lenses were one of the elements that made the idea work.'

As with *Sex Comedy*, a number of the film's interiors were shot at the recently refurbished Kaufman Astoria Studios in Queen's, the East Coast base of Paramount in the silent and early sound periods. There were also some well-chosen New York locations; the conference scene was filmed upstairs in the offices of one-time Fox head Spyros K. Skouras on West 51st Street. Since 1964, this had been part of the John Jay College of Criminal Justice. Woody would return to this location, using the fake 'mediaeval' office of Darryl F. Zanuck's former secretary for an eventually cut scene in *Radio Days*. The scenes involving Zelig, Eudora and her sister, Meryl, were shot mostly around Teaneck in Bergen County, New Jersey, a location favoured some 70 years before by D.W. Griffith and the old Biograph Company. Woody has since recalled that the shooting of the film was relatively easy, it was the post-production which proved difficult. *Zelig* took nearly three years of development and production - nine months for the editing alone - and 'There was a point', said Willis, 'when I thought we were never going to finish, a point when I thought I was going to go nuts. I have never worked so hard at making something difficult look so simple.'

Critics, staggered by the sheer brilliance of the exercise, were almost uniformly won over, though many long-time Allen fans expressed disappointment at the film's lack of strong dialogue scenes, character development or real story. But, at the opening at the 599-seat Beekman Theatre in July 1983, *Zelig* broke the existing house records and there were lines halfway round the block. In its second week, the film shot to number one position in *Variety's* Box Office chart - a first for Woody - and, during its 14-week New York run, it took nearly $700,000 at that one cinema alone. Vincent Canby described *Zelig* as 'a summation and a perfection of methods and ideas that have been turning up in all his films ... He, rather than any of his more conventional mainstream contemporaries is the premier American film-maker of his day.' Jack Kroll in *Newsweek*, while describing the film's hero as 'the Great Gatsby of Schlemiel', was similarly encouraging. Pauline Kael, almost inevitably, dismissed *Zelig* as 'a masterpiece only of its kind ... like a teeny carnival you may have missed - it was in the yard behind the Methodist church last week'. There were also inevitable comparisons with *Citizen Kane* and intimations, in many quarters, that Woody had, finally, become 'his own man'. All of which represented his best all-round reviews since *Manhattan*.

Broadway Danny Rose *Broadway Danny Rose* is a deceptively slight, black-and-white, New York-based shaggy dog story about a small-time agent and former stand-up comic who specializes in the oddest of the odd no hope clients. His stable includes a blind xylophonist, a one-legged tap dancer, a one-armed juggler, a roller-skating penguin, a lady glasspiel act and a bird called 'Peewee' which picks out 'September Song' on the piano.

Danny's one 'normal' client, a passé, overweight, Italian-American crooner, Lou Canova (Nick Apollo Forte), is a fifth-rate talent with aspirations to third, whose stock-in-trade - a painfully schmaltzy medley of oldies - convinces Danny he's worthy of a nostalgia boom cash-in on an upcoming NBC special with Milton Berle. Danny's efforts to promote Lou tell us as much about the unkind vagaries of show business as about Danny himself: if by some miracle of talent or *chutzpah*, one of his clients ever does get a move up the ladder, it is only to dump Danny in favour of a more powerful management. Early in the film Danny is seen trying to book some of his acts into Weinstein's Majestic Bungalow Colony in the Catskills, where Woody had made his own 16-year-old amateur debut, performing magic tricks. But the only act in which the manager is interested is a comic who has already had a small success and moved on.

The story is framed within a series of mostly light-hearted reminiscences by a group of Danny's old associates - seven veteran Borscht-belt comedians who join up regularly at the Carnegie Deli on 7th Avenue. Here, enjoying a round-table, strictly Kosher snack, they inevitably fall to gossiping, swapping improbable stories of the old days and the people who struggled to make it in show business. The film's anecdotal format is somewhat reminiscent of Louis Malle's *My Dinner with Andre* (1981) and both the scenes with the comics and the story proper - related in a sequence of affectionate and increasingly risible flashbacks - are lit from within by the mystique of old Broadway and a regret for a show-biz ambience which has long since passed.

Although Woody's comic apprenticeship came some time after the end of the waning vaudeville boom, he did rub shoulders with any number of those entertainers who inhabited that world, several of whom appear in semi-auto-biographical roles in the movie. Six of the alternating story-tellers - including Sandy Baron who tells the best and longest anecdote - had been real-life comics, while the seventh member of the group, Woody's manager, Jack Rollins, once worked out of a tiny office like the fictional Danny, though in Rollins's case, at the top of the Plaza Hotel where his only client was Harry Belafonte. Filming of these scenes encompassed two whole days at the Deli. The owner Leo Steiner, playing himself in the movie, reported that after the film came out business was even brisker than usual.

The film's other main story-line involves Lou's mistress, Tina Vitale (Mia Farrow), a bouffant bleach-blonde, replete with Brooklyn accent, tight slacks and dark glasses, who is a Mafia widow, now dangerously 'cheating' on her would-be 'fiancé', gangster Johnny Rispoli (Edwin Bordo). When Lou gets a chance to audition his stuff for Berle with a date at the Waldorf, it falls to Danny (echoes of Woody's ghost-writer role in *The Front*) to 'beard' for him and get Tina to the show, without arousing the suspicions of Lou's wife.

Eschewing the experimentation of his preceding movies in favour of a warm glow of show-biz recognition, the film fairly bristles with in-jokes and deft parodies, like the interpolation of a grainy television talk show, presided over by Joe Franklin, a 30-year veteran of WOR-TV, and Milton Berle, hilari-ously guying his own image as a blonde-wigged Cinderella in Macy's Thanksgiving Day parade. Woody, a great admirer of Berle (who, in his heyday, was known as 'Mr Television') had first met the older comedian as a boy of 15 at the Circle Magic Shop where they had swapped card tricks. Remembering Berle's kindness, he promoted the comic's cameo in the movie as both homage and fond payback. Berle, unaware of the way Woody pares his footage to the bone, was disconcerted later to discover that his full day's work on the film had been reduced to a mere guest bit.

Danny's attempts to get Lou's career off the ground are beset with quite wonderful improbabilities. Lou is temperamental, has a drink problem and, wrote Richard Corliss, mixes 'the repertoire of Vic Damone with the sexual charisma of Buddy Hackett'. Danny though, has ultimate faith in him and, with the possibility of his opening for Berle at Caesar's Palace, Danny brushes up Lou's act to include 'My Funny Valentine', complete with a special up-to-the-minute lyric about the moon landing.

Danny is sweet and likeable, but a loser, perpetually shoved aside by a dangerous world, clinging to the old-fashioned virtues of loyalty and straight dealing, and camouflaging his nervousness with bustling energy, fake optimism and one-liners. Like the agent Jerry Wexler in *The Floating Lightbulb*, Danny tries to come across like a hot shot but, also like Wexler (whose biggest client was a talking dog), he is only 'an ever-hopeful huxter', almost saint-like in his dealings with rarely grateful clients.

The character of Danny is thought to have been inspired at least partially by Woody's very first manager, Harvey Meltzer, older brother of one of his former classmates. Although the relationship was finally strained (Woody left Meltzer after five years for Rollins and Joffe), Meltzer is affectionately immortalized as the good-natured Danny, while the latter's ornamented Runyon-esque patter ('Might I interject one concept at this juncture?') is also reputedly drawn from life. With his sub-Dale Carnegie catch-phrases and a philosophy borrowed from his saintly Uncle Sidney, Danny begins to come across as a sort of 'radical innocent' like Chaplin. He may have his dark side - he can be sly and lacking in courage - but possesses an essential purity which compares well with the corrupt and insensitive folk who inhabit his world.

When Tina, after a spat with Lou, refuses to attend his concert, Danny is delegated to change her mind. Lou won't sing without her and, unaware of what he's getting into, Danny accompanies her to the Mafia mansion. But Johnny, given the brush by Tina, swallows iodine and his hit-men brothers, convinced Danny is the guy who's been sending Tina a white rose every day, give chase, threatening to chop off his legs. Escaping into the Jersey Flatlands (a locale where 'The Family' traditionally bury their victims!), the couple get lost, are put on the right track by 'Superman' (an actor making a shaving-cream commercial nearby) and boat it back across the Hudson. But, far from being safe, they are finally snatched and taken to a deserted warehouse. Not at all admirably, Danny fingers the hapless Barney Dunn (Herb Reynolds), 'The World's Worst Vent', as Tina's 'white rose' suitor. Danny imagines him safe aboard a cruise ship, but Barney, a chronic stutterer, has been cancelled and he gets badly beaten up. Happily, the cops catch the guys who did it and, conscience-struck, Danny pays Barney's hospital bills and takes him on as a client. Although Woody refuses to over-sentimentalize, the denouement of the film is infinitely touching. Despite his claim that he generally tends to think 'mechanics' rather than 'motivation' and stays well within his minimal histrionic range, the emotiveness of the final scenes, give or take what some have seen as a tacked-on happier ending, are cued in by the beautiful sequence where Lou, egged on by Tina, breaks the news that he's signed with another agent. The camera scarcely moves from Danny's anguished, uncomprehending face and we must agree with Woody's own view that 'it's a nicely acted moment'.

The sequences at the very end of the film are a return to the sweetness we discovered in the earlier stages of the story. Heartwarmingly, though he scarcely makes a living from his clients, Danny throws them a Thanksgiving dinner (frozen turkey pieces!) to show them how much he cares. This takes place in his own frowsy apartment where, amidst the falsely cheerful gathering of lonely tenth-raters, Tina, unable to settle for either Lou or her subsequent date, the shaving-cream actor, calls on him. Still bitter over her part in Lou's duplicity, Danny shows her the door. But, realizing he must accept her as she is, he pursues her down the street. Their final coming together - in long shot and immeasurable moving - takes place right in front of the Carnegie Deli, the very location where, years later, the whole of this improbable tale will be told and retold by the assembled comics. It is here that Danny is subsequently afforded the ultimate testimonial to a great-hearted human being - having a sandwich named after him (cream cheese on a bagel with marinara sauce). Such was the affecting verisimilitude of this occurrence that Leo Steiner was inspired to create a real 'Danny Rose' sandwich - a corned beef, pastrami and coleslaw colossus, plus a customized doggy bag with every order! (Danny is reputedly the only fictional character, apart from *Blondie's* 'Dagwood Bumstead' to be thus honoured.)

With its captivating Italianate score, and engaging performances, *Danny Rose* reminds one how cherishable Woody's films can be when dealing with matters closest to his own earlier experience. Although the cars, clothes and casual, free-wheeling camera style suggest the immediate present, the story proper is told entirely in flashback, and a clue to its period may be found in that significant reference to the moon landing. The film also harks back to an even earlier era, that of such Damon Runyon stories as 'The Brain Goes Home', the character comedies of Preston Sturges and all those genial old movies about vaudeville no-hopers, like *Little Miss Broadway* and *It All Came True*.

A major asset of the film is its imaginative use of Mia, cast against type as a sassy, gum-chewing moll, tottering on spiked heels and with a hairdo, quipped *Newsweek*, 'like a leaning Tower of Pizza' and her eyes concealed for much of the movie behind outsize shades. This was because, as Mia confessed to critic Gene Siskel, her eyes were otherwise 'not tough enough' to play a woman like that. When Tina *does* appear with scrubbed face and her hair in a towel, she suddenly looks beautiful, innocent and refined, as if, symbolically, she had been cleansing out her past.

The character's genesis lay in one of the regular outings Woody and Mia had made, some time earlier, to a favourite uptown Italian restaurant, whose gum-chewing, chain-smoking owner wore sun-glasses 'even when it's two in the morning' and 'a six foot high bouffant hair style'. Woody made mental notes, recapitulating them later when he had the idea for the film and needed a convincing foil for his own character. It was a type Mia had long wanted to play and the voice, she said, came from a secretary at Orion who, along with a couple of similarly accented friends, she recorded in her kitchen on Central Park West. She also ran and re-ran *Raging Bull*, gorged on pasta and wore large foam pads under her costume to make her own slight frame more curvaceous.

Small-part casting followed Woody's by now-established pattern of eschewing well-known actors who could convince in their roles in favour of faces and personalities who fit. Thus Howard Cosell (ex-*Bananas*) turns up again, as himself, at Berle's table, and Gerald Schoenfeld, real-life boss of Schubert Theaters, is cast against his own, apparently gentle personality, as the unscrupulous agent, Sid Bacharach. Irving Selbst, who also plays an agent, was, in reality, in the men's clothing business and went on to play the (finally cut) role of Jackammer in *Radio Days*. Joie Gallio, Beverly Hills High School-graduate daughter of Joey Gallio and a talented stage performer, also has a small role as a fortune-teller's assistant. Amongst the acts in the film is Gloria Parker, a Brooklyn Academy of Music graduate, who had become a noted 'glasspiel' artist. She had learned this extraordinary skill from her Czech grandfather. As for the role of Lou Canova, it had originally been mooted for, amongst others, Robert de Niro, Danny Aiello and Sylvester Stallone. Aiello, named by Woody as his 'sixth favourite actor', recalled being so devastated at losing the part, that he 'went into a room and I cried for two whole weeks'. Woody recompensed him with the second male lead in *The Purple Rose of Cairo*. Nick Apollo Forte was a Connecticut-based singer, actually an ex-fisherman, who pressed his own records, made his living as a cocktail pianist and had never acted in his life. He had also, he confessed, never seen an Allen film, but was discovered when one of the casting people came across his album, *Images*, in a New York store.

The film itself has a wonderful informality. This was Gordon Willis's penultimate film with Woody 'and we wanted a rough-looking appearance which gave us lighting freedom - I didn't have to wait for the sun. Here I could shoot on the inspiration of the moment.' Woody's insistence that bright sunlight detracts from depth of contrast meant that, as on a number of previous occasions, he and Willis would find themselves waiting around for hours during exterior shooting for overcast skies to return. During one shoot in New Jersey, according to Eric Lax, they went off for a glass of wine and forgot to call in. Producer Robert Greenhut, unamused to find a blocked-off highway, police in attendance and a 75-strong crew, but no director or cameraman, designated assistant director Thomas Reilly to dog Woody's footsteps thereafter.

Danny Rose was the first of Woody's films to be released exclusively in the US by Orion, rather than through its previous agreement with Warners. The original deal had called for what was said to be an unprecedented 'parallel sovereignty', leaving Orion, theoretically, free to act as a sort of boutique studio, developing movies for Warner release. But a series of hits (*Arthur*, *10*, *Caddyshack*) was followed by some flops and the relationship with Warners, increasingly strained, finally broke down. On the look-out for a distribution company they could truly control, Orion and its partners bought out the ailing Filmways for $16m, with HBO (Home Box Office) chipping in with $10m, and leaving Orion in charge of distributing its own pictures.

A significant bone of contention between the two studios had been Woody's contract which did not sit too well with the Warners hierarchy. Their own money, they felt, was being used to indulge a potentially unprofitable talent. The fate of *Danny Rose* would be proof, if any were needed, that Woody's films were now geared, more than ever, towards an increasingly 'selective audience'. The film's US rentals of $5.5m (budget $8m) were in no way comparable with Orion's chief 1984 hits, *The Terminator* and *The Woman in Red*. Against this, however, must be set the company's decision to promote the movie as a limited-run, art-house offering.

Critics, though, swooped on the film with barely disguised glee. Richard Corliss in *Time*, found it as 'appetizing as a pastrami-on-wry sandwich', while Vincent Canby, comparing its story structure to Conrad, called it '... a love letter not only to American comedy stars and to all those pushy hopefuls who never quite made it to the top in show business, but also to the kind of comedy that nourished the particular genius of Woody Allen'. Almost alone, Pauline Kael in *The New Yorker*, complained of the film's 'curdled Diane Arbus bleakness' and that it was 'the only time a Woody Allen picture has made me feel he was writing down - trying for a crowd pleaser'. She also compared it unfavourably with the 1959 British movie, *Expresso Bongo*.

Danny Rose received its UK première at the 1984 Edinburgh Festival, where even the gag 'Two taxicabs collided. Thirty Scotchmen [*sic*] were killed' was taken in good part. London reviewers were likewise well disposed. Iain Johnstone (*The Sunday Times*) considered it to be, after *Annie Hall*, Woody's 'second funniest film to date'. Richard Combs (*Times Literary Supplement*) felt that Danny's 'ultimate redemption through his love for Tina has a genuine pathos that makes this Allen's most moving, and possibly his best film'. Writing after the event, David Shipman, not a Woody Allen fan, thought the film 'sweet and likeable ... probably his best picture, with pathos and wistfulness happily replacing the old ego-jokes'. More expensive than *Zelig*, but picking up profits in overseas territories, *Danny Rose* remains, on constant re-viewing, a particularly heartening combination of good humour, eccentricity and charm - qualities which, in Woody's very next movie, would be returned to the audience in spades.

The Purple Rose of Cairo *The Purple Rose of Cairo* is an enchanting romantic fable which again questions the nature of fantasy versus reality and the efficacy of dream as a mirror image for life and society. It also examines the very nature of cinema itself and, by inference, its audience, as well as being a sharply observed study of New Jersey folk during the Roosevelt era. Cecilia (Mia Farrow) is a romantically yearning short-order waitress, struggling to support herself and her boozy, unemployed slob of a husband, Monk (Danny Aiello). To alleviate Monk's brutality and the pressures of long hours at the diner where she works, she escapes into a life of fantasy at her local bijou movie theatre, 'The Jewel'.

Cecilia has conceived a crush on an up-and-coming movie star, Gil Shepherd (Jeff Daniels) - or rather, his on-screen shadow 'Tom Baxter'. Baxter is but one of the improbable characters in a romantic RKO comedy, *The Purple Rose of Cairo*, whose fragmented plot we can only guess at from the enticing clips shuffled dexterously before us. We do glean, however, that our hero is a naïve adventurer, explorer and poet, fascinated by the legend of 'The Purple Rose' which, it has been said, was painted for an Egyptian queen at the behest of the Pharoah who loved her. Tom, who has been 'adopted' by a bunch of glitzy Manhattan socialites, is a charmingly innocent combination of Howard Carter, Frank ('Bring 'em Back Alive') Buck and the Henry Fonda character in *The Lady Eve*. With his safari suit, sola topi and riding breeches he cuts an incongruous figure.

During Cecilia's fifth visit to 'The Jewel', Tom, intrigued by her presence yet again in the stalls, unexpectedly steps out of the screen to confront her - causing pandemonium in the audience and noisy vituperation from the rest of the on-screen cast. Cecilia is bewildered but delighted by this odd turn of events and the film proper then turns into a scintillating duel between what should be (the 'finite' story played out in precise terms 'night after night' on screen) and what, in an ideal world, ought to be (the dream becoming reality - if you wish it strongly enough).

Quite unaware of the pain to come, Cecilia sweeps the still safari-suited Tom off to a deserted amusement park, romance and concealment, while the rest of the on-screen cast begin to question their own validity in the established narrative. Meanwhile, the manager is called, some audience members demand their money back, the wires to Hollywood are jammed with panic announcements, anarchy reigns. At the height of the commotion, the manager threatens to stop the film and thus - the actors in it. 'Yes, but you don't know what it's like to disappear!' wails Henry (Edward Herrman), while the other cast members are, understandably, irate at Tom's summary disruption of the story.

The thin dividing line between reality and dream, as intimated by Henry's subsequent aside, 'You see, we're reality, *they're* a dream!' has been a popular staple of fantasy cinema. *Cairo*, in turn, is a reworking of another variant on the theme, Woody's *New Yorker* story 'The Kugelmass Episode'. In this, a New York Jewish professor of humanities, through the medium of a magician's cabinet, enters the pages of *Madame Bovary*. Kugelmass not only falls in love with the heroine but spirits her back to the 'real' world, putting her up, unbeknownst to his flesh-and-blood wife, at the Plaza Hotel! The idea of Kugelmass turning up as an unidentified character in classroom copies of the Flaubert novel all over the country is reflected in *Cairo*, where clones of Tom are trying to leave the story in every movie theatre where the film is being shown.

Woody decided to rework the idea in terms of cinema because, as he noted to Christopher Frayling, it was 'a good graphic for me'. But the story's starting point could have lent itself just as well to any medium. *Cairo*, said Woody, was 'just a funny notion that occurred to me one day, and within 48 hours all the developments fell into place'. In working on the script, however, Woody got stuck about half way through. He decided to start writing something else, coming back to *Cairo* when he got the idea of introducing the 'real' actor, Gil Shepherd, into the story. Very simply, the object of the movie was 'to show that we all have to choose between reality and fantasy. And, of course, we're forced to choose reality, because the other way lies madness.' But this also has its pit-falls and, as Cecilia finds to her cost, 'reality hurts you'.

As the film characters continue to quarrel among themselves, each assumes recognizable traits of his or her nightly behaviour in the story. This latter has come to resemble a glossy champagne comedy by Mark Sandrich or Mitchell Leisen. Woody is wittily observant of the film types and screwball situations of the genre, as individually or *en masse*, these characters lose their cool and begin to improvise wildly.

Meanwhile, back in New Jersey, Cecilia and Tom embark on a romance just as sweetly innocuous as the one in the film-within-the-film. Tom is an innocent abroad, as much so in Depression-era New Jersey as he was in the screen story. 'Well, now you're going to get a champion roll in the hay' promises Dianne Wiest as the heart-of-gold hooker Emma who briefly becomes Tom's self-appointed guide. 'What?', exclaims her ingenuous client, 'there's hay in the *bedroom*?' All he knows of sex has been airbrushed from his character's consciousness by the Hollywood Production Code, which in turn has ensured that nothing he does on screen could be remotely true to life.

Gil is also something of a fiction, actually an ex-cabby called Herman Bardebedian, and while Tom continues to spout the romantic nonsense which squares with his on-screen character, Gil has more of the 'Aw Gee' practicality of the down-to-earth guy. Though reluctant to leave the safe confines of Hollywood - where he is about to star in a biopic of Lindbergh - Gil is persuaded to take flight to New Jersey to see if he 'can't control his own creation'; through all of this, Woody's view of the film city and the (implied) idiots who work there is as teasing as ever.

Gil and Tom represent another of those games Woody likes to play with questions of identity - or lack of it - posing such questions as 'Is this person a different person from the other person? Or merely the same person?'- as in Pirandello's *As You Desire Me* and Hitchcock's *Vertigo* - who just *appears* to be different? Critic Richard Roud, while praising the acting of Daniels, actually cast doubt on the notion of whether Tom and Gil are really a double role at all, or, in true Pirandello terms, two separate extensions of a single personality.

It is however, in the final scenes of the film that the true differences between Gil and Tom are revealed. Having accomplished his set task - persuading Tom back on screen where he belongs - Gil deserts Cecilia in a way Tom, one feels, never would. But how could a screen idol's career survive a public romance with an ordinary New Jersey housewife? Tom, kinder, more romantic than his 'creator', did after all offer her a way out. Why not join him up there on the screen? Well, she does briefly agree to follow him, and Tom's return to his own world becomes a triple illusion, since, in climbing back into his own story, Tom is forced like Cecilia to change in size from one shot to another, passing in the process from 'real' to unreal, from colour to black-and-white! But that glamorous, unreal, monochrome, cinematically accelerated world is not for her. 'We'll live on love', Tom assures her. 'That's just movie talk', she reminds him gently.

At the end of the film, Cecilia is left to nurse her loneliness, gazing tearfully at the screen, now luminous again with the images of Astaire and Rogers in *Top Hat*. It is a heartrending wind-down to a story which seemed to demand a happier one. But it was the possibility of this downbeat coda which, according to Woody, attracted him to the idea in the first place. He had, in fact, shot an even bleaker ending - one in which Cecilia, bereft of both Tom and Gil, does not even have the final solace of 'The Jewel' to escape to. Instead, in the very last shot we see Cecilia's tearstained face, gradually fixing into a tentative smile at the on-screen antics of Fred and Ginger.

Cairo replaced *Stardust Memories* as Woody's own favourite amongst his films. 'It was the one', he said, 'which came closest to my original conception', and critics referred to it as his 'coming of age' or 'transition' film. Although he has claimed that 'there's nothing exotic about it', *Cairo* is, in fact, the clearest exposition yet of a romantic-poetic vision in Woody's work, deploying themes and narrative ideas drawn from the whole gamut of film and literary tradition.

The picture's most obvious inspiration, though, is *Sherlock Jr* (1924), a classic comedy described by René Clair as 'the screen equivalent of Pirandello'. In a reversed situation from Woody's film, Buster Keaton, as a lowly projectionist, climbs or 'hallucinates' into the cinema screen to help solve a crime which has been baffling the film-within-a-film protagonists. Woody, however, has persistently denied that *Sherlock Jr* was in any way an influence, pointing to the fact that the idea of Cecilia stepping into the screen in *Cairo* had been an afterthought. Keaton, anyway, was by no means the first to exploit the convergence of immediate 'reality' into film-within-film, and one may also point to Jean Cocteau's *Orphée* (1950), with the dreamer meeting his love on the other side of the 'magic mirror'. For mirror read cinema screen, where the Depression no longer exists and, wherein, as in *Orphée*, we have the age-old conflict between the 'real' world and the mythical, 'the surreal eventuality of an unknown destination which may either benefit or destroy'. As in *Through the Looking Glass*, Cecilia is a dreamer whose dreams become, albeit momentarily, a reality through the very act of stepping beyond. Woody would offer us a further variation on this theme in *Alice*, while since *Cairo*, at least a dozen recent movies and any number of TV commercials, have exploited the latter film's basic device.

In an attempt to explain why *Cairo* failed to be more popular, Woody has suggested that the picture, like *Zelig* and *Radio Days*, 'fell somewhere between the categories of commercial movie and art film'. He also agreed that the lack of a really optimistic ending (unlike the thematically similar *Splash!*) was a major bar to commercial success. In other ways, the film is not told conventionally. Although the central story is in colour, its texture is washed out and unglamorous, in accordance with its Depression-era ambience, and it is the shimmering black-and-white film-within-a-film which affords the story its glamour and visual beauty. This is the reverse, say, of *The Wizard of Oz*, where Dorothy fantasizes in Technicolor (her unconscious state), but lives her 'real' life in the monochrome Kansas farmlands. *Cairo*'s $13m cost, encompassing a virtual 50 per cent reshoot, was also, in terms of Woody's then normal average, somewhat inflated for an art film.

Another problem for some audiences was the absence, for only the second time in one of his pictures, of Woody himself. He was, though, as a number of critics noted, present in spirit and, given that Cecilia was, according to Woody, loosely based on his cousin Rita when young, she is one of the three characters, along with Eve in *Interiors* and Marion in *Another Woman*, with whom Woody claims he most closely identifies! One may also note how closely the gestures and intonations of Mia in several of her films with Woody had already begun to mirror his own. Pauline Kael, though significantly praising Mia's performance in *Cairo*, suggested that she did not in general 'challenge the Allen persona' in quite the same way as Diane Keaton had done and, interestingly, Woody has said he had almost used Diane in *Cairo*.

Mia is, obviously, less of a kook than Diane, alternately tough and ethereal - her waif-like appearance somewhat at odds with some of the 'steely survivor' roles she has played in films like *Danny Rose* and *Hannah and Her Sisters*. In comparison with Diane, she has displayed a wider range and was helped in *Cairo*, Mia said, by the fact that Cecilia was the one character she had played which came closest to her own personality.

Mia's performance is matched by Daniels - engagingly brainless in both of his roles - though *Cairo* had, in fact, started shooting with Michael Keaton in the parts. Keaton had accepted the film at a fee of $250,000 (a quarter of his then usual) just for the chance to work with Woody. But ten days into shooting, he left the project, ostensibly, said Woody because although funny, Keaton was coming over as 'too contemporary a character'. Whatever the actual reason, Keaton's manager, Harry Colomby, described the situation as a case of 'mutual miscalculation on both sides' - though the parting was, reportedly, friendly. In despair, Woody, under pressure from the studio, nearly rewrote the roles for himself, but 'I'm not the matinée idol type'. When Woody failed to sign Kevin Kline, caster Juliet Taylor suggested Daniels, hot from his role in *Terms of Endearment*.

Other cast members include Stephanie Farrow, sometime stand-in for Mia, as her on-screen sister (and fellow waitress at the diner), while another sister, Prudence (of Beatles' 'Dear Prudence' fame), is credited as 'Art Department Co-Ordinator'. Broadway impresario Alexander Cohen is film producer 'Raoul Hirsch', George J. Manos, an associate of Rollins and Joffe, plays a press agent, while future leading lady Glenne Headly (the then-wife of John Malkovich) is one of the hookers in the brothel scene. Veteran film favourite Van Johnson, and Broadway names Zoe Caldwell, John Wood and Milo O'Shea turn up as actors in the film-within-a-film. Woody's major discovery was Dianne Wiest, a respected stage performer with a few minor films to her credit and, the second he met her, he said, 'She lit up the room! The minute she walked in there was something terrifically special about her. And I knew I had to use her!'

Principal photography commenced in early November 1983, on locations ranging from Jersey City and Bertrand Island Park to Piermont Village, a bleak town on the Hudson River, 15 miles north of New York. The shoot there stretched from a scheduled ten days to a chaotic three-and-a-half weeks. This was due to the early arrival of winter blizzards, just after the storm windows had been removed from the main street shops, ready for filming. For the sake of authenticity, store fronts and window displays had been altered in advance, the shopping area was sealed off and many locals suffered huge financial losses. Even seven months after the crew's arrival, reported Nick Rosen in London's *Sunday Times*, contractors were still trying to put the town back to normal.

The film's most important location, 'The Jewel', required a fake frontage to be constructed in Piermont, but the bulk of the movie theatre sequences involved The Kent, a dilapidated last-run picture house, on Avenue H and Coney Island, built right next to a freight trestle. It was, recalled Woody, 'one of the great meaningful places of my boyhood', and was torn down shortly after the completion of the movie. The bordello scenes with Wiest and Headly were shot on West 71st Street, on a site now utilized by the Grace and St Lutheran Church as a shelter for the homeless in winter. It would also be used for the (finally cut) 'Astonishing Tonino' episode in *Radio Days*. The deserted carousel and switchback sequences were shot in January 1984 in Prospect Park, Brooklyn. But, as so much of the filming turned out cold and windy, part of this location was recreated at the Kaufman Astoria. *Cairo* was, in fact, the first movie to shoot on the studio's newly refurbished 'B' stage. Here Woody directed a number of the film-within-a-film sequences. For the scenes where Gil and Tom appear on screen together a series of mattes was required, though, in several instances, Woody opted for the straightforward use of a double (David Weber). In either event, the results were virtually seamless.

Like Woody's four previous pictures, *Cairo*'s year-end rentals ($5.1m) were barely over a quarter of the US revenues generated by *Annie Hall* and *Manhattan*. The film's American failure was due, it was thought, not only to public antipathy to *Cairo*'s 'pessimistic' ending but to the lack of 'any clear, consistent message' from the critics. That said, both Vincent Canby and Rex Reed (*The New York Post*) raved, while Pauline Kael, for once, offered an unusually positive review for an Allen movie. None of which helped the picture to ultimate commercial success and, as Woody has wryly noted, the box-office progress of his films, with a few exceptions, usually follows a set pattern: enthusiastic front-office predictions, based on the first few days' takings, followed by a sharp audience decline. It is something which, by his own admission, *also* happens to Bergman!

Although, in a year dominated by *Out of Africa*, *Cairo* failed to win an Oscar in any category, Woody did receive a Golden Globe Award for his script. Yet again, the film's biggest success was in Europe. *Cairo* broke the all-time record at two smaller London cinemas and the 1985 theatre high at several others. It went on to win the BAFTA Award for Best Film and Screenplay and was named Best Foreign Film by the London Critics' Circle. In France, following a phenomenally popular *hors concours* screening at Cannes, *Cairo* won a César Award and the Prix Moussinac for Best Foreign Picture.

8

All in the Family

1986-9: Hannah and Her Sisters to Oedipus Wrecks

Hannah and Her Sisters In July 1985, Woody signed a further three-film contract with Orion which included a clause prohibiting the screening of his movies in South Africa. The deal, which was non-exclusive, called for one film a year following on from the completion of *Hannah and Her Sisters* which started shooting in November 1984. The studio had just enjoyed an unexpected box-office bonanza with the release of *Amadeus* in September, even though, at the end of 1985, it was reported that this was the only one of its 11 releases of that year to make more than $10m in North America. The company had now gone three years without a really big hit and in February 1986 Orion posted a net loss for 1985 of $32.9m.

Orion's fortunes began to rally, however, with the success of *Platoon* and *Hannah* and, although the latter's $35.5m US gross in no way compared with *Platoon*'s $134m (rentals $66.7m), the financial benefits of both films would be a significant reason for a rise in the company's stock.

Hannah and Her Sisters was described by Woody as one of his 'novels on film' and was, at 107 minutes, his longest movie to that date. It was also to be the first in a quartet of 'family' films - two warm, two bleak - which Woody would make through the mid to late 1980s. *Hannah* and *Radio Days* deal, respectively, with middle-class WASP and lower middle-class Jewish concerns, while simultaneously reflecting elements of Woody's extended family relationships with Mia and semi-comic recollections of his Brooklyn childhood. The succeeding films, however, represent a return to the grimmer ambience of *Interiors*. *September* echoes the edgy mother-daughter relationship of that film, while *Another Woman* delineates the married state as an increasingly sterile partnership from which all but the observance of an elementary courtesy has been eliminated.

If *Hannah* suggests an on-screen equivalent of the Mia-Woody relationship at its warmest and creatively most fulfilling, to what extent do the two later films, along with the subsequent *Oedipus Wrecks*, reflect an association which was already beginning to run its course - not to mention the sombre musings of a film-maker, once more at an artistic crossroads, faced with the imminence of fatherhood, the passing of his fiftieth birthday and an increasingly uncertain showing at the box-office?

The success of *Hannah*, however, signified, at least for the present, a more optimistic Woody. The film, he said, was intended as a 'romanticized view of Mia' and connections between the actress and her screen character seem obvious - a factor played upon by the film's publicity. Hannah, deceptively frail in appearance, is an image of womanly perfection and 'peaceful efficiency' who is actually the linchpin to a large and, in many ways, problematic family. Like Mia, she has an actress mother, a director father, a partner who can't stand the country, an ex-husband who is in the media and, most importantly, she is a successful actress in her own right who neglects her career in order to spend more time with her children.

Since much of the film was shot in the large 11-room Central Park West apartment which Mia had formerly shared with her mother, Maureen O'Sullivan, and since seven of Mia's children also appear in the film, one might be forgiven for drawing further real-life inferences. In addition, O'Sullivan plays the mother of the title characters and, as Mia suspected, various of the film's protagonists were drawn from her own family, as well as 'other sisters Woody has known, like Diane Keaton and *her* sisters'. Mia's son, Fletcher Previn, playing a party guest, is addressed as 'Fletcher', two of Mia's adoptive children play Hannah's adoptive children, while the casting of Michael Caine, a long-time friend, as a sort of Woody Allen surrogate and on-screen husband of Mia, affords the enterprise some further home-movie resonances. And, although there would be the inevitable denials that Hannah was, in any way a 'true' portrait, 'I felt it was a complete exposé of herself', said O'Sullivan, 'She wasn't being anything - she was being Mia.'

Hannah and Her Sisters is Woody once more in quasi-Chekhovian mood, treating the various romantic and psychological upheavals of an appealing group of characters over the course of three separate Thanksgivings. Woody had originally wanted the story to cover a single year, unlike the film's acknowledged cinematic model, Bergman's *Fanny and Alexander* (1982), which, likewise, deals with a cultured, theatrical family, united in its predilection for food, sex, love, music and mischief. Although the final shape of *Hannah* was not directly dictated by the Bergman model, Woody did decide to lengthen the period of the film for reasons of pacing, character development and narrative logic. In this way he was able to allow the picture 'to determine its own form, where once ... [he] ... would have been a slave to its influences'.

Although they have similar careers and backgrounds, Hannah's family are not the same tortured souls we encountered in *Interiors* and producer Robert Greenhut, though satisfied with the early reviews, grew increasingly nervous of the audience reaction, especially when critics began to comment on the film's 'Chekhov spirit'. He feared, quite rightly, that publicizing the film as a sort of 'sequel' to *Interiors* would harm the box-office. But, although there *are* a number of parallels, notably in the surface similarities between the title character and the obsessively perfectionist Eve, the family group in *Hannah*, united in spite of petty frictions and jealousies, suffuses the screen with a glow more potent that anything Woody had conjured thus far.

At first, Woody told *The New York Times* 'the film had a simple plot about a man who falls in love with his wife's sister ... [but] I re-read *Anna Karenina*, and I thought, it's interesting how this guy gets the various stories going, cutting from one story to another. I loved the idea of experimenting with that.' Using the Tolstoy as no more than a starting point for *Hannah*'s parallel plot lines, Woody began thinking about a comic exploration of a number of his favourite themes. 'I was able', he said, 'to coalesce these ideas into a tragicomedy about people all linked by ties of blood and marriage'.

Woody's own character, Mickey Sachs, is, like Alvy Singer in *Annie Hall*, a death-obsessed hypochondriac, only more so. He is a high-powered TV producer, striving to get out of the rat race and, in common with a number of other Allen characters, at one point packs his job in. He was formerly married to Hannah, is the chief focus of the film's comic spirit and, though briefly attendant on the other leading characters, seems to stand somewhat apart from the main action. This, though, appears to be a quite deliberate device to position Woody's customary (Jewish) outsider, yet again as the quirky observer of his own and other people's eccentricities.

Woody, originally, had started out with no other idea than that Mickey had once been married to Hannah and had 'this terrible scare'. In the first cut of the film, however, the relationship between the two was not revealed until about halfway through and audiences were confused. Woody duly altered this so that the couple's previous marital situation is realized much earlier.

Mickey shares his 'narrator' role with three of the other characters, notably Hannah's present husband, Elliot (Michael Caine), and it is Elliot, rather than Mickey, who assumes the lion's share of the guilt-ridden, romantically obsessed monologues in the film. It is left to Mickey to encapsulate the film's most encouraging theme, voiced in the final stages of the movie, that 'The heart is a very, very resilient little muscle. It really is'. This makes for an unusually optimistic ending for Woody which a number of observers found something of a compromise.

A degree of this optimism also resides in the heartening resolution of the Elliot-Hannah story. Hannah, in the film's opening sequences, has gathered her family and friends around her for Thanksgiving dinner. The group includes her mother Norma, a one-time musical-comedy star, her commercials-director father, Evan (Lloyd Nolan in his final screen role), and her husband Elliot, a financial adviser to the rock-music industry. He is described, oddly, by Mickey, as a 'loser' and has conceived a crush on Lee, Hannah's beautiful sister (Barbara Hershey), an unfocused drifter and 'perennial student' who attends AA meetings. She has been shacked up with Frederick (Max Von Sydow), a prickly, anti-social, Andrew Wyeth-like artist, who in Woody's words, 'has been teaching Lee about life but making a bad job of his own'.

The idea of Von Sydow for the role had come from casting director Juliet Taylor and, in Woody's original draft, the character was called Peter - changed to 'Frederick' to make him sound more European. Once Von Sydow was in place, the part was altered and enlarged, becoming older and angrier in the process. The presence of Bergman's favourite leading man in the film further augments the customary resonances from that particular source and Woody has named Von Sydow and Geraldine Page as the only actors he has yet directed of whom he found himself in awe.

The third sister, Holly (Dianne Wiest), is also an actress, a former coke addict and unsuccessful. On the side, she runs something called the Stanislavski Catering Company with her actress friend, April (Carrie Fisher). Unlucky in love, Holly is drawn briefly to philandering, opera-loving architect David (an uncredited Sam Waterston) whom she 'loses', as is her wont, to April. Holly is insecure, eccentric, delightful and infuriating by turns, her inability to sort out her life suddenly given an upturn when she finally discovers a hidden talent for writing scripts.

Lee and Holly, to whom Hannah is unwittingly condescending, have always relied on their more practical sister for her stability but, over the next two years, her strength is sorely tested. Elliot, feeling himself superfluous to Hannah's aura of sweetness and perfection, does not surprise us by setting his cap at the sparkling but vulnerable Lee. Meanwhile, Holly all but goes to pieces, Norma and Evan lay into each others' show-biz vanities, while Hannah turns for support to the neurotic Mickey. It is significant that Mia, by her own admission, never really understood Hannah, 'not at the start and not at the finish' - whether she was, indeed, the lovely bulwark of the whole family or had a darker side. Discussion revolved around 'whether Hannah was a good sister or a bad sister', and the fact that neither Woody nor Mia could decide one way or the other or 'find a clear handle on it' finally made the character more interesting.

As with *Interiors* and *Crime and Misdemeanors*, the film is essentially a portrait of artists, commercial or 'pure', while the three leading men in the film represent different aspects of Woody's own persona as those in *Interiors* never seemed to do.

Douglas Brode sees Michael Caine as a sort of British Woody Allen, with his horn-rims and specific obsessions, but, although intriguingly cast, Caine was by no means Woody's first choice, nor was the role specifically written for an Englishman. Unlike a Redford or an Eastwood, Caine was a person, Woody felt, who could suggest weakness and might be induced to cry if a relationship went wrong. Caine took the role to gain 'comic credibility' in the US, but what Woody wanted was his ordinariness and vulnerability. Although he grudgingly let the actor shoot a 'funny' version of one of his scenes, it was the serious one that was printed. Woody has said that he actually had 'a big debate' about the possibility of taking the part of Elliot himself and agreed he could have played it just as easily as Mickey or, indeed, any of the other male roles if not, he admitted, as well. According to Caine, he had asked Woody if he could wear spectacles in the film because 'To me the character is an *alter ego* of Woody' and some observers felt that Woody should have consolidated the roles of Mickey and Elliot and made them one.

Each of the film's characters is seen from a different standpoint, keyed in also by his or her own personal musical motif. Thus, Holly and Lee are both aptly characterized by 'Bewitched, Bothered and Bewildered', April by 'The Way You Look Tonight', David's penchant for opera cues in an appearance by Maria Chiara in *Manon Lescaut*, while Mickey, almost inevitably, is favoured by such jazz greats as Basie and Brubeck. If the Lee-Elliot romance (J.S. Bach) demonstrates the comic potentialities of over-age passion, the romantic exploits of Holly, as befits her edgy, underconfident personality, are altogether more yearning. Anguishing over her career, the soullessness of cattle-call auditions (though Wiest's rendition of 'I'm Old Fashioned' is awkwardly captivating) and the will-he/won't-he tenor of her brief association with David, Holly becomes the character most like the adorable neurotics of Woody's earlier comedies. For all her practical strength, Hannah also has her problems. Her sisters resent her calm beauty, her success, her self-sufficiency, while Elliot wants a woman less intimidating, one he himself can take care of. One of the most touching scenes comes when, after a bitter quarrel, she tells Elliot, tearfully, that she too has 'enormous needs'. 'Well, I can't see them', he replies, 'and neither can Lee or Holly!' In affectionate parody of Mia's real-life child-gathering role, she also wants another baby to add to the four she already has. Two of these were by artificial insemination and very funny is the scene, related in flashback, in which the supposedly infertile Mickey tries to persuade his former writing partner, Norman (Tony Roberts) to donate his sperm!

Although the role of Mickey was not in the original script, Woody felt that a character who 'suffers a lot because he thinks a lot' had its funny side and was worth exploring on screen. Mickey here is used as a darkly comic cipher for such weighty concerns as 'the imminence of death and the meaning of life'. Convinced early on that he has the classic symptoms of inoperable brain cancer, Mickey buys a rifle with which to kill himself. The gun goes off, accidentally, failing to kill him but rousing the neighbours.

Ill health has been a recurring theme in Woody's work and the brain tumour idea had been derived from a real incident, when, during the editing of *Manhattan*, he had lost his hearing in one ear. Reminded, while studying a book on Gershwin, that the composer's own fatal brain tumour had been signalled in exactly this way, Woody had been forced to live through the tensions of awaiting the happily benign results of his hospital tests. Retaining this dark comic tone, in *Hannah* there is also a series of semi-farcical scenes in which Mickey expresses his intention to convert to Catholicism or other religions. Cut, though, was a sequence where he confesses to a priest which, amusing when shot, was excised for reasons of pace.

Although Woody's character retains its ethnic roots - Mickey's ultra-Jewish parents being wonderfully satirized - *Hannah* is, once again, an essentially WASP family portrait, and the hand-picked cast plays with uniform excellence. The oldies, though not central to the story, are particularly well used. O'Sullivan, who had initially refused the role of Norma, described in the script as 'a boozy old flirt with a filthy mouth', would go on to play Mia's mother in the first (abandoned) version of *September*, and also herself, alongside Woody's mother, Nettie Konigsberg, in his uncompleted 'work in progress' documentary, *Two Mothers*. Hershey, in, critically, the most overlooked performance of the three female leads, is much more than just the shallow enchantress the role implies and she and Caine give their scenes together an almost adolescent sense of romantic urgency which is both absurd and touching.

The triumph of the film however, is Wiest. She has the ability to make an ostensibly irritating character infinitely appealing. Neurotic, indecisive, wracked with self-doubt, Holly may be seen as almost a female echo of

Mickey, and we realize quite early on that these two deserve each other. Though he and Holly had a night out together some time back and didn't hit it off, they meet by chance at Tower Records and discover they have a great deal in common. Holly is delighted by Mickey's encouraging reaction to her writing and they fall in love. At the end of the film, the couple are happily married and Mickey, at the third and final Thanksgiving, embraces Holly as she whispers the very last line in the film, 'Mickey, I'm pregnant.' The moment is intensely moving.

Although Woody has said he prefers 'to do smaller films because it's just easier, physically', he found *Hannah* to be one of his most difficult. One of its major problems resided in his ever-increasing practice of creating characters on set, rather than in the script, and shooting in long continuous takes to avoid disrupting the timing of the actors. Michael Caine has recalled that Woody tends to use the camera lens like his own eye, allowing the actors to walk in and out of shot, registering nothing that is not immediately visible: 'This gives his films a strange kind of reality, as though the camera is a voyeuristic intruder that can't manage to see all the action.' But the end result, due to expert camerawork, the spontaneity of players who have often learned their lines within moments of stepping on set, and meticulous cutting, remains the antithesis of theatrical. The deliberately episodic structure, Brechtian chapter headings, flashbacks and spoken asides also serve to enforce an initial view that artifice is taking precedence over inner reality. But our emotional response to the characters and their relationships is total. Only a major film-maker, one feels, would have the confidence, frequently, to shoot a film like a play and still come up with a movie.

Hannah and Her Sisters is at its most cinematic in its ravishing observations of New York itself. In a sequence loosely recalling the opening shots of *Manhattan*, David the architect gives Holly and April a guided BMW tour of his favourite buildings. Instead of Gordon Willis's more studied grey-and-white tones in the earlier film, these are transformed by Carlo Di Palma's warmer Technicolor palette which offers these scenes and the film as a whole, said David Ansen, their 'deceptively casual grace'. Willis had been unavailable (as he would be for *Radio Days*) and Di Palma (who noted later that his ideal working life would comprise one film a year with Woody and one with Bertolucci), would go on to light most of Woody's future work. Woody had, in fact, originally wired Di Palma (as well as a DP who used to work with Kurosawa), offering them the job of lighting *Take the Money and Run*. Neither was free at that time and, at any rate, as Woody later admitted, he would not at that stage have known how to utilize their talents. Woody had been impressed with Di Palma's work on *Blow-Up* and *The Red Desert* and was touched to learn when they finally did manage to work together that Di Palma had kept the original telegram. 'His more muted photographic style' wrote Douglas Brode, was to give 'Woody's recurring concerns a visual freshness', while his almost documentary use of the dolly, starting, say, with a methodical close-up, then dollying backwards to reveal the whole setting, is a process repeated four or five times in *Hannah*, as if the viewer were 'looking for the poetry of the invisible camera, a straightforward witness to events'. It affords the picture a casual look, perfect for its essential style, while the film's subtly nuanced handling of the three female leads, in particular, is worthy of Bergman at his best.

As was Woody's now-established custom, part of the $8-$9m budget was set aside for extensive reshooting and, in fact, only about 20 per cent of his original script ended up in the film, with actors flying back into New York at a moment's notice from places as far flung as London and India. Many of the scenes were rewritten during the reshoot and were, in most instances, completely different from the initial concept. In various of the versions there were more scenes of Mickey and Hannah together, while Tony Roberts also had more scenes in the original, including one in an art gallery. Another cut sequence was a rather explicit, albeit fully dressed, Lee-Elliot sex scene - described by Caine as a 'knee trembler' - and which he thought somewhat out of place in a Woody Allen film! The very beautiful scene where Hannah, in bed with Elliot, tells him that she too is 'fragile' was a later addition.

In the original version, the film ends with Elliot still in love with Lee, even though she has married someone else (her college tutor) and Elliot has gone back to Hannah. Woody has recalled that this idea 'was so down for everyone that there was a huge feeling of disappointment and dissatisfaction every time I screened it' and that his failure with this ending was a lack of preparation for it in the body of the film - 'so I had to put a more benign ending on it and it dissatisfied me.'

Barbara Hershey has said she found the filming a gruelling experience: there were some lighthearted moments but usually it was a very serious set. This view was confirmed by Caine who recalled in his autobiography that it was the quietest set he had ever come across, 'a bit like working in church'. Woody, though, was in his element, noting that it had been the most enjoyable of all his films to make because he had family and friends around him and was able to lunch in nice restaurants he knew well.

Woody has remained ambivalent about *Hannah*, dismissing it as 'a somewhat middlebrow picture'. He points to the lack of an Allenish sting in the tail as a possible reason for both its immense popularity and its artistic 'failure'. The moral of *Hannah*, though, was summed up astutely by Carrie Fisher who noted to *The New York Times*, that 'we can go to shrinks for 50,000 years and know why we do everything and then go back and do it again. You can have your mistakes, and repeat it, too.'

Hannah opened wide, at over 400 US theatres in February 1986. Normally, Woody's films start off in just Los Angeles and New York and then go into specialized release in other key cities. But such was Orion's belief in the picture that, as the company told *Variety*, 'We're selling it more as an entertainment rather than as the latest in the Woody Allen series.' Indeed, the Sutton Theater première in New York was mobbed by 'the beautiful people' who just 'loved it'. The critics were similarly eulogistic. Apart from a few minor cavils about the 'fairy tale' ending and Woody's own character in the movie retreading old ground 'in his continued search for meaning and sense', reviews ranged from 'masterpiece' and 'Woody's greatest triumph' (Rex Reed in *The New York Post*) to Kathleen Corliss in *The New York Daily News* who exclaimed, 'Hurrah for *Hannah*, Woody's latest - and greatest - is really *Manhattan* with a heart.' Even Pauline Kael, while suggesting that Woody 'should take ... a long break from his sentimentalization of New York', dubbed it 'an agreeably skilful movie'. Graham McCann, writing after the event, found it 'inflected by a comic tone that makes it one of the most liberating American movies since the Capra era'.

For many, the film's *hors concours* screening in May 1986, accompanied by a specially filmed interview with Woody, directed by Jean-Luc Godard, turned out to be *the* major event at that year's Cannes Film Festival. Woody saw *Hannah* go on to be his biggest success in Europe since *Annie Hall* and, encouraged by the US box-office, Rank (distributor of Orion's movies in the UK), decided to adopt a different launch pattern from Woody's previous films. After a preview screening at the National Film Theatre in June, *Hannah* opened at Rank's flagship cinema, the Odeon, Leicester Square. Wardour Street pundits felt that opening the film in a theatre traditionally associated with the Bond movies was something of a risk. But *Hannah* proved that anything is possible.

The film achieved a record-breaking West End opening gross as the capital's top earning title, and ended up as Britain's 16th Biggest Money-Maker of 1986. It scored in the US with an initial year's rental of $16.6m and went on to win three Oscars (Best Original Screenplay and Supporting Players - Wiest and Caine), as well as nominations for Best Film, Director, Production Design and Set Decoration. Woody's appearance in the film put him, after an absence of years, among the annual list of Top Money-Making Stars (at 20th), though his role, as the critics had noted, was but one bright ingredient in a glittering even-handed ensemble. Like *Annie Hall*, the picture was widely influential and imitated. Several movies aped its basic family situation and structure (like Ron Howard's *Parenthood*, with Wiest in a virtual re-run of her Holly role) while a group calling itself 'Hannah and Her Sisters' had a chart hit with an upbeat version of 'Bridge Over Troubled Water' in the late summer of 1991.

King Lear A great deal of interest focused on Woody at the 1987 Cannes Festival where, represented by the out-of-competition *Radio Days*, he could also be glimpsed, sporting a Picasso tee shirt and entangled in film strips, in the cutting room 'climax' of Jean-Luc Godard's weird *King Lear*. This had been announced only two days prior to its screening as 'a work in progress'. That it had been apprehensively awaited may be borne out by the generally hostile reviews, summed up by David Robinson of *The Times*, who noted that 'This is the most cynical trick he [Godard] has yet played on his patrons and admirers: a casual assembly of disconnected and mostly nonsensical scenes in which Shakespearean lines occasionally surface without point.' Indeed, the film was less about Shakespeare's *Lear* than a continuing exposition of its director's thesis that 'Instead of writing criticism I now film it.'

Lear is certainly one of the most peculiar enterprises Woody has managed to get involved with, but less important for his own minimal contribution than for the mutual admiration long enjoyed between him and its director. The influence of Godard and the New Wave can be discerned in a number of Woody's movies, from the freewheeling style of his earlier comedies to the wobbling, *cinéma verité*, hand-held camera technique of *Husbands and Wives*.

Although a version of *Lear* had originally been in development, by Godard, at Francis Coppola's ill-fated Zoetrope Studios in Hollywood in the early 1980s, it was not until his return to film-making in Europe that the project finally began to come together. Legend has it that Cannon Films' Menachem Golan, having just attended a screening of Godard's Cannes 1985 festival entry *Detective*, had whisked the director into the nearest coffee bar to emerge, 15 minutes later, with a contract hastily drawn up on a cocktail napkin. *Lear* was to be set in modern-day New York, with Marlon Brando as the King and Woody as the Fool. Godard duly confirmed the participation of Woody around the spring of 1986 when they were filming their *Hannah* interview at the Manhattan Film Center.

Many observers were convinced that the project would never get further than the restaurant doors, and, having failed to interest Brando, Cannon next announced that the film would star Lee Marvin as Lear, a tycoon in this version, running a conglomerate in the US, with Woody as the Fool and a screenplay by Norman Mailer. The latter was 'seduced' into signing by a firm promise that Cannon would finance Mailer's pet project *Tough Guys Don't Dance*. In January 1986 it was announced that Dustin Hoffman would star, while Godard's own preferred choices for Lear - Orson Welles or Joseph Losey - had died, in preference, said the wags, to having to appear in the movie! When Hoffman also demurred, Mailer himself was asked to star. 'He's a natural', enthused Golan, 'he has five daughters and a crazy life.'

Originally, Mailer conceived the film as dealing with a little theatre company attempting to stage a modern version of *King Lear*, with Mailer's daughter, Kate Miller, as Cordelia. American theatre director Peter Sellars was cast as the story's peripatetic 'observer', William Shakespeare V. But, in December, after just one day's filming in Nyon, Switzerland, near Godard's home at Rolle, Mailer and Godard 'agreed to disagree' and Mailer and Kate Miller went home.

The dispute was thought, chiefly, to have hinged on Godard's suggestion that Lear should have incestuous longings for his daughter. 'Mr Godard and I', recalled the writer, 'couldn't pass a piece o'chicken across the table without a major disagreement'. A great deal of the resulting film did, though, adhere to Mailer's original conception, and he and Kate could also be glimpsed at the beginning of the movie, caught by Godard's camera on the terrace of the Hôtel Beau Rivage, as well as explaining both the adaptation and their non-appearance in the scenes which followed.

The script's main departure from the Bard lay in Lear's metamorphosis from an ancient British king to a modern-day mafioso, Don Learo (Burgess Meredith) and the film, when finally shown in its original English language version (but without French subtitles), at Cannes, seemed to have very little to do with Shakespeare at all.

As for Woody, although he had, reputedly, shot 20 minutes of screen time, filmed during a few hours one morning with a skeleton crew, that brief sequence at the end of the picture was all that Godard would ultimately allow him. 'And I felt while I was doing it', Woody recalled, 'this is going to be a very silly movie. A very foolish movie. But I thought, this is for Godard. And I got a chance to meet him.' David Robinson, for one, found Woody's appearance in the film 'reassuring', though Woody had been somewhat bemused at taking direction from a film-maker whose lack of 'traditional reverence for plot and planning' was by this time notorious.

One good result of their collaboration had been Godard's original 30-minute 'video encounter', *Meetin' WA*, which was also screened at the Rotterdam Film Festival in 1988. In spite of a degree of 'owlish recalcitrance' to be noted on Godard's part in the interview, the item was generally well received. But, a victim of Cannon's 1987 cost cutting, *King Lear* never did receive a satisfactory release. Its single screen run in New York netted a mere five-figure take in January 1988 and, apart from post-Cannes screenings at the Montreal and London film festivals and a limited number of showings at the ICA in London, *Lear* remains one of the least known of all Godard's films to English-speaking audiences.

Radio Days Much more favourable attention was devoted to *Radio Days*, an affecting, colourful look at Woody's growing up in Brooklyn in the late 1930s and early 1940s. The story is set against an evocative background of the radio programmes and hit songs of the day and, although a number of movies have used wireless and dance tunes as counterpoint to stories set in that particular period, this vastly entertaining film is possibly the only one where the history of a single *family* is told in direct juxtaposition with the Golden Age of Radio. It is an enterprise which thoroughly justifies Graham Greene's contention that 'Childhood is the bank balance of the writer.'

Woody began filming in November 1985, completing, after extensive reshoots, in May the following year. With its meticulous period setting, amber-toned camerawork and vast canvas, *Radio Days* was, technically, Woody's most ambitious project to that date. The film made imaginative use of the French-developed Louma crane, a flexible mechanism to which the camera is fixed, allowing for very spectacular movements. It had first been used in the US on Spielberg's *1941*. There was also a great deal of tricky effects work, a multiplicity of locations and a huge cast; Woody found it especially difficult to co-ordinate things and retain a thread because the film didn't have a fixed story, being mainly anecdotal in style.

Described by him as a 'big colourful comic cartoon almost a musical but not quite', *Radio Days* is like a series of animated picture postcards, nostalgic, funny and tuneful, which like Gene Saks's film of Neil Simon's *Brighton Beach Memoirs* and Barry Levinson's *Avalon*, also comes across as a warm, Jewish equivalent of such earlier mainstream Americana pieces as *Ah, Wilderness!* and *The Human Comedy*. *Radio Days* offers us the best of two worlds, since it contains a full complement of all-American radio personalities alongside the central linking story of a typical lower middle-class Jewish family of the time.

We follow the latter from the immediate pre-War years through Pearl Harbour and the early stages of the conflict to just beyond the New Year's Eve celebrations of 1943-4, counterpointed by the various streams of popular iconography of the period. Woody had originally planned only to use the songs, showing us exactly where his on-screen *alter ego* Little Joe (Seth Green) was at the time he first heard them. After the first half-dozen examples, however, Woody felt that the idea was getting monotonous and decided to combine Joe's adventures with those of the other listeners and the radio personalities themselves. Although Woody does not appear, he narrates the story in his familiar New York twang as the grown-up voice of Joe, thus acting as a two-way mirror between the listeners and the studio performers, while echoing the immediate sensations of Joe himself, through whose eyes and perceptions the interweaving stories unfold.

Although we are asked to suspend our disbelief in that many of the incidents recalled for us by the grown-up Joe could not have been literally witnessed by his boyhood counterpart, such is the spell of the story-telling that, finally, as with *The Purple Rose of Cairo* and *Zelig*, anything on screen seems possible. This is especially the case when Joe recalls the travails of the film's principal radio character, the struggling actress-cum-cigarette-girl Sally White (Mia) and offers us three quite separate versions of what may have happened on the night she was trapped on the roof of the St Regis-Sheraton Hotel with her radio star lover Roger (David Warrilow). When Joe finally moves into a semblance of that glamorous world - the occasion when his Aunt Bea (Dianne Wiest) and her new beau Chester (Jimmy Sabat) take him to the Radio City Music Hall to see *The Philadelphia Story*, it was, says Joe's grown-up voice, 'like entering Heaven - I'd never seen anything so beautiful in my life'. Beautifully restored in 1979, the Music Hall was, at the time of filming, just as little Joe of the story might have experienced it.

The film starts with an amusing conceit. A pair of burglars, robbing the house of Joe's neighbours, the Needlemans, answer the telephone and become random contestants in a phone-in radio quiz show. Next we are introduced to Joe's family: his parents (Michael Tucker, Julie Kavner), his grandparents (William Magerson, Leah Carrey), Uncle Abe and Aunt Ceil (Josh Mostel, Renee Lippin), cousin Ruthie (Joy Newman) and Joe's unmarried bookkeeper aunt, Bea, all of whom correspond, approximately, to Woody's real-life family and testify to the fact that, as a boy, he and his parents frequently shared with or were billeted on various relatives. Although, yet again, Woody claimed that the film was only 'very loosely' autobiographical, at least one childhood friend has insisted that *Radio Days* is exactly like Woody's real family situation at the time. Facts are considerably changed around for dramatic purposes and the radio shows are mostly generic (to avoid protracted rights negotiations), but certain elements in the film, like the characters' names and the family of Communists living next door, are just the way things were.

Although he himself was raised partly in Long Beach, Woody decided to film the family scenes in Rockaway, a run-down Brooklyn coastal resort to the east of Coney Island. Long Beach, he figured, was too long a daily drive from his Manhattan base. Rockaway, a cold, windy peninsula, 'with mostly turn-of-the-century houses and inhabitants to match' has been popular with film-makers, and had also been Neil Simon's original setting for the Brighton Beach plays, changed by him, finally, because his chosen title, *Far Rockaway Memoirs*, lacked the alliteration he preferred.

For *Radio Days*, an entire block was cleaned and dressed for the filming, with modern signposts removed and some 'new' period façades built over the existing structures. A local newspaper in November 1985 reported that $5 of the film's $16m budget had been expended on these renovations, which was, patently, untrue. Little Joe's house was at Beach 115th Street and, when it was subsequently 'cloned' for interior shooting at the Kaufman Astoria - a little larger than life size and with no ceiling, so that Di Palma could hang the lights - the detail was so precise that the owner's three-year-old daughter, on a visit to the studio, became upset to find what she imagined to be her own home nestling in the middle of a sound stage.

Over the rainswept opening scenes, the adult Joe's voice informs us that each member of the family had a favourite programme. Joe's mother never missed 'Breakfast with Irene and Roger', and Woody uses this glamorous pair as a major link between radio fiction and real life, notably as regards Roger's illicit affair with Sally whom he falsely promises to introduce to the head of his agency. Irene (Julie Kurnitz), meanwhile, joins her husband at the King Cole Room of the St Regis-Sheraton, hob-nobbing with the likes of 'Hemingway' and 'Richard Rodgers'. 'They were two different worlds', the adult Joe recalls. As with *Zelig*, there were newspaper ads for lookalikes to play the various 'real-life' celebrities in the film.

With its 'moderne' art deco furniture and elegant upholstery, Irene and Roger's lavish pad was actually fashioned for the film out of the Paradise Garage in New York's King Street, 'the oldest and best known gay disco in Manhattan', while the idea for these sequences was principally derived from a real-life radio-show couple of the 1930s, Pegeen and Ed Fitzgerald. They began broadcasting from their own apartment in 1937 and were so popular that even President Roosevelt came along to watch. As becomes obvious, Roger and Irene, like the other radio personalities we meet, are some way removed from their ultra-cool, sympathetic on-air roles.

The contrast between the dream figures and their reality is also demonstrated in the vignette about Joe's favourite programme, 'The Masked Avenger', whom Joe fantasizes as a sort of 'cross between Superman and Cary Grant'. He is actually played by the short, bald, chubby Wallace Shawn, an Allen regular who was Diane Keaton's little 'homunculus' of an ex-husband in *Manhattan*. The casting of Shawn reflects the real-life radio 'Superman' of Woody's boyhood who was 'a little budgy man - my height and three times my size, with jowls and baggy eyes. A real pooch of a fellow. That really appealed to me.' Another hero of Joe and his pals is 'Biff Baxter', G-Man of the Air' who, on radio, takes care of the Nazis and the Japs, but is, in reality, just an actor. He is played by Jeff Daniels (Tom Baxter in *Cairo*) and, though willing to do his bit on air, urging his juvenile audience to collect scrap iron and spot Jap planes from the roof, Biff, like Errol Flynn, is denied a more active role in the war on grounds of being categorized 4-F.

Aunt Bea, whose one big dream is to get married, is dated by a number of unsuitable beaux and is addicted to the more romantic kind of programme. In one sequence, she goes out on a date with chunky Stanley Manulis (Andrew Clark) who runs out of gas and stalls his car on Breezy Point. 'Well, what's a girl to do?' murmurs Aunt Bea, about to give way to the inevitable, when 'La Cumparsita' on the car radio is suddenly interrupted by Orson Welles's famous 'War of the Worlds' broadcast! The voice of 'Don Richards', flashing news of the Martian landings 'live' from Wilson's Glen, New Jersey, so panics Mr Manulis that he takes off, leaving Aunt Bea to trudge home six miles in a pea-souper. It is one of the best gags in the film, all the wittier for being based on an actual radio programme of the time.

Joe's father in the film is, perhaps, the most closely recalled character from Woody's childhood. Here is a man ashamed of being a cab driver, a job he keeps secret from his son. He is also full of all sorts of cockamamie schemes to make money, several of which had been actual occupations of Woody's father, Martin. The film character's failure in life and diminutive stature are contrasted with the more expansive Uncle Abe who is a radio sports fan and fish expert. Cousin Ruthie, however, loves romantic boy crooners and, as the grown-up Joe recalls, 'To this day there are certain songs that, no matter where I am, the minute I hear them I get instant memory flashes.'

As the film proceeds, the Sally story is brought into sharper focus, reaching its darkly comic apotheosis in the sequence where, working as a hat-check girl in a Manhattan night-club owned by a notorious mobster, she inadvertently witnesses his slaying by an underworld rival. Having run out of bullets, the killer, Rocco (Danny Aiello), kidnaps her, planning to ice her later, but an ensuing dialogue reveals that they had once lived on adjoining streets in the same Brooklyn suburb.

Rocco and his family decide to help her, and as a result, Sally's subsequent career is happily more successful. She is involved in a funny sequence as a jingle singer for laxatives and, finally, after a course of elocution lessons to get rid of her strong Carnarsie accent, she exploits her now-fake semi-English delivery as anchor-lady for 'The Lady Lydia Facial Cream Hour'. The product is, presumably, imaginary, but Sally's gossip personality, only too reminiscent of real-life models, adds to the fun.

Meanwhile, Joe's mother gets pregnant again, Aunt Bea keeps getting her romantic dreams dashed and Joe's father is forced to reveal to his son his 'secret' occupation. Although the vignetted nature of the narrative does present structural problems, much of the film is very entertaining and a number of interludes are characterized by a nicely mordant humour. This is exemplified by the film's most bizarre sequence - the 'Favourite Sports Legends' radiocast of 'Bill Kern' and his shaggy dog anecdote about 'Kirby Kyle', the lean southpaw pitcher from Tennessee. The accident-prone Kyle was, it appears, also addicted to duck hunting and from season to season continued to run up high scores, even when blind and missing an arm and a leg. Subverted into comic effect by the straight-faced manner of the telling, this odd fable would appear to derive from the real-life exploits of Monty Stratton, one-legged former pitcher for the Chicago White Sox. Brian Mannain from the Rollins-Joffe office, himself a keen amateur player, was co-opted to play Kyle, while former sportscaster Guy Le Bow, now owner of a local radio station, played Kern. The latter character was said to be based on Bill Stern, a radio personality of the 1930s who had been prone to somewhat overheated sports stories.

As a warmly recalled adult view of the past and its sensations, *Radio Days* recalls Fellini's *Amarcord* and, with *Stardust Memories* (*8 1/2*) and *Alice* (*Juliet of the Spirits*), could be said to form part of an unofficial trilogy in homage to the Italian maestro. *Amarcord* is a fond, random collection of boyhood reminiscences set in Rimini in the 1930s. Unlike the film version of *Pennies from Heaven* which captured the darkness but fumbled the escapism of that era, Woody's approach, like that of Fellini, demonstrates how the human condition can be enhanced even in time of war and privation by the popular entertainment of the time.

When the convention *is* broken, as in the quite heartrending sequence near the end of the film where the fate of little Polly Phelps trapped in her Penn Field mine shaft abruptly refuses to be yet another mistily recalled fantasy of the air waves, we are genuinely shocked. But this episode pushes us logically towards an ending as bittersweet and yearning as anything to be found in recent American cinema. As Diane Keaton, in a last-minute guest appearance, hauntingly sings the New Year's Eve night-club number 'You'd Be So Nice to Come Home To', Sally and The Masked Avenger lead their fellow revellers up on to the roof of the St Regis-Sheraton. A vast illuminated top hat begins to rise from behind the flat rooftop and the Masked Avenger, in reflective rather than heroic guise, offers his companions a Chekhovian valediction to a vanishing era and the transitoriness of their own fame. But, as the 'Silver Dollar MC' (Tony Roberts) has drunkenly assured them, 'We have it pretty good, we're the voices all America listens to.' And then, true to his own radio character, The Masked Avenger intones his famous sign-off, 'Beware, evil-doers, wherever you are!' Could little Joe's life and what his older self remembers of it, *all* be nothing but vaguely deceptive figments of the airwaves?

Due to the project's enormous scope, *Radio Days* made use of virtually all of Woody's regular team of actors and technicians. 'It's the biggest cast we've ever had' he told Alexander Walker, 'When we began there were 220 speaking parts, but only 150 appear in the movie. I had to cut the rest, it was running so long, and sit down and write 70 "Sorry, you didn't make it letters" to the bit-part players.' Most of these were selected, said Woody, 'to be cartoon exaggerations of what my real-life people were like' and, as in *Stardust Memories*, a number were chosen for their 'great faces' rather than any professional acting experience.

Woody specifically created the role of Sally for Mia after trying out various other characters with her which she might conceivably have played. Diane was also offered a choice of part but, like Mia, could not have been convincing as a member of the central Jewish family. Amongst the other Allen regulars was Julie Kavner, best known previously for her role as Valerie Harper's sister, Brenda, in TV's *Rhoda*. Woody had seen her some time before on television and thought her very funny, but had lost track of her until she had been suggested for the role of Mickey's assistant Gail in *Hannah*. A big fan of Woody's working methods, Kavner has said that her portrayal of Joe's mother in *Radio Days* rang true because, although born in California, she was able to recognize her own Jewish family in Woody's version - which transcended stereotypes. Another TV name was Rebecca Schaeffer who played the Communist's daughter glimpsed kissing a black man by Mrs Silverman. Schaeffer went on to star in the sitcom, *My Sister Sam*, and, as a cruel coda to the denouement of *Stardust Memories*, would end up in reality murdered by a crazed fan.

Amongst the newcomers to Woody's group were British-born (but French-based) David Warrilow as Roger Draper, discovered in a production of *As You Like It* by set designer Santo Loquasto, and Kitty Carlisle Hart, roped in to sing 'They're Either Too Young or Too Old' after two previous artistes had been filmed but found wanting. Woody's initial choice had been 'someone like Barbara Cook' but in the event Hart offers a highly evocative contribution. She was also meant to replace one of her predecessors singing 'I'll Be Seeing You' against a sequence of Sally kissing servicemen, but this scene was cut.

On-the-spot casting included an old woman at Beach 115th Street who, mistaking Joe's collecting for 'The New State in Palestine' for the genuine article, opened her purse to find some change. Delighted, Woody put her in the picture. The actor originally playing school principal Peters was spotted for this, his first movie role, by Woody while the former was having dinner with his wife in Greenwich Village. Dennis Kear, Woody's stand-in for ten years who had never had a part even as an extra and mainly works in computers, was cast as a passer-by. Fletcher Previn was given the part of Joe's best friend, Andrew and, to complete the 'family' atmosphere, Woody even found room for his accountant in the New Year's Eve scenes at the King Cole Room.

Thierry De Navacelle, who observed the filming over the four months' shooting period and wrote a book on the subject, noted Woody's amazing attention to every detail of production - even to the extent of changing drinking glasses around on set or objecting to a particular shade of red on an actor's shirt. This meticulous concentration on apparent trivia was all-embracing, from the design team's choice of World War II posters on the walls to the garter belt under an extra's WAVE uniform which the camera would never see. The visual style of the movie is very reminiscent of its Felliniesque influences. Initially, Di Palma had tried to effect a contrast between the warm colours of the family scenes and the art deco coldness of the broadcasting studios. After viewing the early dailies, however, Woody took against the idea - which explains a great deal of the subsequent reshoot. The look of the 'War of the Worlds' incident was inspired by the fog scenes from Antonioni's *Identification of a Woman* (1982), which Di Palma had also worked on and Woody admired. The Welles sequence was actually shot in the studio with an 8-cylinder Buick and the crew wearing white masks against the artificial 'fog' effects. Woody wanted to create an atmosphere where you couldn't see too much and which was genuinely frightening. This and other scenes in the film benefit from Di Palma's generally unfussy camera style.

The initial nine-week shoot represented some of Woody's widest ranging East Coast locations to that date. These included Coney Island, Rye Playland, Jersey City Union City, and, of course, Times Square and midtown Manhattan. The Playland 'Fun House', required for a sequence to be shot on 14 February 1986, was eliminated because it looked too depressing and was in urgent need of a paint job. Jersey City, where parts of *Danny Rose* and *Cairo* had been shot, had become a virtual little Hollywood-on-the-Hudson, and had also been used for a recent

European TV movie which replicated parts of the Berlin Wall on Jersey City's Exchange Place!

New York shooting ranged from Rockefeller Center to Central Park Zoo, while the pink art deco restaurant of the King Cole Room was shot at its actual location on East 55th Street. Woody also used the River Diner on 11th Avenue and 37th Street where Di Palma had shot parts of *Offbeat* the previous summer. But the roller rink in the Amusement Park, where Aunt Bea is taken by Mr Manulis, was too small for Woody's purpose and was reconstructed in the studio. The German submarine sequence was shot by the second unit off Staten Island, next to a miniature pier, with opticals added later by R/Greenberg Associates. Originally Woody wanted to use the sub from Wolfgang Petersen's *Das Boot* (1981), but customs legalities proved too complicated and he finally settled for the 15-foot model used by Spielberg for the Japanese sub in *1941*. Woody has recalled that the sequence was enormously hard to pull off and, finally, the only way to make the sub look convincing was to reshoot it, with the aid of a 'binocular matte' - the sub then being seen from little Joe's point of view, with glasses, on the beach. This particular sequence ended the first shoot (21 February) while the crew, without Woody, returned to Breezy Point for the Marconi history of radio sequences, which were subsequently cut.

Also excised was an elaborately shot vignette, set in the 1920s, about a Houdini-like escapologist, 'The Astonishing Tonino', who is chained and hurled into the icy waters of the Atlantic. His exploits were to be intercut with an anchorman, posted along the Jersey shoreline, giving, thanks to the 'miracle' of radio, an on-the-spot rundown of the event. While shooting on the Rye locations for these sequences the producers became increasingly depressed when, although dark enough for a set-up, Woody, with 70 extras standing by, still refused to shoot because 'the beautiful reddish light on the horizon was deemed unsuitable for the mood of the scene'. He finally shot from the end of the pier with the camera facing the opposite direction. As it happened, the sequence's place in the story was finally taken by the episode with the burglars.

Woody had actually entered the Kaufman Astoria for four weeks, from 17 January, starting with the King Cole roof scenes and the roller-rink mock-up. Other sequences there included the Polly Phelps scenes, on Stage 'G', and a cut episode, 'Nick Norris - Private Detective' and several of the music-show scenes. Some of these were filmed with direct sound, a technique almost never used nowadays, musical numbers generally being pre-recorded and inserted during the editing. But the radio shows of the 30s were live. 'In those days', said Woody's arranger, Dick Hyman, 'There was this wonderful uncertainty of a live performance. Woody wanted some of the same live quality like in the period.' Among his exceptions to this approach were Jessica Dragonette's 'Italian Street Song', where the acoustics didn't fit, and a sequence shot at the old Savoy Manor Ballroom in the Bronx. This involved Mia singing thinly but charmingly, 'I Don't Want to Walk Without You, Baby', during a USO concert. She had actually pre-recorded two versions for the lip-synching on set but, according to Caryn James in *The New York Times*, the lighting was wrong and the tempo too fast. This meant that Woody had to reshoot the sequence a few days later, rebuilding the set and recalling a hundred extras for the purpose.

By the end of the first shoot, Woody had exposed 120,000 feet of film, averaging less than 2,000 feet a day. The reason for this relatively low ratio is that he tends not to cover himself, using few takes, filming only what he might need. Editing as he went along, Woody made his official move to his Park Avenue post-production suite on 23 January. Reshoots began on Stage 'G' on 25 April with 40 new pages and 20 new scenes. One of these was a sequence called 'Radio Players of the Air', in which Sally is seen to be hopeless in the role of Irina in *The Three Sisters*. Cut, though, was a scene explaining that she couldn't be fired, because she was sleeping with the sponsor. Woody also shot a scene of an old actor reciting the final soliloquy from *Macbeth* and re-recorded his own voice-over, with a new running order. Cut also were the original *La Règle du Jeu*-like introductory shots - a sequence where each actor is used by the camera to introduce another and which, said Navacelle, Di Palma photographed as if it were a ballet. Woody, finally, only used a portion of this sequence, with another voice-over and some additional scenes to introduce little Joe's family more succinctly. Retakes of the St Regis roof scenes meant bringing David Warrilow back from Paris because Roger's original rooftop 'seduction' of Sally looked fake. Woody also made a change to the scene where Sally addresses camera, telling her own story. This was now shown to the accompaniment of the grown-up Joe's narration. Last to be shot were the gangster scenes - the slaying at the El Morocco night-club, written the day before filming. These were intended as a stopgap when Woody found he had insufficient pages to shoot due to Dianne Wiest's absence at her father's funeral. The new scenes included Sally and Rocco in the car, and the scene with Rocco's mother, played by veteran actress Gina De Ángelis, who had literally just come out of hospital and was persuaded reluctantly to take the part. Filming finally wrapped on 9 May 1986.

Despite rough spots due to budgetary limitations, *Radio Days* was well praised for its success in conjuring up the specific flavour of an era. Woody, though, has maintained that his original concept was a film even grander, funnier and more moving in design and that the result 'fell short in every important way'. The critics were almost evenly divided. 'Woody Allen', wrote a jubilant Larry Swindell in the *Star-Telegraph*, 'is really the Charles Dickens of American cinema and my hunch is that *Radio Days* is Woody's *David Copperfield*.' Carpers included Pauline Kael who scoffed that 'The Movie is centered on a preadolescent boy, and there are places where you think he directed it.' Initially, the film looked like a smash. Opening at number 10 in the *Variety* charts, it averaged more in its first week than *Platoon* had done and which would go on to be Orion's biggest money-maker ever. But, after almost nine weeks *Radio Days* slipped away, grossing $12.9m to a year-end net of only $6.4m. Inevitably, it went on to achieve its greatest popularity in Europe, notably in Sweden and Italy, holding the number one spot in Rome for ten weeks in the summer of 1987. The film's UK première took place at the Cinema '87 event at the Brighton Festival, with Dianne Wiest in attendance. British reviews were mainly warm - *Sight and Sound* being representative in finding the film charming but 'as accomplished as it is vaguely antiquated, reminiscent of nothing so much as Woody's first film, *Take the Money and Run*'.

September As a token of the esteem in which Woody was now widely held, he was invited in 1987 to replace Orson Welles as one of the ten honorary members of the American Academy and Institute of Arts and Letters. He was still also in demand to contribute to projects other than his own. One of the more singular offers emanated from Erato Films' Daniel Toscan Du Plantier, former general manager of Gaumont, who during that year asked Woody to direct a version of *La Bohème* at Cinecittà, in Rome. As Du Plantier told me, in January 1995:

> I spoke to Woody Allen three or four times, always in New York. I was very keen for him to do the movie and I asked my former wife, Marie-Christine Barrault, who had worked with him, to arrange a meeting. There is, I think, a generic closeness between Puccini and Woody Allen's movies and the idea was to make it modern, in the times of today. But although he was really interested in the idea and enthusiastic, he was still under exclusive contract to Orion Pictures and I don't think he wanted to commit himself. Since the legal solution seemed insurmountable, finally, I went with my old friend Luigi Comencini who made the film with Barbara Hendricks.

By October 1986 Woody was heavily involved with *September*, the idea for which had been on the stocks for some years. Though perceived by some observers to be a loose reworking of *The Seagull*, the film also posits the theme, according to Woody, that 'when a traumatic incident occurs in one's life, there are those who are wrecked by it and others who are virtually unaffected'. Woody expressed himself less interested in the incident itself than 'the long-time responses' and thought the subject, dealing broadly with 'the bonds that link and tether' might be suitable for a small chamber piece or 'play on film'. This was designed as a deliberate antidote to the large scale and stressful experience on *Radio Days*, being a project which could be 'shot indoors, with no bad weather, fewer actors and fewer sets' but which would still be essentially cinematic.

Direct inspiration came from Mia who suggested to Woody that her 65-acre estate in Bridgewater, Connecticut might be 'a great setting for a little Russian play, like Chekhov or Turgenev'. In fact, Woody originally intended to shoot the film in and around Mia's house at Frog Hollow Farm or, even Vermont, but the scheduling meant that it would have to be done in winter, in the cold and with bare trees. It was with some relief to Woody that the weather broke and he was able to instruct Santo Loquasto to recreate the setting entirely at the Kaufman Astoria.

A stripped-pine, Swedish-style country-house interior was constructed in the middle of a sound stage. In the original design, trees and shrubs were clearly visible through the windows but Woody, finding this idea phoney and preferring to focus attention inwards, decided that, with the aid of curtains, shutters, Venetian blinds, etc., all overtly visual, though not aural, intimations of the world outside would be deliberately excluded. Woody has said that, like *Interiors*, the house in *September* was a key character in the story and in this case was actually the inspiration for the script. In the set design Loquasto was encouraged to go for 'a warm and homey look with a lot of perspectives'. By shooting throughout with a red filter and with the middle section of the film taking place during a power breakdown, Di Palma was able to indulge Woody's growing predilection for the 'dark look'. Indeed, they were both so delighted with the film's visual aspects, that Di Palma was later to name *September* as the best picture he and Woody have made together.

The 'stylistic motif', said Woody, was easier to control in the studio, and the film's concentrated atmosphere would be the nearest he had yet come to an intimate TV drama. This was emphasized by the fact that he decided to shoot in continuity, a method he generally dislikes, because several of the cast had pressing subsequent engagements. It did allow him to reshoot unsatisfactory sequences instantly, cutting as he went along. Technically, he also managed to avoid the usual problem of dialogue movies with their repeated close-ups and often static camera.

Filming proceeded, noted Thierry De Navacelle, with 'the same atmosphere of complicity and quiet intensity' as had been enjoyed on *Radio Days* and the initial shoot was completed in January 1987. Alas, Woody, after cutting it all together, was disappointed with the result, but also realized that structurally the film did not lend itself to minor readjustments. As the summer-house interior was still in place, he decided, in his own words, 'to put a match' to the original version and refilm the whole project from start to finish.

Although Mia and Dianne Wiest were to retain their original roles, Maureen O'Sullivan, again playing Mia's mother, was, according to reports, hospitalized with pneumonia and had to be replaced. But as Woody has more recently revealed, the actress, cast on Mia's suggestion, was simply not positive enough in conveying the comic flair and flamboyance which she has in real life and which Woody had hoped to capture on screen. He finally cast Elaine Stritch after seeing her on TV. Charles Durning, playing Mia's lovelorn neighbour, reportedly had a long-standing commitment elsewhere and was replaced by Denholm Elliott, but Woody, who considers Durning 'a tremendous actor', also felt him to be miscast.

Elliott had originally had the part of O'Sullivan's physicist husband; this character was now played by Jack Warden. Sam Shepard, who had already replaced Christopher Walken, one of Woody's favourite actors, on the earlier shoot, was now felt to be unsuited to his part. This particular role finally went to Allen regular Sam Waterston. The revised version of the picture was put together in less than a month ('Same performance, more money!' quipped Elliott, philosophically), the result being a film which many critics found overly bleak and too heavily influenced by its sources. Finally, though, just like *Interiors,* it was to garner almost as many approving comments as dismissals.

September's central drama is propelled by the psychological problems of a lonely, recently sick girl, Lane (Mia) whose unreturned passion for a neighbouring tenant and her love-hate relationship with a semi-monstrous mother spark off an exploration of Woody's usual concerns - linked here to a not-too-hazy recollection of a real-life Hollywood scandal. Woody, in the film, would appear to be getting deep into the very roots of his own identity crisis and (apparent) self-hatred. But the pivotal figure is not the traditional Jewish 'monster' mother of the later *Oedipus Wrecks* , but a gravel-voiced WASP whose idea of committed motherhood is to have let her fatherless, teenaged daughter take the rap for the long-ago murder of her one-time gangster lover.

This element of the story has been taken to refer to the slaying of Johnny Stompanato Jr in April 1957 by 13-year-old Cheryl Crane, daughter of film star Lana Turner. Woody has said that, although 'aware' of the Turner-Crane affair, this was not his primary inspiration, even if there are still enough point-ers in *September* for one to note the obvious parallels.

In *September*, Lane is a born victim and the casting of Mia in this role is intriguing. Although the film echoes a quite different mother-daughter rela-tionship, Mia's very presence serves to reflect our knowledge that she is also the daughter of a movie star, albeit a minor one, who had actually played her character's mother in the original abandoned version of the film. Although the role had required little actual rewriting, Stritch is, of course, a very different kind of actress than O'Sullivan. Happily, though, similarities between Mia-O'Sullivan and the film's characters go no further than the original mother-daughter casting and, as Mia's biographers perhaps justifiably com-plained, 'one gets the feeling that Allen would be better off leaping into his own troubled relationship with his mother ("the castrating Zionist") rather than diffusing it through Farrow's perspective as the daughter of an actress.'

Woody, quite obviously fascinated by the linchpin resonances of real life versus fiction, dangerously offers his own overt speculations on the case. The twist in *September* is that Lane finally reveals it was her mother, Diane, who actually squeezed the trigger - an idea based on the doubts thrown up by Stompanato's brother (*re* the fatal stabbing) at the time of the original Cheryl Crane murder trial. Although well into her thirties, Lane is still wracked with the deep pain her mother has caused her and, having failed at nearly everything else in life, she also muffs suicide.

In the process of unravelling the truths (or half-truths) of Lane and Diane's story, Woody again plays games around one of his persistent themes - the way people are against the way they would like to be considered, and the some-times inane lengths to which they will go to avoid the actual truth about themselves being revealed. This idea is put explicitly into the mouth of Stephanie (Dianne Wiest), a resident of Philadelphia who has come to stay with Lane for the summer to try and sort out her feelings about her marriage. Stephanie, taking the old mediaeval view that our bodies are a collection of humours which reveal our true character, mentions in conversation that her husband is a radiologist: 'He takes X-Rays, but I never let him take them of me, because if he looked inside, he'd see things that he wouldn't understand and he'd be terribly hurt.'

Three other characters also find themselves in a state of high old indecision. One is the middle-aged, English-accented Howard (Denholm Elliott), a widow-er and former teacher, who had hit the bottle after the death of his beloved wife. He is revealed in the film's very first scene closeted in a 'tutorial relationship' with Stephanie, coaching her in French. He later teaches her how to play pool, but, unlike some other 'educative' figures in Woody's films, Howard is a professional, uninvolved emotionally with the object of his improvement. Instead, he is in love with Lane and has taken on the role of unofficial analyst and father substitute. In his voluntary assumption of healer and guide to this troubled young woman, he has also managed to find belated comfort for his own grief.

Lane is recovering from a doomed relationship with a married man who has finally gone back to his wife. 'I always felt there was a fatal element of hunger in your last affair', says Diane with cheerful cruelty and, as always, the mother has her daughter's number. Lane is now almost compulsively intent on repeating her mistakes, fastening her romantic obsessions on Peter (Sam Waterston), a personable neighbour who rents a guest cottage on Lane's estate. Peter is a Madison Avenue type now trying to fulfil his 'true vocation' - writing a serious book on 'survival'. In one of the film's wryer interludes, he is distracted by Diane who asks him to ghost her 'autobiography'.

Peter admires 'survivors' like Diane and to Lane's increasing consternation, begins to rationalize the killing of Diane's lover on the grounds that it 'is a book in itself'. But no matter how much Peter may try to justify it, the putative autobiography represents the characteristic 'sell-out' of the 'pure' artist to the demands of popular art - that uneasy schism which, in Woody's view, divides the two distinct strands of his own cinematic output thus far.

Stephanie, likewise, is edgily drawn to Peter and, as she later confesses to Lane, she has been leading him on without assessing the consequences. Lane hasn't been able to work for two years and can only clear her debts by selling her summer home and moving back to New York. Her mother, she insists, had given her the house but Diane, her career on the wane and her doggedly loyal husband Lloyd (Jack Warden) in tow, now announces her plan to move back. This confrontation takes place right in front of the potential buyers, as the tearful Lane also has to deal with the discovery of Peter and Stephanie embracing passionately in the kitchen.

Moments like the above, abetted by Stritch's enjoyable extroversion, suggest that Woody, with only a little manipulation, could well have directed *September* towards 'serious comedy' along the lines of *Hannah*. Indeed, the opening scene - slatted sunlight in a pine-panelled parlour and the softly murmured French lesson on the sofa - intimates a much cheerier film than the one we actually see. The early scenes are sun-streaked, relatively optimistic but, symbolically, a storm and a power cut serve to open up the repressed feelings which struggle painfully to the surface.

The central part of the film ('The Second Act') takes place in an indistinct candlelit gloom and consists of a series of intensely written, meticulously orchestrated dialogues. The single exception is Diane's fragmented soliloquy at the ouija board where, dissolving into her cups, she tries to conjure up the shade of her late first husband Richard.

If Diane remains the character most untouched by the storm-wracked progress of the drama, it is, ironically, the person who appears to be the most anchored in the film who, with night set in, expresses the gravest doubts about man's uneasy role in the scheme of things. Lloyd is fiercely protective of Diane but, in a moment of self-revelation, confesses to Peter that it is actually *he* who gains the most reassurance in his marriage to *her*, rather than the other way around. Lloyd once worked at Los Alamos, 'on a project unrelated to the atomic bomb', and is concerned with nothing less than the eventual collapse of the whole universe. How can one treat a simple family tragedy with any depth of emotion or insight when the whole future of the stars and the planets is so demonstrably out of control?

The predominant theme of the film, however, is guilt - the guilt which Lane feels over the killing for which, at the age of 14, she was once held responsible, or the apparent lack of guilt felt by her mother who, having done maximum damage yet again to their relationship and Lane's life, breezes off to Palm Beach at the end of the film, with Lloyd dutifully trotting along behind. When Lane finally faces Diane with having squeezed the trigger on her gangster lover, it is obvious that Diane has either protected herself with a convenient amnesia over the incident or that it happened just as the jury decided it had. 'There are probably things I would do differently if I had to do them over', she snaps, 'but I don't!' There, succinctly, is the very *image* of a survivor.

The film's final act, though emotionally fraught, is once again, visually sunny. The cool sepias and muted browns of the establishment take on a delicately tea-stained look. The blinds are still drawn, but there is bustle and movement, a feeling of things about to be done, of people going some place. Lane has been to an extent, reborn. She has got the 'truth' of her hideous secret off her chest, which, taken together with her recent declaration to Peter, does offer a form of catharsis. Her relationship with her mother is unsolveable, given Diane's unshakeable belief in living in the present. But Lane's touching and tactful rejection of Howard's proposal to her and her realization that Stephanie who, in spite of her 'lapse' is unwilling to sacrifice husband and children for Peter, also reassures her. 'In a few days it will be September', says Stephanie, 'It's gonna be OK' or, as Woody has suggested, 'they are entering the fall of their lives'. At the end of the film, the two young women are revealed sitting side by side in the kitchen making plans to spend some time together in New York.

September is an uncompromising, intimate, minimalist drama from which all humour, except for the bright corncrake utterances of Elaine Stritch, has been deliberately excluded. The film is beautifully acted, with Mia especially moving as the over-emotional, still childlike Lane, all too fragile and lacking in self-worth, with her metal-frame spectacles, Rossetti hairdo and a clothes sense which resembles, says Diane, that of 'a Polish refugee'. Stritch, as the main purveyor of the screenplay's mordant Hollywoodisms, is rather diverting, her non-glamour girl casting being Woody's nervous method, no doubt, of distancing his movie from the real-life characters the screenplay otherwise suggests. Wiest offers another of her highly affecting portraits as the sweet-tempered, bewildered, finally resolute Stephanie. And it is a tribute to her professionalism that, while shooting Woody's second version, Wiest was also appearing on the Broadway stage and had to leave the set every day at 3pm.

Although reasonably satisfied with the second version Woody has said that he would actually have liked to have filmed the story a third time in order 'to make some experiments and just see if other relationships can develop. But, of course, that's pure fantasy.' He was, though, more realistic in predicting the film's reception: 'I knew full well it wouldn't make a dime, not a dime.' *September*'s quiet four-city opening in the US in December 1987 ushered in a reasonable $5,715 per-screen average (five times more than for the simultaneous Columbia opener *Leonard VI*). Although the film went on to play some months at New York's Paris Theater and also enjoyed a small college following, in most places in the US it just wasn't shown. For once, with an Allen movie, overseas screenings failed to turn it into a profit maker.

Another Woman Due to the extensive reshooting on *September*, Woody missed his proposed August start date for *Another Woman*, which did not commence filming until 12 October. The film revolves around Marion Post (Gena Rowlands), a distinguished philosophy professor, who finds herself, aged 50, at a moment of personal reassessment. She is director of undergraduate studies 'at a very fine women's college', is married to a safe, successful cardiologist, Ken (Ian Holm), and has a 16-year-old stepdaughter, Laura (Martha Plimpton), to whom she is devoted. With friends, talent and a comfortable lifestyle, she has a great deal to be thankful for but, as Marion begins to look at her life, we begin to realize that things are not as they seem.

Taking a sabbatical to write a book, Marion sets to work quietly in a small downtown apartment. It is this move away from her natural environment which propels her into a severe post-menopausal crisis. The trigger is her discovery that one of the central heating vents has a direct link to the psychiatrist's

consulting room next door. Reluctantly at first, Marion feels drawn to the disembodied voices she hears, notably that of a disturbed young woman who is
heavily pregnant, troubled about her marriage and impelled towards thoughts
of suicide.

The origin for this story was a comedy idea which Woody had had some
years before - the story of a man living in a room with thin walls who over-
hears a woman talking to an analyst about what troubles her. Discovering that
the woman is beautiful and, having been a party to her most intimate secrets,
he contrives to meet her, becomes her 'dream man', solves her problems and
makes her wishes come true. Woody then began to question the eavesdropping
idea on grounds of taste since, 'even in the most benign Chaplinesque way it
seemed wrong'. Years later, he took the script out again and decided to make
it a more serious story of a woman who eavesdrops on another woman whose
sister is having an affair with her husband. The listener then goes home to discover her own husband is having an affair with her sister. Woody thought the
idea too much like Hitchcock, but did use aspects of the sister story in *Hannah*.
For years, according to Eric Lax, Woody was haunted by this basic theme and
eventually he came up with the story we see. Marion, in this version, said
Woody, is a woman who 'has kept everything personal in her life totally
blocked out' but, finally discovers she can no longer do so. The things she has
been suppressing, like 'the sounds of her inner turbulence, start literally to
come through the walls to speak to her'. That was the starting point for the
film, though the idea of Marion's future actions being instigated by hearing the
girl through the air vent, had been suggested by Mia.

Although initially optimistic about the project, Woody still felt he might
have been better served making it a lighter film. After its disappointing reception, he suggested that he should have made two movies - one a money-making
comedy with himself and Mia or Diane Keaton as the protagonists, and another film, more serious, which would not do so well. But 'I wasn't good
enough', he said, 'to have it rise to the level I wanted.'

The role of Marion was, apparently, intended for Mia, until fate in the
shape of her actual pregnancy with Woody's first (and only) child, Satchel,
intervened. Recently, Woody has suggested that, although not specifically
written for her, Rowlands, whom he considers 'one of America's greatest
actresses', *was* his first choice, as she had also apparently been for the part of
Diane in *September*. The disturbed girl was to have been played by Dianne Wiest
who dropped out due to personal problems. After filming started with
Rowlands and Jane Alexander in the key roles, Woody replaced the latter with
Mia, and her pregnancy was written into the script. This change now allowed

him 'to explore the issue of having children'. Mia actually gave birth in the middle of shooting and had to play her later scenes with a fake stomach. Other cast changes involved Ben Gazzara replaced by Holm and Frances Conroy instead of Mary Steenburgen, as Marion's sister-in-law, Lynn.

The disturbed girl is identified (on the credits, but not in the film) as 'Hope', due to her perceived resemblance to Gustav Klimt's 'elegant pregnant nude' of that name. This the two women discuss, after Marion, neglecting her own work to stay abreast of 'Hope's' ongoing 'confession', encounters her 'by chance' in a local antique store. It is Hope, in fact, who seems to be leading Marion on, acting 'in some way as an incarnation of her own inner self' showing her where she can find out things about her past life and what she has become. Even before the meeting, Marion, motivated by the voices, has already embarked on a recollective journey. It is here that the influence of Bergman - his way of conjuring a person's life in a manner that is dreamy and associative, rather than linear - is again keenly felt. Although Woody has denied the link, the obvious model here is *Wild Strawberries*, even down to the ticking clock motif which opens the film and which Woody had previously used in *Stardust Memories*. Woody utilizes the Bergman film's central idea and basic structure to present us with a soberly cruel vision of life's disappointments.

Through heightened reality, flashbacks, dream sequences and fantasy encounters, Marion's journey ultimately becomes a not entirely comfortable voyage of self-discovery. It is also, like *Stardust Memories*, though on a colder, more cerebral level - a journey into the mind. Woody has admitted that 'the cerebral nature' of the characters themselves led to a more 'frozen' aspect in both *Another Woman* and *September* and made them difficult to sympathize with.

Woody and his cameraman Sven Nykvist had discussed ways in which the dreams and flashbacks (which take up about a third of the story) could be made to appear different from the rest. It was finally decided to shoot semi-realistically, in the same style as the other scenes. This allowed for maximum fluidity in transition between the various sequences 'in the way daydreams slip in and out of daily life'.

In the present, Marion visits her elderly historian father (John Houseman), recently widowed, and she is shocked by his proposal to dispose of her late mother's artefacts. These possessions bring Marion into contact with memories she does not altogether welcome. She is reminded in particular of her mother's predilection for Rilke who once intimated that 'beauty is nothing but the beginning of terror'. Other symbols obtrude, like the black panther in its cage at Central Park Zoo ('That image could only be death') and a theatrical mask from a performance of *La Gioconda* - also a death symbol - which Marion had given as a present to her suicidal first husband Sam (Philip Bosco), who had been her college tutor, much older than herself. During this earlier relationship, Marion had had an abortion because she wasn't 'ready' for children. Similar ambivalent feelings about Marion's character are conveyed through her relationship with her brother Paul (Harris Yulin), a failed writer who idolizes Marion but also hates her, according to her sister-in-law, because Marion is her father's favourite and has always put her brother's literary efforts down.

Marion also recalls her affair with the passionate Larry Lewis (Gene Hackman), a novelist friend of Ken's, the memory conjured up for her at the time he first told her that he loved her. An emotional man, where her husband Ken is charming but cold, Larry is the only person to whom she has expressed her true feelings. With his vision and geniality, expansively delineated by Hackman, we are exposed to the film's life force, the affirmative character to be found, at least once, within the relative bleakness of Woody's more serious films. Larry had once asked Marion to run away with him - but safeness is all. Hers has been a life of lost chances, fashioned out of convenience and security.

Finally, Marion, increasingly obsessed with Hope, follows her through the streets and contrives an 'accidental' encounter. She invites the young woman to lunch - a fateful occasion, since it is in this same discreet restaurant that Marion simultaneously discovers Ken enjoying an intimate meal with her close friend Lydia (Blythe Danner). In all of this - a story which contains intimations of the break-up of four different couples' marriages - it is the one union which, at the outset, seemed most secure, which is now the most endangered. The seeds for its failure may be laid within the character of Marion herself. Judgemental and unemotional, she has led a cool, cerebral life, has gradually alienated everyone around her but, like Hope, she is prey to self-deception and has convinced herself she is just the opposite.

During her single lunchtime conversation with Hope, Marion does most of the talking and Hope just listens. In a curious reversal of their preordained roles, Hope seems to have taken on the guise of analyst; and, significantly, as if 'cured' by the problems of someone 'unhappier' than herself, Hope stops her sessions soon after, leaving no forwarding address.

Although *Another Woman* has more bite and humour than his previous 'serious' efforts, there is a classical rigidity in Woody's approach, especially in conveying the cool, almost overwrought perfection of the central couple's environment and the scrupulously sexless refinement of their marital relationship. We do, though, find a degree of optimism in the ending when Marion, having weighed up her life experience thus far, finally turns our thoughts to the ambiguities inherent in the film's title. This may refer to Hope, the strange young woman with whom Marion is obsessed, but meets only once, to the 'other woman' Lydia, with whom her husband is having an affair, or to yet 'another woman', the one inside Marion herself whom she has been assiduously suppressing for years. Deciding to strike out on her own, in a new apartment, Marion takes final reassurance from reading Larry's new novel and is comforted that the principal character is based on her. For the first moment in a long time, she has a feeling of peace.

Another Woman is at its best in its well-observed view of cultured Manhattanites with their studied passion for poetry, drama, opera and intellectual conversation, elements central to a film which is always fascinating, well acted, complex and austere. As usual, Woody is excellent at conveying the accoutrements of that lifestyle, while even the things his characters leave unsaid distances them even further from the working-class Jewish protagonists of his comedies.

The film's very Allenish concentration on death and dying was perhaps a significant element in its lack of commercial success. Indeed, John Houseman, as Marion's dying father, gives every impression of being on his last legs and did, in fact, die soon after completing his part in the movie. The mood is augmented by the look of the film - the browns and dull greens of an autumnal New York give it an almost monochrome quality. After numerous discussions with Nykvist, it was finally decided against shooting in black-and-white which Woody felt would give the film 'a sense of restraint'. To get the autumnal tone he wanted, there were enormous problems and Woody shot a full two hours of costume tests before he was satisfied. The neat oatmeal interiors, artistically shadowed, convey an atmosphere of almost Dreyer-like barrenness. A notable exception to this is the sequence in the antique store where the idea of 'Hope' is reflected by a genuine splash of bright colour. The store is hung with Tiffany lamps and partitioned with stained-glass screens, including a reproduction of Munch's 'Death and the Maiden', across which the camera lovingly pans, reminding us of this painter's role as a recurring cipher in Woody's work.

Another Woman is a perfect vehicle for Nykvist, working with Woody for the first time. Nykvist would be the cameraman on this and Woody's two subsequent pictures, while Di Palma was recuperating from a stomach operation. Unlike Gordon Willis, who is concerned with the full frame and not, specifically, with the actors, Nykvist is the ideal interpreter of actor-driven movies, like those of Bergman, framing every scene to illuminate the performers' faces - a style described by him as 'two faces and a teacup'. Woody, however, has said he is less at ease with the close-up than Bergman and, although *Another Woman*, like *Crimes and Misdemeanors*, makes imaginative use of the device, he tends to use it very sparingly and almost never for comedy. Nykvist, said Woody, was less happy, at least on the latter picture, with Woody's enthusiasm for warm colours and the 'dark look'. 'But their faces look like tomatoes!' Nykvist complained. Later, as Woody recalled to Stuart Jeffries, 'he got to like it. But even now the lab doesn't believe how dark I want the film.'

Principal photography was completed in January 1988, with Woody and Susan Morse working weekends and evenings to prepare an early rough cut. Woody was so pleased with the result he became convinced it was his real breakthrough as a dramatic film-maker and could be released exactly as it was. A series of reshoots were, however, set for the spring which Woody worked on during a break from filming Oedipus Wrecks. In the two-week wait for these, he also started the screenplay for Crimes and Misdemeanors. Robert Greenhut recalled that he and production manager Joe Hartwick were often driven mad by Woody's perfectionism on Another Woman, exemplified by a scene, already shot, which Woody decided to rewrite and shoot again on the very last day of filming. This required a new location, at the Union Theological Seminary in Manhattan which stood in for a classroom of Marion's college. The production had taken a great deal of Greenhut's inge-nuity to keep within budget and, like several of Woody's 'new' scenes, the sequence was ultimately cut. Woody also had trouble with the film's opening sequence which originally had Marion coming out of a neighbourhood deli with supplies for her new office, and walking along the street. This was to be accompanied by a voice-over of Marion 'introducing herself and explaining her work'. Woody intended to capture it all in a long master shot but, after a dolly track was laid on the sidewalk and Woody, on the camera seat, had him-self dollied through the shot, he suddenly changed his mind. The equipment which had taken two hours to set up was dismantled and the crew sent home. Instead, Marion, in the film's pre-title sequence, simply enters her apart-ment, accompanied by an introductory monologue, prior to setting off for her new workplace.

Alas, at early screenings for friends and close associates reaction to the film was lukewarm, several observers using words like 'cold' and 'boring'. Woody was especially stung by one of the subsequent criticisms of the pic-ture, that, like his previous film, the characters were deemed to be 'too old' to experience the kind of sexual/romantic problems they had in the story!

As with September, reviews were mixed. Richard Schickel who had been 'very positive' about its predecessor, raved, insisting that Another Woman demonstrated a 'lucidity and compassion of an order virtually unknown in

American movies'. To Woody's dismay, Vincent Canby, his most loyal supporter, published the only thoroughly downbeat notice he'd ever given him. Canby, in essence, felt that the film missed because Woody was making a movie about people he didn't really understand or know about. Similarly discouraging were Pauline Kael in *The New Yorker* and Amy Taubin in *The Village Voice*.

Denied Woody's usual New York showcase, the Beekman, *Another Woman* opened on only four screens in the US, grossed a little over $1.6m in 81 days and then sank, almost without trace. It opened the following July at three minor London cinemas, and did enjoy a modest run before going to video. Some of the British reviews were mostly ungrudging, but *Screen International*, echoing an increasingly general view of Woody's recent achievements, warned 'As Woody Allen retreats even further into Ingmar Bergman's navel, there's a danger he'll lose not only his funny bone but also his audience.' Through all of this Woody remained unshakeable, insisting, dishearteningly for his fans, that he wanted to spend less time acting and more just directing - the main reason he'd been absent from the screen for three films in a row.

Oedipus Wrecks The good news was *New York Stories* which had its roots in a conversation Woody had had with Robert Greenhut a couple of years previously. As Greenhut told Kathryn Kirby in *Films and Filming*, Woody had shared with him 'some short story ideas that he had absolutely no outlet for ... but he didn't want to attempt them as a feature film.' Although there was talk of incorporating several of Woody's stories into one picture, it was finally decided to make up a feature comprising three separate segments, each about 40 minutes long and made by three different directors, one of whom would be Woody. The film would reflect his admiration for the compendium movies of the 1940s, like *Tales of Manhattan*, and, although he would be the catalyst for the project - and the first to complete his segment - Woody was freed from the responsibility of sustaining an enterprise which, just like *Everything You Always Wanted to Know About Sex*, might not offer sufficient episodes of like quality.

Originally, Woody wanted to share the film with two European directors, but Greenhut persuaded him towards a more commercial, American triumvirate, especially since *New York Tales* (as it was first known) would comprise a series of featurettes, unrelated except for the common link of being set in New York and dealing with various aspects of the power of love.

There was no difficulty in finding any number of film-makers who, like Woody, had story ideas which they were unable to expand into feature length. This had been the thesis behind Don Boyd's *Aria* (1987) which delineated how ten directors reacted to different pieces of music in the operatic repertoire.

Although Woody had been approached to contribute, scheduling and/or other problems had ruled him out. For *New York Stories* Greenhut settled on Woody, Martin Scorsese and Steven Spielberg. When Spielberg was forced to back down due to completion problems on *Who Framed Roger Rabbit*, the final choice fell on Francis Coppola, a film-maker more closely identified with the city. In embarking on his segment, Coppola was to claim that 'New York is almost an unnamed character in the story.'

Shot at various times through 1988, these three short films were made with all their directors' usual dedication. But doubts about the project's commercial possibilities worried Orion, and the package was taken on by Disney subsidiary Touchstone (though it would be released by Warners in the UK) which agreed to finance it largely because 'the reputations of the directors outweighed any risks that might be inherent in a project like this'. Despite Greenhut's contention to the contrary, the film did not exactly set the box-office alight - a $10.8m US gross returned a net of $4.7m against an estimated negative cost of $19m plus $6m p & a. Greenhut's insistence that the film be presented less as a feature than as 'three distinct films by very distinguished film-makers' intimated what audiences could expect.

Woody's segment, the final one in the film, survived the experiment best. Called *Oedipus Wrecks*, it is the ultimate Jewish mother's joke and based on an idea he had had some time before. 'It'll be the *Gone with the Wind* of Israel', he joked. The opening story, *Life Class*, from Scorsese, was, said the director, 'the dramatic section, the part where everyone goes out to buy their popcorn'. Filming was completed by Scorsese in September, after wrestling with the final stages of *The Last Temptation of Christ*. Many critics actually enjoyed his contribution, a loose update of Dostoyevsky, reserving the majority of their put-downs for the middle segment, Coppola's *Life Without Zoe*. In this writer's view, however, the Coppola is a slight, though charming fable, and the Scorsese a bit of a bore.

As originally stipulated, each segment is concerned with the effects of love on the central characters, and each is carefully scripted, beautifully acted and stylishly shot by master cinematographers - Nestor Almendros, Vittorio Storaro and Sven Nykvist, respectively. All three filmlets are shot through with the warmth of their directors' individual perceptions of New York, each film-maker acting as a sort of unofficial spokesman for the city. In *Oedipus Wrecks*, familiar landmarks - from 42nd Street to Orchard Beach - again demonstrate for us where Woody is at and what he is about, though, ironically, it is left to Coppola to extol the ritzy, uptown world of the Sherry Netherland and Woody's favourite stamping ground, the Russian Tea Room.

Woody's milieu in the film is a more professional and workaday environment, transformed into the setting for an essentially Jewish, mother-ridden, blackly comic nightmare.

Sheldon Mills (Woody), a 50-year-old Jewish lawyer in an ultra-WASP firm, is engaged to divorced mother-of-three Lisa (Mia) - and it may be significant that the characters' first names are the same as those for the 'human' spiders in the missing segment from *Sex*! Sheldon is plagued by his domineering, over-possessive mother, Sadie Millstein - a hilarious turn by Mae Questel, the original off-screen voice for Olive Oyl and Betty Boop. Questel was, in fact, concurrently recycling the latter character for *Who Framed Roger Rabbit*, and had, at first, been reluctant to take on the role of Sadie. She was about the 30th actress Woody interviewed and, not having personally met her when she came in to record her vocal contribution to *Zelig*, he was now immediately struck by her resemblance to his own mother. 'She was authentically the character that I had written', insisted Woody to *The New York Times*, 'the energy, the tone of voice, the right amount of sarcasm without being obnoxious.' Another actress, Jessie Keosian, who played the role of Sheldon's 'Aunt Ciel' was actually Woody's childhood biology teacher and turned up after Juliet Taylor had canvassed a number of old folks' homes for suitable people of the right age. 'She had never acted before in her life', said Woody, 'She was just wonderful.'

Sadie in the story is a persistent source of embarrassment to her son, wingeing endlessly about his gentile girlfriend, his bald spot, his hiatus hernia, his sucking on a blanket in childhood, his Aryanized surname, and offering constant complaints about him in public. She and the film's theme are, ironically, characterized by the old vaudeville number, 'I want a Girl Just Like the Girl That Married Dear Old Dad' and, when Sheldon and Lisa take Sadie and Lisa's children out on the town, they end up at a magic show where, like the hapless Professor Kugelmass, she is persuaded to step into a magician's cabinet. Sheldon has often expressed the wish that his mother would just *disappear* and now, through the magician's inadvertent artifice, she obligingly does so!

Sheldon hires a private detective called Flynn (Paul Herman) to track Sadie down, but without success. At the same time his life begins to improve. No sooner though, has Sheldon learned to relax, than Sadie suddenly reappears out of the clouds, as a vast Oedipal vision, looming down over the top of the Chrysler Building like a long-lost Jewish relative of the Goodyear Blimp! It is a brilliant concept and direct inspiration for the gag came to Woody in a characteristically roundabout way. As he told Silvio Bizio in August 1990:

Once, long before I did *New York Stories*, I was sitting in my apartment looking up at the sky and I was listening to a jazz record [soprano saxophonist
Sidney Bechet] ... and I thought to myself, 'Wouldn't it be wonderful if I
could see that musician in the sky playing music and, you know, only I could
hear this musician playing it for the whole city?' and I thought 'Wouldn't that
be a good image for a movie?' and gradually that evolved from many
thoughts into 'Wouldn't it be embarrassing if my mother was there?' ... and
that's how it came.

From her aerial vantage point the giant Sadie maintains constant vigil over
Sheldon's activities, telling him to wrap up warm, and giving a running commentary on his shortcomings - to which the whole population of New York
and the media become party. Mayor Ed Koch (in a gag cameo) pronounces on
the problem on TV and, at one point, but with farcical results, Sheldon
attempts suicide by putting his fingers in a lamp socket. Finally, just like the
protagonists of *Alice* and *Play it Again, Sam*, Sheldon seeks help from an
unorthodox 'magical' quarter, in this case a woman called Treva Marx (Julie
Kavner), a mystic and breaker of spells.

Treva, though a fake, is sweetly well meaning and there is a funny, tender
scene where Sheldon, returning to his apartment to find a 'Dear John' letter
awaiting him from Lisa, slowly unwraps the remains of a chicken dinner Treva
has sent home with him. To the utterly romantic strains of Jerome Kern's 'All
the Things You Are', Sheldon takes out the chicken leg, inspecting it and sniffing it wistfully, as an expression of rapture gradually suffuses his face. It is as
if a great light had illuminated things, with Sheldon resignedly acknowledging
the victory, through bodily sustenance, of the Jewish girl over the *shiksa*. Only
when Sheldon has become engaged to Treva, the woman in the story who *most*
resembles his mother, does Sadie relent and everything go back to normal.

As in many another cinematic exposition of stifling Jewish maternalism,
Oedipus Wrecks suggests that one's problems may end the moment the mother
figure is eliminated. Sheldon (except in his wildest fantasies) does not go so
far as the George Segal character in *Where's Poppa?* by actively seeking his
mother's death. For him, the simple act of 'disappearance' is enough. Also, like
all good Jewish fables, it turns out in the end, that mother knows best. In her
skyscape 'Cheshire Cat' persona, Sadie has become a symbol of the 'all-seeing
eye' which assesses our actions and judges our sins. It is an idea central to the
theme of Jewish guilt and Jewish persecution (or, in Woody's case, persecution
mania!) - given its most felicitous outlet here in the sequence where Sheldon
has his boyhood bedwetting discussed on the evening news - while the shots of

Sheldon being chased through the streets by the New York media not only echo *Stardust Memories*, but, oddly, anticipate Woody's own very public exposure in 1992-3.

'I must say I'm quite happy with the way it came out', said Woody, 'but then forty minutes is a very *controllable* length.' *Oedipus Wrecks* garnered him some of his best all-round reviews since *Hannah*, especially in Britain. 'Kafka meets Sophocles over the East River', quipped Philip French in *The Observer*, while John Mortimer suggested the story could have been written by Gogol.

Initial filming had taken place over a three-week period in and around the reshoots for *Another Woman*, but *Oedipus Wrecks* was itself subject to 'a monumental number of reshoots', as well as numerous attempts with Nancy Bernstein and R/Greenberg Associates to get the effects of the giant mother exactly right. 'It was fun', Woody told Stig Björkmann, 'and Sven shot it correctly, but it was a long time getting it to work up there. You know, to get the proper way of tapering her off. That was a big nuisance.' Woody was equally meticulous in minor details, rejecting the expensive smart lawyer's suits originally obtained for him by costume designer Jeffrey Kurland. After viewing the dailies for the film's opening scene - where Sheldon talks directly to camera in his psychoanalyst's office - Woody felt the look went against his received image and would be unacceptable to the audience. He reshot the monologue with coat off and tie loosened, perched on a small Queen Anne chair instead of the large overstuffed leather one of the original takes. Woody had actually promised no reshoots on the movie but, as he reasoned to Greenhut, 'No, no, reshoots are what you do after a picture is *completed*. These are revisions.'

Questel was to recall that her original four-week contract, with all the rewrites and recalls, was to run into six months since, impressed by her ability to improvise, Woody encouraged her to use up unlimited footage and 'say some terrible things', making the role of Sadie even more monstrous. In spite of what has been held to be Woody's ambivalent feelings about his own mother, he was to deny that Sadie was based on 'any specific person'. He was also quick to point out that the aggressive, overbearing traits of the film's character exist in many mothers, not just Jewish ones, and are invariably 'motivated from genuine affection - a deep love really.'

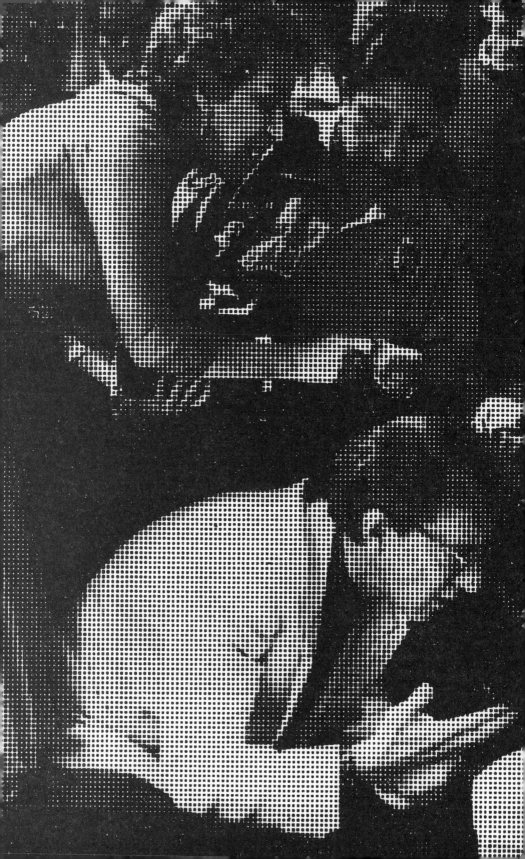

9

God, Guilt, Sex, Death, the Whole Damn Thing

1989-92: Crimes and Misdemeanors to Shadows and Fog

Crimes and Misdemeanors Concurrent with *New York Stories*, Woody was also represented by the 20-minute dance drama *Dimitri*, derived from his Benchleyesque *New Yorker* sequence 'A Guide to Some of the Lesser Ballets'. Set to the music of Verdi by choreographer Stanley Holden, former character dancer with the Royal Ballet, it was premièred by the Los Angeles Chamber Ballet at the Japan American Theatre, on 16 February 1989. Containing spoofs of *Petroushka* and *Giselle* to point up the extreme silliness of classical ballet plots, it was produced on a shoestring $20,000 and made possible through the good offices of Woody's friend and erstwhile co-star, Paula Prentiss.

Meanwhile, in the summer of 1988, Woody had combined a family vacation in Europe with scouting locations for a movie he had in mind, reputedly a Yank-in-Europe plot to be filmed by Sven Nykvist in Norway or Sweden. This plan came to nothing, as did a more bizarre project with which Woody had been, reportedly, in negotiations with Clint Eastwood. A Western(!), it was to have been written by Woody, who would play the baddie, with Eastwood directing and playing the hero. First mooted in the Fall of 1988 and expected to go before the cameras in 1991, this odd idea has yet to get going, possibly due to Woody's apparent insistence that it all be shot in the New York borough of Queens! Woody told me that reports of the plan were 'just not true, the story is false', but of all the unrealized possiblities which he *might* have considered, an Allen-Eastwood link-up is surely the most mouthwatering!

Woody's actual Fall Project '88 finally got underway in New York in early October, with Nykvist again transposing some deft Bergmanesque flourishes on to a story of typical angst-ridden Woody Allen Manhattanites. On this occasion, the result was a dark, witty, moral comedy which many considered Woody's most satisfying full-length work since *Hannah and Her Sisters*.

Unlike *Hannah*, with its interlocking family stories, *Crimes and Misdemeanors* is virtually two films in one, its parts tenuously associated through a single character and only briefly touching until they converge for the film's adeptly-written final sequence. This is the wedding reception given for the daughter of the blind rabbi Ben (Sam Waterston), who is the link between the tales - the unofficial 'confessor' to one of the film's two main protagonists and brother-in-law to the other.

The confessionee is Judah Rosenthal (Martin Landau), a distinguished oph-thalmologist and public benefactor who has been trying to extricate himself from a burned-out affair with a hysterical former air hostess, Dolores Paley (Anjelica Huston). She is threatening to expose him as an embezzler, and rat on his infidelity to his wife, Miriam (Claire Bloom). This section of the film seems uneasy because Huston, with her imposing build and implicit strength of character, is not the actress who instantly springs to mind for the role of an unstable clinging vine. Woody has explained the casting on the grounds that he was deliberately looking for someone who was 'big and impressive' and with just 'enough craziness and anger' to be interesting. Huston does evoke our sympathy and, with Dolores as the catalyst, the story lapses, quite divertingly, into melodrama. This occurs when Judah's black-sheep brother, Jack (Jerry Orbach), intimates that he and some associates will 'straighten her out'.

Judah, an aesthete, is appalled, but, remaining discreetly *in absentia*, he agrees to go along with the plan to murder Dolores. The details of his mis-tress's 'removal', intercut with flashbacks to happier times, are neatly woven into the proceedings. The contrast between the two brothers - one cultured, one roughneck - is mirrored in the parallel story, which deals with Clifford Stern (Woody), an unsuccessful documentary film director, and his brother-in-law Lester (Alan Alda), a smug and narcissistic millionaire TV comedy producer. Lester is also the brother of rabbi Ben, and *Brothers* was Woody's own favourite of over 20 titles he had previously considered.

Although Clifford's professional bag is stories about child hunger and toxic waste, he is also addicted to Hollywood films of the 1930s and 1940s. In this he is abetted by his young, fatherless niece, Jenny (Jenny Nichols) for whose cultural education he is making himself responsible. The film clips we see serve as both thematic links between the two main stories and comments on key moments in the action. They also point up Woody's recurring fascina-tion with fantasy versus reality and offer ironic illustration of the artistic chasm between the bleak *cinema verité* creations of Clifford, the social realist film-maker, and the more popular entertainment 'manufactured' by Lester.

Lester hires Clifford to make a documentary about himself - 'The Creative Mind At Work' - which Clifford reluctantly undertakes in order to finance his smaller, personal film on Professor Louis Levy, a largely unregarded philosopher of the human spirit who finally shakes Clifford out of his narrow 'artist's' pose by committing suicide. In the interim, Clifford falls for the Lester film's associate producer, Halley Reed (Mia Farrow), a wistful-looking but ambitious divorcée, who appears to share similar artistic aims and outlook as Clifford. Clifford, though, is fired from the film, after intercutting Lester with clips of Mussolini and Francis the Talking Mule!

Judah, like Clifford, is an 'educator' - his more cosmopolitan aspect apparently inspired by Louise Lasser's tax-lawyer father - and, in the flashbacks, he gently allows his own culture to wash over the untutored Dolores. The antithesis is Lester whose only brief - notwithstanding his Harvard degree - is to entertain. Untouched by self-doubt, Lester further counterbalances his brother Ben who remains the most morally convinced character in the film. The sweetness of Ben, his acceptance of his imminent blindness, and his placement as more than just a mere sounding-board for the morally wavering Judah, are elements conveyed with grace and charm by Waterston.

The film devolves on a series of moral choices and their consequences, and the way the problems of Clifford are juxtaposed against the darker tones of the parallel story. The anxieties of Judah are exacerbated by the fact that he is not a religious man ('God is a luxury I can't afford'), but is still subject to the spiritual conditioning of his childhood. 'The eyes of God are on us, always' says Judah's scholarly Orthodox Jewish father Sol (David S. Howard), who appears in the flashbacks to earlier times. 'And what were God's eyes like?' muses Judah, 'unimaginably penetrating and intense eyes, I assumed.'

Woody has readily acknowledged that 'eyes' were, in fact, the starting point for the story which, as he explained to Stig Björkmann, contrasts one man (Judah) 'whose vision is fine, but his emotional vision, his moral vision is not good', with another (the rabbi Ben) who is 'blind to other things, to the realities of life … *Crimes and Misdemeanors* is about people who don't see. They don't see themselves as others see them. They don't see the right and wrong situations. And that was a strong metaphor in the movie.'

As Judah lapses into conscious-struck apathy and alcoholic excess over the summary despatch of his mistress, his almost obsessive compulsion for tangible punishment becomes central to the story. The Dostoyevskian resonances of Woody's punning title also turn on the idea that, if the law fails to punish a man for his misdeeds and if he doubts the existence of God, then he must, perforce, take that responsibility upon himself.

Another theme, the contrast between 'real' and popular art, touched on in previous Allen films, is given added complexity through the idea that the documentaries which Clifford makes and which impress Halley, might be the key that will unlock her emotions and lead her to him. However, despite her initial apparent contempt for Lester and his questionable values, it is *his* extrovert persistence which finally pays off.

Clifford, by Lester's standards, is a loser, and the film makes the point, quite matter-of-factly, that the successful are in every way happier. Even Judah, though briefly haunted by 'little sparks of his religious background' has also connived *successfully* at murder and once he realizes that fear of discovery and even feelings of guilt may pass, one sees him, finally, almost untouched by it all. The cynicism of this idea, suggested Pauline Kael, was 'symptomatic of the Reagan eighties' - further exemplified by the way Clifford is left as the real victim of the story; jobless, unsuccessful and unloved; this is the only time in any Allen movie where his character had failed, even momentarily, to get the girl.

The film moving between the immediate present and various recollections of the past, is a virtually seamless exercise in cinematic sleight-of-hand. In eschewing old-style cue-ins to flashback, like soft-focus dissolves or deliberate mood breaks, Woody again fosters the idea that past and present may be subjectively indivisible. The model is, once again, *Wild Strawberries* and Judah's recollective visit to the house he was brought up in is a virtual shot-for-shot reworking of Professor Borg's return to his boyhood home in the Bergman film.

Judah is subjected to an almost Dickensian confrontation with the figures of his past, his adult presence hovering on the fringes of a *Pesach Seder* attended by, amongst others, his father, his radical schoolteacher aunt, May (Anna Berger) and his boyhood self (Garrett Simowitz). The table discussion turns on the fate of the six million who died in the camps. Conjecturing on the reason why so many of the murderers got away with it, Aunt May insists, cynically, that 'Might makes right' and 'History is written by the winners'.

Woody's view of the concentration camp as a 'metaphor for life' (a line cut from *Manhattan*) is an ongoing theme and even his early films are brimful of dark 'Nazi' jokes, drawn from his night-club act. In *Crimes and Misdemeanors*, Professor Levy is a central figure and, like the late novelist and chemist Primo Levi, he is a concentration-camp survivor who has become a philosopher on the nature of forgiveness and survival. When the film came out, lawyers acting for the Levi estate contacted Woody to enquire whether the professor's pronouncements and tragic suicide were intended to reflect Levi's in real life. Woody denied that Levi was an inspiration, the character's genesis to be found in the old 'existential murder mystery' he had been working on as the embryo for *Annie Hall*. In that script, however, Woody had defined the professor as a man who, given his specific philosophy, could *not* have committed suicide - so murder became the key. The role of Professor Levy is played by New York psychiatrist Martin Bergmann who improvised his own lines, and these do carry very strong echoes of Primo Levi's humanist philosophy.

At the Waldorf wedding party which closes the film Clifford, nursing his wounds over the revelation of Halley's affair with Lester, retires to an unoccupied room where Judah, a fellow guest, discovers him. Judah tells Clifford that he has 'a great murder story, a great plot' which, as he relates it, turns out to be the film we have just seen. However, in this version, the man in the story wakes up to find the sun shining and the weight which has been pressing on his conscience ... miraculously lifted. Both the man in the story and, it is implied, Judah himself, have escaped punishment or, at least, punishment in the Dostoyevskian sense as implied by Woody's ironically distorted title.

Clifford suggests to Judah that only by turning himself in can the man in the story afford the enterprise a truly tragic dimension. But real life, says Judah, just isn't like that - 'that's fiction, that's movies'; 'If Frank Capra had made this film in 1945', Landau told Sheila Johnston, 'my character would have confessed to his wife, and given himself up as the music swelled. But this is about now, and it's somewhat cynical. In not coming to terms with things, Woody Allen allows people to draw their own moral conclusions.'

In American cinema, the unpunished crime is a relatively recent narrative concept and, even in the late 1980s, Judah's 'final solution', and the (implied) strain of misogyny to be discerned in the story's thesis, aroused controversy. Landau was to confess himself unnerved that men in the audience were actively rooting for his character and appalled at the hair-raising stories related to him when researching his role by real-life adulterers of his acquaintance. 'There is no question', he said, 'that men often want to get rid of their mistresses if they could find a way. I found a lot of men in Judah's situation. Some were doctors, like him, living on a knife edge ... I drew on everything I had to make Judah real. I thought it was the worst nightmare a man can have.'

As one would expect, the performances are first rate. Woody, looking older and now bearing an uncanny resemblance to Stan Laurel, gives a touching account of the archetypal loser. Mia plays up to him beautifully, subtly suggesting the paradox of a young woman who knows what she wants but has a disturbing way of convincing herself and others that she wants something entirely different. Alan Alda (who, as a writer-director, has been described as 'Middle America's answer to Woody Allen') goes, amusingly, against his customary all-round good-egg persona - and has recalled how much he welcomed the opportunity to play 'a complete shit'. But the film's most compelling performance is Landau's. As a man who has made the irreversible decision not to be 'blown by ethics' he turns in the most rewarding piece of work he has yet done on screen.

Woody had completed the first draft of the screenplay, mostly in hotel rooms (and on hotel stationery!), during the family's European tour. He has said that he had enormous problems with the film's structure, a task not made any easier by his insistence on keeping the two main strands of the story separate. Part of the problem was eventually solved by the music - Bach and Schubert for the 'serious' scenes, Cole Porter, Rodgers and Hart *et al.* for the comedy - but more importantly by shooting the film as if it were two different movies. Even within this context, Anjelica Huston was given only her own sections of the script to read, while the actors playing Judah's family were kept in the dark about Dolores. Indeed, according to a mutual acquaintance, 'Claire Bloom, for one, was very disconcerted. She told me she *never* had a proper script. She arrived there to film the first day and asked Woody Allen what she was supposed to do, and he said, "Oh, you know, just say what you like. Make something up." She was very good in it, though.' Pressed for her personal comments on the filming, 'I have really nothing whatsoever to say about Woody Allen', Bloom told me, 'I disagree with you over the merits or demerits of *Crimes and Misdemeanors*. I thought it mindless and spurious, and Woody Allen's rediscovered Jewishness quite repellent. The film - or my part of it - was shot in New Jersey, in a small and hideous town on the Hudson. I am not a fan, as you can see.'

Landau, who takes a warmer view, did receive a finished screenplay, delivered in great secrecy, with a tentative offer, originally, of the Orbach role. Woody and Juliet Taylor had been impressed by his supporting performance in *Tucker* and, after Landau had actually accepted the part of Jack, Woody decided to test him for Judah. Woody noted later that Landau came across instantly as that character and 'Of all the actors I've ever worked with, he gives expression to my dialogue exactly as I hear it.' Although keen to do the part, Landau was worried that in the original version of the script Judah had no redeeming feature. 'Why on earth', he complained, 'would people want to spend time watching this asshole?' Woody hired him on the spot and, acceding to Mia and Landau's urgings, agreed to make changes. There were numerous revisions to Landau's scenes with Huston, while another change was in the actor initially playing Jack who, after two days, was replaced by Orbach.

Other problems became evident when Woody viewed the first rough assembly in March 1989. Although encouraged by the film as a whole, he felt that the original Clifford-Halley story just 'didn't work'. In the event, Woody would throw out nearly 50 per cent of his first cut, comprising mostly, his own and Mia's segments. 'I wasn't happy with it', he told Nigel Andrews in July 1991, 'It wasn't sharp enough or funny enough. So I completely rewrote it and brought in the Alan Alda character, who was brand-new at that point.' He also decided to strengthen the early scenes between Judah and Dolores, making her less hysterical and turning two sequences into one. The Cliff-Jenny relationship in the original version was much stronger, as were the scenes involving Clifford's widowed sister Babs (Caroline Aaron). The first Clifford-Halley story had Cliff making a documentary at a psychiatric nursing home for retired vaudevillians, including Clifford's own parents. Halley, a social worker involved with the geriatrics, is on the staff. Cliff falls in love with her, but she is both married and having an affair, and, at one point, he and Jenny trail her lover across Central Park. Near the end of the film Cliff poses as a TV producer in order to move on his affair with an aspiring actress (Sean Young), and is caught with her, *in flagrante*, at the wedding party.

Woody, initially, rewrote and reshot ten scenes, altering the details of the Clifford-Halley story, eliminating the roles of Sean Young and Halley's lover, transforming the Alda role into more of a comic character and reducing Darryl Hannah as actress 'Lisa Crossley' to an uncredited cameo. According to Jami Bernard in *The New York Post*, it was rumoured that Woody had cast Hannah 'just so he could stage a few love scenes with her. They did retake after retake'. Finally, she appeared, only briefly, in the release version, as Lester's date, at the TV series launch party. Woody also had trouble with the sequence where, after viewing Hitchcock's *Mr and Mrs Smith*, Cliff and Jenny emerge from the Bleecker Street cinema into the street. Woody reshot the scene on at least 15 separate occasions, incorporating various changes, but the line he was trying to illustrate (Clifford's 'Oh, God, sunlight - traffic') was finally unused.

The Clifford-Jenny episodes were loosely based on Woody's relationship with his sister Letty. She is eight years younger than himself and they have retained their early closeness. As with a number of women Woody knows and respects, he has often used Letty as a sounding board for his film ideas. In the movie, Jenny is Cliff's one real friend and, in the original (cut) ending he tells her that 'The future of the world is in little girls.' At one point Woody had decided on an uplifting sequence to cap the film. This was to have been set in a movie theatre, where Cliff and Jenny go to see a whizz-bang Technicolor musical with Esther Williams. However, taking his cue from his dissatisfaction with *Hannah*, he decided against making the ending of *Crimes and Misdemeanors* 'too happy'.

Visually the film is much warmer than *Another Woman* and Nykvist's fluid camera style combines with Santo Loquasto's interior design to conjure some striking painterly images.

Opening in the US in October 1989 to some of Woody's best reviews ever, *Crimes and Misdemeanors* was also considered sufficiently weighty for three distinguished theologians to discuss the film seriously in *The New York Times*. It was to stay in the box-office charts for 19 weeks to a gross of $17.6m and made a further $2m the following year. This was Woody's best showing in North America for some time and Orion's second biggest moneymaker of the year, though the film's $8.5m net against an estimated negative cost of $13m plus $7m p & a seemed altogether less sanguine. Woody's reputation however had never been higher. He came out as the fourteenth top director in *Première* magazine's annual list of the 100 most powerful 'movers' in Hollywood. In a poll organized by the American Film Institute, leading critics named him second only to Scorsese amongst the best American film directors of the 1980s. (*Manhattan*, though released in 1979, was runner-up to *Raging Bull* as favourite film.) All of this suggested, amidst heavy rumours that Orion might be unwilling to renew his contract, that Woody's clout, at least for prestige purposes, was as strong as ever.

Alice In early November 1989, Woody had already begun work on *Alice*, 'a whimsical non-realistic contemporary comedy', he said, 'about a wife who goes through a remarkable set of experiences at a critical point of her life'. He saw the film as a sort of comic counterpoint to *Another Woman*, wherein a similar kind of heroine 'comes to examine her life, in a different way, but still with a similar purpose'. Woody apparently got the idea for *Alice* when he found himself being treated for a painful stye in his eye by a downtown acupuncturist. The treatment, said Woody, involved manipulating a cat's whisker in the tear duct. Although it didn't work, he was immediately struck by the thought that any number of rich and sophisticated women did believe in the acupuncturist's various treatments and made a beeline for his door.

This basic premise - that each one of us, no matter how sophisticated is constantly searching for a 'magic cure-all' - began to be linked in his mind with his observations of the numerous well-to-do women he'd seen around the environs of his Upper East Side apartment - going out, wearing beautiful fur coats, taking their kids to school, having lunch, coming home from lunch but giving little indication of the kind of lives they led in between.

The result is an odd little fable about a well-cushioned, but anxious, Manhattan housewife, Alice Tait (Mia) who, happily if unexcitingly married for

16 years to a wealthy, self-satisfied Yuppie, Douglas (William Hurt), devotes her days to shopping, pedicures, lunching and gossiping with the girls. Although she has come to accept this leisured lifestyle, Alice, like some earlier Allen characters, is fretful about the ordinariness of her life and suffers about not helping other people. She is also troubled by her erotic feelings for tenor saxophonist Joe Rufilho (Joe Mantegna), a fellow-parent she meets at her children's kindergarten.

Alice is also prey to what Woody seems to see as the non-working woman's favourite pastime - hypochondria - and, seeking relief for a bad back, she visits the establishment of a mysterious acupuncturist and herbal doctor called Yang (Keye Luke). The captivating strains of 'Limehouse Blues' cue in Chinatown where Dr Yang advises Alice it is not her back, but her head and her heart which are troubling her.

Through drugs, Himalayan herbs and even hypnotism, Yang grants Alice the gift of invisibility and magical access to the experiences of her past. She is propelled into a dream world where she observes without being observed, confronting a vision of her husband working away at his office and reliving the night when he first proposed. Other herbs precipitate Alice into fantasy encounters with the ghost of her long-lost love, Eddie (Alec Baldwin), a would-be painter, who was killed in a car crash after she had rejected *his* proposal of marriage. She also glimpses her younger self and her parents - naval officer father (Patrick O'Neal) and her mother (Gwen Verdon), a third-rate movie actress who, although grateful to wed when the studio dropped her contract, drank herself to death on margaritas.

Too nervous to keep a date with Joe, Alice calls up the ghostly presence of Eddie to advise her. Eddie whisks her, Peter Pan-like, over the rooftops of a nocturnal New York and they end up dancing once more in the long-burned-out shell of the Moonlight Casino, scene of their youthful amour and now illuminated, exclusively, by 'lunar spotlight'. Alice also enlists in a creative writing course, but is fobbed off by old friend, TV executive Nancy Brill (Cybill Shepherd) who tells her, quite bluntly, that her 'little middle-class story ideas' scarcely match up to the mass audience's propensity for melodrama and sex. One's recognition that Alice lacks the talent to further her literary ambitions is also voiced by another of the film's ghostly apparitions - Alice's 'Muse' (a suitably bedraggled Bernadette Peters) who appears, like Marley's Ghost, in order to persuade her to concentrate on what is important.

Meanwhile, Joe and Alice become lovers but, thanks to her herbally induced power of invisibility, she discovers that Joe still has something going with his ex-wife Vicki (Judy Davis), a high-powered business woman. Making use of the powers that Alice has granted him also, Joe, alas, does what he has always wanted to do - eavesdrop on Vicki's sessions with her analyst. These reveal that she still loves Joe. Alice then witnesses her husband's affair with an office colleague and, in the confrontation that follows, it emerges that Douglas has been cheating on her for years.

Alice's metamorphosis is finally engineered through her own devices and from the seeds of the do-goodery which lie at the roots of her character. Inspired by a screening of Louis Malle's *India*, she goes off to work with Mother Teresa in Calcutta, returning some time later to do social work among the ethnic community in downtown New York. If we accept that the film is clearly satirizing Mia's earlier real-life flirtations with transcendentalism, her propensity for good works and adoption of Third World orphans, it is done with affection.

The story of *Alice* is conjured out of Woody's long-time fascination with illusion and magic and his view that these and a number of other 'fads' have tended to take the place of religion in many people's lives. The film would also appear to be dependent on a number of literary sources - Dickens, Lewis Carroll, J.M. Barrie and Frank L. Baum - while, at the same time, reflecting the popularity of some recent Hollywood movies, notably the late 1980s cycle of ghost films and stories of characters stepping back in time and reviving their youth.

Although he has said that, in his opinion *Alice*, like *Hannah*, was compromised in that he ended it 'incorrectly', the film is almost a summing up of Woody's work thus far, anthologizing a number of the concerns which have intrigued him. There is, for instance, the theme of change - the idea that people can improve themselves, and have a better life if certain opportunities appear to them. Against this must be set a darker view, exemplified by Dr Yang's line 'Freedom is a frightening thought' - an existential axiom which was to recur in *Manhattan Murder Mystery* - with the strong implication that, in certain circumstances, change and liberation may be less than benign. Or, as someone says in *Husbands and Wives*, 'change is death'.

Alice's retrospective journeyings remind one of several Allen movies which have utilized this device. These sequences are lit by Carlo Di Palma to suggest, yet again, that present, past and even future may, in ideal circumstances, be indistinguishable. Once more Woody deals with lost illusions, blindness versus sight, innocence and guilt. Intriguingly also, *Alice* reflects his little publicized interest in clairvoyance and psychic phenomena. (During his first marriage, Woody had briefly lived in a small apartment on West 75th Street, an address once inhabited by famous 'psychic explorer' Sir Arthur Conan Doyle. According to his friends of that time, Woody was himself gifted with psychic powers.)

Finally, the film is an almost worshipful homage to Mia, although Geoff Andrew was not alone in seeing her as 'little more than a female surrogate for Woody's own persona'. For her performance as Alice, Mia won the National Board of Review's Best Actress citation for 1990.

In a July 1991 interview with Nigel Andrews, Woody said that Juliet Taylor would regularly receive casting submissions from players who, on the surface, would never be thought of as likely participants in an Allen movie. The opportunity to do something which 'tries to be a grown-up film' was obviously appealing to actors. Although such names do not necessarily 'resonate at the box-office' (as with Madonna, say, in *Shadows and Fog*), the attraction of being in one of his films meant that Woody could cast someone like Patrick O'Neal in a wordless bit; directors James Toback and Bob Balaban as, respectively, a professor of scriptwriting and Alice's diminutive admirer, Sid Moscowitz, and 84-year-old Keye Luke in his final screen role. Joe Mantegna is interestingly cast as the good-natured Joe Rufilho, the role necessitating his flying back and forth from Italy (where he was concurrently shooting *Godfather Part III*) in order to complete Woody's reshoots. There was also a debut cameo for Australian supermodel Elle Macpherson in a scene where Joe uses the cloak of invisibility to watch her undress! As for William Hurt, Woody received a call from his agent, saying he'd 'love to do something' in one of his pictures and 'when he came in', said Woody, 'he knew exactly what that character was to begin with ... He was fun to work with, and he did a great job.'

Woody's working title for *Alice* had been *The Magical Herbs of Dr Yang*, but he felt that this gave away too much of the plot. His notes to the crew suggested that the film should be very stylish, use a wider colour spectrum than usual and have 'a nice cartoon quality, to some degree like *Radio Days*'. The very elaborate trick work was put in the hands of Randall Balsmeyer and Mimi Everett whose design and technical skills had already been utilized by a number of New York-based film-makers such as Spike Lee and the Coen brothers. Their skills had also been responsible for Patrick Swayze passing convincingly through solid objects in *Ghost*.

Balsmeyer and Everett found themselves instantly challenged by Woody's emphatic insistence that the film's visual effects should do nothing to 'overpower the acting' or get in the way of his direction. The usual techniques of mattes and mirror shots were unsuited to Woody's established practice of shooting mainly in long continuous takes. Due, it is thought, to Woody's experience with bad looping on *Casino Royale*, he has, on his own films, generally insisted on production sound only. He is known to post-synchronize rarely - 'I don't believe in it', he has said, and so, although Balsmeyer and Everett had pioneered some of the latest techniques in motion-controlled camerwork, this was initially ruled out due to the bulky equipment and noise. To circumvent these problems, Balsmeyer settled on a lock-and-pan technique, allowing fluid camera movement in scenes until a specific effect was introduced. Woody has recalled, though, that, as usual with special effects, he found it all something of an ordeal and somewhat protracted, often finding himself in a position of having to cut a number of shots which had taken all day to make: 'After agonizing work we did finally have to get a camera with a computer. The whole process was very, very difficult', he told Stig Björkmann - and was not helped by the restricted $12m budget at a time when the average New York film cost was $23.5m. For the invisibility sequences, Balsmeyer went for a version of the soft-screen mattes he had employed in *Dead Ringers*: 'To make people appear and disappear we used a soft-edged light, as they would usually disappear from the feet up. The last visible part was their head and that would fade.'

He also managed to convince Woody that, by using a soft split-screen technique, he could keep Alec Baldwin's ghost transparent at all times, without interfering with the performance of the actors. 'We could always photograph the ghost and whoever else was involved all together', said Balsmeyer, 'get the matching background shots and put the ghost in as a percentage exposure.'

For the sequence where Alice and Eddie fly off into the night sky, Balsmeyer employed Preston Cinema Systems' Gyrosphere, a gyro-stabilized camera mount, shooting background plates for the flying effects from a helicopter. This was supervised by Bob Harman, the flying-rig specialist from the *Superman* films, who suggested the use of blue screen to composite the actors. Balsmeyer erected the screen at the Kaufman Astoria and, as he told Dan Scapperotti in *Cinéfantastique*:

We were able to erect an 80-foot track for the camera to move on, which ultimately turned the sequence into a motion-control shoot. We built a platform 8 feet high, 8 wide and 80 feet long that we laid dolly track on. We set up our motion-control rig on that. We suspended the actors on flying rigs about twelve feet off the end of the track so that they could be made to rise and fall and swivel by an operator above them, like marionettes.

Later, in the lab, the disparate elements were joined together to form a composite impression of the characters in flight. The result of all this meant that the flying sequences in *Alice* 'felt part of the same movie rather than some bolted-on special effects.'

Filming had begun in November 1989 but, after shooting for only six days, Woody felt that the work thus far had missed the essential quality he was looking for and that he had virtually no usable footage. In despair, he even conceived the fantasy of having himself hospitalized, so Orion could claim on the insurance. Woody shot and reshot the movie, maddened by small details like a wrong camera angle in a sequence filmed on Madison Avenue or the sudden glimpse of Mia's white dress under her deep-red coat as she walked across Central Park. The white dress ruined the aesthetics of the scene, he complained. 'All this obsession, it isn't perfectionism', he admitted, 'It's obsession, compulsion - and all of that is no guarantee that the film is going to be any good.' And yet, at approximately $100,000 a day, Woody's films at that time were still relatively cheap by average standards.

By the end of shooting, Woody did in fact have to check himself into hospital. By this time he had reshot about half the movie. After viewing the first rough cut, he also rewrote and reshot the beginning and the end, feeling that he had put insufficient emphasis on Alice's selfish, consumerist lifestyle and the undercurrent of Catholic guilt which in the final stages of the film will impel her to go to Calcutta. At one point, Woody included a voice-over letter in which Alice informs her well-read radical sister, Dorothy (Blythe Danner), that she will be coming back to the US. Considering that this failed to bridge the gap satisfactorily between the old lifestyle and her more selfless one, he decided to show this visually, returning Alice to work with the homeless in a milieu far removed from her comfortable Manhattan. Woody finished editing the movie one morning in May 1990 and, in the afternoon of the same day, immediately began the first draft of what would become *Shadows and Fog*. This he completed before starting work on Paul Mazursky's *Scenes from a Mall* in June.

Although more clearly angled to popular success than any of his recent films, and heralded, in some quarters, as Woody's first 'New-Age' comedy, *Alice* grossed a mere $5.9m ($3.3m net) in the US. It also did less well than expected in some other territories, but Columbia, which distributed in France, succeeded in turning the film into a major event in that country. Opening in February, *Alice* shot straight to the number 3 spot in Paris, emerging as the city's fifth top crowd-puller of 1991. Woody's opinion of the film, that it turned out only 'Average ... average to what I had conceived of' may be taken, as usual, at less than face value. Although not one of his major works, it must be counted as an at least unofficial Christmas present to all those loyal fans of the lighter Woody.

Scenes from a Mall It is arguable that *Alice* might have done a great deal better than it did, had the film's release not coincided with the still increasing problems of Orion. The studio's inability to provide sufficient funds for promotion and distribution had seriously undermined the box-office expectations of several movies. Although bolstered, in February 1990, by a $175m distribution deal with a product-hungry Columbia (guaranteeing theatrical and video rights to an unspecified number of future films), ripples of discontent within the company began to surface with the abrupt departure of several key executives.

By late summer, Woody had completed his stint on *Scenes from a Mall*, his first leading role in another director's movie since 1976. Not that he had been short of offers: intriguingly, only a short time before, he had been the personal choice of high-profile lawyer (and subsequent Mia Farrow supporter) Alan Dershowitz, to play him in the film version of Dershowitz's best-selling book on the Claus Von Bulow case, *Reversal of Fortune*. 'We wrote to Woody Allen', recalled Dershowitz, 'and he would have been great. But he said he couldn't do justice to the role. I was [finally] played by an actor called Ron Silver who couldn't stop waving his hands all over the place.'

In *Scenes from a Mall*, Woody found himself working under a director, Paul Mazursky, with whom he has often been thematically linked, and many observers discerned similarities in style and content between *Mall* and a number of Woody's own movies.

The film's origins lay in Mazursky's own observation that the lives of many people, which used to take place in the streets and town squares, had, in recent years, been transferred to the shopping malls. 'Whatever can happen in your life', said Mazursky, 'can happen in a mall. This seems particularly true in Los Angeles where people walk around practically in their underwear.'

Woody and Bette Midler are Nick and Deborah Fifer, an affluent West Coast couple about to celebrate their sixteenth wedding anniversary with a dinner party - he's a successful products endorsement sports lawyer; she's a noted marriage-guidance specialist and best-selling author. Although Mazursky and his co-writer, future director Roger L. Simon, offer a convincing view of the married state, essentially, the film deals with the theme of marital 'truth and consequence' - that curious compulsion of one or both members of a partnership to confess to an affair.

In spite of its massive 2600-strong support cast of bit players and extras, *Mall* is basically a two-hander, depending exclusively on one's response to its stars. Each plays, intriguingly, against type. Woody as Nick, is forceful, fastidious, professes Yuppie values, is committed to 'scientific fatherhood' and actually *prefers* LA to New York. Midler, pleasantly ample and well scrubbed, also reverses her more raucous image to become, at least at the outset, positively subdued.

The film begins with Nick and Deborah, apparently happy together, waving goodbye to the kids who are off on a skiing trip, and instantly embarking on a celebratory quickie. However, their post-coital trip to the Beverly Shopping Center, ostensibly to buy *sushi* for the evening's festivities, rapidly turns into a free-for-all of hostility and accusation, followed by forgiveness and maudlin reunion - until a fresh misunderstanding sparks off further recrimination and disruption. Just like Woody in his own films, Mazursky makes full play of his characters' wittily observed gastrophiliac obsessions and overt fashion fetishism. 'You look like my Aunt Minna in that dress!' says Nick, as Deborah disports herself in a lurid orange number, while Nick (unacceptably for Woody's fans!) is got up in a modest 'dork knob' pony tail, round tortoiseshell specs, in lieu of the familiar hornrims, and what looks suspiciously like a left-over Russian blouson from *Love and Death*. He later changes into a white designer jacket, fancy shirt and smart slacks. 'I was stunned when I saw how I was supposed to dress!' lamented Woody, 'Nick dresses in a way which to me and my usual characters would be appalling. It was atrocious but perfect for the person I played, a lawyer in LA.'

Alternating heart-to-heart exchanges with some well-orchestrated mayhem, the film delineates the gap which exists between private intimacy and public show and the way that in extreme circumstances (as with the lives of celebrities) these may be seen to converge. Mazursky also makes a number of valid points about the commercialization of Christmas and other popular traditions and the bland ironing-out of ethnic and/or 'pure' culture into a patina of middlebrow acceptability. The film's title, however, implies less a society where product (or product placement) has superseded good taste in art than a titular and thematic cross-referencing, though in comic terms, to Bergman's *Scenes from a Marriage* (1974). As with some of Woody's own films, Mazursky's approach demonstrates ways in which the respective concerns of the Swedish master may be transposed on to a corresponding American setting.

Although the film's protagonists are well-to-do West Coast Jewish, they could just as easily be typical Woody Allenish WASP Manhattanites. What is interesting, however, is that two stars of such contrasting comedic talents as Bette Midler and Woody should be so convincingly cast as a couple. If Woody has the slight edge, it is undoubtedly due to his more contained acting style and a somewhat better-written role (in which one suspects, of course, his own personal elaborations on the script). Midler gives a very warm performance and has one genuine highlight - when she and Woody step out on to a tiny café-bar dance-floor, she softly singing, he whistling, to the strains of Cole Porter's 'Easy to Love'.

Plans to shoot in the actual Beverly Center in LA were reportedly ruled out due to Woody's refusal to film in southern California. Scouts were duly dispatched to Long Island, upstate New York and New Jersey. Over 1000 malls were considered, ranging even as far afield as Canada. Although there were a number of linking shots to the real Beverly Shopping Center, much of the filming took place in the recently completed Stamford Center, in Connecticut, whose dramatic modern architecture, six-storey edifice and sleek, mirrored escalators were perfect for the stylized cathedral of consumerism which Mazursky and Simon had in mind. Set designer Pato Guzman also constructed an enormous two-storey replica on a 26,000-square foot sound stage at the Kaufman Astoria. The result was artfully lit to obtain the curious impression of 'flat lushness' the subject demanded. 'We were trying to convey deep emotion', said cameraman Fred Murphy, 'Therefore I used chaotic lighting to create the look of non-lighting'. Only the eagle-eyed would realize that the film was not all shot at the Beverly Center itself.

Midler has recalled that the film was a great deal of fun and that Woody, in unaccustomed lighter mood, did everything he could to keep her spirits up. Freed from the responsibility of writing and directing, Woody was also in his element. 'The whole environment was very pleasant', he recalled, 'It was substantially different from my kind of movie sets which are quiet and riddled with anxiety.'

He reported himself 'amazed' by the amount of preparation Mazursky went in for, compared with his own more spontaneous way of working. This included extensive prior consultation with the actors and technicians and Mazursky taking his cast, said Woody, 'to every location, so we could look at it before the film started. He knew where the camera was going to be. He did a lot of homework. Everything went very smoothly for him and it was fun.'

Scenes from a Mall was opened by Buena Vista on 1039 screens in the US in March 1991. Reviews were mainly dismal and, although it was noted that the film was breezily free of the sentimentality which had marred the concurrent *LA Story*, many critics voiced regret either that the picture had not been written and directed by Woody or that Mazursky had not managed to bring the same satirical edge to it that he had to his previous Bette Midler vehicle, *Down and Out in Beverly Hills*. None of which made *Mall* an obvious box-office attraction and its colossal failure at the wickets - gross $9.3m/rentals $4.2m, against a reported (but, one hopes, apocryphal!) estimated negative cost of $34m - suggested that Woody had little box-office lure, except in his own movies.

On its opening in Paris, *Mall* zoomed straight to the top of the box-office charts. In January 1991, *Elle*'s women readers had polled Woody into third place as their 'most potent fantasy lover', after Alain Delon and Arnold Schwarzenegger(!), and *Première* magazine, in July, was to reveal Woody to be France's ninth most popular star (he came twelfth in Britain). Finally, though, *Mall* failed to equal the brilliant French success of *Alice* and in other territories was not much liked. The film's failure was held to be at least partially responsible for Disney's disappointing third quarter net (a 31 per cent drop on the previous year) and, indeed, since November 1990, only two of the company's 16 releases had performed above break-even or out-and-out flop level.

Shadows and Fog Although it had been announced in August 1990 that Woody would be making his next three films for Orion, there was widespread speculation that he was ready to switch studios. His apparent unhappiness with his film-making salary was what had prompted, it was thought, his brief flirtation with Disney. Ever since *New York Stories*, Disney subsidiary Touchstone had reportedly been trying to lure Woody away from Orion though he had turned down their offer of the uptight vacationing shrink role (eventually played by Richard Dreyfuss) in *What About Bob?* Reports, however, that he would move his operations to that company had to be tempered with the probability that he would not enjoy the same creative autonomy as before. There was also a degree of resentment within Disney, it was said, over his $5m fee for the disastrous *Mall*.

When talks with Fox also foundered, Woody, as expected, signed a new non-exclusive pact with Orion. This called for three further films, in two of which, at least, Woody would star. The first was *Shadows and Fog* - at one point known as *Fog and Shadows* but in either case an acknowledged titular reference to Alain Resnais's classic Auschwitz documentary *Nuit et Brouillard* (1956).

The movie was shot over a three-month period, from 19 November on, entirely at the Kaufman Astoria. Here, Santo Loquasto had constructed an elaborate eighteenth century-style European city set, complete with cathedral, cobbled streets, bridges, ponds and grimy garrets. This presented enormous logistical problems for the camera crew because, as Woody has since recalled, after one week's filming under normal circumstances, they would obviously have run out of bits of set to shoot on. However, filming in black-and-white and in 'fog', they 'found that by judiciously moving around things and switching things we were able to do the whole thing on a single set'. Prior to the shooting Woody and Di Palma did a half-day of tests, trying out various kinds of lighting and film stock. They 'came to the conclusion that the film would be served best by being shot non-realistically with very dramatic backlight'. Shooting mainly in a series of quite long, pre-meditated takes, with actors often in half-light or silhouette and by allowing each scene 'to dictate its own form', the film achieved a very atmospheric, poetic quality, ideally suited to its given sources. But, although held to be influenced by the so-called German Expressionist films of the 1920s, Woody has insisted that the style of the picture was preordained by the subject matter and the way Americans of his own background imagined the Europe of the period. He denied that the result was, in any way, a homage.

Alice and *Shadows and Fog* were just two of the 139 movies to be shot in NewYork during 1990 but, ten days into the shooting of *Fog*, the customary hectic activity enjoyed by the US industry in NewYork suddenly ground to a halt. The hold-off was due to a breakdown in contract negotiations between the Hollywood studios and the East Coast branch of IATSE, representing the technical crews in the city. Such was the affection and respect, however, in which Woody was held by local industry workers that he was, almost uniquely among major film-makers, allowed to continue filming unmolested.

When Woody had announced to Orion that he wanted to film *Fog* exclusively in the studio in black-and-white, 'the entire company nearly had a heart attack. But they have been very good sports.' They needed to be, since soon after the film's completion in early 1991, it was being widely reported that Orion, desperately trying to stave off imminent Chapter 11 bankruptcy proceedings, might be unable to release any of its new product, nor indeed, to sanction the commencement of Woody's 'Fall Project 1991'.

By this time, the company was over $500m in debt, nearly double its movie earnings for 1990. The euphoria over the box-office successes of *Silence of the Lambs* and *Dances withWolves* had to be weighed against the fact that foreign and video rights to these were controlled, under its February cash deal, by Columbia. This meant effectively that any revenues due to the more successful films would be barely sufficient to meet debt repayment and interest charges, let alone the average $10m per film required to promote and market the ten titles still in post-production limbo - soon to include *Shadows and Fog*.

While awaiting the go-ahead for his next project, Woody kept himself busy shooting a series of five commercials, on a $3 budget, for the Communist-run Italian Co-op. This was the country's biggest supermarket and hypermarket chain, based in Bologna. Apart from his earlier appearances in magazine and poster promotions - undertaken for very little money, but with a view to getting his name and face known to a wider public - this was a brand new venture for Woody, for which he would receive nearly $1m.

Filmed in New York and Rome from June on, over a four-and-a-half month period, the commercials starred popular Italian comedian Roberto Benigni but otherwise featured American actors who just *looked* Italian. Woody did not appear, claming he wouldn't be convincing as an Italian consumer. Photographed by Di Palma, with some of Woody's usual crew, and running at less than one minute each, the first four ads were showcased at the Venice Film Festival, in September, Woody's contract stipulating that they could not be shown outside Italy. (Three years previously, he had also been asked to come up with an advertising idea for Campari. When, in early 1991, he finally submitted his script, it was rejected as 'too sexy' - Woody had set it in a brothel.)

His immediate problems were solved, however, when, having successfully negotiated to forego his two remaining films for Orion, he signed a new deal with TriStar, which company also undertook the belated release of *Shadows and Fog*. In 1989, TriStar and its sister studio, Columbia, had been jointly acquired for $34.4m by Japanese electronics giant Sony. The latter was, ironically, Orion's major creditor and responsible, through Columbia, for the distribution of Orion and TriStar's product world-wide.

Although there were media jibes about Woody's 'ingratitude' to the company which had given him so much freedom, the transfer of his Untitled Pictures Inc. to TriStar had actually been masterminded by Mike Medavoy, a former top talent agent and one of the original founders of Orion, who had become central to the company's favourable links with Hollywood's big creative names. He had left Orion in March 1990 to become chairman of TriStar. In July 1992, Arthur Krim and Eric Pleskow would also quit Orion, the studio they had helped establish in 1978 and, with none of the original team still in place, the company, barred under US post-bankruptcy regulations from actively financing its own movies, relinquished its role as a major producer.

With Woody's first film for TriStar nearing completion, the company took the unusual step of opening *Shadows and Fog* in Europe prior to its release in the US. This was thought to reflect both Orion's previous difficulties in setting a North American playdate and Woody's enduring popularity in Europe, especially in Paris, where the film had its world première in February 1992. *Le Figaro* noted the occasion as 'a way of homage to the nation that was the first to hail him [Woody] as more than a highly gifted comic'. But, although it reached third place at the Paris box-office in its second week, the film dropped quickly, failing, like *Mall*, to equal the success of *Alice* the previous year. After an out-of-competition screening at the Berlin Film Festival, *Shadows and Fog* did do 'nicely' elsewhere, said Woody, notably in Italy where it won the David Di Donatello Award for the year's best foreign film. Its US release in March generated a mere $2.7m gross ($1.2m net) or fewer than one million admissions. It did not turn up in Britain until February 1993, where it attained a total gross of only £87,622.

At least part of the trouble was the subject matter. With its character names derived from Woody's 1973 playlet *Death*, *Shadows and Fog* is both a spoof on Hollywood's recurrent obsession with serial killers and a means by which Woody could examine, in more darkly comic terms than before, a number of his prevailing themes - God, guilt, paranoia, 'death and one's position in the Universe', the Jew as victim and psychoanalysis. Woody has suggested that *Shadows and Fog* is the closest he has ever come to 'a definitive, dramatic metaphor' on the theme of death that is equal to Bergman's *The Seventh Seal* and adds that 'existential subjects to me are still the only subjects worth dealing with'. That said, the fact that *Shadows and Fog* doesn't quite come off may be due to any number of factors, not least its almost too slavish imitation of the old UFA studio thrillers and German 'street' films of the late 1920s. The devoted assimilation of their distinctive art direction, high-contrast lighting techniques and even performance levels, somehow gets in the way of the story-telling. The film swiftly turns into a game of 'Spot-the-Old-German-Movie', while Woody, with his shapeless suit and ultra-short haircut, gives every impression that Zelig is alive and well and living in Mitteleuropa.

Shadows and Fog is set in an unidentified Everytown, presumably German, though the money is in dollars and the modes of address English. Owen Gleiberman in *Entertainment Weekly* was not alone in remarking that Woody's fictional city looked like Prague, describing the setting as 'Kafkaland' - a mood quickly established by the use of 'The Cannon Song' from *The Threepenny Opera* and the distinctively Murnau-lit composite street design, oozing with abstract night and fog. Originally, Woody had played with the idea of using classical scoring, possibly Grieg which was, of course, a presiding musical motif of the film's thematically most striking model, Fritz Lang's *M*. After completing *Fog*, however, Woody began to play some Kurt Weill tunes which, interspersed with a couple of vintage Jack Hylton dance band numbers, 'just seemed to fit in perfectly'.

The predominant theme of the film is summed up by the Allen character's line, 'The night is a free feeling' - the idea that once you get out into the night, deprived of your normal daylight protections, civilization is gone. It is a classic metaphor in the darker works of fiction and if the plot of the movie follows the established conventions of earlier models with an almost too meticulous attention to the clichés of the form, it does so with a great deal of visual imagination.

The film from the outset is wreathed in a miasma of doom. A strangler is loose, appearing out of the post-Expressionist opening montage as an indistinct, shadowy figure at the top of a flight of stone steps or lurking round walls. Street lamps glimmer, buildings loom, shadows distend and fog creeps as various victims, including a night watchman and a shady pathologist, meet sticky ends. The film, like the play it is based on, posits the idea of a neighbourhood, wrote Francine du Plessix Gray, 'decimated by some mysterious force that remains undiagnosed and unnamed'. The murderer, a constant threat, is revealed, albeit nebulously, as a malevolent composite of mediaeval death's-head, Max Shreck's Nosferatu, Paul Wegener's *Der Golem*, Lang's *M*, 'The Vampire of Düsseldorf' and Jack the Ripper.

Max Kleinman (Woody) is a humble hardware clerk, so cringing in his manner that he addresses his tyrannical boss, Mr Paulsen (Philip Bosco), as 'Your Majesty'. He is treated like scum by his fiancée, Eve (Kate Nelligan), his well-rounded landlady (Camille Saviola) badgers him to marry her, and he is torn this way and that by the increasingly threatening demands of two rival vigilante groups, each of whom want him to join them. He is initially reluctant to commit himself - the living embodiment of Nietzsche's famous phrase: 'A man with no plan is not a man.'

A number of suspects present themselves: Kleinman's peeping tom boss, his friend the doctor, several passers-by and even poor Kleinman himself. Disturbed that a neighbour called Mintz, a *mohel* who performs 'quality circumcisions', has been carted off with his family for questioning, Kleinman goes voluntarily to the police station to intercede. 'Nobody's guilty of anything, are they?' he asks, plaintively. Alas, Kleinman's presenting himself to the police serves only to make the authorities aware of his existence.

Meanwhile, a circus is encamped on the outskirts of town. A sword swallower (!) called Irmy (Mia), upset that her lover, the Clown (John Malkovich) is cheating on her with the wire walker, Marie (Madonna), packs her bags and leaves. She is befriended by a prostitute (Lily Tomlin) and given shelter for the night in a brothel. Here, a wealthy student Jack (John Cusack) persuades her to turn a trick for $700 - a vast sum to Irmy, but everyone, according to the story, has a price.

The murders continue through the night. The hapless Kleinman wends his way home through the gloomily-lit city. By chance, he meets Irmy. There is no romance between them but, alone together in the night streets, they become mutually protective. She also persuades Kleinman to give her night's earnings to the Church, and in so doing, he is brought once more to the attention of those looking for a convenient scapegoat. With the tacit approval of the police, Kleinman is put on 'trial' by the vigilantes who threaten to string him up there and then. But he escapes, and having taken refuge, like Irmy, in the brothel, eventually finds himself at the circus. Here he saves his new friend from the murderer, with the help of a magician called Irmstedt (Kenneth Mars). Kleinman, who has been fired from his job, gratefully accepts a new position - as magician's assistant.

The bare bones of the plot suggest a rather trite composite of several early European movie cycles. Woody's film, like those which inspired it, explores the darker side of human nature and, by inference, that of a specifically middle-European culture which, certainly during the period where the film is set, was, wrote historian Jeffrey Richards, 'peculiarly obsessed with death, madness and twilight'. The circus (or 'carny') story, for instance, provided a perfect blend of the tawdry and the sinister while, that classic serial killer plot, Fritz Lang's *M*, had used the role of the child murderer and his summary comeuppance at the hands of a criminally-inspired kangaroo court, as a cipher for the rise of Nazism. As in Lang's film, the motif of the 'Citizens' Committee as an alternative to the orthodox legal process, demonstrates how anti-Semitism, vigilantism and hysteria may provide the seeds for extremist political acts.

Kleinman is referred to by an associate, Simon Carr (Wallace Shawn), as this 'slimy, creeping vermin, more suited to extermination on this planet'. He emerges subsequently as a sort of Raskolnikov figure, leaving behind him all the 'clues' necessary to convict him but, unlike his Dostoyevskian forebear, having committed no crime commensurate with his intrinsic feelings of guilt. 'We are all guilty in the eyes of God' was one of the predominant themes in *Crimes and Misdemeanors* and, once again, it is a very Hebraic concept, seized upon here by the unorthodox forces of law and order who recognize in Kleinman a shambling advertisement for an essentially Jewish culpability. Finally, though, like Kafka's *The Trial*, which Woody has said it 'would be great fun to be able to do one day', the film is not a political work *per se* but about one man's inability 'to control events or to understand his own destiny'.

Significantly, during his flight, it is with other outsiders that Kleinman derives most comfort - from the gypsyish circus folk and the warm, life-affirming prostitutes who, although they sell 'love' also have the capacity to give it. The film is also very good at embracing, once more, such autobiographical resonances as Woody's penchant for magic and long-time status as an amateur magician. The capture of the murderer in the circus tent, for instance, is a terrific routine - an audacious effect which takes the breath away. Magic is used as a cipher for Kleinman's escape from cruel reality, much in the way that the real-life Woody, as a child, hid in his room at home, practising his skills away from the prying eyes of his family.

Woody also gently lampoons the widening maternal concerns of Mia, as in the Chaplinesque scene where she forces the Clown to assist her in 'adopting' the baby of a recently murdered waif (Eszter Balint). Unlike their more recent screen roles, however, neither Woody nor Mia's character can be interpreted here as 'true' reflections of their real-life personalities. 'If you see me on the screen like the character in *Shadows and Fog*', Woody insisted to Sean Mitchell in *The Los Angeles Times*, 'schlepping around, fumbling around, it isn't me. It just isn't. There may be some elements of me in it, but they're ... exaggerated for comic purposes.'

With its superior production design, authentic costuming and some skilful use of the Louma crane, *Shadows and Fog* was, at $14m, one of Woody's more ambitious efforts. Stephen J. Spignesi, a staunch Allen supporter, suggests that it 'may very well be the most beautiful film he has ever made'. But, although there were encomiums from the likes of Vincent Canby and Jim Kline, most US critics gave the film short shrift, complaining in most instances of its typical Bergmanesque discursions on art and illusion and the way in which its all-star cast was wasted in an apparently negligible exercise. Christopher Tookey in London's *Daily Mail* accused Woody of 'self-aggrandisement' in gathering such weighty names around him; a recent biographer, Tim Carroll, was to enquire whether Woody might be 'taking some sort of perverse pleasure in tempting all these high priced stars to come and work for "scale" in a movie about whores' and treating his old nemesis, Hollywood, as the metaphor for a whorehouse!

The cast, though, is one of the film's more intriguing elements, the acting being exercised on a number of different levels - from Woody's semi-comedic, if somewhat embarrassed, turn as Kleinman and the naturalistic performances of Mia and Cusack, to the florid, Pabst-like histrionics of the prostitutes (great energizers whenever they are on screen) and the Brechtian 'theatrical' style of the vigilantes and the police. Notable amongst the latter group is the film's most bizarre character (extrapolated from *Death*), the shaven-skulled clairvoyant, Spiro (Charles Craigin) who can identify a suspect simply by sniffing him.

Among a number of bright vignettes is the long-serving Julie Kavner giving a vibrant turn as the embittered haberdasher who had been jilted by

Kleinman when he discovered the truth about her 'hysterical' pregnancy. Donald Pleasence (his name misspelt on the credits) pitches in with an enjoyable 'Come on, suspect me' performance as the pathologist - an authentic figure from early German horror films - collecting the organs of his charges as 'an opportunity to study something about the nature of evil'. Pleasence, like many another Allen cast member, confessed himself bemused at receiving only his own pages and, as he told me, in December 1993:

> I never read the script, nobody read the script. I think they were kept locked in Woody's safe, so I was interested to see the film when it came out - to see what happened. And, even then, I wondered! And what you see is what I shot, more or less ... I can't remember anything particularly funny happening, except, when, in one scene we had together, he comes in and he says, 'Have you heard about Schmidt?' I forget the actual name of the person, but I said, to him, 'Who's Schmidt? I mean, I don't know anything about Schmidt. Who *is* he? If I've got to talk about Schmidt I need to know something about him.' And Woody said, 'No, no, that's not necessary, it doesn't matter that you know about Schmidt.' And I thought, 'Well, that *is* a funny way of directing a picture!'

Some other cast members, on the other hand, actually welcomed this evasiveness about the story. 'During production, Woody was approving and supportive', recalled Lily Tomlin, 'and it was great to have the freedom and relief of not being responsible to make those decisions about what the character would be doing at any given moment. The only bad thing was that I had to smoke cigarettes in the movie and I got violently sick.'

Few of the players, though, had much chance to develop their characters beyond a useful thumbnail-sketch level, while Kate Nelligan, Fred Gwynne and, even, Madonna, offer cameos which are scarcely that. Although the very idea of Madonna appearing in an Allen movie grabbed full media attention, her role as 'the most voluptuous woman in the circus' lasts barely a minute. Woody's representatives were strenuously to deny mischievous reports of dissension on set and, amidst rumours that Madonna had been drastically edited from the film, Woody instantly leapt to her defence. 'Not a frame of her has been cut', insisted his publicist, Linda Hintelmann, 'Nor has that ever been contemplated. She's first rate in the film'. But there *were* a number of casualties, including David Strathairn, Steven Keats and Stephen Mendillo. Pleasence:

I do remember that, after I'd done my scenes, some time later, I was called back to reshoot them again with completely different actors. They were small-part actors, and whether it was that they were no longer available or that he wanted to change them, I don't know. But it was a question of the location of the scene that he wanted changed, which is why he had to bring me 3000 miles to do a retake! The dialogue was more or less the same. There were *some* rewrites, but what really struck me was the idea of some guy taking his mother along to the film and he was no longer in it. I mean, he would understand if it was all very different, but it was exactly the same scene, with a different actor, and he had come along to see someone else in the part - I mean, like 'Who is this fellow?'

In spite of its lowering images, *Shadows and Fog* is still essentially a comedy, with a liberal sprinkling of gastrophilic gags and intimations of the old slapstick Woody. 'Everybody loves illusions', says the magician, Irmstedt, 'Needs them like he loves the air' and in Woody's painstaking recreation of a strange, almost illusory world, he uses cinematic sleight-of-hand and received sources to conjure a fearful vision of a city on the edge of nightmare which, through the channels of hopefulness and magic, is turned, finally, into something far lighter.

10

Crimes & Whispers

1992-5: Husbands and Wives to Mighty Aphrodite

Husbands and Wives Woody's second release of 1992 was *Husbands and Wives* which, dealing as it does, with the problems of marital breakdown and a middle-aged man's relationship with a much younger woman, could not have been better (or worse!) timed had it been scripted from life. Coinciding with the extensive media coverage given to the dramatic break-up of the Allen-Farrow partnership, the film gave rise to all manner of speculation as to the eerie parallels between on-screen narrative and actual events.

News of the crisis, which had been bubbling under the surface for some months, burst upon an unsuspecting world in the second week of August and even succeeded in knocking the Republican convention at Houston right off the front pages of *Newsweek* and *Time*. Indeed, during much of that week, CNN's 'Headline News' made reports of Mia and Woody's very public squabbles their main story.

Revelations about Woody's affair with Mia's 21-year-old adopted daughter, Soon-Yi Previn, not to mention all the other accusations and counter-accusations, were meat and drink to the media. Psychologists and journalists theorized and, as the old saw about life imitating art was duly trotted out, Woody's movies, short stories and early night-club routines were deconstructed for clues. As the ensuing court appearances and media reports quickly attested, his personal life was beginning to look like a parody of his films, rather than the other way around. It was, averred one of Mia's biographers Joe Rubin 'the celebrity scandal of the decade'.

As was soon made clear, the couple had begun to withdraw from one another around the time of Mia's recent pregnancy, although, as friends and co-workers, they were, for some time afterwards, still very much an item. During the family's annual European tour, in the summer of 1991, it was rumoured that Mia and Woody were scouting locations for a movie to be made in the west of Ireland. But the film which did subsequently emerge, the New York-based *Husbands and Wives*, was seen as both a reflection and anticipation of real-life events and was instantly examined for pointers. 'Crimes and Whispers' quipped *Time* at the height of the 'scandal', and this punning phrase could just as well have been applied to the film itself.

So, which came first - the love affair or the movie? Unsurprisingly, Woody was swift in his denials. The screenplay, he insisted, was 'a made-up story', written years before, 'with no autobiography in it all all'. In fact, he had, at one point, considered playing the Sydney Pollack character, while Mia had been offered the choice of either leading female part. 'And, for a couple of weeks', Woody told Nigel Andrews, 'she was going to play the Judy Davis role, and then decided ... that she would rather play the other because the schedule fell better for her.' That said, it is significant that both the Mia and Davis characters are women undergoing the agonies of marital breakdown and that the husband in *each* case dallies with a woman much younger than himself. As *The New York Times* suggested, this was probably the first film ever to be made about a scandal before the scandal had actually taken place!

Although there *are* a number of apparent similarities between the plot of the film and its real-life equivalent, a great deal of the speculation may be put down to pure media hype. More accurately, the movie may be seen to mirror problems encountered by each one of us in our search for love and lasting companionship. True, the two central characters, Gabe and Judy Roth (Woody and Mia) are a professional middle-class couple who split up in the story - due, not entirely, to Gabe's admittedly unconsummated infatuation with a 20-year-old student, Rain (Juliette Lewis). True, also, that Gabe and Judy say things to each other which several observers have taken as all-too-painfully drawn from life, and that, at nearly all times, they are seen to be wearing the same kind of shapeless (but expensive?) 'hand-me-down' outfits in which Woody and Mia were frequently photographed around town. And true, besides, that the couple live in Manhattan (like most of their recent screen characters) and that their friends in the film are played by real-life friends, like Nora Ephron and John Doumanian as party guests, Sidney Pollack in the second male lead and costume designer Jeffrey Kurland as the unseen interviewer/analyst. But, after a while, attempts to draw real-life inferences from the film become blurred in mere guess work. The fact that various of the characters are writers, culture vultures, sexually frustrated and pay regular visits to their shrinks, does not make them unique to the films of Woody Allen!

Since all of Woody's films rely on a degree of revision and readjustment throughout filming, one's suspicion that the Soon-Yi affair may have, at least marginally, influenced the story's development remains inescapable. *Husbands and Wives* had started shooting in November 1991 and Woody's relationship with Soon-Yi, he later admitted, had begun in September. Although they had previously accompanied each other to sporting events - like the Knicks' game to which Gabe takes Rain in the film - and Woody had gotten Soon-Yi an extra role in *Scenes from a Mall*, there is no reason to suppose that their friendship turned serious any earlier than later reported. If, though, as it was also suggested, Mia had discovered those notorious nude snaps of Soon-Yi during the actual filming - or rather, seven days before the completion of principal photography - this can only lead to further conjecture as to which of the film's scenes carry 'after the event' resonances. Mia, it was reported, had gone on making herself available for reshoots, even though she and Woody were already in dispute. It could scarcely be Mia's fault if, as *The New York Times* later suggested, her 'washed-out appearance' and 'somnambulant acting' in some parts of the film had been due to the fact that she had come upon the Soon-Yi photos only two days before she was due to shoot the scene where Judy tells Gabe she no longer loves him.

Basically, the film deals with the discomforts of both marital and extra-marital relationships. The catalyst is the bombshell presented to Gabe and Judy by their best friends, Jack and Sally (Pollack and Davis): the couple have decided to split up. Gabe takes the news in his stride, leaving Judy to bear the brunt of the shock. Subsequent scenes expose her insecurities - about sex, other women, male untruthfulness and her own marital relationship. She is described as a 'passive-aggressive' and even Judy's architect first husband (played by former Yale president Benno C. Schmidt) categorizes her in flashback, as a 'poor me' type who always gets what she wants.

In a dramatic departure from previous Allen form, the above scenes, and, indeed, the rest of the film, are shot by Carlo Di Palma like a fly-on-the-wall TV documentary, with a dizzying hand-held technique, long takes and intrusive close-ups. The camera jerks and jumps, following the characters from room to room or marooning them behind pillars and doors. Although the colour tones retain a warm, orangeish glow, the often agitated camera work serves to set the characters and their surroundings somewhat off balance, as if their anxieties and neuroses were being cruelly editorialized. Woody has said that he was aiming at 'a jagged, nervous feeling' because he wanted the audience to feel that 'the internal, emotional and mental states of the characters are dissonant'. The first scene where the hand-held camera turns for a full five minutes, was to be the most talked about in the film.

Significantly, the camera is at its calmest when focusing on Jack's subsequent mistress, Sam (Lysette Anthony) and Judy's nice, square, editor friend, Michael

(Liam Neeson), who are the most 'normal' characters in the film. Although 'you do sacrifice composition, some pretty lighting', agreed Woody, he found that shooting on the wing in a nervous, rough-edged manner, without worrying too much where individual characters were at any given time and often jump-cutting from one scene to the next, represented 'a very, very exhilarating weapon in the arsenal of film-making' - one he would repeat, to a lesser degree, in *Manhattan Murder Mystery*.

Woody has said that the technical approach to the film started with the idea that content, rather than perfection of the frame was the important thing, the result being that, after just doing general lighting, Woody was able to allow the actors to move where they wanted, confident that Di Palma would be able to pick them up. Scenes were shot with no prior camera rehearsal, operator Dick Mingalone simply being instructed to take up the camera and keep pace with the actors as best he could. The end result of this was that the filming was cheaper and faster: it required only three days of reshoots instead of Woody's usual month or so, and it was the first time in years that he'd come in under budget.

Much was made of this striking departure from the formalized, carefully composed set-ups of Woody's more recent movies and, at times, the film suggests a throwback to the *cinema verité* techniques of John Cassavetes or the French New Wave. Although not entirely successful - some audience members complained of feeling 'nauseous', while Pauline Kael dismissed the device as a 'stunt' - most of the cast found the technique liberating. The added realism also extends to the dialogue. There is, virtually, for the first time in an Allen film, a deal of bad language and it is the first film which Woody had directed in which his on-screen character is heard to say 'fuck'.

As in previous Allen films, the audience is invited to share the role of off-screen 'analyst', as various of the characters unburden their problems direct to camera. The device serves to cue in a series of revealing flashbacks, like Gabe's first meeting with Judy at a beach party in the Hamptons, recalling a similar sequence in *Annie Hall*. The off-screen 'listener' also acts as a sort of subjective sounding board for Gabe's present romantic problems, including his inability to cope with Rain's disconcerting narrative of her father-fixated sex life.

Gabe is a professor of creative writing and his attraction to the free-spirited Rain is as much due to her literary promise as her precocious sexuality. One of Gabe's problems in his relationship with Judy is that she wants children (she already has a daughter from her first marriage) and he does not - a situation which seems to stand in rough parallel with Woody's reported real-life opposition to Mia adopting any more children. Woody's contention during the subsequent court hearings that their off-screen relationship had ceased to be a sexual one, is also obliquely referred to. When the film couple's marriage is in its last stages of unravelment and Gabe tells Judy he's now prepared to give her a child, it is already too late. 'You use sex to express every emotion but love!' she accuses, which is perhaps the most painful line in the film.

Judy, initially perceived as a 'doormat', is, we are told, a 'succubus' with reserves of grit. She once wrote a thesis at Radcliffe on Bauhaus architecture and now works for something called *Night Magazine* - these scenes having been shot at the offices of *Artforum* on Bleecker Street. Judy also writes poetry on the side and is thrilled by the enthusiastic reaction of Michael, having already earmarked him for the 'cerebral and inhibited' Sally. Judy, however, is drawn to him herself, and, after a brief fling with Sally, Michael marries Judy after her divorce from Gabe. Ironically, it is the couple who first split up, Sally and Jack, who get back together, while Gabe, of all the principals, is left alone. His is the last voice we hear, the last face we see, and it is his loneliness plus his own failure with relationships that the film, finally, is about. 'Can I go now? Is it over?' are Gabe's plaintive last words to the off-screen analyst.

In the course of the film, it becomes relatively easy to empathize with both couples. Sally, long married to Jack, is sexually unresponsive and, by her own admission, too hyperactive mentally even to relax in bed with Michael to whom she is actually attracted. Jack, meanwhile, initially relishes his live-in relationship with sweet and sparkly aerobics teacher Sam, who regenerates him with healthy exercise, good sex and all those enjoyable (and therefore 'sinful') things like daft videos, which Sally would never have at home. It is only a matter of time, however, before Jack is again hankering after Sally. 'Look, some people are not constituted to be single', he confesses, 'I mean, how long can you discuss aerobics and the Zodiac?'

Gabe, meanwhile, has already tried to deflect Judy's growing suspicion that his interest in Rain is anything but educative. 'They don't want old men', he reassures her. 'I think an old man does better than an old woman', she replies. Audiences were quick to pick up on Gabe's equally illuminating line to the camera/analyst when he confesses that professors are 'notorious at seducing their pupils. It's a cinch'. It may also be worth noting that in the August 1992 edition of *Cosmopolitan*, a canvas of 700 college women revealed that slightly more would prefer to go to bed with the 'cerebral and wimpish' Woody than the more muscular Sly Stallone!

Rain is a great admirer of a story Gabe once wrote, 'The Grey Hat'. She now begs him to let her read his unpublished novel, and, 'to clarify certain feelings Gabe [has] about human relations', scenes from this are duly acted out as an amusing interlude. However, when Rain later tells Gabe she is upset by some of his 'attitudes' in the book and then leaves the only copy in a taxi, it is the beginning of the end. Gabe, confiding in Jack, falls to discussing some of his more bizarre sexual relationships; Jack gently reminds him that Judy, his wife, is still the ideal - 'the first sane woman' Gabe was ever involved with. This judgement though, is given the insider's lie since, in her scenes with Gabe, Judy comes across as nervy, anxious and erratic; according to Gabe, she is only 'stable on the surface'. If we accept the myriad 'clues' in the film to Woody and Mia's off-screen relationship, to what extent was he aware, in structuring the role to fit her, that he might be effecting something in the nature of a character assassination?

A strain of bleak misogyny, fuelled by some hilarious politically incorrect one-liners, noticeably surfaces in the episodes involving the unfortunate Sam. Feminist critics' ire was aroused by the fact that both Jack and Gabe regard Sam as an airhead - a view exemplified by the occasion when Jack, exasperated by her chirpy but pitiful attempts to hold her own at a party infested by smart Manhattan intellectuals, manhandles her out of the house. This sequence climaxes with Sam screaming and staging an attention-grabbing sit-down in the street outside. When filming began, Lysette Anthony recalled, Sam was 'hilarious ... a vulnerable angel. But Woody reshot it to make me obnoxious. The scene got incredibly violent. I couldn't sleep for three days. I'm not exaggerating ... there were people with their mouths open, going "My God, we've never seen this much violence in a Woody Allen movie!" '

Gabe's waspishness with Rain à propos her 'politically correct' opinions on his novel, and the exposure of Sally's ball-breaking put-downs of subservient admirers also hint at that stream of overt male chauvinism of which Woody's feminist detractors had earlier accused him. And yet, as Davis noted to Geoff Andrew in February 1993, 'Many men find it difficult to write female characters, as if they didn't recognize that we are the same animal - the mysterious feminine! He's written some fantastic roles; it's extraordinary that a man wrote Another Woman with such empathy.'

The role of Sally is presumably the one for which Woody had been in negotiations a short time before with Jane Fonda. The possibility came to nothing when the actress refused to change what he has described as her 'astronaut wife's haircut'. Although also toying briefly with the idea of Dianne Wiest, Woody, impressed with Judy Davis's handling of her smallish part in Alice, was inspired to rewrite Sally specifically for her. As Davis was to recall, she found the role 'irresistible', later revealing to Cahiers du Cinema that it was 'the best and most important part' she'd had in an American picture.

The casting of Pollack is also something of a master-stroke. Jack is twitchy, sexually frustrated, earnest and intolerant and, in a number of ways, not all that admirable - but, in Pollack's hands, he is also vulnerable, funny and sympathetic. Woody has recalled that he thought of Pollack for the role after seeing him in *Tootsie* and, 'fortunately, he was tremendous from the minute he read it and I never had to give him a line of direction, ever'.

Both Davis and Anthony have spoken of Woody's lack of writer's vanity in encouraging them to improvise - even though he has since claimed that, although free-moving in style, most of *Husbands and Wives* only sounded like improvisation because 'they were so good they seemed to be making it up'. But he did allow the actors to embellish, and 'add words here and there to make the dialogue more colloquial'.

Woody had begun filming on 4 November 1991, on the campus of Columbia University's Barnard College, an élite all-women's liberal arts establishment, with student extras dressed in Woody's favourite browns and greens, instead of their customary black. The early scenes featured Woody, as Gabe, in scholarly tweeds, trying to make a date with his most promising student, Rain played, initially, by British actress Emily Lloyd. Although Woody had auditioned a number of American girls - including *Buffy the Vampire Slayer* star Kristy Swanson - he had cast Lloyd due to his admiration for her debut performance in *Wish You Were Here* (1987). Lloyd had expressed herself 'overwhelmed' to be in an Allen movie but, shortly into the filming, Woody replaced her with *Cape Fear* discovery, Juliette Lewis. 'It was my fault', he said, 'I put too much burden on her, particularly in trying to get her American voice right.' Although Woody has described Lewis as 'a wonderful actress' and 'very gifted', it is this writer's view that, as she also demonstrated in *Cape Fear*, she has such a *peculiar* acting style that she throws the film slightly off key.

Problems also arose in early December when one Mustafa Majeed, a notorious black activist with a reputation for terrorizing film sets, twice disrupted filming and, claimed crew members, tried to sting Woody for a $100,000 'donation' to leave him alone. The disruptions only ceased when Woody reported Majeed to New York mayor David Dinkins who issued a restraining order. After a brief period exerting similar tactics on Harlem construction sites, Majeed and his followers returned to the fray and, in April 1994, brought a mob of 150 demonstrators on to the New York location of Woody's telefilm remake of *Don't Drink the Water*. Majeed, who had originally filed a human rights complaint against Woody's production company, was said to be incensed at the lack of black and latino faces in his films. Although not entirely justified, this specific criticism has been persistently levelled against Woody, a factor rationalized by him on the grounds that, small roles apart, he just doesn't 'know the black experience well enough to really write about it with any authenticity'. (Spike Lee, a long time admirer of Woody who, ironically, has also been intimidated by Majeed, has frequently voiced his ambition to be the first African-American to play a leading role in an Allen film.)

Filming was otherwise relatively smooth, though subject, as ever, to Woody's perfectionism. On one occasion he embarked on a late-year foray to Long Island for a single day's shooting outside a clapboard beach house just off Dune Road in East Hampton. Here he was confronted by a bright and breezy locale, with perfect blue skies. Increasingly depressed by this picture-postcard aspect and with no sign of the weather worsening for the sequence he had in mind, Woody, with his crew and dozens of extras standing by, refused to roll the cameras. Finally, he moved his unit back to Manhattan, at a rumoured write-off of $200,000. As for the New York shooting, Woody, in accordance with his subject matter, gave the city a harder, grittier look, mostly devoid of the lovingly captured landmarks which had characterized his earlier films.

Principal photography was completed on 20 January, in preparation for a fall release. But, faced with the massive media coverage generated by the subsequent 'scandal', TriStar's publicists grew increasingly nervous. As Woody's first official project for the studio, much was hanging on the outcome. *Shadows and Fog* had still not opened in a number of overseas territories and, in Italy, the reported refusal 'on moral grounds' of voice-over artist Oreste Lionello to undertake his usual chore of dubbing Woody also hinted at a not-entirely-unforeseen Catholic backlash. A subsequent report in late August 1992, revealed that Co-op Nordemiglia was cancelling the fifth and final ad of Woody's original 1 billion lire ($850,000) advertising contract.

Even back home, what has been described as 'the public disgrace of one of liberal America's staunchest cultural icons' also led to questions about Woody's professional future. But, despite an initial outbreak of nerves on the part of Sony's Japanese owners, it began to appear as if his new movie might still hit the box-office jackpot. After the film's world première at the Toronto Film Festival in September, TriStar changed its mind about a discreet opening at Barnard College, releasing it earlier than planned and, unprecedentedly, for an Allen movie, on 865 screens - instead of in just key situations as Orion might have done. The film also had a $6m marketing budget - roughly three times more than for Woody's previous few movies - while media analysts predicted that it could well achieve a record $20m net in the US and restore, if mostly for the wrong reasons, Woody to the forefront of 'commercial' directors. At the last minute, however, TriStar got cold feet. All promos and parties were cancelled and, as usual, Woody made no attempt, personally, to plug the picture, even though he'd intended to. In this case, there was probably no need: *Husbands and Wives* was so hot by this time that a print on its way to Dallas to be screened for Liam Neeson was hijacked *en route*. Despite the immediate intervention of the FBI, bootleg copies were soon changing hands at $200 apiece.

Although there was apparent barracking on both East and West coasts (even for the trailers!), the film opened to a first five days' ticket sales of $3.5m, a record for an Allen film in North America. Audiences were quick to spot the 'real-life' resonances and, reported Gill Harley in *The Sunday Express*, either met the film with uncomfortable silence or 'giggled and hissed' as Mia's 'frumpy looking character' asked Woody, 'Do you ever hide anything from me? Feelings? Longing?' To which he replies 'No, do you?' Much press mileage was made out of Woody's line, 'I've always had a penchant for what I call *kamikaze* women. They crash their plane into you, and you die with them', while even hardened New Yorkers, it was said, squirmed in their seats at the off-screen analyst's question, 'Have you been honest with your wife?' and the various references to 'pliable girl students'. 'There are a lot of parallels there', wrote Doug Vaughan in *New York Magazine*, 'and, as you watch the film, each line takes on a new meaning'. Indeed, the April 1993 video version contained additional footage which, once again, wrote Stephen J. Spignesi, had 'people trying to decode every line and scene in the film for insight into the whole vile mess'.

With a few notable exceptions, reviews for the film were Woody's best since *Hannah*, but it soon became obvious that, although scandal may boost newspaper circulation and TV programmes, it does not necessarily resonate at the box office. *Husbands and Wives* dropped from the charts within five weeks, to a disappointing 1992 gross of $10.5m ($5m net), while even the somewhat cynical concurrent reissue of the May-September-angled *Manhattan* failed to draw the crowds. Woody did go on to receive his tenth Oscar nomination for Best Original Screenplay (second only to Billy Wilder with 13), and Davis was cited as Best Supporting Actress. Neither won, although Woody did accept the Best Screenplay nod from BAFTA, as well as from the London Critics' Circle, noting that the British 'have been very, very supportive of my films down the years'.

Husbands and Wives, rushed into the release spot originally intended for *Shadows and Fog*, had actually achieved a three-day opening gross of £78,738 in seven London cinemas - the highest ever for an Allen film in Britain - and went on to a total take of £888,481. It also played 19 weeks in the Paris top ten. '*Husbands and Wives* made about what any Woody Allen film makes', Woody told his friend, journalist Denis Hamill, 'A loyal audience. Some expected it would make more because of the controversy, and when it didn't, considered it a flop.'

Indeed, although the worldwide gross of around $28m (against an estimated negative cost, according to Woody, of $12m) was to push the film into slight profit, its reception in America was a further reminder that Woody's relationship with the box office had long been ambiguous. Orion, which had posted a net loss of $312m on revenues of $491m, for 1991-2, had recently revealed that Woody's 11 films for the company had cost around $100m to produce but had earned back an aggregate of only $60m in the US. *Hannah and Her Sisters* had accounted for roughly a third of the total, but, though it was said finally to have grossed somewhere over $40m since its first release, the film's actual net was only $18.2m. If one sets this against its estimated negative cost of $9m, plus editing, prints, advertising and interest charges, even the success of Woody's biggest post-*Annie Hall* grosser fails to look optimistic. Slow returns on video, plus Woody's persistent refusal, until recently, to have his films shown on commercial television, have also served to deprive his backers of much needed revenue. What was required, at this point, was a significant change of direction.

Manhattan Murder Mystery Amidst continuing speculation that Woody's personal problems might sink his deal with TriStar, he was already at work on his next picture. Touted under such titles as *Dancing Shiva* and *The Couple Next Door*, it finally emerged as *Manhattan Murder Mystery* and reunited Woody with co-writer Marshall Brickman for the first time since *Manhattan*. In the interim, Brickman had directed several films, including *Lovesick* (1983) and *The Manhattan Project* (1986), the former utilizing a variant of the 'ghostly guide' idea from *Play it Again, Sam*. *Manhattan Murder Mystery* was also a reworking, principally, of Woody and Brickman's original script ideas for *Annie Hall*.

Woody had originally got the idea for the film when he was living on Park Avenue and had shared the floor of his apartment with an elderly couple. At one point he had to go away to play 'the hungry i' night-club in San Francisco and, returning about six weeks later, he called upon the husband who told him, far too cheerfully, that, in Woody's absence, his wife had fallen out of the window to her death. 'And I thought to myself', recalled Woody, 'how could he be so unaffected by it? And it always stayed with me.' Woody decided it might be very interesting for an average New York couple (but not a 'sleuthing' couple) to come home one evening and happen upon a possible murder which they start to investigate.

In an early draft, a college professor, Dr Levy, had been found dead, apparently due to jumping from an office window. Annie and Alvy, aware of the professor's life-affirming character, refuse to believe it was suicide and investigate. The Levy character was then dropped - though reinstated, loosely, in *Crimes and Misdemeanors*, where murder, agreed Woody, was less relevant to the plot than the opportunity it afforded to explore 'all the religious and philosophic ruminations' relating to it. In their next draft, Woody and Brickman had the pair, just as in *Annie Hall*, meeting in front of a movie theatre, with her being late and him not wanting to go in after the film has started. In this version, the couple then go home, stopping off on the way at Zabar's delicatessen for bagels and cream cheese. They get into the elevator with their new neighbours - one of whom, the husband, is already planning to murder his wife.

As Woody noted at the time, he felt the idea to be an insubstantial genre piece not worth devoting a year to. Woody and Brickman then spent two months trying to develop their ideas into the framework of a Victorian farce to be set in England or Boston but, the day before the actual writing was due to start, Woody, put off by the setting and the idea of working again in costume, changed his mind. *Annie Hall* began to take shape along the lines we see in the movie.

Meanwhile, the original script resurfaced as a project on a number of occasions and, in 1991, Woody once more intimated that he would 'love more than anything to do a murder mystery. That would be my gift to myself.' In spite of his frequent put-downs of Hitchcock ('an airport read, none of them had any real content at all') and his astounding claim that he'd only ever read one good murder thriller (Ira Levin's *A Kiss Before Dying*), he has remained fascinated with the genre. Woody once named *Double Indemnity* as his all-time favourite film and clips from it were to be a significant element in *Manhattan Murder Mystery*. Soon after, 'I spoke to Marshall Brickman', he recalled, 'and said "Why don't we try and whip this into shape?".' Although the pair made a few minor readjustments, their original script was to remain 'pretty much' the same.

Principal photography began in New York in September 1992, with a cast including Alan Alda, Anjelica Huston and Woody himself. Mia, who was originally to co-star (and would subsequently sue Woody, under a 'pay or play' deal for her $350,000 fee), had been replaced five weeks prior to filming by Diane Keaton. Indeed, as Woody told Steve Kroft of CBS *Sixty Minutes*, Mia had become so convinced that she was going to do *Manhattan Murder Mystery*, that she unexpectedly telephoned him in the second week of August to check on the start date and the imminent costume fittings. She had, apparently, made an appointment for these on the very day *after* she had been alerted to Woody's alleged sexual molestation of the couple's adopted daughter, Dylan!

Although it might be fascinating to conjecture what Mia might have done with Diane's 'amateur sleuth' role in *Manhattan Murder Mystery*, the film, as originally planned, would have had Mia as the sober, intelligent half of the team, refusing to believe that their neighbour's wife had been murdered, while Woody was to be the 'detective', the one with the jokes, dragging a reluctant Mia along with his enthusiasm. Normally, said Woody, he would have altered the script to suit Diane but, because it was so tightly plotted, they simply swapped roles, with Woody transformed into the straight man, a solemn spoilsport, on the imminent verge of an anxiety attack, and Diane playing the more buoyant, fanatical half of the partnership, hilariously putting new pep into the couple's marriage by involving her husband, unwillingly, in her amateur sleuthing. Without altering a single word of the screenplay, said Woody, Diane's strong comic persona was sufficient to change the film's whole perspective.

Apart from her cameo in *Radio Days*, Diane, mainly due to her yen to do more serious roles during the 1980s, had not worked with Woody for 14 years. Her stint on *Manhattan Murder Mystery* got off, almost inevitably, to a bumpy start. A week into filming, Woody told her there was a problem. 'He said it just wasn't good', she recalled to Marcelle Clements in *Lear's* magazine, but after working with her coach, Marilyn Friend, Diane steeled herself to return to the set: 'Of course, I was completely terrified. But Woody also is very clear. He says, "You'll shoot it again". That's the great thing about him, he's totally honest, non-sentimental.' As Diane has also noted, she had no qualms about playing a woman in her forties in a film which addresses the subject of marriage and ageing head-on. There are, in fact, any number of jokes about middle age, failing eyesight and the possibility of losing one's partner to a younger rival. Diane said she actually relished her on-screen conflict with the more glamorous Anjelica Huston: 'I never had more fun hating somebody. Jealousy, envy, I love that, especially of another woman.'

Manhattan Murder Mystery continued shooting through the winter of 1992 and, although confessing to feelings of guilt at 'wasting almost a year on something which was pleasurable ... but not significant', Woody, who has referred to the events of 1992-3 as 'horrendous', later said that having a film to do, especially a comedy, had been 'a life-saver'. Filming, in fact, passed off without incident, bar a late November report that armed thieves had absconded with $35,000 in actors' salaries from the offices of Woody's production company. Originally to première at an *hors concours* screening at the 1993 Cannes Film Festival, *Manhattan Murder Mystery* was withdrawn along with a handful of other US movies at the last minute, for reasons insufficiently explained. It did subsequently play successfully at Venice prior to its US release in August. TriStar took the step, unusual for an Allen film, of holding nationwide previews in advance of its 268-screen opening. Initially, the film was well received taking $3.04m in its first week, a higher per screen average than for *Husbands and Wives*. Of 49 leading US critics, 28 were predominantly in favour and only one, Terence Rafferty of *The New Yorker* was to offer a completely downbeat review. There were some complaints about the slimness of the plot and Woody's decision to persist with the hand-held camera technique from *Husbands and Wives* - 'Like being on board a yacht or something', said one British critic - which, 'Coupled with the new film's deliberately drab decor and its taste for glaring overhead light' afforded the proceedings, wrote Janet Maslin in *The New York Times*, a somewhat 'unhelpful flourish'.

While regretting, like a number of critics, that Woody had not simply opted for 'an actual years-on sequel' to *Annie Hall*, Maslin saw Woody and Diane this time around as 'a nagging, hopelessly neurotic Nick and Nora Charles ... conjuring up the rapport these two shared so memorably several lifetimes ago'. Although Woody, at one point, *had* contemplated a follow-up to *Annie*, he had finally decided against it, considering the idea 'exploitative'.

This time around, Diane as Carol, though still something of a kook, is less blithe than Annie and, in Marcelle Clements's words, 'more elegant, perhaps, not pretending to be a girl but an attractive and witty woman'. It is Woody as Larry, rather, with his hypochondria, dietary concerns and typical phobias, who seems most recollective of a moment when both these attractive stars were at their zenith as insecure but engagingly comic icons of their time.

The starting point of the story is the supposed murder of the couple's new neighbour, Lillian House (Lyn Cohen) by her philatelist, cinema-owning husband Paul (played by former Broadway producer Jerry Adler). The two couples live on the same floor and have only just met; the situation plays up the idea of apartments with paper-thin walls, which, said Woody, 'makes it possible ... to bring out the proximity of these two worlds - the daily life of the main characters, played by Diane and myself, and the murder plot'.

Unable to convince either Larry or the police of her suspicions, Carol is aided in her detective work by playwright pal Ted (Alan Alda) who has long had a crush on her, while Larry, a fiction editor at Harper's, is being vamped by clever but predatory author Marcia Fox (Anjelica Huston). As a means to her ends, Marcia offers to help improve Larry's poker skills and the scene set in the Café des Artistes, where he performs a practice run for her benefit, demonstrates the prestidigitatous Woody of earlier years once more at his hilarious best - a deft routine which prompted spontaneous applause from preview audiences.

Although, quipped Woody, there is 'no hidden meaning - or, even, meaning' - in the film, *Manhattan Murder Mystery* does revolve around many of its author's usual interests, like sport, old songs and movies, and makes sly comments on contemporary society and the universal angst of the average Manhattanite. He also offers us some of the same moral points which cropped up in *Crimes and*

Misdemeanors, albeit wittily subverted to the requirements of comic melodrama. There are some wonderful in-jokes - like the supposedly dead wife turning up on a bus labelled 'Vertigo'. The idea of the amateur sleuth as a voyeur was, of course, the central thrust of Hitchcock's *Rear Window*, a classic thriller to which *Murder Mystery* was by Terence Rafferty unfavourably compared. The fact that Larry is a publisher, and two of the other main characters writers, impels us towards those bright, informed, Upper-East-Sider exchanges which have long delighted those on Woody's wavelength and helped fuel the dyspepsia of his detractors.

Almost in spite of the persistent use of Di Palma's nervous hand-held, the film is often wonderful to look at. One recalls the bold, swooping helicopter shot, at the opening of the movie, with the whole panoply of Manhattan laid out before us, or the rapturous overhead view of the George Washington Bridge, with its majestic illuminated suspensions, over which Larry and Carol speed in frantic pursuit of the chief suspect's car, as he leads them on a nerve-jangling jaunt to a hellish New Jersey steel smelting factory. Best of all is the climactic sequence: a dazzling pastiche of the final hall-of-mirrors shoot-out from *The Lady from Shanghai*, while that very movie is being projected on screen in a downtown fleapit!

The film's wide-ranging New York locations also include Lincoln Center, all lit up at night; the murky interiors of the old Chelsea Hotel; the Hotel 17 on the East Side; the '21' Club; The National Arts Club and such favourite Allen haunts as Elaine's and Madison Square Garden, for a New York Rangers hockey game. But the New York streets, on this occasion, are virtually empty and devoid of local colour. As Woody explained to Jean-Michel Frodon in *Le Monde*, 'I filmed the streets the way they were. I didn't try to create or recreate a particular atmosphere ... I wanted to avoid anything *outré* or symbolic. I wanted my characters to be as ordinary as possible.'

That said, the dialogue is agreeably aphoristic and Woody's timing of some funny one-liners seems to have lost nothing with the passing of years. Alan Alda as the amused, romantically-inclined participant in what may or may not be a genuine murder investigation brings his affable talents to bear on some quite touching scenes with Diane. As for Diane, her no-nonsense histrionics and refreshingly uncosmeticized appearance augment her character's daffiness and almost childlike enthusiasm to perfection. Of the four principals, Huston has the least developed role but, as the 'brains' of the group her playing is spot on.

Bullets over Broadway Public conjecture over Woody's film future continued through the first half of 1993, as the ongoing feud with Mia ran its course. On 7 July, Manhattan Supreme Court judge Elliott Wilk, in a highly critical 33-

page ruling, dismissed as 'frivolous' and without merit Woody's suit for custody of the couple's three shared children, and restricted his future access. He was also ordered to pay Mia's $1m legal costs. Woody, who had already expended $2m on the case, had also, according to reports, made a voluntary $1m payment to Mia in September 1990 to cover health and educational expenses for Moses, Satchel and Dylan. This amount was reportedly part of Woody's $7m fee for appearing in a Japanese television commercial.

In early May 1994, Woody lost another round in the battle when the courts upheld the previous ruling that he was 'not a fit parent'. Happily, the Connecticut state attorney, acting on recommendations from a Yale-New Haven medical team, had already dropped the more serious charge of child abuse which, to be fair, Mia insisted she had never personally set in motion.

Briefly, after the publication of the Yale findings, the New York newspapers were, mostly, pro-Woody and it says much for his well-entrenched position as a widely popular and even beloved entertainment icon that his reputation did not suffer, finally, much more that it did. Notwithstanding such doom-laden prophecies as that of Manhattan divorce attorney Raoul Felder - to the effect that 'He can put his career in an envelope and mail it to Roman Polanski' - it seemed obvious, for the immediate future, that Woody would continue to make films, if in circumstances somewhat different from before.

On 21 July came the surprise announcement that TriStar had amicably agreed to forego the third and final film in Woody's existing contract. This was to enable him, it was reported, to take up an offer from old friend Jean Doumanian's recently founded Sweetland Films which was holding out better financial terms, both in costs and director's fees. The budgetry hike, reported *Variety*, could be as much as 25 per cent over his deal with TriStar.

The new three-picture contract was negotiated with the blessing of Mike Medavoy, whose personal friendship, suggested insiders, still put TriStar in the front line for at least domestic distribution. TriStar, after three strong years, however, was just embarking on a rocky box-office ride following on from the exodus of several high-profile executives from the company. Medavoy himself was to relinquish the chairmanship of TriStar in January 1994 - a move rumoured to have been brewing for the previous two years. In October he became co-founder and chief executive officer of a new production venture, Phoenix Pictures and named Woody as one of the film-makers he would love to bring into the company.

Jean Doumanian, a former model, had first met Woody when he was appearing as a stand-up at Mister Kelly's in Chicago in the early 1960s. In 1980 she had been signed as a $15,000 a week producer on *Saturday Night Live* and Woody is rumoured to have been the driving force behind Doumanian's brief stint on the show during which she had been responsible for launching the careers of Joe Piscopo and Eddie Murphy. She had formed Sweetland to handle the American end of the Nykvist-directed Foreign Language Oscar-nominee *The Ox* (1992) and had subsequently put together a multi-million-dollar line of funding for further TV and theatrical projects from both US and European sources.

Woody's sister, Letty Aronson, a one-time teacher of emotionally disturbed children and, latterly, vice-president of the Manhattan Museum of Television and Radio, had also been associated with Doumanian on *Saturday Night Live*. She became vice-president of Sweetland in December 1992. According to Aronson, Woody and Doumanian had long talked of joining up professionally and, although industry eyebrows were raised at the very idea of Woody leaving the security of a major studio to make movies with an as yet untried independent, a number of associates insisted that the new deal made perfect sense.

To counteract his failing box office, Woody had been gradually changing his views about personal publicity. He did, for instance, slip quietly into London in August 1993 to promote *Manhattan Murder Mystery* in advance of its January 1994 release. Seven years before he had also been persuaded to hire publicist Leslee Dart to help raise the profile of his films, though resisting, she complained, every good idea she had. 'The irony is', said Woody, 'that I've done more publicity since my personal crisis of the past year than in all the years combined. Because I've been forced to.' None of this helped *Husbands and Wives* to ultimate box-office success in the US, and it was a moot point whether *Manhattan Murder Mystery* would fare any better. In fact, the film's North American gross ($11.3m against an estimated negative cost, according to Woody, of $13-14m) was little more than for its predecessor. In Europe, however, the pattern of reversing the domestic trend for Woody's films, was yet again repeated. *Manhattan Murder Mystery* grossed nearly $8m in France, where it also received a César nomination as Best Foreign Film. It briefly topped the box-office charts in London, Rome and Madrid (it was Spain's eleventh biggest money-maker of 1993-4), and did excellent business in Germany and Latin America. Its £920,523 gross in the UK was 'very good' for a Woody Allen film, TriStar's Stephen Oliver told me, but, then, the film 'was rather more commercial with a very good cast'.

The extensive speculation about Woody's future film plans came, at a time, ironically, when his international critical reputation had never been higher. In France he had long been spoken of in the same breath as Cocteau and Camus and, in the recent massive two-volume *50 Ans de Cinéma Américain* (1992), not only were Woody's cultural references studiously examined, but the writers devoted 11 pages to him - compared to John Ford's meagre four.

Alice, noted Woody, had achieved more admissions in the French capital in 1991 than in the whole of the US put together, and the breakthrough he had achieved with *Annie Hall* in places like Switzerland, Sweden, Israel and parts of Asia, had guaranteed an ongoing popularity. Every one of his films since *Annie* had taken more money outside of America and, almost in spite of the scandal, he had continued to be a major draw in strongly Catholic Italy where even the chequered *Shadows and Fog* had helped restore the fortunes of its local distributor, CDI. Much of Woody's success outside the US was still linked, obviously, to his popularity as an actor and, in a recent survey (July 1991), he had emerged as the world's 23rd most bankable star, in 'presale' terms, of the 300 stellar names in the canvas.

Woody is by no means the first American film-maker to have enjoyed a greater popular success outside of his own country and, were it not for concerns for his family, he would like nothing better, he told Clive Hirschhorn, than 'to make a film in French, in Paris, but it would take three or four months to shoot and I don't want to be away from the children that long ... '. He still receives numerous approaches for acting jobs, even recently, for a Shakespeare play, but 'I turned it down', he said, 'I just couldn't do it'. Should even offers from these sources fail to materialize, he would, he says, be perfectly happy just sitting at home, writing novels or plays. Whether we believe him or not is up to us, though it is to be hoped that the pictures will still be made and the kind of controls Woody has been able to exercise over his work will continue unabated. 'I think I will go on making movies of my own choice with no problem', he told Denis Hamill in April 1993, 'I'm not in the least concerned about my career.'

Indeed, *Bullets over Broadway*, the project which kicked off the Sweetland deal, began filming in and around New York in late September. It was co-scripted by Woody and Doug McGrath, who had recently adapted the remake of *Born Yesterday*. Woody had met McGrath through a mutual friend and, after offering him the choice of five possible story ideas, began working with him on the screenplay, in January 1993. The result of their joint labours was a witty, gritty comedy, set during Prohibition in the Roaring Twenties, about putting on a play on Broadway. Woody was to describe *Bullets* as 'a comedy with a serious point to it, a philosophical point', packed with hilarious set pieces which are 'seen from a modern viewpoint'. It also included gangsters and shoot-outs (something of a return to his first movie, *Take the Money and Run*) but, as with *Manhattan Murder Mystery*, he now found the scenes of violence and gunplay difficult. 'It's a form of brutality that's completely alien to me', he told *Le Monde*, 'That scene [in *Murder Mystery*] was necessary to the plot, but I'd never have managed it without the help of Orson Welles!'

Bullets over Broadway completed principal photography in 11 weeks and, while the film was still editing, Woody embarked almost immediately on his TV remake of *Don't Drink the Water* which began shooting on a four-week schedule in April 1994. Transmission was set for December, by which time a second TV movie had been agreed upon. This was to be *Powers of Attorney*, from a legal thriller novel, to be directed by Woody, but scripted by Alan Rosen. There was also an off-Broadway show - three one-act comedies (*An Interview* by David Mamet, *Hotline* by Elaine May and Woody's *Central Park West*), under the blanket title, *Death Defying Acts*. This was presented by Jean Doumanian and Julian Schlossberg, on 6 March 1995, at the 500-seater Variety Arts, after a brief try-out in Stamford, Connecticut. The plays were directed by Michael Blakemore, with virtually identical casts, and the critical view was that Woody's contribution, the longest of the playlets, came off best. Some reviewers, though, found the 'real-life' resonances in *Central Park West* to be 'unsavoury' and 'uncomfortable'. Mainly due to Woody's contribution, *Death Defying Acts* became the longest running off-Broadway opener of 1995, and there were plans to tour the show in October of the following year.

Aside from this mind-boggling flurry of activity, there remained the release problem of *Bullets over Broadway*. Although it was reported that Woody had not expected to spend more than his usual budget, still well below the now $30m (plus $15m p & a) Hollywood average, Doumanian had raised $20m in foreign money - for a film, reportedly to cost $19m - Woody's biggest budget to that date. However, the movie had been completed without a firm contract for distribution - a first for Woody and, in the current climate of his career, a calculated risk.

Notwithstanding reports that the Hollywood majors had discreetly distanced themselves from Woody during his recent troubles, there were, according to Doumanian, at least four offers for the film. The release of *Bullets over Broadway* would be, finally, entrusted to Miramax, an unconventional New York-based distributor, founded by the buccaneering Bob and Harvey Weinstein expressly to handle such provocative independent titles as *The Piano* and *The Crying Game*. In late 1993, the brothers Weinstein had successfully completed an estimated $80m 'killer deal' for the acquisition of Miramax by Disney. Miramax, though, would still operate autonomously, in regard to marketing and distributing its own movies and, in June 1994, acquired the US and Canadian rights to *Bullets over Broadway* - despite being denied a preview of the completed film. Disney, meanwhile, were reported to be 'thrilled' to have Woody under what already began to look like a long-term aegis.

The Weinsteins, after viewing the picture, expressed themselves delighted and much was made of the fact that this would be the first Allen movie to be sold world-wide to independent distributors. Miramax also succeeded in obtaining international sales rights, in addition to domestic distribution. At the same time, sources said, the company had agreed to pay off the now estimated $20m cost of the film, thus taking the onus off Sweetland and the original backers. It was to be noted, however, that, in terms of Woody's recent record, the 'deal could be more about prestige than black ink' - a situation somewhat alleviated by enthusiasm in Europe. Bac Films instantly put in a bid for French distribution, in spite of the $4m asking price (the price paid was actually $2.8m with a minimum p & a commitment).

Bullets over Broadway is an archetypal backstage comedy thriller which, initially, owes something to the characters and ambience of the 1927 Philip Dunning-George Abbott stage hit *Broadway*. It also pays affectionate homage to such later 'putting on a show' entertainments as Noel Coward's 'Star Quality', the Al Jolson musical *Go Into Your Dance* and *All about Eve*. One of the characters - a former pants salesman turned producer (played by Jack Warden) is called 'Julian Marx', an obvious play on the director 'Julian Marsh' in *42nd Street*, while the gangster sequences pay lip-service to that vigorous cycle of fast-edited rat-a-tat-tat crime thrillers which heralded in the early sound period. The film is neither terribly original nor as excruciatingly funny as perhaps it ought to be, but it *is* very enjoyable, taking its chief thrust (as in *Broadway Danny Rose*) from the traditional close links between American show business and organized crime.

It also has some pertinent things to say about art vs commerce/art vs life/sex vs love and Woody's avowed aversion to the kind of artist who 'creates his own moral universe' by assuming it as his God-given right to do as he pleases - purely on account of any talent that artist may or may not have. Above all, the film deals with the way that amateur, untrained talent may often prove more effective, in practice, than professional trained skills.

The play in question is being backed by a big-time mobster, Nick Valenti (Joe Viterelli), with the unshakeable proviso that his moll, a bird-brained night-club chorine, Olive Neal (Jennifer Tilly), play a top-featured role. The story's neat central idea is that the hapless Olive's appointed hit-man bodyguard, Cheech (Chazz Palminteri) becomes so disenchanted with what he sees and hears in rehearsal, that he begins offering unsolicited advice on the script. 'You don't write like people talk', is Cheech's constant complaint. At first his interpolations are resented by the play's author-director, David Shayne (John Cusack), a somewhat overwrought Pittsburgh boy trying to make good on the Great White Way. Then like the cast, he begins to realize that this unwelcome attendant on the somewhat frayed rehearsals at the old Belasco Theater actually talks a lot of horse sense. Streetwise and intuitive, Cheech has the natural ability to put his finger on the very pulse of what's wrong with the play - a pretentious piece of wordy, over-cerebral psycho-drivel called *God of Our Fathers* - and, working in surreptitious collaboration with its credited (but less talented) author, he briskly transforms it into a copper-bottomed hit!

Along the way, Woody fills out the story with some predictable but highly diverting situations. David, for instance, cheats on his nice regular girl friend Ellen (Mary-Louise Parker) with temperamental fading stage-star Helen Sinclair (Dianne Wiest). The vowel-fracturing Olive, struggling to encompass her ludicrously miscast role as the play-within-a-play's lady psychiatrist, embarks on a flirtation with British-born leading man Warner Purcell (Jim Broadbent), an actor laddie of the old school. Loveable but ridiculous, he comes replete with elaborate corsetry and a gargantuan eating compulsion. Helen clashes with perky second lead Eden Brent (Tracey Ullman) and Ellen has a brief, compensatory fling with failed playwright and left-wing Village philosopher, Sheldon Flender (Rob Reiner).

Against all this, Woody and his team create a wondrous looking and sounding portrait of a bustling 1920s' Manhattan. The film is a visual feast, from its Times Square opening - actually a black-and-white cut from the period which was digitally colorized to match - to the art deco apartments and hallways, the artily-lit street scenes, speakeasies and newsstands, vivid backstage milieu and darkly comic waterfront shoot-outs. It is a highly romanticized recreation of a vanished age, bathed in a deep red, sepia and yellow glow by cameraman Carlo Di Palma, designed and costumed to the nines, the sound track awash with the kind of insouciant golden standards which nostalgia buffs adore.

Locations for the film ranged from an empty ballroom at the New Yorker Hotel, previously used for the El Morocco scenes in *Radio Days* and now reconstructed as the 'Three Deuces' night-club, to an unoccupied unit in the Tudor City building in Manhattan, standing in for Olive's over-decorated art deco apartment. Helen's richly appointed, somewhat cluttered art nouveau establishment was fashioned out of an actual house on Riverside Drive, and the billiard parlour, where David and Cheech do most of their writing, was constructed out of an old warehouse. Although the actual Belasco frontage on 44th Street was used for exterior shooting, the rehearsal and performance interiors were shot inside the Cort Theater on 48th.

A couple of scenes were also filmed in Greenwich Village, while the more ambitious sequence, where mob hit-men speed along a Manhattan street with machine guns blazing, was actually shot in the Williamsburg neighbourhood of Brooklyn, real-life childhood stamping ground of gangster Bugsy Siegel. The scene where David declares himself to Helen, and she first utters her famous catch phrase, 'Please - don't speak. Don't say a word ...' was shot in Central Park. Filming on a grey, muggy day with a completely flat sky, Woody was in his element: 'We don't shoot outside on sunny days, and haven't in twenty years. On an overcast day like that, when you have flowers in the background - or any colors for that matter, you get a very rich saturation that you don't get on a sunny day.' As a result of which, the scene appears to burst with colour as David pours out his passion for the tempestuous Helen.

Woody had also intended shooting the opening-night party scene, at the end of the movie, in Central Park, but this was ruled out due to prohibitive overtime costs. Instead, Woody changed the locale to a restaurant where the windows were blacked out and the cast and crew paid their normal daily rates. Being set in the 1920s, the film had already proved more costly than usual, especially since Woody - to the relief of many fans - had decided to dispense with the more economic but too modernistic hand-held camera technique of his two previous films.

Although the story was, according to Woody, 'strictly made up' and the character of Cheech a pure fiction, he has admitted that David was intended as himself in a younger, more handsome guise. At one point, Woody did consider playing the role himself and he and co-writer McGrath conceived of David as 'a college professor, an academic at heart but one who fancied himself as an artist and occasionally wrote a play to prove it'. McGrath was, apparently, all in favour of Woody taking the part, but Woody, feeling 'it fell slightly more naturally to a younger person', resisted.

Impressed by Cusack's natural playing as the student in *Shadows and Fog*, Woody cast him in the role of David. Though tending to shout a lot, he emerges as a taller, more personable representative of Woody, even down to some of the inflections, hand-wringing, anxiety attacks and lines he has to utter. Cusack, though, is much more than a mere Woody Allen clone - not only on account of their physical differences but because David is an artistic failure, in complete antithesis to Woody's high-powered media heroes of more recent vintage. In the end, David opts for a settled life with long-time inamorata Ellen, back in Pittsburgh where he doesn't have to prove himself as an artist.

Although Woody has said he had no actors in mind when he wrote the screenplay, the casting is virtually foolproof. Viterelli, a relative newcomer to films and a self-confessed fan of Damon Runyon and the 1920s, was cast on the strength of his performance in *The Firm*, while Broadbent was brought to Woody's attention by Juliet Taylor after she'd spotted him in the British film, *Enchanted April*. Broadbent has said that he particularly relished Woody's way of working mostly in long, continuous takes in long shot, and the fact that 'all the principals are on the same rate of pay, so you don't get stars lording it and pulling the usual stunts'. Dianne Wiest, who would win a Best Supporting Oscar for her performance and was honoured, in the same category by the New York, Los Angeles and National Society of Film Critics, plays Helen as a well-judged composite of a number of stage and screen legends of earlier days. With her slightly Anglicized accent and highly theatrical manner (both on and off stage), Wiest makes her scenes seem a great deal better than they actually are. Palminteri as Cheech is lethal but oddly likeable, an articulate rough diamond, paraphrasing the odd line from *This Gun for Hire* and offering some salient views on the failures of formal education. He is used in the film to play up the contrast between the striver (David) who simply adopts the artist's pose, but would readily compromise to get his play performed, and the genuine artist (Cheech), who has a passion for his work and will kill if necessary to see his true vision fulfilled.

Following the precedent of *Goodfellas* and *The Godfather* films, a number of the actors playing racketeers in the movie were the genuine article. 'And oddly enough' Woody told Colin Brown, 'they're graceful with dialogue and can speak and be believable. Sometimes they're more graceful than actors who have studied for 20 years.' One of Nick Valenti's henchmen in the film was actually at school with Woody: 'He was the neighbourhood gangster where I grew up in Brooklyn - a gun-toting gangster at 16 who then went off to prison.' As for Palminteri, latterly both actor and sensitive writer of plays and film scripts, he was so like the character, as Woody had envisaged him, that it was no surprise to discover that he 'had a racket kind of background' and had known a number of real-life mobsters personally.

The stand-out performance, though, comes from Tilly as the sexily brainless Olive who so appals Cheech with her thespian ineptness that, convinced she is hell-bent on ruining 'his' play he does what any self-respecting dramatist *ought* to do - takes her for a ride! In the original script, said Tilly, 'She was simply told she wasn't ready for Broadway and quietly dumped' but, in the film, the actress's climactic waterfront exit - counterpointed by a near subliminal snatch of 'Up the Lazy River' - is both chilling and hilarious. (Ironically, in fact, one journalist had the temerity to ask Woody if the idea of his bumping off an actress on screen was meant to symbolize a proxy revenge on Mia Farrow!). Olive, like a number of the other characters, is compounded in cliché - but her 'rise' from night-club floosie to feature role in a Broadway play is given impetus by the sassy conviction and sheer delectability of Tilly's playing. 'After the first five minutes on set', recalled Tilly, 'I realized that Woody not only wants you to improvise, it became apparent to me he wanted Olive to never stop talking. He had this idea about Olive, he said, "She's in her own little world and it just revolves around her and she just talks and talks and talks." '

Cusack and the other cast members also welcomed the opportunity to improvise, and it is certain that the prestige value of working with Woody has not diminished with the years. Dianne Wiest accepted her role in *Bullets*, sight unseen, because she said 'I feel like I get to go on adventures with Woody that I couldn't get to go on with any other filmmaker.' Any number of actors would also subscribe to that view, though Woody appears to remain staunch in his predilection for employing high-powered names to often minimal effect. Harvey Fierstein for instance, is reduced to two brief moments as David's agent, while the originally announced Alan Arkin was to disappear entirely.

Bullets over Broadway, as befits its flamboyant theatrical setting, is Woody playing very much to the gallery. This would be reflected in the film's world première at the Venice Film Festival, in September 1994. European critics were virtually unanimous in their praise, as were most of those who saw the picture at its equally favourable showing during the New York Film Festival, in October. The film's subsequent two-screen US opening achieved an impressive $86,062 three-day gross - a higher per screen average than for any concurrent release. Of 45 leading New York & LA critics, 37 gave *Bullets* the thumbs up. 'A bright, energetic comedy!' enthused Janet Maslin in *The New York Times*, while Mike Clark of *USA Today* dubbed it 'an opulent rib-tickler worthy of its screaming-neon title'.

There were, as for *Manhattan Murder Mystery*, reservations about the featherlight plot, and a number of critics echoed Clark's observation (*vis-à-vis* the apparent parallels in the film) 'about talent and acceptable public behaviour often being at odds'. *Bullets* appeared also to be one for the fashion-conscious, who noted how closely the satin boudoir slips and other accessories at Anna Sui and Ghost already resembled some of Jeffrey Kurland's dazzling Oscar-nominated costumes for the film. As Kurland told me:

I made a big study of the movies and magazines, a quite extensive research into the period, what it must have been like, with hindsight, to be there, back at that time, the 1920s. I spent a great deal of time in museums and libraries and I must have looked at many, many hundreds of photographs and books of the period. And we wanted to get that look, for it to be a very accurate picture, with very authentic costuming - not just 'Oh, yeah, *that* looks like the 1920s' - but it had to be true to the setting of the writing, of the piece - which, again, was filled with whimsy. And we had to reflect that, needed to express that world, that feeling. So I got hold of all sorts of cottons and chintzes and linens and other materials they used then, with lots of fringes and furbelows, and we went for the kind of cut and authentic style and colours they used in that era.

By year's end, however, the picture, in admittedly selected screenings, had gen-erated a mere $8.6m gross at the US box office, though it did emerge as Miramax's third top money-maker of 1994, after *Pulp Fiction* and *The Crow*. But, the film's commercial prospects improved, dramatically, in the run-up to the Oscars. With nearly three years gone by since the height of the 'scandal', Hollywood was in forgiving mood. *Bullets* received seven nominations (the same as for *Hannah*) which, apart from those already mentioned, were for Best Director, Original Screenplay, Art Direction and the Best Supporting contribu-tions of Tilly and Palminteri. Although Wiest was the only winner, post Oscar euphoria boosted the weekly box office by 35 per cent and helped push the film towards a final US gross of around $13.5m.

On its Paris opening in January 1995 *Coups de feu sur Broadway* (*sic*) had also notched up an immediate first week's take of $497,664. Woody, assisted by Charlotte Rampling, went on national TV to promote the picture and saw it score a nearly $2.5m gross in the French capital alone. By the first week of April, *Bullets* had already bettered its domestic returns in only seven overseas territories, looking, potentially, like Woody's best 'crossover' prospect since *Crimes and Misdemeanors*. It opened a month later in the UK to almost over-whelmingly positive reviews. '*Radio Days* meets *Some like it Hot*', enthused Carole Allen on *London Newstalk*, while 'Rush to see it!' urged Derek Malcom in *Cosmopolitan*, 'This is the best dish Allen has served up for some time'. The capital's top film attraction during its first two weeks, with a further seven weeks in the London top ten, *Bullets* eventually achieved a British gross of just over £1m, going on to a total worldwide take of $37.6m.

Mighty Aphrodite In February 1994 Woody had been reported scouting locations in Venice for a movie to feature Soon-Yi - possibly the old American in Europe idea he had been planning prior to *Crimes and Misdemeanors*. He had actually begun work on a new screenplay in January, but the film which did emerge, *Mighty Aphrodite*, was shot, on a 10-week schedule, in New York, New Jersey and Sicily from 3 October, followed by a sequence of reshoots in February 1995.

A contemporary romantic comedy, it starred Woody as a sports journalist, Lenny Weinrib, married to self-centred art gallery owner Amanda (Helena Bonham Carter). The couple have an adopted son, Max (Jimmy McQuaid), who, Lenny becomes convinced, is 'so bright and charming and funny' he must be the offspring of very remarkable parents. This aspect of the story was inspired, said Woody, by his own fond observations, years before, of his adop-tive daughter Dylan - his conjectures abut her true parentage becoming linked, some months later, with the germ for a funny story about a character who becomes so obsessed with the idea of falling in love with his adopted son's real mother that he sets out to find her. At the end of his search, though, Lenny, in the film, is dismayed to discover that, far from being a 'saint with a 150 IQ', Max's mom is actually the multi-pseudonymous Linda Ash (Mira Sorvino), alias 'Judy Cum', a sweet-natured but bubble-headed hooker and porn actress with the face of a model, the legs of a wading bird and the language of a truck driver. Reassured by her still-evident regret at having given up the baby, Lenny decides to 'rescue' this fallen angel, endow her with polish and find her a suitable mate, but in so doing, he and Linda have to deal with her cutting-up-rough pimp, Ricky (Dan Moran), as well as the embarassing evidence of her former 'film career'!

Lenny also has to cope with Amanda's suspected infidelity with smooth operator Jerry Bender (Peter Weller) and, while making a number of witty and only slightly sceptical comments on middle-class marriage, non-biological parenthood, tutorial relationships, art, society and morality in general, the story is punctuated by a series of nightmare sequences and flashbacks to Ancient Greece - filmed at the open air Teatro Greco in Taormina - where an amphitheatre company, in classical masks and robes, is performing *Oedipus Rex*.

This location, originally carved from the flank of Mount Etna, has served in recent years as the site of the annual Taormina Film Festival, which Woody, from his attendance with *Bananas* in 1971, had remembered as an 'unspeakably beautiful place, and I'd always hoped I could return'. With a few period-enhanced amendations by Santo Loquasto, the Teatro proved ideal for Woody's purpose, and the chanting Chorus, aided and abetted by a finger-wagging 'Cassandra' and an Ansafone 'Zeus' (a device derived from *God*) is brought vividly back to droll New York Jewish-accented life to comment and advise upon the foolish foibles of present-day lovers and warn against Lenny's hubristic attempts to assuage his curiousity and deflect a preordained destiny.

'I wanted to stylize the chorus', said Woody, 'I didn't want these guys to wander in like they're going to buy newspapers, but instead I wanted them to have a certain amount of choreographed motion, as the choruses of that time did. And for that you need a choreographer'. For this purpose, Woody hired Graciela Daniele, who had worked on *Bullets over Broadway*, and , although the Chorus do step out of period to perform a couple of musical comedy standards, they are all the funnier for keeping their movements loosely in accord with the established pseudo-Graeco style of the earlier scenes. With their masks and gowns, the Chorus may also be taken as a self-satirising reference to the Bergamanesque 'Death' symbol which Woody had decided to cut from

the climactic Southampton beach scenes in *Interiors*. They are led by an ubiq-
uitous conscience figure (F. Murray Abraham), while other players in the
tragedy include Jack Warden as 'Tiresias', Jeffrey Kurland as 'Oedipus' and
Olympia Dukakis as 'Jocasta'. The modern cast includes Michael Rapaport as
Kevin, a young boxer, and Claire Bloom, albeit briefly, as Amanda's mother.
Hot young actress Lili Taylor was, though, a casualty of the editing.

New York filming ranged from the Upper East Side, for the Weinribs' first
apartment, as well as Linda's exotically detailed whore's pad, fairly bristling
with sex toys and phallic knick-knacks, to a loft on Mercer Street, in the
Tribeca district of Manhattan, for Lenny and Amanda's second home. As usual,
Loquasto's interior design for these settings does much to reflect the basic
personalities and social aspirations of the respective owners. For Amanda's
main workplace, Woody used the ChristenRose art gallery on West Broadway,
in Soho, while other locations included Madison Square Garden, the bandshell
in Central Park, the Roxy restaurant in Times Square and the FAO Schwartz
toy store on 58th Street, midtown Manhattan. There were also forays to
Quogue, in the Hamptons, the New Jersey Turnpike and, for the first time
since *Sex Comedy*, Woody also took his unit to Tarrytown, in New York State.
This was for the sequence where Linda, smarting over her stalled romance
with Kevin, finally meets the man of her dreams, a dashing helicopter pilot!

The film was shot, by Di Palma, in characteristic dark tones and , inasmuch
as Woody is still frequently accused of playing a one note fiddle, from the visual and design point of view the changes on his movies have been rung with
quite remarkable originality. As Jeffrey Kurland recently told me:

> No project is ever the same. *Mighty Aphrodite* was my 14th consecutive film
> designing for Woody - Woody's Untitled '95 is the 15th! - and it could eas-
> ily have been 14 or 15 different directors, each film is so different. With
> the Chorus costumes for *Mighty Aphrodite*, which were period, we used all
> natural colours and materials, all cottons and silks and things, it was all
> very painterly, over-dyed and painted. We had trims made and painted, and
> we applied paints to leathers and bronzes - they cast the buckles and
> insignia and everything in bronze, which were put on after. I wanted it to
> look like the authentic article, just like things used to be in those days, to
> be accurate as far as what we know of that period. So, although it was a
> very whimsical idea, I wanted it to *look* like somebody's idea of those
> times. I don't know if you're familiar with the work of Alma-Tadema, who
> is a favourite artist of mine. His Neo-Classical style had a great impact on
> me - all those drapes, flowing robes, togas and such, which are quite

spectacular. And so I tried to imitate his style, that sort of strange Victorians' idea of what the Greek and Roman times were like. Which, of course, is how a lot of people have come to see the Ancient World.

The wit and inventiveness of *Aphrodite*'s production and costume design are, indeed, assets, though without the intrusions of the Greek Chorus, the basic story would be slim, indeed. The film also suffers from a number of glaring structural flaws - most importantly, the fact that Max, around whose implied 'genius' Lenny's quest for heritage revolves, remains insufficiently established as a person to offer us very much more than a cursory peg upon which to hang the mechanics of the plot. Young Max is sweet, clean-cut and charming, but apart from a handful of scenes in which Lenny fusses over him, plays ball, takes him to the gym and showers him with presents, we do not, in fact, learn very much else about him - a weakness of development which *Radio Days* apart, would appear to the the traditional fate of juveniles in Woody's movies.

Other characters, except for the three leads, are similarly short changed. The relationship between Linda and Kevin, though momentarily endearing, has no sooner got under way than it's over, the script is wasteful of Jack Warden's otherwise amusing turn as a blind New York street beggar, and Peter Weller's few appearances as Amanda's sleazeball backer (and would be seducer) fail to give any real inkling as to why she should be so strongly tempted. On the other hand, the scenes between Amanda and Lenny/Lenny and Linda are minor triumphs of the comedian's art, particularly the latter, wherein Woody and Sorvino enjoy one of the most felicitous and likeable mismatch teamings since Woody and Diane captivated world audiences in *Annie Hall*.

As for the central marital relationship, it is not only thoroughly convincing, and, ultimately, poignant, but it reverses the more recent trend in Woody's movies by establishing Amanda as the socially (and culturally) superior half of the partnership, while Lenny reverts, to some extent, to the archetypal 'loser' figure of Woody's earliest comedies: the blustering yet unconfident romantic, the little man with great hopes but undefined aspirations, modest in stature and with ineffably middle brow tastes.

Miramax, already in place to handle domestic distribution, acquired the international rights to *Aphrodite* in late July from their Dutch-based owner, Sweetland BV. Negotiations had taken longer than usual, reportedly due to interest from competing distributors - a situation fuelled by the, to that date, encouraging $20m plus overseas gross of *Bullets over Broadway*. *Aphrodite* received a world premiere *fuori concorso* screening on 1 September at the 53rd Venice International Film Festival, where, in acknowledgement of his reputation in Europe, especially Italy, Woody was honoured, *in absentia*, with a Golden Lion for long-term career achievement. European reviews for the film were, if anything, even warmer than for its predecessor, Jean-Michel Frodon in *Le Monde* suggesting that judging by the spontaneous gales of laughter and applause which greeted the film throughout the screening, any other honour Venice might bestow would clearly be an irrelevance.

Other critics agreed that had the film been in official competition it would surely have won a prize in its own right, certainly as regards the actors - most notably the Harvard educated Sorvino, who had met Woody earlier, when she auditioned briefly and unsuccessfully for the TV remake of *Don't Drink the Water*. Cast against previous type, she appears as an Amazonian bimbo, towering, like several of his former leading ladies, high above Woody. With blondeish streaked hair, spiked heels, skin-tight dresses and fluffy sweaters from which she is constantly threatening to erupt, she delivers her lines in highpitched, flatly uninflected Minnie Mouse tones which the actress, apparently, based on a friend of her mother's.

According to Sorvino, she had researched her role by walking around Philadelphia (Linda's former stamping ground) for three days 'in character', and talking to strippers and 'a lot with Sandy Bitch, a porno actress, and she impressed me with the enthusiasm with which she spoke of her activities. She did so, without embarassment, using the word "profession" with considerable pride.' Immediately before filming, Sorvino received from Woody just a single instruction: 'I don't want a glimmer of intelligence to show through because not only is she dumb but she's stupid'. Describing Linda as 'the best comedic role written in the past 25 years', the actress added that getting a part in an Allen movie was like a 'gift from God', and she found Woody 'enormously sympathetic and easy to work with'. Sorvino made a virtual clean sweep of the year's Best Supporting Actress nods from the US Critics, culminating with a Golden Globe Award and an Oscar.

Following further screenings at the Toronto and Chicago Film Festivals, *Mighty Aphrodite* on its 19 screen, six city US opening in late October, achieved a top per screen weekend average gross of $17,184. Indeed, early New York audiences echoed Venice by breaking into spontaneous cheers and applause, though this favourable reception came in spite of widely reported protests by the city's powerful Spence-Chapin Adoption Agency, which objected strongly to Woody's treatment of the film's subject matter, and in particular, the characterization of Linda.

Apart from their near consensus on Sorvino, American reviewers, unlike their European counterparts, were split down the middle, a number prefering to review recent events in Woody's life rather than the work in hand. Syndicated columnist Maureen Dowd, in fact complained that *Aphrodite* reminded her of 'a campaign film', but Janet Maslin in *The New York Times* compared the picture favourably, in terms of fantasy, with *Alice* and *The Purple Rose of Cairo*. Todd McCarthy in *Variety* highlighted Sorvino, the film's vintage song score, and Di Palma and Loquasto's success in affording the film 'a particularly warm look', but did take Woody to task for his continued predilection for 'having very young women fall in love with him and his anxiety about having children: the latter seems like an issue he should have long since dealt with, while the former feels a tad unbecoming at this point'.

The gags, it was agreed, were well up to par, McCarthy especially savouring the scene in the story's preamble where Lenny, in trying to pick a name for his adopted infant son, is prompted into reciting 'a funny but dubiously close-to-home laundry list' of just those kind of arty celebrity icons about whom Ike Davis had once waxed lyrical in *Manhattan*. And to those who always preferred to see (and hear) Woody in familiar guise, the comic counterbalance of erudition, romanticism, self-deflation, proudly worn neuroses and generosity of spirit was once again very much to the fore.

By the end of 1995, however, the film had grossed little more than $5m. Much, as usual, would rest on the picture's reception elsewhere - 'My films are so much better in Europe', Woody once joked, 'The dubbing covers up all my mistakes'. *Aphrodite* opened there in January/February 1996, briskly topping its US take in Italy and posting Woody's biggest ever first day gross in France. It had already received a couple of encouraging advance screenings at the London and Southampton Film Festivals, and its UK release followed a major month-long European city tour by Woody and his New Orleans Jazz Band, which, as the New York Jazz Ensemble, had released its first professional album, *The Bunk Project*, in 1993. The tour climaxed at London's Royal Festival Hall and, along with selective media promotions by Woody himself, the packed to capacity gigs afforded *Mighty Aphrodite* a more than usually helpful box-office profile.

Afterwords Taken within the context of the last two or three years, it would appear that Woody's already formidable workload had been spurred by the events in his life, rather than hindered by them. Certainly, he is not short of future plans. According to a 1987 report, he already had ideas, treatments and even full-length screenplays put by to guarantee his next dozen movies - work, said Woody, which would keep him busy until at least the end of the century.

He has said, for instance, he would love to do a movie featuring Diane Keaton, Judy Davis and Dianne Wiest - 'the three most exciting actresses there are for the moment' - and there is also a possible project about the birth of jazz, as opposed to a story which merely depends on jazz scoring or a musician hero. This is an idea Woody has been playing around with, for some time, and it would take the story from the early years in New Orleans, right on through Chicago, New York and Paris. He has not yet put the project in motion because, as he told Stephen Farber, 'I've been too lazy to get out of New York' - and, although 'it could be wonderful' and he has a number of ideas for the script, he has never got down to the actual writing because 'I can't do it for less than a lot of money'. Another plan, announced in October 1994 and something of a departure, would be a non-fiction documentary about his ongoing child custody battles with Mia. Woody, though, said he would not make up his mind until after the pending appeals had been settled. He was also waiting, it was reported, to find out what Mia herself had to say in her upcoming autobiography. Prior to this possibility, Patsy Kensit and Dennis Boutsikaris had already played the roles of 'Mia' and 'Woody' in a two-part Toronto-based mini series, *Love and Betrayal: The Mia Farrow Story*. Although Mia had taken legal steps to try and stop it, Woody took the idea less seriously. 'I hope I'll be cast in an interesting way', he quipped. Aired on the US Fox Channel on 28 February and 2 March 1995, the film went as far as it could, while still adhering to the known 'facts' of the Allen-Farrow story.

By March 1995, Woody was hard at work, as an actor only, on a two-hour TV update of Neil Simon's famous Broadway hit, *The Sunshine Boys*. Co-starring Peter Falk and Sarah Jessica Parker, it was produced and directed by John Erman for Hallmark Entertainment/CBS. Previously filmed for the big screen in 1975 with George Burns and Walter Matthau, and as an MGM-TV pilot with Red Buttons and Lionel Stander the following year, the new version had Woody as the more fastidious of the story's two veteran Vaudevillians (the Burns role), with Falk as his shambling former partner. The telefeature's chief departure lay in transforming the key role of the Falk character's slickly earnest agent nephew into a *niece,* and such was their confidence in the material and quality cast, Hallmark had reportedly considered offers to have the result released theatrically. As for his immediate directing plans, Woody had long talked of a large-scale musical, at one point to star Diane Keaton, and, in embarking on his all-star $20m plus *Everyone Says I Love You*, it looked as if the dream was, finally, coming to fruition. 'I don't like to discuss this', he had said in July, 'because I don't know if I can *make* a decent musical. Should it look like the problems are overwhelming, I'd like to switch gears without too much embarrassment'.

Woody was reported putting the finishing touches to his script during that year's Venice Festival and, in spite of his usual bid for secrecy, the Italian media managed to leak certain elements of the film's plot which appeared to revolve around a traditional close-knit Jewish family with a half-crazy grandfather who lives in Paris. The cast included Tim Roth, Judy Davis, Goldie Hawn, Alan Alda, Bette Midler, Lukas Haas, Ed Norton, Natalie Portman and Drew Barrymore. In the story's Italian interlude, Woody and Julia Roberts were father and daughter, with Roberts casting her spell on a young Venetian count - played by fast-rising local heartthrob Kim Rossi Stuart. Woody began two weeks' filming in Venice, on the 11 September, in the environs of the famous Teatro della Fenice, on Campo San Fantin (tragically destroyed by fire, in late January 1996, shortly before Woody was due to appear there with The New Orleans Jazz Band). Other locations included the Lido, the fish market and the gardens and villa of Venice Festival benefactor Count Volpi di Misurata. After some further shooting in New York, Woody completed the film's 14-week schedule in Paris. 'The Paris locations were all touristy sorts of places', Robert Greenhut told me, 'We filmed in front of the Ritz Hotel quite a bit, and the Palais de Chaillot for a party scene. There was no studio work and the New York filming was also all on location, except for one sequence, part of an apartment, which we shot, not at the Kaufman Astoria, as Woody usually does, but at the Chelsea Pier Studio, on 23rd Street'.

A further possiblity mooted at this time was *A Jew in Love*, a proposed collaboration between Woody and Spanish director Fernando Trueba - a film for that country's most powerful producer, Andres Vicente Gomez. There were also ideas for several new comedies and a number of personal projects, any one of which, said Woody, would 'go for the highest sensibility' and conceivably afford him the 'masterpiece' he claims to have eluded him and which would rank him, he hopes, alongside such idols as Buñuel and Bergman.

To his admirers that longed-for masterpiece has already been made, though, with characteristic modesty, Woody would be the first to deny it. 'I can sneeze backwards, I can balance on an eye', he asserted, in one of his early routines - a moment of wry surrealism which intimated, notwithstanding his own professed limitations, that, where the true artist is concerned, anything is possible.

Nor is he unduly worried, he says, about being remembered. 'Someone once asked me if my dream was to live on in the hearts of my people', Woody told William Geist in *Rolling Stone*, 'and I said I would like to live on in my apartment... You drop dead one day, and it means less than nothing if billions of people are singing your praises... You'd be better off with a couple of years' extension'.

Filmography

Note: Woody Allen functioned as writer-director on all of the following, except where otherwise stated. Although his own films, until recently, were each billed as 'A Jack Rollins-Charles H Joffe Production', since Joffe's semi-retirement in the late 1970s the logo has become pseudonymous with Woody's Untitled Productions Inc. This latter is an autonomous unit, most of whose key personnel have been with Woody for over two decades. Joffe still manages Woody's career and he and Rollins retain their contractual links, but the films are now produced under the aegis of Jean Doumanian's Sweetland Films.

Abbreviations: *s.s.* - shooting start; *e.n.c.* - estimated negative cost; *US/Can r.* - US and Canadian rentals (Canada usually providing about 15 per cent of the Noth American total). * means updated from original release year, latter's figures in brackets; *dir.* - director; *pr.* - producer; *scr.* - screenwriter; *ph.* - director of photography; *des.* - production designer (or pre-1971, art director); *ed.* - editor; *spec f/x.* etc - special effects; *cos.* - costume designer; MPAA, BBFC - US and UK censorship ratings; *US/Can gr.* - gross when rental not known, or around double to 2.5 times rental figure, latter being the amount accruing to distributors after exhibitors' fees and other expenses have been deducted; *AA* - Academy Award winner. *Note:* To illustrate the complex relationship between box office takings and *e.n.c.* , a single example will suffice. *Take the Money and Run* achieved domestic rentals of $2.59m + (foreign) $450,000 = (world total) $3,040,000. E.n.c.was $1.53m + p & a (prints and advertising) $1,275,000 + distributors' fees $680,000 + bank loan interest $165,000 = (total cost) $3,650,000. Thus the film, though popular, lost $610,000 on first release, only breaking even with the help of reissues, TV and video sales, about 7 years later.

WHAT'S NEW, PUSSYCAT?/QUOI DE NEUF, PUSSYCAT? (US/FRENCH)
1965 (June. *UK*: Aug); *s.s.* 15 Oct 1964 (Paris and environs; Studios Boulogne-Billancourt); *e.n.c.* $4m ($3m b.) *US/Can r.* $8.7m* ($7.1m. 5th Top Money-Maker); 108 mins (from 120); Famous Artists/Famartists/UA

Dir. Clive Donner; *pr.* Charles K. Feldman; *scr.* Woody Allen, loosely adapted from *Lot's Wife* by Ladislaus Bus-Fekete; *ph.* Jean Badal (Technicolor); *des.* Jacques Saulnier; *music* Burt Bacharach; *ed.* Fergus McDonnell; *spec f/x.* Bob MacDonald; *cos.* Gladys de Segonzac; MPAA (R); BBFC (X).
Cast: Peter Sellers (Fritz Fassbender); Peter O'Toole (Michael James); Romy Schneider (Carol Werner); Capucine (Renée Lefebvre); Paula Prentiss (Liz Bien); Woody Allen (Victor Shakapopolis); Rita (Ursula Andress); Edra Gale (Anna Fassbender); Catherine

Shaake (Jacqueline); Jess Hahn (Perry Werner); Eleanor Hirt (Sylvia Werner); Nicole Karen (Tempest O'Brien); Jean Paredes (Marcel); Michel Subor (Philippe); Louise Lasser (The Nutcracker); Françoise Hardy (Secretary); Richard Burton (Man in Bar).

WHAT'S UP, TIGER LILY? (US/JAPANESE)

1966 (Sept. *UK*: June 1976) Orig: *Kizino Kizi/Kagi No Kagi/Key of Keys* (Japan, 1964); 94 mins; Toho. First US version: *A Keg of Powder*.

Dir. Senkichi Taniguchi; *pr.* Tomoyuki Tanaka, Makoto Morita; *scr.* Hideo Ando; *ph.* Kazuo Yamada (Tohoscope, Eastmancolor).

Revised: Jan-Feb 1966 (New York); 79 mins (Video version 4 secs cut); Saperstein-Bercovitch/Benedict Pictures Corp./American International; *exec pr.* Henry G. Saperstein; *prd. conception* Ben Shapiro; *assoc pr. & special material* Woody Allen; *scr, vocal dubbing* Woody Allen, Frank Buxton, Len Maxwell, Louise Lasser, Mickey Rose, Julie Bennett, Bryna Wilson; *music* The Lovin' Spoonful; *superv ed.* Richard Krown; MPAA (PG); BBFC (A).
Cast: Tatsuya Mikashi (Phil Moskowitz), Miye Hana (Terry Yaki), Akiko Wakayabashi (Suki Yaki), Tadao Nakamaru (Shepherd Wong), Suzumu Kurobe (Wing Fat), and Woody Allen, China Lee, Kumi Mizuno, Louise Lasser.

CASINO ROYALE (US-UK)

1967 (*UK*: April. *US rel.* Apr); *s.s.* 10 Jan 1966 (UK, Ireland, Paris, West Berlin, Shepperton, Pinewood, MGM-British Studios); *e.n.c.* $12m ($6m b.); *US /Can r.* $10.2m (3rd Top Money-Maker) 131 mins; Famous Artists/Columbia.

dirs: John Huston, Kenneth Hughes, Val Guest, Robert Parrish, Joseph McGrath (Richard Talmadge, Anthony Squire); *pr.* Charles K Feldman, Jerry Bresler; *scr.* Wolf Mankowitz, John Law, Michael Sayers (*uncred*: John Huston, Terry Southern, Peter Sellers, Val Guest, Billy Wilder, Joseph Heller, Ben Hecht, Woody Allen, Orson Welles, Frank Buxton, Dore Schary) from the novel by Ian Fleming; *ph.* Jack Hildyard; *addtl ph.* Nicholas Roeg, John Wilcox (Panavision, Technicolor); *des.* Michael Stringer, John Howell, Ivor Beddoes, Lionel Couch & *uncred.*, Vincent Korda; *music* Burt Bacharach, Herb Alpert; *ed.* Bill Lenny; *spec f/x.* Cliff Richardson, Roy Whybrow; *cos.* Julie Harris; MPAA (P); BBFC (U).
Cast: Peter Sellers (Evelyn Tremble), Ursula Andress (Vesper Lynd), David Niven (Sir James Bond), Orson Welles (Le Chiffre), Joanna Pettet (Mata Bond), Daliah Lavi (The Detainer), Woody Allen (Jimmy Bond), Deborah Kerr (Widow McTarry), William Holden (Ransome), Charles Boyer (Le Grand), John Huston (M), Kurt Kasznar (Smernov), George Raft (Himself), Jean-Paul Belmondo (French Legionnaire), Terence Cooper (Cooper), Barbara Bouchet (Moneypenny), Jacqueline Bisset (Miss Goodthighs).

TAKE THE MONEY AND RUN

1969 (Aug. *UK*: Oct 70) *s.s.* 17 June 1968 (San Francisco); *e.n.c.* $1.53m ($2m b.); *US/Can r :* $2.59m; 85 mins; Palomar-ABC/Cinerama Releasing Corp.

pr. Charles H. Joffe; *exc pr:* Sidney Glazier; *co-scr.* Woody Allen, Mickey Rose; adapted from un-produced stage play by W. Allen; *ph:* Lester Shorr; (Technicolor); *des.* Fred Harpman; *music* Marvin Hamlisch; *superv ed.* James T. Heckert; *eds:* Paul Jordan, Ron Kalish; *ed consultant* Ralph Rosenblum; *spec f/x.* AD Flowers; *cos.* Erick M. Hjemvik; MPAA (M); BBFC (A).

Cast: Woody Allen (Virgil Starkwell), Janet Margolin (Louise), Marcel Hillaire (Fritz), Jacqueline Hyde (Miss Blair), Lonny Chapman (Jake), Jan Merlin (Al), James Anderson (Chain Gang Warden), Ethel Sokolow (Mother Starkwell), Henry Leff (Father Starkwell), Jackson Beck (Narrator), and Louise Lasser (Kay Lewis)

DON'T DRINK THE WATER (US/CANADIAN)

1969 (Nov; *UK:* TV only); *s.s.* 10 Mar 1969 (Miami, Quebec, Studio City, Miami); *e.n.c.* $8m; *US/Can r:* $1.03m est; 98 mins; Joseph E. Levine/Avco Embassy

dir. Howard Morris; *pr.* Charles H. Joffe (*exec. pr. uncred.* Frederick Brisson); *co-scr:* R.S. Allen, Harvey Bullock (*uncred:* Marshall Brickman), from the stage play by Woody Allen; *ph.* Harvey Genkins (Movielab-colour); *des.* Robert Gundlach; *music* Pat Williams; *ed.* Ralph Rosenblum; *cos.* Gene Coffin; MPAA (G); BBFC (None).

Cast: Jackie Gleason (Walter Hollander), Estelle Parsons (Marion Hollander), Ted Bessell (Axel Magee), Joan Delaney (Susan Hollander), Michael Constantine (Krojack), Howard St. John (Ambassador Magee); Daniel Meehan (Kilroy), Richard Libertini (Fr. Dobney), Pierre Olaf (Chef), Avery Schreiber (Sultan), Phil Leeds (Sam), Mark Gordon (Mirik), Dwayne Early (Donald), Joan Murphy (Airline Clerk), Martin Danzig (Miskin), Rene Constantineau (Organ Grinder), Howard Morris (Getaway Pilot).

BANANAS

1971 (May. *UK:* Sept); *s.s.* 4 May 1970 (New York, Puerto Rico); *e.n.c.* $2m; *US/Can r.* $3.5m; 82 mins; Rollins-Joffe/UA.

pr. Jack Grossberg; *scr.* Woody Allen, Mickey Rose, loosely suggested by the novel *Don Quixote, USA* by Richard Powell and the story 'Viva Vargas' by Woody Allen; *ph.* Andrew M. Costikyan (De Luxe Colour); *des.* Ed Wittstein; *music* Marvin Hamlisch; *assoc prd & superv ed:* Ralph Rosenblum; *ed.* Ron Kalish; *spec f/x.* Don B. Courtney; *cos.* Gene Coffin; MPAA (OP); BBFC (AA).

Cast: Woody Allen (Fielding Mellish), Louise Lasser (Nancy), Carlos Montalban (General Vargas), Natividad Abascal (Yolanda), Jacobo Morales (Esposito), Miguel Suarez (Luis), David Ortiz (Sanchez), Rene Enriquez (Diaz), Jack Axelrod (Arroyo), Howard Cosell, Roger Grimsby, Don Dunphy (Themselves).

PLAY IT AGAIN, SAM

1972 (May. *UK:* Oct); *s.s.* 4 Oct 1971 (San Francisco, Paramount Studios, Hollywood); *e.n.c.* $1.3m ($1.6m b.); *US/Can r.* $5.8m* ($5m); 97 mins (*reissue:* 84 mins); Rollins-Joffe/Apjac/Paramount.

dir. Herbert Ross; *pr.* Arthur P. Jacobs; *scr.* Woody Allen from his stage play; *ph.* Owen Roizman (Technicolor); *des.* Ed Wittstein; *music* Billy Goldenberg, Oscar Peterson, Max Steiner, Herman Hupfeld; *ed.* Marion Rothman; *cos.* Anna Hill Johnstone; MPAA (PG); BBFC (AA).

Cast: Woody Allen (Allen Felix), Diane Keaton (Linda), Tony Roberts (Dick), Jerry Lacey (Bogart), Susan Anspach (Nancy), Jennifer Salt (Sharon), Joy Bang (Julie), Viva (Jennifer), Suzanne Zenor (Discotheque Girl), Diana Davila (Museum Girl), Mari Fletcher (Fantasy Sharon), Michael Green, Ted Markland (Hoods).

EVERYTHING YOU ALWAYS WANTED TO KNOW ABOUT SEX*
(*BUT WERE AFRAID TO ASK)

1972 (Aug. *UK*: Mar 1973); *s.s.* 3 Jan 1972 (LA and Culver City Studios, Hollywood); *e.n.c.* $2m; *US/Can r.* $8.8m* ($8.5m; 10th Top Money-Maker); 87 mins; Rollins-Joffe/Brodsky-Gould/UA.

pr. Charles H. Joffe; *scr:* Woody Allen (& *uncred* Marshall Brickman); suggested by the book by Dr David Reuben; *ph.* David M. Walsh (De Luxe Color and b & w); *des.* Dale Hennesy; *music* Mundell Lowe; *superv. ed.*: James T. Heckert; *ed.* Eric Albertson; *cos.* Arnold M. Lipin, Fern Weber, Western Costume (LA); MPAA (R); BBFC (X).

Cast: Woody Allen (Fool, Fabrizio, Victor, Sperm), John Carradine (Dr Bernardo), Lou Jacobi (Sam), Louise Lasser (Gina), Anthony Quayle (King), Tony Randall (Operator), Lynn Redgrave (Queen), Burt Reynolds (Switchboard), Gene Wilder (Dr Ross), and Jack Barry, Toni Holt, Robert Q. Lewis, Pamela Mason, Regis Philbin (Themselves), Erin Fleming (Girl).

SLEEPER

1973 (Dec. *UK*: May 1974); *s.s.* 30 Apr 1973 (Monterey, California; Denver and Boulder, Colorado; Mojave Desert; Rocky Mountains; Culver City Studios, Hollywood); *e.n.c.* $3.1m ($2m b.); *US/Can r.* $8.3m* (1973: N/A); 88 mins; Rollins-Joffe/UA.

pr. Jack Grossberg; *co-scr.* Woody Allen, Marshall Brickman; *ph.* David M. Walsh (De Luxe Color); *des.* Dale Hennesy; *music* Woody Allen, with the Preservation Hall Jazz Band and The New Orleans Funeral & Ragtime Orchestra; *ed.* Ralph Rosenblum; *spec f/x.* AD Flowers, Gerald Endler; *cos.* Joel Schumacher; MPAA (PG); BBFC (A).

Cast: Woody Allen (Miles Monroe), Diane Keaton (Luna Schlosser), John Beck (Erno Windt), Mary Gregory (Dr Melik), Don Keefer (Dr Tryon), John McLiam (Dr Agon), Bartlett Robinson (Dr Orva), Chris Forbes (Rainer Krebs), Marya Small (Dr Nero), Peter Hobbs (Dr Dean), Susan Miller (Ellen Pogrebin), Lou Picetti (MC), Brian Avery (Gerald Cohen), Spencer Milligan (Jeb), Spencer Ross (Sears Swiggles).

LOVE AND DEATH

1975 (June. *UK*: Oct) *s.s.* 23 Sept 1974 (France, Hungary, Malfilm Studios, Budapest); *e.n.c.* $8.5m ($7.5m b.); *US/Can r.* $7.4m*($5m); 85 mins. Rollins-Joffe/UA

pr. Charles H. Joffe; *exc pr*: Martin Poll; *ph.* Ghislain Cloquet (De Luxe Color); *des.* Willy Holt; *music* S. Prokofiev; *ed.* Ralph Rosenblum, Ron Kalish; *spec f/x.* Kit West; *cos.* Gladys De Segonzac; MPAA (PG); BBFC (AA).
Cast: Woody Allen (Boris), Diane Keaton (Sonja), Zvee Scooler (Father), Despo Diamantidou (Mother), Sol I. Frieder (Voscovec), Olga Georges-Picot (Countess Alexandrovna), Harold Gould (Anton), Henry Czerniak (Ivan), Feodore Atkine (Mikhail), Beth Porter (Anna), Lloyd Battista (Don Francisco), James Tolkan (Napoleon), Jessica Harper (Natasha), Alfred Lutter III (Young Boris).

THE FRONT

1976 (Sept. *UK*: Jan 1977) *s.s.* 15 Sept 1975 (New York); *e.n.c.* $3.5m; *US/Can r.* $5m; 94 mins; Ritt/Rollins-Joffe/Persky-Bright/Columbia.

dir., pr. Martin Ritt; *exec. pr.* Charles H. Roffe; *assoc. pr.* Robert Greenhut; *scr.* Walter Bernstein; *ph.* Michael Chapman (Metrocolor); *des.* Charles Bailey; *music* Dave Gruslin; *ed.* Sidney Levin; *cos.* Ruth Morley; MPAA (PG); BBFC (AA).
Cast: Woody Allen (Howard Prince), Zero Mostel (Hecky Brown) Herschel Bernardi (Phil Sussman), Michael Murphy (Alfred Miller), Andrea Marcovicci (Florence Barrett), Remak Ramsey (Hennessey), Marvin Lichterman (Myer Prince), Lloyd Gough (Delaney), David Margulies (Phelps), Joshua Shelley (Sam), Norman Rose (Network Attorney), Charles Kimbrough (Committee Counsel), M. Josef Sommer (Committee Chairman), Danny Aiello (Danny La Gattuta), Georgann Johnson (TV Interviewer), Scott McKay (Hampton), David Clarke (Supermarket Owner), J.W. Klein (Bank Teller).

ANNIE HALL

1977 (Apr. *UK*: Sept) *s.s.* 10 May 1976 (New York, New Jersey, Los Angeles, Pathé Studios, Manhattan); *e.n.c.* $4m ($3m b.); *US/Can r.* $19m* ($12m); 93 mins; Rollins-Joffe/UA.

pr. Charles H. Joffe; *exec. pr.* Robert Greenhut; *co-scr.* Woody Allen, Marshall Brickman; *ph.* Gordon Willis (De Luxe); *des.* Mel Bourne; *music* various; *anim.* Chris Ishii; *cos.* Ruth Morley; MPAA (PG); BBFC (AA). *AA*: Best Film, Director, Actress, Original Screenplay.
Cast: Woody Allen (Alvy Singer), Diane Keaton (Annie Hall), Tony Roberts (Rob), Carol Kane (Allison), Paul Simon (Tony Lacey), Shelley Duvall (Pam), Janet Margolin (Robin), Colleen Dewhurst (Mom Hall), Christopher Walken (Duane Hall), Ronald Symington (Dad Hall), Helen Ludlam (Grammy Hall), Mordecai Lawner (Alvy's Dad), Joan Newman (Alvy's Mom), Jonathan Munk (Alvy aged 9), Marshall Mc Luhan, Dick Cavett, Truman Capote (Themselves).

INTERIORS

1978 (Aug. *UK*: Nov) *s.s.* 24 Oct 1977 (New York City; Southampton, Long Island); *e.n.c.* $10m; *US/Can r.* $4.6m; 91 mins (video: 83 mins); Rollins-Joffe/UA.

pr. Charles H. Joffe; *exec. pr.* Robert Greenhut, *ph.* Gordon Willis (Technicolor); *des.* Mel

Bourne; *music* source only; *ed.* Ralph Rosenblum; *cos.* Joel Schumacher; MPAA (PG); BBFC (AA).
Cast: Kristin Griffith (Flyn), Mary Beth Hurt (Joey), Richard Jordan (Frederick), Diane Keaton (Renata), E.G. Marshall (Arthur), Geraldine Page (Eve), Maureen Stapleton (Pearl), Sam Waterston (Mike), Henderson Forsythe (Judge Bartel).

MANHATTAN
1979 (Apr. *UK*: Aug) *s.s.* 17 July 1978 (New York, New Jersey; Filmways Studios, Harlem); *e.n.c.* $8m plus; *US/Can r.* $17.6m*($16.9m); 96 mins; Rollins-Joffe/UA.

pr. Charles H. Joffe; *exec. pr.* Robert Greenhut; *co-scr.* Woody Allen, Marshall Brickman; *ph.* Gordon Willis (Panavision, b & w); *des.* Mel Bourne; *music* George Gershwin (adapt and arr. Tom Pierson); *ed.* Susan E. Morse; *cos.* Albert Wolsky, Ralph Lauren; MPAA (R); BBFC (AA).
Cast: Woody Allen (Isaac Davis), Diane Keaton (Mary Wilke), Michael Murphy (Yale), Mariel Hemingway (Tracy), Meryl Streep (Jill), Anne Byrne (Emily), Karen Ludwig (Connie), Michael O'Donohue (Dennis), Gary Weis (TV Director), Kenny Vance (TV Producer), Damion Sheller (Isaac's son, Willie), Wallace Shawn (Jeremiah), Bella Abzug (Guest of Honour), Tisa Farrow, Victor Truro, Helen Hanft (Party Guests).

STARDUST MEMORIES
1980 (Sept. *UK*: Dec) *s.s.* 11 Sept 1979 (New York City; Oyster Bay, Long Island; Ocean Grove, N.J.; Filmways Studios, Harlem); *e.n.c.* $9m ($8m b.); *US/Can r.* $4.1m* ($3.65m); 89 mins; Rollins-Joffe/UA.

pr. Robert Greenhut; *exec. pr.* Jack Rollins, Charles H. Joffe; *ph.* Gordon Willis (b & w); *des.* Mel Bourne; *music* Dick Hyman and various; *ed.* Susan E. Morse; *cos.* Santo Loquasto; MPAA (PG); BBFC (AA).
Cast: Woody Allen (Sandy Bates), Charlotte Rampling (Dorrie), Jessica Harper (Daisy), Marie-Christine Barrault (Isobel), Tony Roberts (Tony), Daniel Stern (Andy), Amy Wright (Shelley), Helen Hanft (Vivian Orkin), John Rothman (Jack Abel), Anne De Salvo (Sandy's Sister), Joan Newman (Sandy's Mother), Gabrielle Strasun (Charlotte Ames), David Lipman (George), Bob Maroff (Jerry Abraham), Leonardo Cimino (Sandy's Analyst), Eli Mintz (Old Man), Robert Munk (Boy Sandy), Sharon Stone (Pretty Girl on Train).

A MIDSUMMER NIGHT'S SEX COMEDY
1982 (July. *UK*: Sept); *s.s.* 22 Jun 1981 (New York City; Rockefeller Estate, Westchester N.Y.; Kaufman Astoria Studios); *e.n.c.* $7m; *US/Can r.* $4.5m; 88 mins; Rollins-Joffe/Orion/WB (*UK*: Col-EMI-Warner).

pr. Robert Greenhut; *ph.* Gordon Willis (Technicolor); *des.* Mel Bourne; *music* Felix Mendelssohn; *ed.* Susan E. Morse; *anim. effects.* Kurtz & Friends, Zander's Animation Parlour; *cos.* Santo Loquasto; MPAA (PG); BBFC (AA).
Cast: Woody Allen (Andrew Hobbes), Mia Farrow (Ariel Weymouth), José Ferrer

(Professor Leopold Sturgis), Julie Hagerty (Dulcy Ford), Tony Roberts (Dr Maxwell Jordan), Mary Steenburgen (Adrian Hobbes).

ZELIG

1983 (July. *UK*: Oct) *s.s.* 19 Oct 1981 (New York, New Jersey and Kaufman Astoria Studios); *e.n.c.* $6.5m; *US/Can r.* $6.8m* ($6.5m) 79 mins (incl. 5 mins credits); Rollins-Joffe/Orion/WB (UK: COL-EMI-Warner).

pr. Robert Greenhut; *ph.* Gordon Willis (b & w and colour); *music* Dick Hyman and various; *ed.* Susan E. Morse; *visual f/x.* Joel Hyneck, Stuart Robertson, R/Greenberg Associates; *des.* Mel Bourne; *cos.* Santo Loquasto; MPAA (PG); BBFC (PG).
Cast: Woody Allen (Leonard Zelig), Mia Farrow (Dr Eudora Fletcher), Garrett Brown (Actor Zelig), Stephanie Farrow (Sister Meryl), Will Holt (Rally Chancellor), Sol Lomita (Martin Geist), John Rothman (Paul Deghuee), Deborah Rush (Lita Fox), Marianne Tatum (Actress Fletcher), Mary Louise Wilson (Sister Ruth), Patrick Horgan (Narrator), Susan Sontag, Irving Howe, Saul Bellow, Bricktop, Bruno Bettelheim, John Morton Blum.

BROADWAY DANNY ROSE

1984 (Jan. *UK*: Aug) *s.s.* 20 Sept 1982 (New York, New Jersey, Kaufman Astoria); *e.n.c.* $8m; *US/Can r.* $5.4m* ($4.8m); 86 mins; Rollins-Joffe/Orion (*UK*: Rank).

pr. Robert Greenhut; *ph.* Gordon Willis (b & w); *des.* Mel Bourne; *music superv:* Dick Hyman; *songs*: Nick Apollo Forte & various; *ed.* Susan E. Morse; *cos.* Jeffrey Kurland; MPAA (PG); BBFC (PG).
Cast: Woody Allen (Danny Rose), Mia Farrow (Tina Vitale), Nick Apollo Forte (Lou Canova), Sandy Baron, Corbett Monica, Jackie Gayle, Morty Gunty, Will Jordan, Howard Storm, Jack Rollins, Milton Berle, Joe Franklin, Howard Cosell, Sammy Davis Jr (Themselves).

THE PURPLE ROSE OF CAIRO

1985 (Mar. *UK*: July); *s.s.* 9 Nov 1983 (New York City; Piermont Village, NY; New Jersey; Kaufman Astoria); *e.n.c.* $13m; *US/Can r.* $5.1m; 82 mins; Rollins-Joffe/Orion. (*UK*: Rank).

pr. Robert Greenhut; *ph.* Gordon Willis (De Luxe Color and b & w); *des.* Stuart Wurtzel; *music* Dick Hyman & various; *ed.* Susan E. Morse; *optical effects* R/Greenberg Associates/The Optical House, NY; *cos.* Jeffrey Kurland; MPAA (PG); BBFC (PG).
Cast: Mia Farrow (Cecilia), Jeff Daniels (Tom Baxter/Gil Shepherd), Danny Aiello (Monk), Dianne Wiest (Emma), Camille Saviola (Olga), Irving Metzman (Theater Manager), Stephanie Farrow (Cecilia's Sister), David Kieserman (Diner Boss), Juliana Donald (Usherette), *Purple Rose* cast: Edward Herrman (Henry), John Wood (Jason), Deborah Rush (Rita), Van Johnson (Larry), Zoe Caldwell (The Countess), Eugene Anthony (Arturo), Ebb Miller (Band Leader), Karen Akers (Kitty Haynes), Annie Joe Edwards (Delilah), Milo O'Shea (Father Donnelly), Peter McRobbie (The Communist).

HANNAH AND HER SISTERS

1986 (Feb. *UK*: July) *s.s.* 18 Oct 1984 (New York; Turin, Italy; Kaufman Astoria); *e.n.c.* $9m ($8m b.); *US/Can r.* $18.2m* ($16.6m); 107 mins; Rollins-Joffe/Orion (*UK*: Rank).

pr. Robert Greenhut; *ph.* Carlo Di Palma (Technicolor); *des.* Stuart Wurtzel; *music* various; *ed.* Susan E. Morse; *cos.* Jeffrey Kurland; MPAA (PG-13); BBFC (15). *AA*: Best Orig Scr, Supp Actor (Michael Caine), Supp Actress (Dianne Wiest).
Cast: Woody Allen (Mickey), Michael Caine (Elliot), Mia Farrow (Hannah), Carrie Fisher (April), Barbara Hershey (Lee), Lloyd Nolan (Evan), Maureen O'Sullivan (Norma), Daniel Stern (Dusty), Max Von Sydow (Frederick), Dianne Wiest (Holly), Julie Kavner (Gail), Bobby Short (Himself), Joanna Gleason (Carol), Maria Chiara (Manon Lescaut), The 39 Steps (Rock Band) and *uncredited* Tony Roberts (Norman), Sam Waterston (David).

RADIO DAYS

1987 (Jan. *UK*: June); *s.s.* 4 Nov 1985 (New York; Union City, Jersey City, NJ; Kaufman Astoria); *e.n.c.* $16m; *US/Can r.* $6.4m; 85 mins. Rollins-Joffe/Orion (*UK*: Rank).

pr. Robert Greenhut; *ph.* Carlo Di Palma (De Luxe Colour); *des.* Santo Loquasto; *music* various (superv. Dick Hyman); *ed.* Susan E. Morse; *spec f/x.* R/Greenberg Associates; *cos.* Jeffrey Kurland; MPAA (PG); BBFC (PG).
Cast: Mia Farrow (Sally White), Dianne Wiest (Bea), Seth Green (Joe), Julie Kavner (Mother) Josh Mostel (Abe), Michael Tucker (Father), Julie Kurnitz (Irene), Wallace Shawn (Masked Avenger), David Warrilow (Roger), Joy Newman (Ruthie), Renee Lippin (Ceil), Tony Roberts (Emcee), Danny Aiello (Hit Man), Jeff Daniels (Biff Baxter), Robert Joy (Fred), Kenneth Mars (Rabbi Baumel), Diane Keaton, Kitty Carlisle (Singers) and Woody Allen (Voice of Adult Joe).

KING LEAR (US/SWISS)

1987 (*prem.* Cannes Film Festival 'work-in-progress' screening, May 1987; World Film Festival, Montreal, 30 Aug 1987; LFF 28 Nov 1987; *US*: New York only, Jan 1988; *UK*. ICA, London, Jan 1988); *s.s.* Dec 1986 (Nyon, Switzerland; France, etc.); *e.n.c.* $1.5m; *US gr.* single screen run only, $13,000 est; 90 mins; Cannon Films/Cannon International. (English language)

dir., scr., ed. Jean-Luc Godard; *pr.* Menachem Golan, Yorum Globus; *assoc. pr.* Tom Liddy; *ph.* Sophie Maintigneaux (Colour); *des.* François Musy; MPAA (15); BBFC (15).
Cast: Burgess Meredith (Don Learo), Peter Sellars (William Shakespeare V), Molly Ringwald (Cordelia), Jean-Luc Godard (Professor) Woody Allen (Mr Alien), Norman Mailer, Kate Miller, Léos Carax.

SEPTEMBER

1987 (Dec. *UK*: July 1988); *s.s.* (1st version) 27 Oct 1986 (Kaufman Astoria Studios, NY); (2nd version) Jan-Feb 1987; *e.n.c.* $10m; *US/Can gr.* $486,000; 82 mins; Rollins-Joffe/Orion (*UK*: Rank).

pr. Robert Greenhut; *ph.* Carlo Di Palma (De Luxe Colour); *des.* Santo Loquasto; *music* various (*superv.* Roy S.Yokelson); *ed.* Susan E. Morse; *cos.* Jeffrey Kurland; MPAA (PG); BBFC (PG).

Cast: Mia Farrow (Lane), Sam Waterston (Peter), Elaine Stritch (Diane), Dianne Wiest (Stephanie), Denholm Elliott (Howard), Jack Warden (Lloyd), Ira Wheeler (Mr Raines), Jane Cecile (Mrs Raines), Rosemary Murphy (Mrs Mason).

Orig. Cast: Mia Farrow (Lane), Christopher Walken/Sam Shepard (Peter), Maureen O'Sullivan (Diane), Dianne Wiest (Stephanie), Charles Durning (Howard), Denholm Elliott (Lloyd).

ANOTHER WOMAN

1988 (Oct. *UK*: July 1989); *s.s.* 12 Oct 1987 (New York; New Jersey; Kaufman Astoria); *e.n.c.* $10m; *US/Can gr.* $1.6m; 88 mins (UK: 84 mins); Rollins-Joffe/Orion (*UK*: Rank).

pr. Robert Greenhut; *ph.* Sven Nykvist (Du Art Color/De Luxe); *des.* Santo Loquasto; *music* various; *ed.* Susan E. Morse; *optical f/x*: R/Greenberg Assocs; *cos.* Jeffrey Kurland. MPAA (PG); BBFC (PG).

Cast: Gena Rowlands (Marion), Mia Farrow (Hope), Ian Holm (Ken), Blythe Danner (Lydia), Gene Hackman (Larry), Betty Buckley (Kathy), Martha Plimpton (Laura) John Houseman (Marion's Dad), Sandy Dennis (Claire), David Ogden Stiers (Young Marion's Dad), Philip Bosco (Sam), Harris Yulin (Paul), Frances Conroy (Lynn), Kenneth Welsh, Bruce Jay Friedman, Michael Kirby.

OEDIPUS WRECKS

1989 (March. *UK*: Nov). Woody Allen's segment of *New York Stories* (comprising '*Life Class*', d. Martin Scorsese, '*Life Without Zoe*', d. Francis Coppola, and '*Oedipus Wrecks*'); *s.s.* 21 March 1988 (New York; Kaufman Astoria); *e.n.c.* $19m ('*Oedipus Wrecks*': $6m est); *US/Can r.* $4.7m; *total r.t.* 123 mins; ('*Oedipus Wrecks*': 41 mins); Rollins-Joffe/Touchstone-Buena Vista (*UK*: Warners).

pr. Robert Greenhut; *ph.* Sven Nykvist (Du Art Colour); *des.* Santo Loquasto; *music*: various; *ed.* Susan E. Morse; *spec visual f/x*. R/Greenberg Associates (*superv.* Stuart Robertson, Joel Hyneck); *cos.* Jeffrey Kurland. MPAA (PG); BBFC (15).

Cast: Woody Allen (Sheldon Mills), Mia Farrow (Lisa), Julie Kavner (Treva), Mae Questel (Mother), Shandu the Magician (George Schindler), Marvin Chatnover (Psychiatrist), Mr Bates (Ira Wheeler), Molly Regan (Sheldon's Secretary), Jessie Keosian (Aunt Ceil), Bridget Ryan (Rita), Paul Herman (Detective Flynn), Andrew MacMillan (Newscaster), Mayor Edward I. Koch (Himself).

CRIMES AND MISDEMEANORS

1989 (Oct. *UK*: July 1990); *s.s.* 3 Oct 1988 (New York; New Jersey; Kaufman Astoria); *e.n.c.* $13m; *US/ Can r.* $8.5m* ($6.5m); 104 mins; Rollins-Joffe/Orion (*UK*: Rank).

pr. Robert Greenhut; *ph.* Sven Nykvist (Du Art Color/De Luxe); *des.* Santo Loquasto;

music various; *ed.* Susan E. Morse; *cos.* Jeffrey Kurland; MPAA (PG-13); BBFC (15).
Cast: Caroline Aaron (Barbara), Alan Alda (Lester), Woody Allen (Cliff Stern), Claire Bloom (Mirium Rosenthal), Mia Farrow (Halley Reed), Joanna Gleason (Wendy Stern), Anjelica Huston (Dolores Paley), Martin Landau (Judah Rosenthal), Jenny Nichols (Jenny), Jerry Orbach (Jack Rosenthal), Sam Waterston (Ben), Martin Bergmann (Prof. Louis Levy).

ALICE

1990 (Dec. *UK*: July 1991); *s.s.* 6 Nov 1989 (New York; Kaufman Astoria); *e.n.c.* $12m; *US/Can r.* 1991: $3.3m (*1990*: N/A); 106 mins; Rollins-Joffe/Orion (*UK*: Rank).

pr. Robert Greenhut; *ph.* Carlo Di Palma (De Luxe Color); *des.* Santo Loquasto; *music* various; *ed.* Susan E. Morse; *visual f/x.* Randall Balsmeyer (Balsmeyer & Everett Inc.), Effects House Corp, The Magic Camera Co.; *cos.* Jeffrey Kurland; MPAA (PG-13); BBFC (12).
Cast: Mia Farrow (Alice Tait), Alec Baldwin (Eddie), Judy Davis (Vicki), William Hurt (Doug), Keye Luke (Dr Yang), Joe Mantegna (Joe), Bernadette Peters (Muse), Cybill Shepherd (Nancy Brill), Gwen Verdon (Alice's Mother), Patrick O'Neal (Alice's Father), Julie Kavner (Decorator), James Toback (Professor), Caroline Aaron (Sue), Bob Balaban (Sid Moscowitz).

SCENES FROM A MALL

1991 (Feb. *UK*: April); *s.s.* 11 June 1990 (New York; New Jersey; Los Angeles; Stamford, Conn., Kaufman Astoria Studios); *e.n.c.* $34m; *US/Can r.* $4.2m; 87 mins; Touchstone/Silver Screen Partners IV/Buena Vista (*UK*: Warners).

dir., pr. Paul Mazursky; *co-pr.* Pato Guzman, Patrick McCormick; *co-scr.* Roger L. Simon, Paul Mazursky; *ph.* Fred Murphy (Du Art/Technicolor); *des.* Pato Guzman; *music/music adapts.* Marc Shaiman; *ed.* Stuart Pappé; *cos.* Albert Wolsky. MPAA (PG-13); BBFC (15).
Cast: Bette Midler (Deborah Fifer), Woody Allen (Nick Fifer), Bill Irwin (Mime), Daren Firestone (Sam), Rebecca Nickels (Jennifer), Paul Mazursky (Dr Hans Clava).

SHADOWS AND FOG

1992 (*prem.* Paris, 12 Feb 1992; Berlin Film Festival, Feb 1992; *US*: March 1992; *UK*: Feb 1993); *s.s.* 19 Nov 1990 (Kaufman Astoria, NY); *e.n.c.* $14m; *US/Can r.* $1.2m; 86 mins; Rollins-Joffe/Orion/Columbia-TriStar.

pr. Robert Greenhut; *ph.* Carlo Di Palma (b&w); *des.* Santo Loquasto; *music* Kurt Weill & various; *ed.* Susan E. Morse; *optical f/x.* Balsmeyer & Everett, The Effects House Corp; *cos.* Jeffrey Kurland. MPAA (PG-13); BBFC (15).
Cast: Woody Allen (Kleinman), Mia Farrow (Irmy), John Cusack (Student Jack), Kathy Bates, Jodie Foster, Lily Tomlin, Anne Lange (Prostitutes), Fred Gwynne (Hacker's Follower), Julie Kavner (Alma), Madonna (Marie), John Malkovich (Clown), Kenneth Mars (Magician), Kate Nelligan (Eve), Donald Pleasence (Doctor), Philip Bosco (Mr Paulsen), Robert Joy (Spiro's Assistant), Wallace Shawn (Simon Carr), Kurtwood

Smith (Vogel's Follower), Josef Sommer (Priest), David Ogden Stiers (Hacker).

HUSBANDS AND WIVES

1992 (Sept. *UK*: Oct); *s.s.* 4 Nov 1991 (New York; Kaufman Astoria); *e.n.c.* $12m; *US/Can r.* $5m; 108 mins; Rollins-Joffe/Columbia-TriStar

pr. Robert Greenhut; *ph.* Carlo Di Palma (Du Art/Technicolor); *des.* Santo Loquasto; *music* various; *ed.* Susan E. Morse; *digital f/x*: Industrial Light & Magic; *cos.* Jeffrey Kurland; MPAA (R); BBFC (15).
Cast: Woody Allen (Gabe Roth), Blythe Danner (Rain's Mother), Judy Davis (Sally), Mia Farrow (Judy Roth), Juliette Lewis (Rain), Liam Neeson (Michael), Sydney Pollack (Jack), Lysette Anthony (Sam), Cristi Conway (Shawn Grainger), Timothy Jerome (Paul), Ron Rifkin (Rain's Analyst), Jerry Zaks (Party Guest).

MANHATTAN MURDER MYSTERY

1993 (Aug. *UK*: Jan 1994); *s.s.* 14 Sept 1992 (New York, New Jersey); *e.n.c.* $13.5m; *US/Can gr.* $11.3m; 107 mins; Rollins-Joffe/Columbia-TriStar.

pr. Robert Greenhut; *co-pr.* Helen Robin, Joseph Hartwick; *co-scr.* Woody Allen, Marshall Brickman; *ph.* Carlo Di Palma (Du Art Color); *des.* Santo Loquasto; *music* various; *ed.* Susan E. Morse; *cos.* Jeffrey Kurland; MPAA (PG); BBFC (PG).
Cast: Woody Allen (Larry Lipton), Diane Keaton (Carol Lipton), Jerry Adler (Paul House), Lynn Cohen (Lillian House), Ron Rifkin (Sy), Joy Behar (Marilyn), William Addy (Jack the Super), Alan Alda (Ted), Anjelica Huston (Marcia Fox), Melanie Morris (Helen Moss).

BULLETS OVER BROADWAY

1994 (Oct. *UK*: May 1995); *s.s.* 27 Sept 1993 (New York; Kaufman Astoria); *e.n.c.* $20m ($19m b.); *US/Can gr.* $13.5m* ($8.6m); 105 mins; Jean Doumanian/Sweetland Films/Buena Vista/Magnolia Productions/Miramax (*UK*: Buena Vista).

pr. Robert Greenhut; *co-pr.* Helen Robin; *exec. prds.* Jean Doumanian, J.E. Beauclaire, *co-exec. prds.* Jack Rollins, Charles H. Joffe, Letty Aronson; *co-scr.* Woody Allen, Douglas McGrath; *ph.* Carlo Di Palma (Du Art/Technicolor); *des.* Santo Loquasto; *music* various; *ed.* Susan E. Morse; *cos.* Jeffrey Kurland; MPAA (R); BBFC (15). *AA*: Best Supp. Actress (Dianne Wiest).
Cast: John Cusack (David Shayne), Jack Warden (Julian Marx), Chazz Palminteri (Cheech), Joe Viterelli (Jack Valenti), Jennifer Tilly (Olive Neal), Rob Reiner (Sheldon Flender), Mary-Louise Parker (Ellen), Dianne Wiest (Helen Sinclair), Harvey Fierstein (Sid Loomis), Jim Broadbent (Warner Purcell), Tracy Ullman (Eden Brent).

DON'T DRINK THE WATER (TVM)

1994 (Transm *US*: 18 Dec); *s.s.* 4 Apr 1994 (New York; New Jersey; Kaufman Astoria); *e.n.c.* $3.5m; 92 mins (*transm time*: 120 mins); Daisy Prods/Magnolia Prods/Sweetland Film Corp/BVI and Jean Doumanian Prods/ABC.

pr. Robert Greenhut; *exec prds.* Jean Doumanian, J. E. Beaucaire; *co-exec pro*:
Letty Aronson; from Woody Allen's play; *ph.* Carlo Di Palma (Colour and
b & w); *des.* Santo Loquasto; *music* various; *ed.* Susan E. Morse; *cos.*
Suzy Benzinger.
Cast: Woody Allen (Walter Hollander), Julie Kavner (Marion Hollander), Mayim Bialik
(Susan Hollander), Michael J Fox (Axel Magee), Dom De Luise (Father Drobney), Edward
Herrman (Ambassador Magee), and Josef Sommer, Austin Pendleton, John Doumanian,
Erick Avari, Rosemary Murphy, Robert Stanton, Vit Horejs, Ed Herlihy, Ed Van Nuys, Skip
Rose, Leonid Uscher, Stas Kmiec, Sandor Tecsy, Brian McConnachie, Victor Steinbach,
Frederick Rolf, Elizabeth de Charay, Taina Elg.

MIGHTY APHRODITE

1995 (Oct.; *UK*: April 1996); *s.s.* 3 Oct 1994 (New York; New Jersey; Sicily); *e.n.c.*
$15m; *US /Can gr.* $5.02m (1995 only); 95 mins; Jean Doumanian/ Sweetland/Miramax
(*UK*: Buena Vista).

pr. Robert Greenhut; *co-pr*: Helen Robin; *exec. prods.* Jean Doumanian, J.E. Beaucaire;
co-exec prs: Jack Rollins, Charles H. Joffe, Letty Aronson; *ph.* Carlo Di Palma (Du
Art/Technicolor); *des.* Santo Loquasto; *music* various; *ed.* Susan E. Morse; *cos.* Jeffrey
Kurland; MPAA (R); BBFC (15).
Cast: Woody Allen (Lenny), Helena Bonham Carter (Amanda), Mira Sorvino (Linda Ash),
Michael Rapaport (Kevin), F. Murray Abraham (Leader), Claire Bloom (Amanda's moth-
er), Olympia Dukakis (Jocasta), David Ogden Stiers (Laius), Jack Warden (Tiresias), Peter
Weller (Jerry Bender), Dan Moran (Ricky the Pimp), Jeffrey Kurland (Oedipus).

THE SUNSHINE BOYS (TVM)

1996 (Transm US: April 1996); *s.s.* 13 March 1995; (New York); *e.n.c.* 90 mins (*trans time*:
120 mins); Metropolitan Productions Inc-RHI Entertainment/Inc/Beta Film/Hallmark
Entertainment/CBS.

dir., pr. John Erman; *exe.pr.* Robert Halmi Sr; *scr.* Neil Simon from his play

Shorts & Documentaries

The Laughmakers (1962) Edgewater Prods/ABC; *created and pr.* Robert Alan Aurthur; *dir.* Joshua Shelley; *scr.* Woody Allen; *ph*: Don Malkames (b & w); *des*: Albert Brenner; music: Robert Prince; *ed.* Ralph Rosenblum; *cos*: Larry Komiroff.
Cast: Louise Sorel (Joyce), Paul Hampton (Ted), Sandy Baron (Danny), Louise Lasser (Susan), Alan Alda (Phil), David Burns (Sid), Michael J. Pollard (*uncred*). Untransmitted US TV pilot, revolving around the ups and downs of a failing Greenwich Village improvisational group, for whom talented newcomer Joyce triggers unexpected success. Rediscovered by the American 'Back to Film School' project. UK première at the Plaza Cinema (British Short Film Festival, London) on 31 Aug 1995 (30 mins).

The Politics - and Comedy - of Woody Allen (1971). Orig. *The Woody Allen Comedy Special*. PBS/Channel 13. *dir., scr.*, Woody Allen; *asst dir.* Fred T. Gallo. 1-hour special whose main item was the 30 min 'bad taste' spoof documentary 'The Harvey Wallinger Story', with Woody as 'Wallinger' (Kissinger) and Diane as his wife. Amid controversy, the show was cancelled within hours of its scheduled 21 Feb 1972 transmission. Today, the programme seems facetious rather than scathing, but with some distinctive Allen touches. (60 mins)

My Favourite Comedian (1979) Lincoln Center Film Society (NY); *dir.* Woody Allen; *narr.* Woody Allen, Dick Cavett. Tribute to Bob Hope, screened at the Avery Fisher Hall on 25 April, in front of a celebrity audience. Subsequently at the New York Film Festival, September. Compilation includes clips from 17 movies Hope made between 1938 and 1954 (63 mins).

The Subtle Concept (1980) Toxico Pictures / IDHEC (Paris) *dir., scr., camera op.* Gérard Krawczyk. From Woody Allen's *New Yorker* story 'Mr Big'. *e.n.c.* Ffr 18,240/ US $3000; *ph*. Giacinto Pizzuti (b & w); *des*. Michel Vannier; *music* Max Steiner; *ed.* Alberto Yaccelini. English track. 35mm (21 mins).
Cast: Allan Wenger (Kaiser Lupowitz), Rebecca Pauly (Heather Butkiss), Ed Marcus (Rabbi Weiman), Nicholas Bang (Pope), Daniel Crohen (Sgt Reed), Pierre Benzrihem (Bartender), Patrice Richard, Jean G. Le Dantec (Bodyguards).

Two Mothers. Woody's 'work-in-progress' documentary featuring Nettie Konigsberg and Maureen O'Sullivan has yet to be seen. Mia Farrow suggests it never got further than the cutting room, while Tim Carroll's view is that 'the motivation behind Woody's making of the documentary will remain a mystery'.

Woody on Stage

FROM A TO Z

Plymouth Theater, New York, 20 Apr 1960. Two Act Revue *d.* Christopher Hewett; *pres.* Carroll & Harris Masterson; *chor* Ray Harrison; *Sets, light, cos.* Fred Voepel; *music dir.* Milton Greene; *Music and words* Jay Thompson, Dickson Hughes & Everett Sloane; Woody Allen (incl his sketches 'Hit Parade' and 'Psychological Warfare'), Jack Holmes, Mary Rodgers & Marshall Barer, Paul Klein and Fred Ebb, Herbert Farjeon, Fred Ebb & Norman Martin, Don Parks & William Dyer, Nina Warner Hook, Paul Klein & Lee Goldsmith, Charles Zwar & Alan Melville. 21 perfs

With Hermione Gingold, Elliott Reid, Louise Hoff, Kelly Brown, Stuart Damon, Isabelle Farrell, Michael Fesco, Virginia Vestoff, Alvin Epstein, Borah Kovach, Paula Stewart, Bob Dishy, Beryl Towbin, Larry Hovis, Doug Spingler.

DON'T DRINK THE WATER

Morosco Theater, New York, 17 Nov 1966; *d.* Stanley Prager; *prs.* David Merrick, Jack Rollins and Charles Joffe; *set & light* Jo Mielziner; *cos.* Motley. 598 perfs.

Lou Jacobi (Walter Hollander), Kay Medford (Marion Hollander), Anita Gillette (Susan Hollander), Anthony Roberts (Axel Magee), James Dukas (Krojack), Dick Libertini (Father Drobney), Gerry Matthews (Kilroy), House Jameson (James F. Magee), Curtis Wheeler (Burns), Gene Varrone (Chef), Oliver Clark (Sultan of Bashir), Donna Mills (Sultan's First Wife), John Hallow (Kasznar), Sharon Talbot (Countess Bordoni), Luke Andreas (Novotny), Jonathan Belt (Waiter).(*Medford succeeded by Peggy Cass)

Note: The national company production opened at the Nixon Theater, Pittsburgh, 7 Oct 1968. *d.* Sam Levene; *pres.* Bill Fisher, Bud Filippo, Ken Gaston; *Tech creds* (except *light* Jerome Richland) same as NY; *w.* Phil Foster, Vivian Blaine, Gloria Bleezarde (Hollanders), Gary Krawford (Axel Magee), Walt Wanderman (Fasther Drobney), Roy C. Mansell (Ambassador Magee).

PLAY IT AGAIN, SAM

Broadhurst Theater, New York, 12 Feb 1969; *d.* Joseph Hardy; *prs.* David Merrick, Jack Rollins and Charles Joffe; *decor* William Ritman; *cos.* Ann Roth *light* Martin Aronstein. 453 perfs.

Woody Allen (Allan Felix), Sheila Sullivan (Nancy), Jerry Lacey (Bogart), Anthony Roberts (Dick Christie), Diane Keaton (Linda Christie), Barbara Brownell (Sharon/Barbara), Diana Walker (Sharon Lake), Jean Fowler (Gina), Cynthia Dalbey (Vanessa), Lee Anne Fahey (Go-Go Girl), Barbara Press (Intellectual Girl).(*Allen succeeded by Bob Denver).

Note: National company opened Blackstone Theater, Chicago, 15 Sept 1970, closed
Huntingdon Hartford Theater, LA, 27 Feb 1971. *d*. Ben Gerard; *tech creds* same as NY; *w*.
Red Buttons (Allan Felix), Deborah Deeble (Linda), William Bogert (Dick), Peter De
Maio (Bogey). Subsequently *pres*. Apple Corps Theater Co, 14 May-22 June 1986, *d*. Jack
Melanos, *w*. Neal Arluck (Allan Felix), Wendy Makkena (Linda), Gary Richards (Dick),
John Raymond (Bogey). 35 perfs.

Globe Theatre, London, 11 Sept 1969; *d*. Joseph Hardy; *pr*. David Merrick, H.M. Tennent
and Donald Langdon; *décor* Susie Caulcutt. 355 perfs.
Dudley Moore (Allan Felix), Patricia Brake (Nancy), Bill Kerr (Bogart), Terence Edmonds
(Brian Morris), Lorna Heilbron (Sally Morris), Anne de Vigier (Gillian/Barbara), Jennifer
Clulow (Gillian Lake), Juliet Kempson (Penny), Angela Rider (Au Pair Girl), Vicki
Michelle (Go-Go-Girl), Vivienne Cohen (Museum Girl).(*Moore succeeded by
James McManus)

THE FLOATING LIGHTBULB
Vivian Beaumont Theater, New York, 27 Apr 1981; *d*. Ulu Grosbard; *pr*. Richmond
Crinkley, for the Lincoln Center Theater Company; *set*. & *cos*. Santo Loquasto; *light*.
Pat Collins; *sound* Richard Fitzgerald; *magic design* Robert Aberdeen. 65 perfs &
16 previews.
Brian Backer (Paul Pollack), Eric Gurry (Steve Pollack), Beatrice Arthur (Enid Pollack),
Danny Aiello (Max Pollack), Ellen March (Betty), Jack Weston (Jerry Wexler).
Note: Subsequently *pres*. American Conservatory Theater, San Francisco, 23rd season
1986-7; *artistic dir*. Edward Hastings

The Nuffield Theatre, Southampton, 17 May 1990; *d*. Patrick Sandford; *pr*. Nuffield Theatre
Trust (University of Southampton); *set* Robin Don; *cos*. Nicole Young; *light*. Davy
Cunningham; *magic consultant* Ali Bongo. 25 perfs.
Gian Sammarco (Paul Pollack), Paul Russell (Steve Pollack), Sylvia Syms (Enid Pollack),
Sam Douglas (Max Pollack), Regina Reagan (Betty), Lee Montagu (Jerry Wexler)

CENTRAL PARK WEST
Variety Arts Theater, New York. 6 Mar 1995 (try out Rich Forum, Stamford, Conn., 12
Feb 1995) *d*. Michael Blakemore; *pr*. Julian Schlossberg, Jean Doumanian; *set*. Robin
Wagner; *cos*. Jane Greenwood; *light* Peter Kaczorowski; *sound* Jan Nebozenko. Third play in
multiple bill, comprising 'An Interview' (Elaine May), 'Hotline' (David Mamet) and
'Central Park West' by Woody Allen, under the umbrella title *Death Defying Acts*. 343 perfs,
9 previews to 31 Dec 1995.
Debra Monk (Phyllis), Linda Lavin (Carol), Gerry Becker (Howard), Paul Guilfoyle
(Sam), Tari T. Signor (Juliet)
Note: *Central Park West* is the only Allen one-acter to have been given a prestige capital
city presentation.

For details of Woody's shorter one act plays, see pages 130-33.

On Woody Allen

Woody Allen: An American Comedy (1977) Films for the Humanities, Princeton, N.J. *pr. and dir.* Harold Mantell; *narr.* Woody Allen (30 mins).

Film '78 Special (1978) BBC TV. *intr.* Barry Norman; *pr., scr., pres.* Iain Johnstone; *ser. pr.* Barry Brown. Transm. 7 May. 'Rare' Allen interview on autobiographical nature of *Annie Hall*, non appearance at Oscars, discussing 'Psychiatrists, Diane Keaton, Nixon, fame and sex'. Clips from *Annie Hall, Bananas, The Front, Sleeper, Love and Death,* etc. (30 mins).

Woody Allen (The South Bank Show) (1978) LWT. *exec. pr.* Nick Elliott; *ed.* Derek Bain; *pr. and dir.* Alan Benson. Transm. 7 Dec. Melvyn Bragg interviews Woody Allen with specific attention to *Interiors* (50 mins).

To Woody Allen, From Europe with Love (1980) Iblis Film/BRT (Belg.). *Conc., dir.* André Delvaux; *pr.* Pierre Drouot, Daniel Van Avermaet; *ph.* (Colour) Michael Badour, Walter Van Den Ende; *ed.* Jean Reznikov, Annette Wauthoz; *music* Egisto Macchi. Delvaux's 'Valentine portrait' to Woody revolves around the Oyster Bay, Long Island filming of *Stardust Memories* and subsequent editing at the Manhattan Film Center. Woody also discusses his work to that date, especially his own favourite *Love and Death*. English track (40 mins).

Meetin' WA (1986). *dir.* Jean-Luc Godard. Video encounter between Godard and Woody Allen, at the Manhattan Film Center, Spring 1986, to accompany *Hannah and Her Sisters* to the Cannes Film Festival. Also shown Rotterdam Film Festival, 1988 (30 mins).

Woody Allen: Love, Death, Sex, and Matters Arising (1987) BBC TV *Arena. pr.* Margaret Sharp; *ed.* John Lee; *scr.,pres.* Christopher Frayling. Transm. 13 Nov .In-depth interview, illustrated with clips and contributions from Woody and Tony Roberts, summing up former's relationships and career to that date (50 mins).

Mister Manhattan: Woody Allen (1987) Trebitsch Produktion International Gmbh/ZDF/ ORF/CBS (Ger). *Pr.* Katharina M. Trebitsch; *on-line pr.* Jutta Lieck; *d.* Peter Behle; *ph.* Peter Warneke; *ed.* Ursula Dalchow. Woody interviewed about his life and career by Hellmuth Karasek with special emphasis on *Radio Days* and other Orion movies. Clips from *Radio Days, Hannah, Broadway Danny Rose* and *The Purple Rose of Cairo*. There are also generous illustrations of Woody playing clarinet at Michael's Pub and views of Manhattan, shot in something approaching the Allen style (50 mins).

Woody and Mia (Sixty Minutes) (1993). CBS News. *sen ed.* Esther Libertal; *exec pr.* Don Hewitt. UK transm. 8 April. Prestige multi-item news magazine programme in which Woody gives his side of the 'scandal' to presenter- interviewer Steve Kroft. (60 mins).

Woody Allen (The South Bank Show) (1994) Carlton/LWT. *Ed.* Gordon Mason; *ph.* Les Young; *pr & d.* Nigel Watts. Transm. 1 Jan. Melvyn Bragg interviews Woody on his career and directing style, with reference to his recent troubles and specific attention to *Manhattan Murder Mystery* (50 mins).

Moving Pictures: Woody Allen (1995) Barraclough Carey/BBC TV. *exec pr.* Darlene Wolf; *ser dir.* Saskia Baron; *ser ed.* Paul Kerr; *dirs.* Saskia Baron, Richard Nash; *ed.* Safi Ferrar; Transm. BBC2 2 April. Howard Schuman, in multi-item programme, interviews Woody about his recent troubles and *Bullets over Broadway*.

Film 95 Special (1995). BBC TV. *Intr.*, *scr.*, *pres.* Barry Norman; *ser pr.* Bruce Thompson; *dir.* Liz Ekberg; *ed.* Mike Jackson; Transm. 17 April. Interview with Woody, concentrating on *Bullets Over Broadway*, *Hannah and Her Sisters*, recent troubles and future plans (30 mins).

Production Information

Title	Production Distribution Co.	Shooting start	US release date	Est. neg. cost	US & Can. rentals	Profit/loss comments
What's New, Pussycat?	Famous Artists/UA	15 Oct 64	Jun 65	$4m	$8.7m	$1m over budget, but 5th Top Money-Maker.
What's Up, Tiger Lily?	Benedict Pictures/AIP	(Dubbed version: Jan 66)	Sep 66			Cult success. Moderate money-maker.
Casino Royale	Famous Artists/Columbia	10 Jan 66	Apr 67	$12m	$10.2m	Doubled its budget but 3rd Top Money- Maker US and US and world hit.
Take the Money and Run	Rollins-Joffe/ Palomar/ ABC/Cinerama	17 Jun 68	Aug 69	$1.53m	$2.59m	Small cost, popular and and with selective audience, lost $610,000 on first release.
Don't Drink the Water	Rollins-Joffe/ Avco Embassy	10 Mar 69	Nov 69	$8m	est. ($1.03m gross)	Medium budget, few overseas screenings - significant flop.
Bananas	Rollins-Joffe/UA	4 May 70	May 71	$2m	$3.5m	Low cost - small profit.
Play it Again, Sam	Rollins-Joffe/Apjac/Paramount	4 Oct 71	May 72	$1.3m	$5.8m	Modest budget - world hit
Everything You've Always Wanted to KnowAbout Sex	Rollins-Joffe/ Brodsky-Gould/UA	3 Jan 72	Aug 72	$2m	$8.8m	10th Top Money-Maker, sizeable hit.
Sleeper	Rollins-Joffe/UA	30 Apr 73	Dec 73	$3.1m	$8.3m	$1.1m over budget, but big hit.
Love and Death	Rollins-Joffe/UA	23 Sep 74	Jun 75	$8.5m	$7.4m	$1m over budget - big o'seas Money-Maker.
The Front	Ritt/Rollins-Joffe/ Persky-Bright/ Columbia	15 Sep 75	Sep 76	$3.5m	$5m	Moderate budget - picked up profits in Europe.

Film	Production			Budget	Gross	Notes
Annie Hall	Rollins-Joffe/UA	10 May 76	Apr 77	$4m	$19m	Moderate budget - huge US and world hit.
Interiors	Rollins-Joffe/UA	24 Oct 77	Aug 78	$10m	$4.6m	Medium budget - slight profit-maker.
Manhattan	Rollins-Joffe/UA	17 Jul 78	Apr 79	$8m	$17.6m	Medium budget - world-wide hit.
Stardust Memories	Rollins-Joffe/UA	11 Sep 79	Sep 80	$9m	$4.1m	Medium budget - just over break-even on world-wide basis.
A Midsummer Night's Sex Comedy	Rollins-Joffe/Orion/WB	22 Jun 81	Jul 82	$7m	$4.5m	Modest budget - just over break-even.
Zelig	Rollins-Joffe/Orion/WBm	19 Oct 81	Jul 83	$6.5	$6.8m	Modest budget - small world profit-maker.
Broadway Danny Rose	Rollins-Joffe/Orion	20 Sep 82	Jan 84	$8m	$5.5m	Moderate budget - just over break-even.
The Purple Rose of Cairo	Rollins-Joffe/Orion	9 Nov 83	Mar 85	$13m	$5.1m	Medium-to-large cost - moderate loss.
Hannah and Her Sisters	Rollins-Joffe/Orion	18 Oct 84	Feb 86	$9m	$18.2m	$1m over budget but major world hit.
Radio Days	Rollins-Joffe/Orion	4 Nov 85	Jan 87	$16m	$6.4m	Large budget - US flop, European profits.
September	Rollins-Joffe/Orion	27 Oct 86	Dec 87	$10m	($486,000 gr)	Medium cost - significant loss-maker.
Another Woman	Rollins-Joffe/Orion	12 Oct 87	Oct 88	$10m	($1.6m gr)	Medium cost - significant loss-maker.
Oedipus Wrecks (New York Stories)	Rollins-Joffe/Touchstone-Buena Vista	21 Mar 88	Mar 89	$19m	$4.7m	Over-budgeted and loss maker. Woody's segment under third of total.

Title	Production Distribution Co.	Shooting start	US release date	Est. neg. cost	US & Can. rentals	Profit/loss comments
Crimes and Misdemeanors	Rollins-Joffe/Orion	3 Oct 88	Oct 89	$13m	$8.5m	Medium-to-high cost - world money-maker.
Alice	Rollins-Joffe/Orion	6 Nov 89	Dec 90	$12m	$3.3m	Medium cost - loss-maker US, big hit France and other venues.
Scenes From a Mall	Touchstone/Silver Screen Partners/Buena Vista	11 Jun 90	Feb 91	$34m	$4.2m	Inflated cost - massive flop.
Shadows and Fog	Rollins-Joffe/Orion/Columbia-Tristar	19 Nov 90	Mar 92	$14m	$1.2m	Medium cost - big flop, except some European venues.
Husbands and Wives	Rollins-Joffe/Tristar	4 Nov 91	Sep 92	$12m	$5m	Medium cost - US flop but ultimate profit-maker with $28m overseas.
Manhattan Murder Mystery	Rollins-Joffe/Tristar	14 Sep 92	Aug 93	$13.5m	($11.3m gr)	Average US take for a recent Allen film - hit No. 1 spot in Rome and UK on first release. Big hit in France.
Bullets over Broadway	Magnolia/Sweetland Films/Miramax/Buena Vista	27 Sep 93	Oct 94	$20m	($13.5m gr)	Average US release take, in late year, bolstered by overseas success in 1995.
Don't Drink the Water (TVM)	Magnolia/BVI and Jean Doumanian/Sweetland/ABC TV	4 Apr 94	Transm. ABC Network Dec 94	$3.5m		8.1/12% Nielsen share at prg. start, dwindling to 6.2/10% by end of transmission.
Mighty Aphrodite	Doumanian/Sweetland/BVI/Miramax	3 Oct 94	Oct 95	$15	($5.03m gr: 1995 only)	Anaemic year's end US gross; anticipated Europe major hit.

Selective Bibliography

BY WOODY ALLEN

Complete Prose, Wings Books, Random House, 1991; Picador, 1992, 1995.

Death - A Comedy in One Act, Samuel French, 1975.

Don't Drink the Water - A Comedy in Two Acts, Samuel French, 1967.

The Floating Lightbulb - A Drama in Two Acts, Samuel French, 1982.

Four Films of Woody Allen (Annie Hall, Interiors, Manhattan, & Stardust Memories), Random House, 1982; Faber and Faber, 1983, 1995.

Getting Even, Random House, 1971; W.H. Allen, 1973; Picador 1995.

God - A Comedy in One Act, Samuel French, 1973.

Hannah and Her Sisters, Random House, 1987; Faber and Faber, 1988.

The Illustrated Woody Allen Reader, ed. Linda Sunshine, Jonathan Cape, 1993; Vintage, 1994.

Play it Again, Sam - A Romantic Comedy in Three Acts, Samuel French, 1969.

Side Effects, Random House, 1980; New English Library, 1981, 1988.

Three Films of Woody Allen (Zelig, Broadway Danny Rose, The Purple Rose of Cairo), Random House, 1985; Faber and Faber, 1988, 1995.

What's New Pussycat? novelisation from Woody Allen's original screenplay by Marvin H. Albert, Harmony Books, 1965; Mayflower-Dell, 1965.

Without Feathers, Random House, 1975; Elm Tree Books, 1976; Sphere Books, 1978; Warner, 1988, 1995

Woody Allen on Woody Allen: In Conversation with Stig Bjorkmann, Faber and Faber, 1994.

Woody Allen's Play it Again, Sam: ed/ Richard J. Anobile, with interview by Herbert Ross, Grosset & Dunlap, 1977.

ABOUT WOODY ALLEN

Adler, Bill and Feinman, Jeffrey, *Woody Allen, The Clown Prince of American Humour*, Pinnacle Books, 1973.

Altman, Mark, *A Woody Allen Encyclopaedia*, Pioneer Books, 1991.

Benayoun, Robert, *Woody Allen: A Dèla du Language*, eds Herschner, Paris, 1985; as *WA: Beyond Words*, transl. and introd. by Alexander Walker, Pavilion Books, Michael Joseph, 1986; as *The Films of Woody Allen*, Harmony Books, 1987.

Bendazzi, Giannalberto, *The Films of Woody Allen*, Ravette, 1987.

Brode, Douglas, *Woody Allen: His Films and Career*, Citadel Press, 1985, as *The Films of Woody Allen*, Columbus, 1986; revised and updated as *The Cinema of Woody Allen*, 1991.

Carroll, Tim, *Woody and His Women*, Warner, 1994.

Champlin, Charles and Tseng, Derrick, *Woody Allen at Work: The Photographs of Brian Hamill*, Harry N. Abrams Inc, 1995

Dureau, Christian, *Woody Allen*, PAC, 1985.

Girgus, Sam B. *The Films of Woody Allen*, Cambridge Film Classics, Cambridge Mass, 1995

Groteke, Kristi, with Rosen, Marjorie, *Woody and Me: The Nanny's Tale*, Hodder and Stoughton, 1994.

Guthrie, Lee, *Woody Allen: A Biography*, Drake Publishers, 1978.

Hample, Stuart, *Non-Being and Somethingness* (collected comic strips based on Woody Allen jokes), Random House, 1978.

Hirsch, Foster, *Love, Sex, Death and the Meaning of Life: Woody Allen's Comedy*, Limelight 1990, 1993.

Jacobs, Diane, *... but we need the eggs: The magic of Woody Allen*, Robson Books, 1989.

Lax, Eric, *On Being Funny: Woody Allen and Comedy*, Manor Books, 1977.

Lax, Eric, *Woody Allen: A Biography*, Vintage, 1992.

Lebrun, Michel, *Woody Allen*, PAC, Paris, 1979.

McCann, *Woody Allen: New Yorker*, Polity Press, 1990.

McKnight, Gerald, *Woody Allen, Joking Aside,* Star Books, 1983.

Navacelle, Thierry de, *Woody Allen on Location*, Sidgwick & Jackson, 1987.

Palmer, Myles, *Woody Allen: An Illustrated Biography*, Proteus, distr. Scribners, 1980.

Pogel, Nancy, *Woody Allen*, G.K. Hall & Co./Twayne Publishers, 1987.

Rosenblum, Ralph, and Karen, Robert, *When the Shooting Stops ... The Cutting Begins*, Viking Press, 1979.

Sinyard, Neil, *The Films of Woody Allen*, Magna Books/Bison, 1987.

Spignesi, Stephen J., *The Woody Allen Companion*, Plexus, 1993.

Wernblad, Annette, *Brooklyn is not Expanding: Woody Allen's Comic Universe*, Fairleigh Dickinson, 1992.

Yacowar, Maurice, *Loser Take All: The Comic Art of Woody Allen*, Frederick Ungar, 1979; new and expanded, Roundhouse, 1991.

DISCOGRAPHY

Woody Allen: Colpix CP 488 (1964) Recorded Mister Kelly's, Chicago, March; 37.08mins approximately.

Woody Allen, Vol 2: Colpix CP 518 (1965) Recorded Shadows, Washington, April ; 30.35 mins.

The Third Woody Allen Album: Capitol ST 2986 (1968) Recorded Eugene's, San Francisco, August; 34.59 mins.

Woody Allen: The Nightclub Years, 1964-5: United Artists UA 9968 (1976); 74.59 mins.

Woody Allen: Standup Comic: 1964-1968: United Artists UA-LA 849 - J2/Casablanca Records & Film Works (1978); 74.59 mins.

The Bunk Project The New York Jazz Ensemble (*incl.* banjo *music dir.* Eddy Davis, *Clarinet* Woody Allen) Limelight 514 937-2 (1993). Recorded New York, August 1992. 61.33 mins.

Index

Aaron, Caroline 207
Abascal, Natividad 54
Abbott, George 245
ABC 26-7, 45, 53
Abraham, F. Murray 251
Abzug, Bella 115
The Academy Awards
(Oscars) 13, 23, 93, 97-8, 100, 106, 108, 116, 118, 120, 146, 161, 171, 235, 242, 247, 249, 254
Ackerman, Stanley 51
Adler, Jerry 239
Adler, Larry 85
Agfa monochrome 113
Aiello, Danny 97, 130, 153-4, 155, 177
Albeck, Andy 124, 126
Albee, Edward 130
Albert, Marvin H. 33
Alda, Alan 27, 202, 205-7, 239-40
Alexander, Jane 190
Alice 138, 158, 178, 198, 208-14, 217-20, 232, 237, 243, 254
'All the Things You Are' 198
Allen, Carole 250
Allen, Karen 115
Allen, R.S. & Bullock, Harvey 42
Allen, Steve 7
Alma-Tadema, Sir Lawrence 252
Almendros, Nestor 196
Alphaville 70
Altman, Robert 21
'Am Ufer' ('On the Beach') 106
American-in-Europe 201, 250
The American Academy & Institute of Arts & Letters 183
American Cinematographer 101, 112, 146
American Film Institute Poll 298
American International Pictures (AIP) 40, 70

American Zoetrope Studios 172
Andress, Ursula 32, 36
Andrew, Geoff 210, 232
Andrews, Nigel 206, 210, 228
Anglim, Philip 125
Anhedonia 87
Anna Karenina 80, 165
Annie Hall 14, 55, 61, 72, 74, 84-99, 101, 109, 111, 113-15, 119, 124, 126, 129, 155, 161, 165, 171, 199, 205, 230, 236-7, 239, 243, 253
Anobile, Richard J. 60, 62
Another Woman 14, 20-21, 107, 159, 163, 189-95, 199, 208, 232
Anouilh, Jean 136
Ansen, David 140, 169
Anspach, Susan 61
Anthony, Lysette 229, 232-3
anti-semitism 95
Antonioni, M. 139
Aquinas, St Thomas 80
Arbus, Diane 154
Arkin, Alan 249
Aronson, Letty 207, 242
Arriflex cameras 49
art deco 176, 180, 246
art nouveau 246
'As Time Goes By' 63
As You Like It 179
Astaire & Rogers 122, 158
Astor, Mary 57
Avery, Tex 41

BAC Films (Paris) 245
The BAFTA Awards 107, 116, 161, 235
BBC 13, 132
BNC Mitchell 169
Bach, JS 167, 206
Bach, Steven 100, 110, 112, 115, 125-6
Bacharach, Burt 38
Backer, Brian 130
Balaban, Bob 211

Baldwin, Alec 209, 212
Balint, Eszter 223
Balsmeyer & Everett 20, 211-12
Bananas 38, 44, 50, 52-6, 58, 69, 153, 250-51
Bang, Joy 60
Barnard Ladies' College 132, 233-4
Barnes, Clive 81
Baron, Sandy 150
Barrault, Marie-Christine 119-20, 122, 183
Barrie, Sir J.M. 136, 138, 210
Barry, Jack 67
Basie, Count 27, 167
Baum, Frank L. 210
The Beatles 160
Beatty, Warren 14, 29-30, 79, 126, 138, 141
Bechet, Sidney 198
Beck, Jackson 48
The Beekman Theater 149, 245-6
Begelman, David 84
The Belasco Theater 245-6
Belafonte, Harry 69, 150
Bell, Arthur 124-5
Bellow, Saul 148
Belson, Jerry 83
Benayoun, Robert 100, 104, 105, 136
Benchley, Robert 27, 131, 201
Benigni, Roberto 219
Benjamin, Richard 58, 66
Benjamin, Robert 99-100
Bergen, Candice 42
Berger, Anna 204
Bergman, Ingmar 11, 13, 20, 26, 80, 93, 99, 100-101, 105, 107, 131, 135-6, 139, 161, 164, 166, 170, 191, 194-5, 201, 215, 220, 223, 251, 256
Bergman, Ingrid 62
Bergmann, Martin 205
Berle, Milton 149-50, 153
Berlin Film Festival 81, 220

Bernard, Jami 207
Bernardi, Herschel 84
Bernstein, Nancy 199
Bernstein, Walter 84, 86, 97
Bertolucci, Bernardo 66, 169
Bessell, Ted 43
Bettelheim, Dr Bruno 142, 147
'Bewitched, Bothered and Bewildered' 167
Bialik, Mayim 44-5
Biograph 148
Bitch, Sandy 255
Bizio, Silvio 109, 197
Björkmann, Stig 19, 132, 203
Björnstrand, Gunnar 135
Blakemore, Michael 244
The Bleecker Street Cinema 207
Bloom, Claire 202, 206, 251
Blow-up 139, 169
The Blue Angel 29
Blum, John Morton 148
Bogart, Humphrey 56-9, 61-3, 66, 134
Bogre, Michelle 143, 146-7
Bonaparte, Napoleon 78-80
Bonham Carter, Helena 250
Bonnie and Clyde 41, 48, 50
Bookbinder, Robert J. 108
Bordo, Edwin 150
The Borscht Belt 84, 150
Bosco, Philip 192, 221
The Boston Herald 216
Bourne, Mel 101, 103, 124-5
Boutsikaris, Dennis 255
Bow, Clara 143
Boyd, Don 195
Bragg, Melvyn 22, 104
'The Brain Goes Home' 152
Brake, Patricia 58
Brando, Marlon 23, 172
Braudy, Susan 87, 112

Brave New World 73
Brecht, Berthold 169, 224, 255
Brickman, Marshall 18, 42, 64, 70, 72, 86, 87-8,90-92, 96, 111-12, 114-15, 126, 236-7
Brickman, Miriam 75
Bricktop 143
'Bridge Over Troubled Water' 171
Brien, Alan 117, 135
Brighton Beach Memoirs 174, 176
The Broadhurst Theater 56
Broadbent, Jim 246-7
Broadway Danny Rose 19, 54, 123, 129, 149 55,159, 180, 245
Broccoli, 'Cubby' 35, 37
Brode, Douglas 64, 68, 122, 136, 167, 169
Brodsky-Gould Productions 64
Brooks, Mel 14, 98
Brothers 102
Brown, Colin 248
Brubeck, Dave 167
Bruce, Lenny 27
Buck, Frank 155
Buckley, Betty 20
Buckley, William F. 41
Buffy the Vampire Slayer 233
Bullets Over Broadway 45, 240-50, 251, 253
Bulow, Claus Von 214
The Bunk Project 255
Bunuel, Luis 256
Burne-Jones, Edward 136
Burnett, Carol 26
Burns, George 256
Burrows, Abe 25
Bus-Fekete, Ladislaus 29
Buttons, Red 256
Buxton, Frank 36, 40
Byrne, Anne 115

Caesar, Sid 14, 26, 42
Caesar's Palace 42, 132, 151
Caglione, John 142
Cahiers du Cinéma 232
Caine, Michael 21, 164-5, 167-71
Caldwell, Zoe 160
Camp Tamiment 26
Camus, Albert 242
Canby, Vincent 15, 25, 51-2, 63, 69, 108, 126, 149, 154, 161, 195, 223

Cannes Film Festival 116, 161, 171-4, 230, 238
'The Cannon Song' 221
Capote, Truman 97
Capra, Frank 171, 205
Capucine 29, 32-3
Carlisle, Kitty 179-80
Carnegie, Dale 151
The Carnegie Deli 123, 150, 152
The Carnegie Hall 27
Carney, Art 26
Caron, Leslie 30
Carradine, John 68
Carrey, Leah 175
Carroll, Lewis 210
Carroll, Tim 61, 112, 223
Carson, Johnny 27, 41-2
Carter, Howard 155
Casablanca 57-9, 62
Case, Brian 145
Casino Royale 30, 34-9, 42, 47, 53, 212; novel 34-5, 37; TV segment 34
Cassavetes, John 66, 230
Castro, Fidel 54
The Cat's Pajamas 143
Cavett, Dick 42, 116
CBS 34, 42, 84, 237
Central Park West 130, 132, 244
César Awards 161, 242
'Chameleon Days' 143
The Chameleon Man 142, 144
The Changing Man 143, 144
Chaplin, Charles 7, 11, 55, 62, 114, 141, 143, 151, 190, 223
Chekhov, Anton 11, 1365, 165, 179, 184
Cherrill, Virginia 42
The Chevy Show 26
Chiara, Maria 167
Chicago Film Festival 254
The Chicago Seven 56
The Chicago White Sox 137, 178
ChristenRose gallery 252
Christie, Julie 34
Cinecittà Film Studios 183
Cinéfantastique 212
Cinema '87 183
Cinéma verité 49, 172, 230
La Cinémathèque Française 77, 133
50 ans de cinéma Américain

242
Citizen Kane 147, 149
City Lights 42, 114
The City Neurotic 72
Clair, René 158
Clark, Andrew 177
Clark, Mike 249
Clements, Marcelle 238-9
Cleopatra 35
Cloquet, Ghislain 77, 78
Cocteau, Jean 158, 242
Cohen, Alexander 160
Cohen, Lyn 239
Cohn, Sam 108, 127
The Colgate (Comedy) Hour 25, 59
Colomby, Harry 159
Columbia Pictures Corp 35, 37, 39, 84, 189, 214, 218-9
Columbia University 55, 233
Combs, Richard 155
Comencini, Luigi 183
Commentary 91
Commonweal 140
Le concept subtil see *The Subtle Concept*
'The Condemned' 77
'The Confidence Man' 145
Connery, Sean 35
Conroy, Frances 191
Constantine, Michael 43
Cook, Barbara 180
Coolidge, Calvin 142
La Co-Op Nordemiglia 219, 234
Coppola, Francis 196
Corbett, Ronnie 38
Corliss, Kathleen 171
Corliss, Richard 151, 154
The Coronet Theater 55
The Cort Theater 246
Cosell, Howard 53-5, 153
Cosmopolitan 23, 231
The Couple Next Door 236
Coups de feu sur Broadway 250
Coursodon, Robert 121
The Court Jester 67
Cousteau, Jacques 76
Coward, Nöel 132, 245
Craigin, Charles 224
Crane, Cheryl 185-6
Crimes and Misdemeanors 88, 167, 194, 201-8 222, 236-7, 239-40, 250
Crist, Judith 115, 119

Culver City Studios 70
'La Cumparsita' 177
'Cupid's Shaft' 42
Current Biography 42
Cusack, John 222, 224, 245, 247-8

The Daily Mail 223
Damone, Vic 151
Dancing Shiva 236
D'Angelo, Beverly 97
Daniele, Graciela 251
Daniels, Jeff 155, 159-60, 177
Danner, Blythe 192, 213
Dart, Leslie 142
David Copperfield 183
David Di Donatello Awards 220
Davis, Bette 78
Davis, Judy 13, 209, 228-9, 232-5, 255
Day, Doris 44
Death 69, 130-32, 220, 224
'Death and the Maiden' 193
Death Defying Acts 244
Death Knocks 130-32
Deaton, Charles 71
De Angelis, Gina 182
De Filippo, Eduardo 198
Delaney, Joan 43, 216
Delon, Alain 217
Delvaux, André 123
De Luise, Dom 45
Dempsey, Jack 141, 148
De Niro, Robert 23, 153
Dershowitz, Alan 214
De Sica, Vittorio 66
Dewhurst, Connie 91, 97
Diamond, I.A.L. 29
The Dick Cavett Show 70, 95, 116
Dickens, Charles 183, 204, 209
Didion, Joan 87, 103
Dillinger, John 48, 51
Dinkins, David 233
Di Palma, Carlo 20, 169-70, 176, 180-82, 184, 193, 217, 229-30, 240, 246, 252,
The Disney Organisation 196, 217, 244
Disney, Walt 136
Donner, Clive 30-34, 35
Don't Drink the Water 41-5, 58; play 42-5, 48, 56; TV film 44-5, 233, 244, 253
Dorme, Norman 35, 39
'Dorrie Keaton' 62
Dostoyevsky, Fyodor 79,

196, 203, 205, 223, 244
Douglas, Sam 130
Doumanian, Jean 124-5, 204, 241-2, 244
Doumanian, John 97, 124, 228, 241
Dowd, Maureen 256
Doyle, Sir Arthur Conan 211
Dragonette, Jessica 182
Dreams and Furies 14
Dreiser, Theodore 67
Dreyer, Carl 193
Dreyfuss, Richard 98, 217
Dukakis, Olympia 251
Dunning, Philip 245
Dunphy, Don 53
Durning, Charles 185
Duvall, Shelley 97

The Eamonn Andrews Show 38
Earhart, Amelia 143
Eastlake, Charles Lock 123
Eastman Double X negative (film stock) 147
Eastwood, Clint 13, 126, 167, 201, 258
'Easy to Love' 216
Edinburgh Festival 116, 132, 155
8½ 116, 121, 178
Eisenhower, President Dwight D. 85
El Weirdo 53
The Elephant Man 142
Elle 217
Elliott, Denholm 107, 185-6
Ellison, Ralph 145
Entertainment Weekly 220
Ephron, Nora 93, 228
Equal Rights Amendment (ERA) 110, 115
Erato Film 183
Erman, John 256
Esquire 22-3, 27, 76
Evans, Robert 31, 58
The Evergreen Review 14, 27, 53
Everyone Says I Love You 256
Everything You Always Wanted to Know About Sex (*But Were Afraid to Ask)* 54, 63-9, 71, 78, 101, 195, 197, 254; book 64-5, 68
Existentialism 117, 220
L'Express 146

FAO Schwartz 252
Falk, Peter 84, 98, 256
Fanny and Alexander 164
Farber, Stephen 120
Farrow, Dylan 237, 241, 250
Farrow, John 138
Farrow, Mia 12-13, 21-2, 119, 137-9, 142, 145, 147, 150, 153, 155, 159, 163-4, 166-8, 182, 184-5, 186, 189-191, 197, 203, 205-6, 208-10, 212, 214, 221, 223, 227-32, 234, 237, 240-41, 255-6
Farrow, Moses 241
Farrow, Prudence 160
Farrow, Satchel 190, 241
Farrow, Stephanie 143, 160
Farrow, Tisa 115
fascism 141
FBI 86, 234
Felder, Raoul 241
Feldman, Charles K. 29-31, 33-7, 39, 47
Fellini, Federico 93, 116, 119, 124, 139, 178, 180
feminism 13, 109, 111, 232
Ferre, Governor Luis G. 53
Ferrer, José 137, 139
Fierstein, Harvey 249
The Fifth Dimension 42
Le Figaro 220
film noir 133-4
The Filmmaker 70
Films and Filming 195
Finch, Peter 34
Finkelstein, Sidney 121
Finler, Joel 41, 121
Fisher, Carrie 166, 171
Fitzgerald, E. & P. 176
Fitzgerald, F. Scott 142, 144
The Flatbush Theater 25
Fleming, Erin 77
Fleming, Ian 34, 37
Flynn, Errol 177
'The Floating Lightbulb' 120, 130
The Floating Lightbulb 120, 129-30, 141, 151
Fog and Shadows 218
Fonda, Henry 155
Fonda, Jane 232
Forbes, Bryan 35
Ford, John 242
Forte, Nick Apollo 19, 149, 153
Fox *see* Twentieth

Century-Fox
The Fox Channel 256
Fox, Michael J. 44
'Francis the Talking Mule' 203
Frankenstein 68, 121
Franklin, Aretha 41
Franklin, Joe 150
Fraser, Nicholas 96
Frayling, Christopher 150, 156
French Impressionism 136
French New Wave *see nouvelle vague*
French, Philip 199
Freud, Sigmund 80, 93, 110
Friedman, Dr Dennis 140
Friedman, Lester D. 94, 143
Friend, Marilyn 238
Frodon, Jean-Michel 240, 253
The Front 83-6, 134, 150
Frye, Dwight 68

Gable, Clark 7
Gallio, Joie 153
Gallio, Joey 153
Gallo, Fred T. 71, 75, 77, 89
Garbo, Greta 148
Garrison, Ellen 147
The Garry Moore Show 26
Gaumont Cinémathèque 133
Gaumont Film Productions 183
Gazzara, Ben 191
Gehrig, Lou 125, 146
Geist, William 257
Gelbart, Larry 12, 26
Genesis, The Book of 66
Georges-Picot, Olga 78
German Expressionism 11, 131, 218
Gershwin, George 109-110, 168
Getting Even 133
Gibb, Bill 98
Gilliatt, Penelope 108, 117
Gingold, Hermione 26
Girgus, Sam B. 113
Gish, Lillian 148
Gleason, Jackie 42-3, 84
Gleiberman, Owen 220
The Globe Theatre 57
God 69, 130-32, 251
Godard, Jean-Luc 70, 171-4
Gogol, Nicolai 199
Golan, Menachem 172-3

The Goldbergs 124
Goldblum, Jeff 97
'Golden Age of Radio' 174
Golden Globe Awards 161, 254
Goldenberg, Billy 63
Gomez, Andres Vicente 256
Gone with the Wind 70, 196
Goodhill, Dean 112
Gould, Elliott 64
Graham, Dr Billy 42
Graham, Martha 14
Grahame, Kenneth 136
The Grand Finale 88
Grange, Red 143-4
Grant, Cary 29, 177
Gray, Francine du Plessix 131, 221
Grayson, Kathryn 25
The Great Gatsby 138, 148
Green, Seth 175
Greene, Graham 174
Greenhut, Robert 134, 154, 165, 194-6, 199
Grey (Chaplin), Lita 143
Griffin, Merv 42, 246
Griffith, DW 136, 148
Griffith, Kristin 102
Grimsby, Roger 55
Grosbard, Ulu 130
Grossberg, Jack 49-50, 71, 75
Guest, Val 34-7, 38, 47, 57
The Guggenheim Museum 108, 110
'A Guide to Some of the Lesser Ballets' 198
Guthrie, Lee 111
Guzman, Pato 216
Gwynne, Fred 225

Hack, Shelley 97
Hackett, Buddy 26, 151
Hackman, Gene 192
Hagerty, Julie 137, 139
Hall, Conrad 94
Hall, Diane Keaton *see* Keaton, Diane
Hall, Dorrie 62, 119
Hall family 94, 96
Hallmark Entertainment 256
Hamill, Brian 145, 160
Hamill, Denis 145, 235, 243
Hamlisch, Marvin 50
Hammett, Dashiell 113
Hampton, Christopher 143
Hampton, Paul 27
Hanft, Helen 119

Hanna-Barbera
Productions 42
Hannah and Her Sisters
14, 20-21, 102, 109,
159, 163-72, 179,
187, 190, 199, 201-2,
207, 210, 235-6, 249
Hannah, Darryl 207
Hardy, Françoise 33
Hardy, Joseph 56
Harley, Gillian 235
Harman, Bob 212
Harper, Jessica 97, 119
Harper, Valerie 179
Hartwick, Joseph 194
'The Harvey Wallinger
Story' 56
Hayes, Kerry 145
'Headline News' 227
Headly, Glenne 160
Heaven's Gate 110, 126
Hecht, Ben 30, 36
Heckert, James T. 49, 69
Hefner, Hugh 13
Heller, Joseph 36
Hemingway, Ernest 176
Hemingway, Mariel 110,
112
Hendricks, Barbara 183
Hennesy, Dale 66, 69,
71
Henreid, Paul 62
Henske, Judy 87
Hepburn, Katharine
77
Herman, Paul 197
Herrmann, Edward 156
Hershey, Barbara 166,
168, 170
Hillaire, Marcel 51
Hintelmann, Linda 225
Hippodrome 38
Hirschhorn, Clive 243
Hitchcock, Alfred 19,
157, 190, 207, 237,
240
Hitler, Adolf 144, 146-7
Hoffman, Dustin 58, 83-
4, 115, 120, 126, 136,
173
Holden, Stanley 201
The Hollanders 43
Hollywood Production
Code 157
Holm, Ian 20-21, 189,
191
Home Box Office Inc
(HBO) 154
Hoover, Herbert 142
Hope, Bob 25, 55, 61,
67, 79, 85, 88, 116
Horgan, Patrick 143
Horvath, Odon Von 143
Hot Press 13
Hotline 244

Houdini, Harry 181
House Committee on
Un-American Activities
(HUAC) 84-5
Houseman, John 191,
193
Howard, David S. 203
Howard, Ron 172
Hughes, Kenneth 35
'Human Chameleon'
145
The Human Comedy 174
Hungarofilm 76
'the hungry i' 26, 236
Hurt, Marybeth 102,
107
Hurt, William 209, 211
Husbands and Wives 21,
103, 111-12, 138,
172, 193, 210, 227-
36, 238-9, 242, 254
Huston, Anjelica 202,
206, 237-40
Huston, John 35-6
Huxley, Aldous 73

Hylton, Jack 220
Hyman, Dick 142, 181
Hyneck, Joel 145

'I Don't Want to Walk
Without You Baby'
181
'I'll Be Seeing You' 180
'I'll Get By' 144
'I'm Old Fashioned' 167
'I Want A Girl...' 197
Independent Television
Network 44
The In-Laws 98
L'Institut des Hautes
Etudes Cinémato-
graphiques (IDHEC)
133
Interiors 20, 99-108, 111,
120, 159, 163, 165,
167, 184-5, 251
Irvin, John 22
An Interview 244
It All Came True 153
'Italian Street Song' 182

Jacobi, Lou 43, 65
Jacobs, Arthur P. 58
Jacobs, Diane 61
Jacobs, Tom 45
James Bond 34-5, 39-40,
171
James, Caryn 109, 182
The Japan American
Theatre 201
'The Jazz Age' 142, 144
'Jazz Heaven' 118
Jeffries, Stuart 194
A Jew in Love 256
The Jewish Image in

American Film 94, 143
Joffe, Carol 171
Joffe, Charles H. 21, 26,
29, 31-2, 42-4, 47,
58, 64, 71-2, 75-6,
84, 89, 108, 125, 134,
151, 160, 196
The Johnny Carson Show
41-2, 70
Johnson, Van 160
Johnston, Sheila 205
Johnston, Reginald 45
Johnstone, Iain 155
Jolson, Al 118, 245
Jordan, Richard 103,
107

Kael, Pauline 15, 51,
105, 125, 149, 154-5,
159, 161, 171, 183,
195, 204, 221, 223,
230
Kafka, Franz 55, 91,
131, 199-200
Kagi No Kagi 39
Kalmar and Ruby 121
Kalter, Joanmarie 106
Kalutani, Michiko 141
Kane, Carol 78, 90
Kane, Helen 143
Kanfer, Stefan 91
Karasek, Hellmuth 58
Katz, Lehman 'Lee' 99
Kauffman, Stanley 107,
140
Kaufman Astoria Studios
76, 148, 160, 176,
181, 184, 212, 216,
218
Kavner, Julie 175, 179,
198
Kaye, Danny 26
Kear, Dennis 180
Keaton, Buster 11, 70,
74, 143, 158
Keaton, Diane 12-13,
56-8, 60-62, 64, 72-7,
79, 87, 91-3, 96-8,
101-2, 110-12, 115,
139, 159, 164, 178-9,
190, 237-40, 253,
255-6
Keaton, Michael 159
Keats, Steven 225
Keg of Powder 39
Kelley, Ken 79
Keosian, Jessie 197
Kensit, Patsy 255
The Kent 160
Kern, Jerome 198
Kerr, Deborah 37
Key of Keys 39
Kinescope 67
King Lear 172-4
The Kinsey Institute 64

Kirby, Kathryn 195
Kissel, Howard 124
Kissinger, Henry 56
Kline, Jim 223
Kline, Kevin 160
The Knicks *see* The
New York
Knickerbockers
Koch, Joanne 116
Koch, Ed 198
Kodak monochrome
(Double X) 113
Konigsberg, Allan
Stewart (Woody
Allen) 7-258 *passim*
Konigsberg, Martin 25,
87, 150, 177
Konigsberg, Nettie 25,
168
Konigsberg, Rita 159
Kraft Music Hall 41
Kramer vs Kramer 115
Krawczyk, Gérard 133-4
Krim, Arthur 25, 99-
101, 127, 219
Kroft, Steve 237
Kroll, Jack 15, 107, 149
Kubrick 69-70
'The Kugelmass Episode'
133, 156, 197
Kurland, Jeffrey 199,
228, 249, 251-2
Kurnitz, Julie 176
Kurosawa, Akira 169
Kustow, Michael 133

Lacey, Jerry 57-8, 62-3
Lahr, John 7, 131-2
Lamarr, Hedy 42
Landau, Martin 202,
205-6
Lang, Fritz 51, 69, 221-
22
Langdon, Harry 73
La Rue, Danny 38
Lasser, Louise 27, 33,
40-41, 51, 54-5, 56,
61, 65-6, 91, 102,
104, 119, 177, 202
Lasser, Mrs S.J. 40, 102,
104
Last Year at Marienbad 123
The Laughmakers 27
Laurel, Stan 205
Lauren, Ralph 99
Lavi, Daliah (Dahlia) 35
Law, John 35
Lax, Eric 66, 107, 139-
140, 154, 190
Lazenby, George 35
Leahy, Gaila 54
Lean, David 92
Lear's 238
Le Bow, Guy 178
Lee, China 41

Lee, Spike 211, 234
Lefebvre, Germaine
 see Capucine
Leisen, Mitchell 157,
 255
Lemmon, Jack 98
Lenard, Mark 97
Lennon, John 120
'Leonard the Lizard'
 143
lesbianism 109
Levi, Primo 205
Levin, Ira 237
Levinson, Barry 174
Lewis, Jerry 47
Lewis, Juliette 228,
 233
Lewis, Roger 37
Liebman, Max 26
Life Class (New York
 Stories) 196
Life Without Zoe (New
 York Stories) 196
'Limehouse Blues' 209
Lincoln, Abraham 131
Lincoln, Trebitsch 145
Lincoln Center 88,
 129, 240
Lincoln Center Film
 Society 116
Lindbergh, Charles A.
 142, 157
Lindemuth, James 123
Lionello, Oreste 69,
 234
Lippin, Renee 175
A Little Night Music 135
Lloyd, Emily 233
Lloyd, Harold 70
Loeb, Philip 85
Lolita 110
Lollobrigida, Gina 66
The London Academy
 of Dramatic Art
 (LAMDA) 110
London Critics' Circle
 161, 235
The London Film
 Festival 174, 235,
 255
London Newstalk 250
'The Look of Love' 38
Loquasto, Santo 130,
 142, 179, 184, 207,
 218, 251, 256
Loren, Sophia 29
The Los Angeles
 Chamber Ballet 201
Los Angeles Film
 Critics 247
The Los Angeles Film
 Exposition 97
The Los Angeles Herald 64
The Los Angeles Times
 223

Losey, Joseph 173
Louis Malle's India
 (Phantom India) 210
Louma crane 20, 174,
 223
Love and Betrayal: The
 Mia Farrow Story 255
Love and Death 22, 67,
 74-81, 83, 101, 112,
 123, 139, 215
Love, Death and Food 79
Love, Food and Death 79
The Lovin' Spoonful 41
Lubitsch, Ernst 255
Luke, Keye 209, 211
Lumet, Sidney 108
'The Lunatic's Tale' 121
Lutter III, Alfred 78

MGM-British Studios
 35, 39
MGM TV 256
McCann, Graham 7,
 61, 92, 98, 124, 171
McCarthy, Joseph 83-4
McCarthy, Todd 254
McGrath, Douglas 18,
 243, 247
McGrath, Joseph 35, 37
McKnight, Gerald 101
McKuen, Rod 73
McLuhan, Marshall 93
McQuaid, Jimmy 250
McQueen, Steve 13,
 126
MacArthur, Douglas 85
Macdonald, Philip 14
Maclaine, Shirley 26,
 29
Macpherson, Elle 211
Macrae, Heather 68
Madison Square Garden
 91, 240, 252
Madonna 211, 222, 225
mafia 150-51, 153
Mafilm 76
Magerson, William 175
The Magical Herbs of Dr
 Yang 211
Mailer, Norman 17,
 172-3
Majeed, Mustafa 233-4
Malcolm, Derek 250
Malkovich, John 160,
 222
Malle, Louis 150, 209
The Maltese Falcon 57,
 62, 133
Mamet, David 132, 244
Manet, Edouard 136
Manhattan 8, 13, 18,
 86, 98, 108-16, 117,
 122, 126, 138, 168-
 9, 171, 208, 235-6
The Manhattan Film

Center 172
Manhattan Murder
 Mystery 88, 95, 204,
 210, 230, 236-40,
 242-3, 249, 254
The Manhattan
 Museum of Television
 and Radio 242
The Manhattan Project
 236
The Manhattan
 Supreme Court 240
Mankiewicz, Chris 100
Mankiewicz, Joseph L.
 107
Mankowitz, Wolf 34-8
Mannain, Brian 178
Manos, George J. 160
Mantegna, Joe 209, 211
Mantell, Harold 123
Marathon Street
 Studios see
 Paramount Studios
Marconi, Guglielmo
 181
Marcovicci, Andrea
 85-6
Margolin, Janet 12, 50-
 51, 90, 91
Mars, Kenneth 221
Marshall, E.G. 102,
 106
Marvin, Lee 172
The Marx Brothers 11,
 49, 53, 56
Marx, Groucho 30, 50,
 78, 88, 93, 104, 120,
 131
Maslin, Janet 238-9,
 249, 254
Mason, Pamela 67
Masters and Johnson 69
Mastroianni, Marcello
 29, 65, 121
Matthau, Walter 256
Maxwell, Kenny 40,
 137
May, Elaine 27, 132,
 244
Mayakovsky, Vladimir
 70
Mazursky, Paul 104,
 214-7
Medavoy, Mike 100,
 127, 219, 241
Meltzer, Harvey 151
Melville, Herman 144
Melville, Jean-Pierre
 134
Mendelssohn, Felix 136
Mendillo, Stephen 225
Meredith, Burgess 173
Merrick, David 57, 131
The Merv Griffin Show
 246

Methodists 123, 149
Metro-Goldwyn-Mayer
 Picture Corp (MGM)
 52-3, 100
Michael's Pub 74, 98,
 255
Midler, Bette 215-17
A Midsummer Night's Sex
 Comedy 126, 134-40,
 147, 148, 252
Midwood School 48
Mighty Aphrodite 249,
 250-5
Miller, Arthur 130
Miller, Edwin 36, 100
Miller, Kate 173
Milligan, Spike 38
Minnelli, Liza 41
Mingalone, Dick 230
Mintz, Eli 124
Miramax Film Corp
 244, 253, 250
Miramax International
 Pictures 245
'Mr Big' 133-4
Mister Kelly's 26, 241
Mitchell, Elvis 15
Mitchell, Sean 223
Monaco, James 107
Le Monde 240, 243, 253
Monicelli, Mario 65
Monkhouse, Bob 38
Monroe, Earl 91
Monroe, Marilyn 85
Montagu, Lee 130
Montreal Film Festival
 133, 174
Moore, Colleen 144
Moore, Dudley 57-8
Moore, Stephen 75
Mora, Philippe 141
Moran, Dan 251
Moreland, Arthur 67
Morley, Robert 34
Morley, Ruth 98-9
The Morosco Theater
 42
Morris, Howard 42-4
Morse, Robert 53
Morse, Susan E. 19, 90,
 115, 144, 194
Mortimer, John 199
Moss, Robert F. 120
Mostel, Joshua 175
Mostel, Zero 84
Mother Teresa 210
The Motion Picture
 Association of
 America (MPAA) 65,
 110
The Motion Picture Herald
 see Quigley 'Top
 Money-Making Stars'
Munch, Edvard 105,
 193

Münchausen, Baron 145
Munk, Jonathan 93
Murnau, FW 221
Murphy, Eddie 242
Murphy, Fred 216
Murphy, Michael 85, 109, 115
Murray, Braham 132
The Museum of Modern Art 108, 110
Mussolini, Benito 203
My Apology 130, 132
My Favourite Comedian 116
'My Funny Valentine' 151

NASA 68
NBC 25, 41, 45, 56, 149
NBC Writers' Development Program 25
Nabokov, Vladimir 110
The National Board of Review 211
The National Film Theatre 44, 171, 255
The National Radio Theater of Chicago 132
The National Theatre 133
Navacelle, Thierry De 180, 182, 185
Nazism 115, 147, 177, 204, 222
Neeson, Liam 230, 235
Nelkin, Stacey 111-12
Nelligan, Kate 221, 225
neo-realism 66
The New Orleans Funeral and Ragtime Orchestra 70, 74
The New Orleans Jazz Band 255
The New Republic 121, 139
The New York Daily News 27, 171, 256
New York Film Critics 247
The New York Film Festival 116, 249
The New York Jazz Ensemble 255
New York Knickerbockers 91, 115, 229
New York Magazine 115, 235
The New York Post 161, 171, 207
New York Rangers 240

New York Stories (1989) 195, 198
New York Tales see *New York Stories, Oedipus Wrecks*
The New York State Theater 88
The New York Sunday Times 108
The New York Times 52, 125, 145, 165, 170, 182, 197, 208, 228-9, 249, 254
New York University 25, 154, 156, 195, 201
The New York Yankees 145
The New Yorker 14, 27, 51, 77, 97, 130, 144, 154-5, 238
The New Yorker 89, 92
Newman, Joy 175
Newman, Laraine 124
Newman, Paul 13, 83, 126
'News on the March' 147
Newsweek 15, 149, 152, 227
Nichols, Mike 27
Nichols, Jenny 206
Nicholson, Jack 21, 86, 126
Nietzsche, Friedrich 91, 221
1941 174, 181
Niven, David 36, 39
Nixon, Richard M. 56, 85
Nolan, Lloyd 166
Nolde, Emil 105
Nosferatu 221
nouvelle vague 15, 172, 230
The Nuffield Theatre 130
Nuit et Brouillard 218
'Number 1 Dream Lover' 126
Nykvist, Sven 20, 107, 193-4, 196, 199, 201, 207, 242

007 see James Bond
Obie Award 132
The Observer 199
The Ocean Grove Camp Meeting Assoc. 123-4
Odeon, Leicester Square 39, 171
Odets, Clifford 130
Oedipus Rex 251
Oedipus Wrecks (*New York*

Stories) 146, 194, 195-9
Og 121-2, 125
Oliver, Stephen 242
Olivier, Laurence 67
'On the Beach' see 'Am Ufer'
O'Neal, Patrick 209-10
O'Neill, Eugene 99, 141
Orbach, Jerry 202, 206
Orion Pictures Corp 17, 25, 100, 126, 135, 152, 154, 161, 171, 183, 196, 207, 213, 214, 217, 219, 234, 236, 219-20
Orwell, George 73
O'Shea, Milo 160
O'Sullivan, Maureen 138, 164, 168, 185-6
O'Toole, Peter 30, 32-3
Otto e Mezzo see *8½*

Pabst, GW 223
Pacino, Al 84, 126
Page, Geraldine 101, 105-7, 166
Palminteri, Chazz 245, 248-50
Palomar Pictures International 47, 100
Panaflex (camera) 148
Panavision 112-13
Paramount News 48
Paramount Pictures Inc 58-9, 64, 148
Paramount Studios 59
The Paris 89, 189
Parker, Gloria 153
Parker, Mary-Louise 246
Parker, Sarah Jessica 256
Parrish, Robert 35
Parsons, Estelle 43
Pathé Studios 88
Pauly, Rebecca 133
Peabody Award 56
Penn, Arthur 48
Perelman, S.J. 27
Peters, Bernadette 209
Petersen, Wolfgang 181
Peterson, Oscar 50
Pettet, Joanna 38
Phantom India (*L'inde fantôme*) see *Louis Malle's India*
'Phil Feldman's Hostility 121
The Philadelphia Story 175
Picasso, Pablo 172
Picker, David 52, 70
Pinewood Studios 35

Pirandello, Luigi 11, 117, 157-8
Piscopo, Joe 242
Pius XI, Pope 143, 146
Plantier, Daniel Toscan Du 183
Plath, Sylvia 102
Play it Again, Sam 44, 56-63, 66, 69, 84, 112, 130-31; play 44, 47, 50, 52, 56-63, 57, 87, 131, 198, 236
Playboy 13, 27, 33, 41, 54
Pleasence, Donald 22, 225
Pleskow, Eric 100, 219
Plimpton, George 34
Plimpton, Martha 189
Polanski, Roman 241
The Politics - and Comedy - of Woody Allen 56
Pollack, Sydney 22, 228-9, 232-3
Porter, Beth 22, 77-9, 89
Porter, Cole 143, 206, 216
Powell, Dilys 74
Powell, Richard 52
Powers of Attorney 244
Première 208, 217
Prentiss, Paula 32, 58, 66, 201
Pre-Raphaelites 138
Previn, Andre 138
Previn, Fletcher 164, 180
Previn, Soon-Yi 227-9, 250
Price, Vincent 70
Prince Valiant 67
Le Prix Moussinac 161
The Producers 49
Prokofiev, Sergei 81
Puccini, Giacomo 183
Pulp Fiction 250
The Purple Rose of Cairo 20, 117, 122, 145-6, 153, 155-161, 175, 177, 180, 254

Quayle, Sir Anthony 67
The Query 130, 132
Questel, Mae 142, 197, 199
Quigley 'Top Money-Making Stars' Poll (MPH) 13, 63, 171

R/Greenberg Associates 20, 145, 181, 199
Radio City Music Hall

63, 175

Radio Days 20, 87, 92, 129, 148, 153, 159, 160, 163, 169, 172, 174-83, 184-5, 211, 238, 246, 249, 250, 253

Rafferty, Terence 97, 238-9

Raging Bull 153, 208

Rainer, Peter 140

Rampling, Charlotte 119, 122, 125, 133, 250

Rapaport, Michael 251

Ratoff, Gregory 34

Reagan, Ronald 204

'Red River Valley' 68

The Red Skelton Hour 38

Redford, Robert 13, 126, 167

Redgrave, Lynn 66

Reds 79, 138, 141

Reed, Rex 161, 171

La Règle du Jeu 135, 182

Reilly, Thomas 154

Reiner, Rob 246

Reinisch, Dr June 64

Renoir, Auguste 130

Renoir, Jean 14, 21, 136

Resnais, Alain 218

Reuben, Dr David M. 64, 68-9, 131

Reynolds, Burt 13, 83

Reynolds, Herb 151

'Rhapsody in Blue' 109

Rhoda 179

Rich, Frank 114

Richards, Don 177

Richards, Jeffrey 222

Rilke, Rainer Maria 191

Riot in Cell Block 11 48

Ritt, Martin 83-4, 86

The Roaring 20s 243

Roberts, Julia 256

Roberts, Tony 44, 57-8, 60-61, 90, 96, 110, 120, 132, 137, 140, 168, 170, 179

Robertson, Stuart 145

Robinson, David 140, 172-3

Robson, Eric 145

Rogosin, Lionel 108

Roizman, Owen 60

Rolling Stone 79, 97, 257

Rollins, Jack (Rollins & Joffe) 25-6, 29, 42-4, 47, 52, 58, 64, 84,90, 99, 101, 111, 124, 150-51, 160

Roosevelt, President

155, 176

Rose, Mickey 18, 48, 53, 74

Rosen, Alan 244

Rosen, Harlene 25, 61, 95

Rosen, Nick 160

Rosenberg, J. & E. 85

Rosenblatt, Benjamin 145

Rosenblum, Ralph 9, 44, 49-50, 55, 69-71-4, 76, 80-81, 88-9, 96, 103, 107, 115

Ross, Herbert 58-63

Rossetti, Dante Gabriel 136, 185

Rota, Nino 119

Roth, Henry 145

Roth, Philip 68

Rotterdam Inter-national Film Festival 173

Roud, Richard 126, 157

Rowlands, Gena 189-90

The Royal Exchange Theatre 132

The Royal Festival Hall 255

Rubin, Joe 227

Runes, Richard 89

Runyon, Damon 151-2, 247

Ruth, Babe 146

Sabat, Jimmy 175

Safra, Jacqui 125

Sahl, Mort 26-7, 41

Said, Fouad 48

Sales, Nancy Jo 112

Saltzman, Harry 35, 37

Salvato, Larry 60, 117

Sammarco, Gian 130

Sandford, Patrick 130

Sandrich, Mark 157

Saperstein, Henry 39-40

Sarris, Andrew 81, 108, 126

Saturday Night Live 124, 241-2

Saviola, Camille 221

Sayers, Michael 35

Scapperotti, Dan 212

Scenes from a Mall 214-7, 229

Scenes from a Marriage 214, 219

Schaefer, Dennis 60, 112

Schaeffer, Rebecca 179

Schary, Dore 36

Schickel, Richard 15,

97, 107,140, 194

Schiff, Steven 12

Schlossberg, Julian 244

Schmidt, Benno C. 229

Schneider, Romy 32-3

Schoenfeld, Gerald 153

Schreck, Max 221

Schubert, Franz 206

Schubert Theaters 153

Schumacher, Joel 105

Schwarzenegger, Arnold 12, 70-71, 217

Scorsese, Martin 11, 196, 208

Scott, George C. 21

Screen International 84, 195

'Seems Like Old Times' 96

Segal, George 198

Selbst, Irving 153

Sellars, Peter 173

Sellers, Peter 31-3, 35-8

Selznick, David O. 70

September 15, 22, 126, 140, 163, 168, 172, 183-9, 190-91, 194

'September Song' 149

Seventeen 36, 120

The Seventh Seal 80, 130, 220

Sex 69, 130-32, 209

Shadows and Fog 14, 18, 22, 126, 131, 211, 213, 217-25, 234-5, 243, 247

Shakespeare, William 136, 172-3

Shawn, Wallace 177, 222

Shepard, Sam 22, 185

Shepherd, Cybill 209

Shields, Brooke 94

Shipman, David 155

Shorr, Lester 49

The Sid Caesar Show 26

Siegel, Bugsy 246

Sight and Sound 41, 183

Silver Bear 81

Silver, Ron 214

Silverman, Stanley 132

Simon, Danny 25

Simon, John 14

Simon, Neil 25, 104, 176, 256

Simon, Paul 89, 90

Simon, Roger L. 215, 216

Simowitz, Garret 203

Sinatra, Frank 85, 138

Siskel, Gene 153

Sixty Minutes 237

Skelton, Red 107

Skouras, Spyros K. 148

Sleeper 39, 53, 66, 69-75, 78, 80, 139

Smiles of a Summer Night 135

Socrates 80, 131

'Someone Who'll Watch Over Me' 113

Sondheim, Stephen 135

Sontag, Susan 148

Sophocles 199

The Sorrow and the Pity 93, 96

Sorvino, Mira 250, 252-4

Southampton (Comedy) Film Festival 255

Southern, Terry 36

The Spaghetti Factory cabaret 60

'Spider' sketch 65, 197

Spielberg, Steven 12, 19, 174, 181, 196

Spignesi, Stephen J. 132, 223, 235

Spiner, Brent 124

Springfield, Dusty 38

Springsteen, Bruce 124

Squire, Anthony 35

Stallone, Sylvester 54, 153, 231

Stander, Lionel 256

Stapleton, Maureen 103, 105-7

The Star-Telegraph 183

Star Trek 97, 124

Stardust Memories 12, 15, 61, 89, 95, 98, 109, 116-27, 129, 133-4, 138-9, 141, 158, 178-9, 191, 199, 251

Starkweather, Charles 48

Steenburgen, Mary 136, 139, 191

Steiner, Leo 150, 152

Steiner, Max 63, 134

Stern, Bill 178

Stevenson, Adlai 88

Stokes, Dr Ellwood H. 123

Stompanato, Johnny185-6

Stone, Sharon 13, 124

Storaro, Vittorio 196

'Strange Strawberries' 26

Straithairn, David 224

Stratton, Monty 178

Stravinsky, Igor 81

Streep, Meryl 13, 109, 115

Streisand, Barbra 13,

40, 79, 126
Strindberg, August 81, 109
Stringer, Michael 35
Stritch, Elaine 185-7, 189
Stuart, Kim Rossi 256
The Studio Cinema 108
Sturges, Preston 122, 152
The Subtle Concept 133-4
Sucksdorff, Arne 136
The Sunday Express 235
The Sunday Times 96, 155, 160
The Sunshine Boys 257
Superman 212; radio series 48, 177
Sutton, Martin 109
The Sutton Theater 171
Swanson, Kristy 233
Swayze, Patrick 211
Sweetland BV 253
Sweetland Films 454, 241-4
Swindell, Larry 183
Sydow, Max Von 166
Syms, Sylvia 130

Take the Money and Run 12, 33, 47-53, 55, 71, 100, 169, 183, 243
Talmadge, Richard 32, 35, 37
Tati, Jacques 65, 74
Taubin, Amy 194
Taylor, Juliet 160, 166, 197, 206, 211, 247
Taylor, Lili 251
Tchaikovsky, P. 81
Teatro della Fenice 256
Teatro Greco 251
Technicolor 73, 113, 148, 159, 169, 207
'Ten Best' lists 98, 100, 108
The Thalia 89, 96
'They're Either Too Young or Too Old' 179
Thomas, Kevin 49
Thomas, Philip 111
'Three Little Words' 122
The Threepenny Opera / 'The Little Threepenny Music' (Dreigroschenoper) 221
Tilly, Jennifer 245, 248, 250
Time 42, 44, 81, 97, 114, 140, 154, 227-8
The Times 39, 140, 172
The Times Literary

Supplement 155
'Tin Pan Alley' 142
To Woody Allen, From Europe with Love 123
Toback, James 210
Toland, Gregg 147
Tolstoy, Leo 79-80, 165
Tomlin, Lily 222, 224
Tony Awards 130
Tookey, Christopher 223
Toronto Festival of Festivals 234, 254
Touchstone Pictures (Disney) 196, 217, 255
Tours Henri Langlois Encounters 133
Tracy, Spencer 75
The TransAmerica Corp 100
Treacher, Arthur 42
Trebitsch, Ignacz see Lincoln, Trebitsch
TriStar Pictures Inc 218-9, 234, 236, 238, 241-2
Trueba, Fernando 257
Truman, Harry S. 85
Tucker, Michael 175
Turgenev, Ivan 184
Turner, Lana 185
Twentieth Century-Fox Corp 34, 58, 127, 148
Two Mothers 172

USA Today 249
Ullman, Tracy 246
United Artists Pictures Corp (UA) 25, 35, 47, 52, 58, 70, 74-5, 97, 99-100, 108, 111-12, 115, 124-6
Universal Newsreel 144
Universal Picture Co Inc 68
Universum Film Aktiengesellschft 220
Untitled Pictures (aka Productions) Inc 219
'Up the Lazy River' 248
Updike, John 13

Variety 27, 29, 32, 44-5, 100, 149, 171, 214, 254
Variety Arts Theater 244
The Vatican 133
Vaughan, Doug 235
The Venice Interntional Film Festival 135,

219, 238, 249, 253, 256
Verdi, Giuseppi 201
Verdon, Gwen 209
'The Vicar of Bray' 145
The Village Gate 26
The Village Voice 124, 126, 194
Viterelli, Joe 245, 247
Vitti, Monica 66
'Viva Vargas' 53
The Vivian Beaumont Theater 129-30

Walken, Christopher 22, 91, 185
Walker, Alexander 179
The Wall Street Tennis Club 90, 96
Walsh, David M. 66
Walters, Matthews 132
War and Peace 76-7, 78
The War of the Worlds 177, 180
Warden, Jack 185, 187, 245, 251, 253
Warner Brothers Inc 48, 62, 100, 142, 144, 154, 196
Warrilow, David 175, 179, 182
Waterston, Sam 20-22, 102, 107, 166, 186, 201-03
'The Way You Look Tonight' 167
Wayne, John 13
'We Need the Eggs' 96
Weber, David 161
Weegee 108
Weaver, Sigourney 96
Wegener, Paul 221
Weill, Kurt 221
Weinstein, Bob and Harvey 244
Weinstein's Majestic Bungalow Colony 149
Welch, Raquel 66
Weller, Peter 251, 253
Welles, Orson 14, 26, 36-7, 114, 173, 177, 180, 183, 243
Wells, H.G. 70-71
Wenger, Allan 133-4
Westerbeck, Colin L. Jr 140
Western project 201
Weston, Jack 130
What's New, Pussycat? 29-42, 35, 40, 104 novelization 33
'What's Nude, Pussycat?' 33
What's Up, Tiger Lily? 39-

42
Widmark, Richard 29
Wiest, Dianne 13, 157, 160, 166-8, 171-2, 175, 182, 185-6, 189-90, 232, 246, 248-50, 255
Wild Strawberries 191, 204
Wilder, Billy 36, 235
Wilder, Gene 67
Wilk, Judge Elliott 240
Williams, Andy 34
Williams, Esther 207
Williams, Tennessee 130
Willis, Gordon 19-20, 94, 101, 102, 105, 112-13, 117, 125, 136, 146-8, 154, 169, 193
Wilson, Dooley 63
Wison, Edmund 145
Winkler, Irwin 85
Wood, John 160
Woody Allen 42
Woody Allen: An American Comedy 123
'Woody Allen Looks at 1967' 42
Woody Allen's Fall Project 1991 218
Woody Allen's Fall Project 1978 125
Woody Allen 'Untitled' (Fall Project) 1995 252
Woody et les Robots 72
Wright, Amy 119
Wurtzel, Stuart 171
Wyeth, Andrew 166
Wyler, William 19

Yacowar, Maurice 27, 40, 58, 64, 131
'You'd Be So Nice to Come Home to' 179
Young, Sean 111, 207
'Young at Heart' 85
Youngman, Henny 67
Your Show of Shows 43
'You're the Top' 142
Yulin, Harris 166-7, 192

Zanuck, Darryl F. 148
Zelig 15, 73, 135, 140-49, 155, 159, 175-6, 197, 220
Zimmerman, Paul 69